ARKANA

Exploring Reincarnation

Hans TenDam was born in The Hague in 1943. He studied psychology and pedagogy at the University of Amsterdam, graduating in 1968. Since 1970 he has been an independent management consultant, involved in management and organization development, conflict resolution, reorganizations and strategic planning and management, and he has published many articles on strategic thinking and methodology. He has worked for business, non-profit and government agencies in the Netherlands, the EEC, Turkey, New Zealand and Brazil. Hans TenDam has published books on the difference between occultism and mysticism, the way that oracles work (or don't), the Tarot and reincarnation. He trains psychotherapists in past-life therapy and is a great believer in intuition, as well as a staunch supporter of common sense, methodical analysis and hard work.

HANS TENDAM

Exploring Reincarnation

Translated from the Dutch by

A. E. J. WILS

ARKANA

ARKANA

Published by the Penguin Group
27 Wrights Lane, London W8 5TZ, England
Viking Penguin Inc., 40 West 23rd Street, New York, New York 10010, USA
Penguin Books Australia Ltd, Ringwood, Victoria, Australia
Penguin Books Canada Ltd, 2801 John Street, Markham, Ontario, Canada L3R 1B4
Penguin Books (NZ) Ltd, 182–190 Wairau Road, Auckland 10, New Zealand

Penguin Books Ltd, Registered Offices: Harmondsworth, Middlesex, England

First published 1990
10 9 8 7 6 5 4 3 2 1

Excerpts from 'Little Gidding' from *Four Quartets* by T. S. Eliot, copyright 1943 by T. S. Eliot
and renewed 1971 by Esme Valerie Eliot, reprinted by permission of Harcourt Brace
Jovanovich, Inc., Orlando, Florida, USA; and by permission of Faber and Faber Ltd, London.

Filmset in 10/12 pt Bembo

Made and printed in Great Britain by
Richard Clay Ltd, Bungay, Suffolk

Contents

Foreword

Of all the subjects grouped together under the general heading of 'the paranormal' – telepathy, extra-sensory perception (ESP), precognition, and so on – reincarnation seems by far the most dubious and preposterous, and the least acceptable to men of common sense. This was certainly my own feeling when, in the late 1960s, I was asked to write a book on 'the occult' by an American publisher. To tell the truth, I was inclined to feel that the whole subject was probably the outcome of fantasy and wishful thinking. That view very quickly altered as I settled down to the systematic study of paranormal phenomena, and realized how many reliable witnesses have vouched for their reality. Andrew Lang pointed out that most people who have seen ghosts are not hysterics, but 'steady, unimaginative, unexcitable people with just the odd experience'. The philosopher Leibniz was one of the many people who saw Father Joseph of Copertino rise off the ground while praying and float around like a seagull, while scientists, poets, and philosophers witnessed Daniel Dunglas Home performing similar feats in the nineteenth century. The conclusion seemed unavoidable: human beings possess 'powers' of which they are normally unaware, but which can be released in certain unusual states of consciousness.

Such a definition of 'the paranormal' struck me as both rational and comprehensive – a simple extension of our recognition that great artists, in moments of inspiration, can produce works that have a touch of the superhuman.

However, in due course – about three-quarters of the way through *The Occult* – I found myself confronted with the problem of 'the realm of spirits' and life after death. I had been interested in 'spiritualism' as a child – my grandmother was a member of a spiritualist church – and had decided, at the age of 16 or so, that it was gross superstition. Now, as I settled down to studying the evidence, I had to admit that that view was an oversimplification, and that in just a few cases the evidence for life after death is positively overwhelming.

I felt vaguely embarrassed to have to admit that some of the evidence was so powerful for it was, in a sense, quite irrelevant to my central thesis about man's 'hidden powers'. After writing about the evidence for 'survival', I ended the chapter with a hasty postscript on the subject of reincarnation. This I found even more embarrassing, because it seemed to fly in the face of our common-sense belief that our personalities are, to a large extent, a product of our bodies and our genetic inheritance. At a fairly late stage of my research, I came upon Professor Ian Stevenson's book, *Twenty Cases Suggestive of Reincarnation* (1966), and was deeply impressed by it. Unless Stevenson was a liar, or distorted his information with total disregard for accuracy, then it certainly looked as if the evidence for reincarnation was as powerful as the evidence for telepathy or ESP. On the surface, some of the cases sound preposterous:

A boy named Ravi Shankar, born in July 1951, later gave details of his murder in his previous existence; this may explain the continuation of memory (i.e. because being murdered must be a fairly memorable experience); as a child of 6 he was killed and beheaded by a relative (aided by an accomplice) who hoped to inherit the property of the child's father. Ravi Shankar actually had a scar on his neck resembling a long knife wound. A child named Jasbir claimed to be a man who had been given poisoned sweets, and had died as a result of a fall from a cart in which he had sustained a head injury.

And so on, each case apparently more unbelievable than the last. Yet Stevenson's documentation is unexceptionable, being presented with an exactitude that makes it sound like a sociological thesis.

Since then I have come across a number of other cases that have seemed to me virtually beyond criticism. Yet although I have written subsequent books on fields of the paranormal that deeply interest me – poltergeists, psychometry, life after death – I have deliberately avoided the challenge of writing a full-length book on reincarnation – not only because the amount of research involved is so daunting, but because I am still unable to fit reincarnation into my general picture of the paranormal. This is why, when a friend in Amsterdam told me that a Dutch psychologist had written the most comprehensive book on reincarnation ever attempted, and that he possessed a chapter in English translation, I eagerly demanded to see it. And when I had read it, I wrote to Hans TenDam and pressed him to get the remainder translated, so that I could try to find a British publisher. When he finally wrote to tell me that it had been accepted, I was as delighted as if it had been one of my own books.

This is, I think, *the* great definitive work on reincarnation; it is hard to imagine it ever being superseded. In recent years there have been many impressive and balanced works on reincarnation – notably Stevenson's vast *Cases of the Reincarnation Type*, (1975–83), Ruth Reyna's *Reincarnation and Science* (1975), and a number of remarkable studies of 'hypnotic regression', such as *Encounters with the Past* by Peter Moss and Joe Keeton (1979). These works are not open to the objection directed at earlier books, such as those of Joan Grant, which could be too easily dismissed as mere romantic fantasy or self-deception, but their authors might still be attacked on the grounds that they are obviously emotionally committed to their subject. In chapter 9 of the present work, Hans TenDam remarks wryly: 'The reader who does not believe in reincarnation but has managed to get this far anyway will be happy to observe that even my credulity has limits' (see below, p. 196). Yet it seems to me that the whole merit of the book is that it makes no appeals to credulity. It is obvious that TenDam *does* accept the reality of reincarnation – I know this from speaking with him – but he has written not as a believer, but as a detached observer who simply wishes to present the most comprehensive picture of a vast subject. Some readers may find the approach in the early chapters a little too cool and detached, but if they persist they will find themselves richly rewarded. As far as it is possible to make reincarnation plausible, TenDam has done it. The book will join Myers' *Human Personality and its Survival of Bodily Death*, Tyrrell's *Personality of Man* and Mavromatis's *Hypnagogia* as classics of the paranormal.

Colin Wilson

Preface: The Origin and Aim of this Book

The subject of reincarnation is on an upswing. Many new books have been written about it and older works are being reprinted. This is hardly surprising, considering the generally growing interest in spiritual subjects. To some this heralds a breakthrough to a more spiritual society, possibly under the auspices of Aquarius. To others it signals the superstition which thrives during worrying periods of transition. Nietzsche has already christened our time the age of superstition, although he regarded such periods of cultural decline as breeding grounds for superior individualism.

Reincarnation is a controversial subject; so this is a controversial book. Controversial subjects are often both attacked and defended with irrelevant and inappropriate arguments. The confusion, speculation, emotions, and insinuations they attract don't exactly help to make them less controversial.

Why is reincarnation controversial? Perhaps because it belongs to a highly sensitive area of thinking: the no-man's-land between religion and science. Formerly, knowledge was the province of theology, philosophy, or the intermediate gnosticism. A reflective person attempting to discover the truth about himself and the human condition turned to these three forms of speculation. The main tension in that classical approach was between revelation – knowledge gained from a higher level of reality in special states, and dialectics – knowledge shaped by the reasoning human intellect. The advent of modern science created a new tension, namely between pure intellectual activity and the systematic examination of observable phenomena. The expanding sciences used the dialectic tool of human reason to sharpen their own methodology and to create the apparatus of mathematics to analyse and test the structure of phenomena.

Science found many old concepts obsolete, irrelevant, or simply unprovable. But many important human questions, for the time being or in principle, appeared to be impossible to examine scientifically. The question of the meaning of life, just to mention a small example, fell to religion. In the course of time a territorial division was more or less clearly defined, but with a good deal of irritation on both sides and without a definite settlement, as the question of abortion shows, or the attempt to forbid the teaching of evolution in school because it conflicts with the literal meaning of the Bible (as if there were such a thing as literal meaning).

All the same, a global division of territory did take place in the nineteenth century. The natural was allocated to science and the spiritual to religion and philosophers. If people are confronted with phenomena running across this division they react with alarm, irritation, indignation, and repudiation. The first of such phenomena was *animal magnetism,* closely related to what we know now as hypnosis. At the time the matter was disposed of effectively. Thought to be a natural force resembling the newly discovered electricity, it was assigned to the field of science and experimentation since it was an ordinary natural process and no business of religion. Science then pigeonholed it as suggestion, thereby declaring it to be normal, therefore insignificant, and therefore illusory. This intellectual hattrick has only recently given way to a more serious consideration of the phenomenon.

Spiritualism was the second spoilsport. To scientific minds it suggested a return to the dark middle ages, while the religious were alarmed that the mysteries of life and death were suddenly the object of experimentation. An area subjected to such enormous pressure from two sides easily falls prey to confusion, thus contributing to its own downfall. All the same, spiritualism has come out of it better than magnetism. Countless people continue to believe and to be active in it. In the aftermath of wars in particular, many people on both sides of the divide desire to make contact. After the First World War spiritualism enjoyed a tremendous revival.

Spiritualism triggered parapsychology, still a discipline of a somewhat doubtful standing in the eyes of many scientists. Many disclaim it, often with nonsensical opinions about it.

As hypnosis has recently been gaining greater acceptance and scientific attention, the original magnetism was never completely suppressed.

The explosive increase of *past-life recall* during the last two decades is the third wave of phenomena refusing to be pigeonholed. In a sense, reincarnation is a revival of magnetism, for at first the most important means of recalling past lives were magnetic and hypnotic. In a way it also signals a comeback for spiritualism, as this book will show.

Reincarnation stands out from most other spiritual, mystical, and occult subjects because of its rapidly growing field of empirical evidence. Reports of people recalling past lives when brought into the right state are proliferating. Past-life therapists from all over the world may meet for the first time and within half an hour discover common experiences and common challenges, indulging in the same type of (sometimes heated) discussion that practitioners from other new disciplines pursue.

Hypnotic regression has long been the main tool for past-life recall, but it is rapidly being replaced by methods which avoid, or employ only weak, trance induction, sometimes enabling people to have vivid recall of past-life episodes within a few minutes. This makes reincarnation no longer a matter of belief in general (religion), or of belief in the revelations and insights of the enlightened or initiated (gnosticism), but an area of human experience.

However, many books, often reprints, still use philosophical arguments to make reincarnation plausible. They either quote famous people, or refer to traditional religious and spiritual authorities, or to the more recently initiated (even themselves). Even if this literature is interesting, its main value now is historical. The empirical material in print at present comprises about 10,000 regressions of 2,000 people. The unpublished material in the form of tapes and notes made by those working in this field will be by now at least triple that amount. And work in progress means that even these figures will rapidly become outdated.

People having apparent memories of their own past lives is an area of experience like any other. We need neither doubt that these experiences are what they profess to be, nor believe that they are beyond sober analysis and criticism. I easily accept past-life recall, because I have had such experiences myself and have hundreds of times observed other people having them, but I don't take them for gospel.

We should be grateful for the transition of a theme from the sphere of revelation and faith to the sphere of experience, although unfortunately this gives us no short cut to the truth. Like other areas of human experience, the data are rich, divergent, sometimes confusing, sometimes contradictory, usually uncertain, and often over- or underestimated or distorted by prejudice. However, when large numbers of people have similar experiences, patterns may be discovered. At such a stage a broad inventory and classification study is far more useful than minutely detailed studies of individual cases. For instance, we may look for the similarities and differences. Do patterns emerge? How are they to be interpreted? What are the most acceptable hypotheses?

There are certainly interesting patterns in the data emerging about past-life experiences. Amidst confusion and uncertainty a number of trends become visible, which this book attempts to sketch. On the strength of the evidence reported here, I conclude that this is a highly interesting empirical area of great practical and theoretical value. This study attempts to arrive at a conceptual framework which accords with, or at any rate does not conflict with, the empirical data gathered to date. Obviously the newness and immaturity of the subject, particularly of the publications and studies, warrant only tentative conclusions. But, on the strength of the present material and with a little reflection, many old ideas on reincarnation can be sifted. Whether reincarnation does exist, or exists only in a certain form, at least this will be clear after reading this book: many ideas about reincarnation are inaccurate or absurd.

I shall make many specific references to both the older and most recent literature on the subject so the reader may consult the sources for himself and draw his own conclusions. The book describes existing ideas and practices and tests ideas against the empirical material available at present. The growing body of evidence refutes many old ideas about reincarnation and especially about karma. New ideas are developed that seem to fit known data better.

The first book giving a sympathetic but analytic treatment of the subject was *The Problem of Rebirth* by Ralph Shirley (1924). The second book in this vein is *Reincarnation, Based on Facts* by Karl Muller (1970). The third is *Reincarnation: Ancient beliefs and modern evidence* by David Christie-Murray (1981). My own book differs from these others in three respects:

1 The range and depth of the survey of existing literature.
2 The inclusion of recent regression experiences and experiments and the rise of past-life therapy as an effective psychotherapeutic discipline.
3 The development of paradigms and theory in accordance with the empirical material. The refutation of many speculative, religious and esoteric ideas.

The only author so far to have made useful attempts at formulating a theory has been Gina Cerminara, but her work has effectively been limited to the Cayce readings. The present book refers extensively to case studies but gives no extensive case accounts from regressions, therapies, or spontaneous recall. More specifically, it features:

1 A systematic comparison, and a rational as well as empirical evaluation of soul-body hypotheses, ranging from materialism to metempsychosis.
2 A systematic treatment of all interpretations of apparent past-life recall.
3 Extensive references.
4 Rational and empirical argument instead of mystic and esoteric treatments.
5 Introduction of new paradigms with regard to regression levels, death experiences, types of connections between lives, types of reincarnation patterns, life planning, ego-inflation, etc.
6 A theoretical explanation of apparent lives as animals.
7 A personality theory in accordance with reincarnation phenomena.
8 The first comprehensive treatment of regression techniques, stressing the non-hypnotic ones.
9 A consistent framework for past-life therapy.

The first two parts are a summary of existing literature. The third and fourth part give my own analysis and interpretation of past-life material. Chapters 15 and 16 are largely based on my personal experience as a past-life therapist, and the experiences of colleagues.

The many developments in the field, including in my own practice, warrant a separate book on the methodology of past-life therapy. I am working on this.

Note on text references

References in the text give the author and the year of the first edition of each book in order to give a clear historical framework to the development of ideas about reincarnation. The page indications, however, may refer to a later, still available edition of the book, which is mentioned in the bibliography. For example, (Jinarajadasa 1915: 12) refers to page 12 of the eighth printing in 1973 of Jinarajadasa's book originally published in 1915.

PART I *Ideas*

1 The Hypothesis of Reincarnation

Many people believe in reincarnation or find the idea acceptable. We usually associate it with Hindus or Buddhists. Reincarnation is thought to be a typically eastern idea and almost everyone in India is supposed to believe in it. This knowledge is as common as it is inaccurate. Many city-dwellers in India are familiar with the idea, but most villagers have never heard of it. Moreover, the ideas in India about reincarnation are highly contradictory. Many Indians believe in karma: behaviour in the past life determining this life. But what about those who believe your last thoughts determine your next life, or worse still that your present life is dependent on whether your family had the right people perform the right rituals for the right fees at your death?

Western believers in reincarnation, dramatizing their minority position, usually assume that 99 per cent of Europeans do not believe in reincarnation and consider it an Asian superstition (see, for example, Desjardins 1977: 22). But the situation in the west also differs from what we imagine: belief in reincarnation is widespread. In a 1969 Gallup poll Catholics and Protestants from 10 western countries were questioned about religious matters including reincarnation (Head and Cranston 1977: 486). In the Netherlands 10 per cent believed in reincarnation, 55 per cent did not and 35 per cent didn't know, giving the Netherlands the lowest number of believers. The percentages of believers in reincarnation were as follows:

The Netherlands	10%	Austria	20%
Sweden	12%	Greece	22%
Norway	14%	France	23%
England	18%	West Germany	25%
United States	20%	Canada	26%

Presumably religious people are more inclined to believe in reincarnation than others. But then again, reincarnation is not a part of the

Christian faith. Many consider it to be in conflict with it. The number of believers in reincarnation is more likely to have increased than decreased during the last 15 years, owing to the general tendency towards alternative spiritual ideas. A *Sunday Telegraph* poll in 1979 found 28 per cent of British adults believing in reincarnation. *The Times* found 29 per cent in 1980 (Fisher, 1985). This means an increase of 10 per cent in the 10 years since 1969. In 1982 a Gallup poll found 67 per cent of Americans believing in life after death, and 23 per cent in reincarnation. In 1978 an opinion poll by a leading TV network in Brazil found that 78 per cent of Brazilians believe in reincarnation. They top the bill.

So a great many people believe in reincarnation. Why? The majority undoubtedly because they've been brought up to believe in it. But in the final analysis belief is based on experiences, reflections, and arguments that convince people of its plausibility. Limiting myself here to the sources of belief in reincarnation in western societies, I will peruse the literature published on the subject during the last 150 years, and find out what world-views and philosophies subscribe to belief in reincarnation. The next chapter deals with its occurrence in other cultures. The third chapter describes the reincarnation philosophies of two important esoteric schools of thought.

Six sources of modern belief in reincarnation

The translation of *Sanskrit texts* in about 1820 led to the discovery of classical Indian culture, the earliest source of belief in reincarnation in our society. Although relatively few people read these texts, they had enormous influence. Sanskrit proved to be the oldest language in the Indo-European group, so ancient Indian culture provided the oldest retrospection into our own cultural past. Max Mueller translated and studied many ancient Indian texts, and did much to popularize them. Classical Hindu texts influenced many thinkers, while Buddhism influenced many others, such as Schopenhauer who defined Europe as the continent dominated by the incredibly narrow idea that there was no such thing as reincarnation. The main discovery was, however, that India is apparently the cradle of European thought.

The second source of belief in reincarnation is the French spiritist *Allan Kardec*. Kardec became convinced that mediums really communicated with the dead, and that some of the dead gave sensible answers to sensible questions. He questioned several mediums exhaustively about conditions on the other side and came across the subject of reincarnation. His well-known work, *The Spirits' Book* (1857), contains a number of questions and answers about reincarnation.

These ideas about reincarnation were strongly challenged. First of all, many people did not believe in such methods. Second, many who did, and themselves asked questions on the subject, received different answers from the dead. Spiritualist groups who accepted reincarnation received communications about reincarnation, and groups rejecting it received communications discounting reincarnation. This created such confusion among the incarnated that it caused a schism in the world of international spiritualism. The 'spiritists' did believe in reincarnation and the 'spiritualists' did not. Most of the English and American groups were converted to spiritualism, refuting reincarnation, while the Continentals (including the Brazilians), mainly influenced by Kardec, accepted reincarnation.

Many considered Kardec's spiritism revealing, but others fiercely criticized the method and content of his work. The main criticism was that his strong personality influenced his mediums by suggestion. But if his books portray his seances with any accuracy, most questions were hardly suggestive. Interviewing trance mediums, however, remains a debatable method. While consulting mediums and noting down their answers is an interesting procedure in itself, it can hardly be classed as serious research. Interestingly, however, his work is the only book about reincarnation before 1911 that fits in surprisingly well with the modern empirical regression material.

The third important source of belief in reincarnation was *theosophy*. Theosophy probably did more than Kardec's spiritism to extend views on reincarnation and make the concept acceptable because, at least in its heyday, it was more cosmopolitan and socially active and had greater cultural and intellectual prestige than spiritualism. Blavatsky provided the founding publications, while Annie Besant and above all Leadbeater provided the elaborations. They will be discussed in chapter 3.

Theosophy tied in with Indian philosophy as the title of an early theosophical work, *Esoteric Buddhism* by Sinnett (1883), reveals. According to the theosophical leaders, the 'Masters' who inspired the movement lived in the Himalayas. Consequently, the rise of theosophy renewed interest in Indian culture and religion, even in India itself.

Theosophy is gnostic, esoteric, its knowledge being revealed in a higher mental state to special prepared people. Spiritual discipline leads to crossing a threshold known as initiation, which gives direct access to the truth, or to those who know the truth. The theosophists have a more mystical, grandiose concept of reincarnation than Kardec. Their main criticism of his work was that it lacked esoteric vision and a deeper understanding of karma. According to Shirley, Allan Kardec did have considerable influence on the development of theosophic thought, although the theosophists never acknowledged this (Shirley 1924: 173).

Theosophy spawned a great number of other gnostic schools. Many called themselves theosophical, but many others worked under their own often fancy names. One such school, probably the most serious, was Rudolf Steiner's anthroposophy, with its own doctrines of reincarnation and karma. There is abundant gnostic propaganda literature. Literature is gnostic if written by people who have gained access to an inner source of knowledge. A gnostic does not believe in swallowing somebody else's opinions (at best second-hand knowledge) but in gaining personal access to the source of immediate knowledge (first-hand knowledge). If a person sufficiently develops his inner sense, he may arrive at the truth on his own. Technically speaking, this implies a profound development of the intuition, and a limitation of the intellect to elaborate what is discovered intuitively. A gnostic values his inner insights above traditional revelations of others, but also above sensory evidence and common-sense reasoning.

What gnostics think is always similar to what other gnostics think, yet always different. Gnostics exhort others to use their gnostic concepts and recipes to acquire personal first-hand knowledge, and find out for themselves what the gnostic master has already found out. As a result of this paradox, all gnostic literature is propaganda. Gnostics are led by higher intuition, not by observation and the intellect.

The theosophical and especially the anthroposophical views are gnostic, like the views of other self-professed esoteric writers (for example, Lewis Spence and Max Heindel in America). They discourage research into past-life phenomena, developing instead reincarnation theories based on the insights and inner experiences acquired by approved mystics, occultists, and initiates. These form the foundation for the continual reinterpretation of the existing gnostic concepts and literature.

Albert de Rochas in Paris developed a fourth approach, based on research, which was to become the most important source of past-life knowledge. In 1898 de Rochas noticed that subjects put into trance were fully able to recall past experiences. He discovered he could even instruct them to go back to early childhood and birth. When he took his subjects even further back, they had experiences clearly coming from past lives (de Rochas 1911). His work aroused great interest among theosophists. Colonel Olcott, a founding member of the theosophical movement, visited de Rochas and was impressed with his experiments. Maurice Maeterlinck, a well-known theosophical writer, devoted space to de Rochas in his book about death. All the same, the theosophists did little with de Rochas' work, probably because he was no theosophist, did not speak on behalf of a school of initiates, and was simply conducting experiments. Moreover, he discovered an intermission between lives of only decades, strongly contradicting the theosophical doctrine of intermissions of 1,600, 1,300 and 1,200 years.

Esotericists, like theosophists, were against him because they disapproved of the use of magnetism or hypnosis to put people in trance. People in such trances supposedly lost their ego and power of judgement, becoming passive and submissive, easily led by the hypnotist. After all, man has to become less dependent and more conscious. The spiritualists, too, fiercely contested the work of de Rochas, trotting out the charge of suggestion.

Although there is much to be said for these views, the criticism is not entirely warranted, particularly the idea that a hypnotist easily influences the content of a regression. It is usually difficult, if not impossible, to influence what people see or experience. Often a remigrant cannot answer simple questions about the time and area he lived in, even when the hypnotist and any others present are mentally shouting it to him. In regressions where consciousness becomes divided or elliptic (the present consciousness remaining intact as observer of the past life being relived), the remigrant later describes the sometimes great conflict between the two states of consciousness about some specific information, and the inability of the present consciousness to influence the part recalling a past life. Good examples are to be found in Moss and Keeton (1979).

De Rochas' work so much contradicted theosophical concepts that it never gained ground in theosophy. Even theosophists who were impressed with it kept a safe distance. Van Ginkel (1917), for instance, thought that regression would become a method for past-life recall in the future. Another esotericist, Encausse, writing his occult works under the name of Papus, in about 1920 published *La Réincarnation*, an amazingly abstract and rambling book, which mentions de Rochas only in a footnote at the end, saying his work is interesting.

The discoveries of de Rochas are in even closer agreement than those of Kardec with modern empirical evidence.

The successors to de Rochas were John Bjørkhem in Sweden and the psychiatrist Alexander Cannon in England. Cannon had academic standing: nine European universities awarded him degrees. Cannon regressed almost 1,400 volunteers. He accepted reincarnation only slowly, but conceded at last that 'Freud has been outflanked by reincarnation'. Cannon's work stimulated Morey Bernstein (1956), whose famous case, Bridey Murphy, triggered modern interest in regression and regression therapy. Fisher's estimate that past-life therapy has since been responsible for healing hundreds of thousands of people (Whitton and Fisher 1986: 62), may be an overstatement, but the total number may be well towards 100,000.

The fifth source of belief in reincarnation was *Edgar Cayce* who operated midway between spiritualism and hypnotic regression. By means of self-hypnosis Cayce put himself into deep trance, in which he drew from an expanded consciousness. He was his own inspirator and guide, as it were. People seeking advice about their own problems or those of their children were also given information based on the experiences and lessons of past lives. Cayce himself answered general questions on subjects including reincarnation. Hundreds of his cases illustrate Cayce's concept of reincarnation. The main reason why it was taken seriously is because data of individual cases could sometimes be checked and because his other statements about people were usually accurate, even if he had never met them. On the whole he had great success advising people on health and career problems. This made him more convincing than the average sensitive. Many books contain samples from his readings about reincarnation, and about karma in particular.

The writings of people with *spontaneous recall of past lives* form a sixth source. The first book of this kind to become popular was *Winged Pharaoh* by Joan Grant (1937). She has described other lives in highly readable books, giving vivid impressions of life in earlier times. The spiritualistic aspect of her often unintentionally therapeutic work, and her collaboration with Denys Kelsey led also to past-life therapy (Kelsey and Grant 1967). Joan Grant says relatively little about the mechanism of reincarnation and karma, but she vividly describes conditions after death and the interaction between the living and discarnates.

Second Time Round, by Edward Ryall (1974), is one of the few recall books the more critical investigators in the field take seriously. Els Brouwer's unpretentious book gives a relaxed, pleasant impression of what it is like to recall past lives (Brouwer 1978). Such books are not in themselves convincing proof that reincarnation exists, although they may be rich in obscure historical facts confirmed later.

These, therefore, are the modern sources of western belief in reincarnation: the Indian religions, spiritualism, theosophy followed by comparable esoteric movements, regression experiments, Edgar Cayce and spontaneous past-life recollections.

Recent literature

Most of the mentioned sources have been enriched with new editions during recent decades. Little important new spiritualistic literature on the subject has been published, with the exception of Karl Muller's *Reincarnation, Based on Facts* (1970), and David Christie-Murray's *Reincarnation: Ancient beliefs and modern evidence* (1981). Muller collected an amazing number of cases of past-life recall, including many from relatively unknown spiritualistic sources, but, unfortunately, his book received little attention.

Theosophists have done little original work in the field of reincarnation and karma. Their main concern has apparently been to elaborate and popularize their source books. However, some people inspired by theosophy have written interesting books for the general public. First of all, there is the well-known *Reincarnation: The Phoenix Fire Mystery* (Head and Cranston 1977), already a classic, in which the authors exhaustively compiled almost every statement ever made about reincarnation by writers of every description in all kinds of culture, religion, and philosophy. Secondly, Ian Stevenson, perhaps the only real scientist ever to concern himself with the subject, has extensively researched cases of spontaneous past-life recall in young children. He has reported it in a series of impressive books (see bibliography). Chapter 5 returns to his work. Most theosophical books, however, attempt to make reincarnation acceptable by general arguments sprinkled with popular theosophical insights.

Regression techniques lay dormant until the publication of *The Search for Bridey Murphy* (Bernstein 1956). The story about this book is a book in itself. It had merciless reviews and according to public opinion was adequately refuted. Meanwhile, the refutations have in turn been refuted, and it has been clearly demonstrated that Bernstein's book was the victim of the no-man's-land between the church and science (see, for example, Cerminara 1967). A scientist weighed all the evidence for and against and concluded the facts to be incontrovertible. He then went on to explain these by the generous hypothesis of super-ESP (super-extra-sensory perception), a hypothesis that can never be disproved and is therefore as useless as it is impartial (Ducasse 1960). All the same, Bernstein's book did arouse a great deal of interest in regression. His work was inspired not by Albert de Rochas, but by Alexander Cannon and possibly by Ron Hubbard, the founder of dianetics and scientology. Hubbard developed non-hypnotic regression techniques expressly intended to further mental health. Hubbard's influence has been mainly indirect since his techniques are applied within a rigid organizational framework protected by church status, copyright, membership pressures, and other strict procedures. However, much work has been done by ex-members of his movement.

In Cornwall, Arnall Bloxham used hypnosis to regress people to past lives. He taped the sessions and published *Who was Ann Ocken-*

den? (1958) about the past-life sessions of a prolific subject. A BBC television programme later examined a number of these regressions containing historically verifiable material (Iverson 1976). Another Englishman, Arthur Guirdham, also published interesting material (see bibliography). One of his patients had since childhood recalled fragments of her life as a Cathar in dreams and spontaneous trance. His contacts with her brought recollections of his own past life to the surface, and he traced the past lives of a larger group of people. He checked historical details with French scholars and found the names of those in question in the Inquisition registers at Toulouse. Historians first refuted but later verified some historical details.

By far the most important modern publications are reports of regressions induced primarily with hypnosis, but also reached by relaxation and visualization only. Some books give excellent descriptions of the induction techniques, proceedings, and the subjects' experiences during such sessions (Moss and Keeton 1979). Often the records are supplemented with historical verification of data from the sessions. (Underwood and Wilder 1975; Dethlefsen 1977; Langedijk 1980).

The work of Helen Wambach seems to me the most important breakthrough, if only because of sheer volume. She successfully regressed 90 per cent of her 1,100 subjects to 5 different lives each, producing summaries of about 5,000 regressions which she analysed statistically (Wambach 1978). She also regressed people to the period immediately preceding the present incarnation. Around 750 people had such experiences, which she classified statistically (Wambach 1979). Many people discovered that proper relaxation and visualization bring about a light trance sufficient to recall past lives (Marcia Moore *et al.*). The Christos experiment is a well-known example of such a method (Glaskin 1974, 1978, 1979).

An interesting recent development is the rise of past-life therapy, a form of regression therapy in which people relive traumatic experiences from past lives to resolve present problems stemming from them (Netherton and Shiffrin 1978; Fiore 1978; Cladder 1983). Interestingly enough, Netherton's method enables people to recall past lives within a few minutes without hypnosis, relaxation, or visualization. Chapters 6, 15, and 16 below describe such techniques and their results in more detail.

Another outcome of the renewed interest in occult and spiritual subjects is the reprint of many related works, for example, with theosophical or anthroposophical backgrounds. Other books treat the history of the subject, dealing with the religious ideas of Hinduism, Mahayana Buddhism, Jainism, various Negro tribes, Indian tribes, the Druses, etc. These are based on the revelations of the founders of the various religions, elaborated theologically by important followers and inevitably institutionalized in rituals. Then there is the synoptic literature which aims, usually without developing its own ideas, to make reincarnation acceptable by referring to cases of past-life recall, putting forward arguments, or quoting famous people not generally known to believe in reincarnation. And finally there is the empirical literature describing past-life experiences, which attempts to analyse them or put them to the test, often using the conceptual framework of modern gnostic literature.

What arguments are used to make reincarnation acceptable? Whoever regards reincarnation as a truth apprehensible to initiates, or conveyed through the higher intuition of higher people, rarely uses intellectual arguments. People are simply and gracefully told how things work, have worked and will work. The sympathetic and understanding reader, invited to follow in the writer's footsteps, will discover the truth of these ideas in due course. Diametrically opposed to these gnostic arguments are the empirical arguments made in a scientific vein (though usually without scientific methodology). These point out that many people think they have recollections of past lives and that such recollections exhibit patterns and regularities. Wambach's work (1978) is the best example.

Then there are the rational arguments. The reasonableness of the reincarnation hypothesis is argued, for example, by pointing out how people start their lives unequal and how unequal are their fates, which is difficult to reconcile with divine justice, or the idea that only one life determines our eternal bliss or damnation. Such arguments only affect the religious-minded. Other arguments, like those regarding child prodigies, are used by materialists who think everything begins with conception and ends with death. How come 4-year-olds are gifted pianists or read Latin or have other extraordinary gifts? An indirect form of rational argument is to point out irrational elements in alternative interpretations.

A classic form of reasoning is to quote authorities. If so many great, important, intelligent, and generally respected people believed in reincarnation, who are we bluntly to reject it? A variant is to demonstrate that all through history most people in most cultures did believe in reincarnation. As you are the exception in not believing, the burden of proof is on you.

Pointing out the inherent reasonableness of reincarnation, referring to authorities and people throughout history believing in it, is a favourite argument in gnostic propaganda literature used to prepare the unconverted for the truth. This is all porch argumentation. Those who already believe in theosophy or anthroposophy, or similar philosophies, can then be transported to the holy place where the argument is in theosophical, anthroposophical, or other esoteric terms. The holy of holies is reserved for those who have been through the affirmative experiences themselves. In esoteric schools, therefore, only initiates or those disciples who are at least far advanced in inner training are able to view their own past lives or those of others.

The reincarnation hypothesis compared with other concepts

The idea that people have already lived before they are born and may live again after they die, is viewed here as a hypothesis, to see where it takes us. We start with a provisional analysis to find out how acceptable or fertile it would be as a working hypothesis. Let us compare the reincarnation hypothesis with alternative hypotheses about the link between body and soul and the question of life and death. What are the general hypotheses, and to what extent does human experience support or contradict them?

Table 1 compares nine general hypotheses about the relationship between soul and body. The first is materialism, including all views rejecting a soul independent of the body, rejecting life and consciousness separate from the physical organism. In materialism the mind is a by-product of the body. Thoughts, feelings, emotions, plans, consciousness develop together with the body and in any case end at death. This idea gained ground during the last century, although the Epicureans had already formulated a similar concept and worked out its moral meaning and existential consequences.

I have chosen the term 'psychic collectivism' to include all ideas regarding the mind as having substance, without being an entity in itself, only being a separate entity when in the (human) body. Many cultures assume that at death the soul leaves the body as a vapour or cloud of vitality which is absorbed by the earth, and so gives new vital energy to plants, animals, and human beings. In this view the soul is vital energy temporarily individualized at birth, when it separates from the encompassing psychic field which then feeds it. At death this field reabsorbs the soul. Fechner offers a philosophical variant of this view (see bibliography).

A modern example of psychic collectivism is the theory of a Dutchman living in France who knew so many details about places where he had never been that it embarrassed him. Because he did not want to believe in past lives, he explained this by the idea that interconnected traces of experiences insufficiently integrated with the rest of the soul disengage themselves after death and start to float in the atmosphere as shreds of mist. People with a similar psyche may pick up these shreds of mist and carry them with them as their own knowledge (Van Nes 1958: 111).

I have chosen 'psychic transfer' as a generic label for concepts related to the Buddhist anatta doctrine, which postulates that at birth people receive the mental and psychic patterns and characteristics left by people who died earlier. After death the resultant psychic characteristics again return to a sort of general fund, to be reassigned to those

Table 1 Soul-body hypotheses

Materialism	*Mind is a by-product of the body*
Psychic collectivism	*Mind is a temporarily individualized vital energy*
Psychic transfer	*Mind goes from the dead to the newborn*
Spiritualism:	
Creationism	*New soul produced by God*
Traducianism	*Soul split off from parents' souls*
Generationism	*Soul produced by parents*
Pre-existence	*Previous existence in soul world*
Reincarnation	*Consecutive human incarnations*
Metempsychosis	*Alternating human and animal incarnations*

about to be born. Roughly speaking, there are two variants: the psychic heritage is more or less arbitrary, or it is inherited from a specific person who lived previously, without the newborn being that person. This doctrine also has its followers in our time. Ironically, some of them accuse Madame Blavatsky of propagating the, in their view, incorrect reincarnation hypothesis through carelessness and misunderstanding, when Madame Blavatsky herself was actually a firm believer in psychic transfer (Blavatsky 1886). Theosophy, however, as the work of Annie Besant and especially Charles Leadbeater clearly shows (see bibliography), gradually but rapidly came to accept the reincarnation concept proper.

Buddhist doctrine compares the succession of embodiments with a candle lighting another candle. One follows the other, but they are quite different. The interesting thing about this comparison is its flaw. After all, reincarnation implies some time between one candle going out and the other being lit. If there is continuity, there is some flame in between lives and thus probably identity.

Rohit Mehta (1977) states that the reincarnating entity is a 'psycho-spiritual compound built up in the course of time', continuing to exist from incarnation to incarnation. There is no compulsion and therefore, in his view, no constant factor linking one incarnation with another. Every incarnation is new and fresh, containing nothing from the past and carrying nothing over to the future. Before this, he states that the individuality keeps creating new personalities to complete itself. Schopenhauer, deeply influenced by Buddhism, states that only the will (whose will? one's own?) reincarnates (Head and Cranston 1977 : 294). Anybody able to make sense of such rambling ideas is welcome to explain them.

Hazrat Inayat Khan, the founder of modern Sufism, came up with a theory combining pre-existence and psychic transfer. The soul's journey down to the earth where she is going to incarnate is long and tiring. Therefore, there are places to rest along the way. The deceased, on the way up, are also on a long and tiring journey and rest in the same rest-stops. Descending souls hear the tales of the ascending souls and later they think these are their own memories of past lives (Van Nes 1958: 112). This seems to be taken from Plato. Chapter 8 will indicate the nonsense of 'long and tiring journeys' in the discarnate state.

Psychic collectivism and psychic transfer are midway between the materialistic and spiritualistic points of view. The spiritualistic approach embraces all concepts which regard the mind as an entity with a separate existence after the body's death: the soul. Spiritualistic ideas may be classified according to their view of the soul's fate after the body dies or its state before and during birth. The latter is more interesting. Three spiritualistic hypotheses assume the creation of the soul at birth:

1 *Creationism* asserting that the soul is created by God (from what?) at birth.
2 *Traducianism* asserting that, during the physical conception of a child, parts of the parents' souls split off and join around the embryo to form a new soul.
3 *Generationism* asserting that human beings possess a special creative power somehow enabling them to create the new soul during a (successful?) sexual act.

Aristotle, for example, embraced creationism, Zeno traducianism. These ideas from classical philosophy recur in Christian theology.

If the soul is not created at conception or birth, it already existed before birth. This leads to the idea of pre-existence: the soul exists before birth in a soul-world. It incarnates in a body and after death returns to the original soul-world, possibly improved or deteriorated. Exceptionally, return to a body is possible. This idea was widely accepted in early Christianity. Reincarnation presumes human souls return many times to human bodies. The characteristic feature of metempsychosis or transmigration of souls is that human souls can enter animals as well.

We may separate these nine general hypotheses into those based on, or analogous to, human experience, and those which represent mental fabrications, unconnected with any experience. Materialism, postulating that human life begins at birth and ends at death, is in this respect a reasonable hypothesis. Many things in life begin and end, and having no contact with people who aren't yet born or who have died is one of life's most intense experiences. The psychic collectivism hypothesis, though more obscure, is also reasonable in this respect. Our world has many analogous phenomena, where a diffused substance (a solution, a vapour, or a suspension) may temporarily have a more fixed form (in a vessel, or absorbed). Apart from this, the first two hypotheses vary considerably in their degree of acceptability. That things have a beginning and an end may be even more abstract, but the materialistic hypothesis is also supported by actual human experience. Our ignorance of an unborn child, and the greater impact of losing a friend or family member through death are real experiences. Materialism thus is more than an intellectual analogy, it corresponds to actual experience. Psychic collectivism is mere analogy.

To imagine psychic transfer, or creationism, traducianism, and generationism, is impossible because they are not based on any real experiences. The Buddhist anatta doctrine at least has historical grounds in being a reaction to the rigid and morbid karma and reincarnation doctrines of the Brahman religion prevalent at the time of Buddha. The other three hypotheses are simply the fabrications of philosophers and theologians attempting to answer a question to which they have no answer.

More important, however, is the question of which experiences clearly affirm or contradict these nine hypotheses. Five kinds of experiences are relevant here:

1 Experiences of death: people who, resuscitated after being clinically dead for some time, recount their experience.
2 Parapsychological research into exteriorization and astral projection.
3 Spiritualistic evidence: communication with the dead, usually through a medium, and not in the context of parapsychological research.
4 Experiences preceding birth: people in regression who recall their birth, the prenatal time in the womb, and sometimes the preceding period.
5 Past-life recall: spontaneous recall with or without a trigger, and recall induced by various regression techniques.

An impressively wide literature covers these five empirical areas, varying from the experiences of the illiterate inhabitants of isolated regions to scientific research at universities (half-isolated regions inhabited by the very literate). Each of these areas reveals such distinct patterns that any serious student will find it difficult to dismiss the available empirical material. Gnostic literature is excluded here. Even if the intellectual standard is high, it remains revelation without evidence, whilst experiences which contradict the adopted gnostic framework are usually ignored or made suspect.

From now on creationism, traducianism, and generationism will be dealt with together. Table 2 is the result of the first testing of the seven points of view against these five kinds of experience.

The materialistic hypothesis, in itself a strong one, is contradicted by all five types of experience. Psychic collectivism and psychic transfer are also contradicted on the whole, although parapsychology gives no definite outcome. Obviously prenatal experiences and past-life recall contradict the idea that the soul is created at birth. The other types of experience give no clear indication about this, although much spiritualistic material refers to a form of pre-existence. Naturally, death experiences say nothing about pre-existence, reincarnation, and metempsychosis.

The parapsychological material is scanty on this point, and the spiritualistic material contradictory. After all, the greatest conflict in the international spiritualistic world is whether reincarnation exists. That the believers are in the majority is irrelevant here. Prenatal

Table 2 Soul-body hypotheses tested against various kinds of empirical evidence

	Death experiences	Psychic research	Spirit-ualism	Prenatal memories	Past-life memories
Materialism	—	—	—	—	—
Psychic collectivism	—	o	—	—	—
Psychic transfer	—	o	—	—	—
Soul originates at birth	o	o	—/o	—	—
Pre-existence	o	—/+	—/+	+	—
Reincarnation	o	—/+	+/—	o/+	+
Metempsychosis	o	—/+	—/+	o	—/+

— : contradicted
+ : affirmed
o : indecisive

experiences give no information about metempsychosis, but they do support the possibility of pre-existence and reincarnation. Finally, past-life recall definitely affirms reincarnation but gives little support to metempsychosis.

The first two are thus reasonable hypotheses, analogous to other empirical facts, but refuted by a great number of specific experiences in this area. The two following hypotheses are mental constructs which, if ever concrete enough to be refuted, are contradicted by the empirical evidence. The only hypotheses that may be considered acceptable in the light of existing empirical evidence are those postulating continuity of the human soul: pre-existence, reincarnation, and metempsychosis, the first having the weakest affirmation, reincarnation the strongest.

Prevailing opinion being largely materialistic (or, in the diluted version, agnostic: we shall never know what happens after death because nobody has ever come back) makes our task relatively easy. If the prevalent belief is not a positive doctrine but a denial, all that is required to refute it are a few convincing cases. If people believe there are no fish in a lake, only one fish has to be caught there to refute the hypothesis. However, refuting a hypothesis is quite different from changing people's minds. (After all, somebody may have put the fish there.)

As past-life experiences form the most specific and convincing material in support of the reincarnation hypothesis, we shall limit ourselves to a review of this material. Alexander Cannon has collected about 500 cases of spontaneous past-life recall (1936), Muller about 700 (1970), and Stevenson about 2,000 (see bibliography). The cases Muller collected are the most interesting because many are complicated and involve remarkable phenomena hardly credible to non-spiritualists. Stevenson has published by far the best-researched cases. Up to now he has described extensive research into about 50 cases of spontaneous recall in children (Stevenson 1966, 1975, 1977, 1980, 1983). Then there are the hypnotists and therapists who induce and guide regression to past lives. These are often recorded. The Englishman Arnall Bloxham made about 400 recordings of the regressions of about 50 people; Bjørkhem, a Swede, has collected about 600 documented regressions and Helen Wambach tops the lot with her 5,000 regressions of 1,100 people.

Alternative explanations of past-life recall

Are there other explanations, apart from reincarnation, for these apparent recollections of past lives? Stevenson, in particular, has been careful to allow for alternative explanations of his cases. Adding to his list some possible explanations for regression, we get eight alternatives:

- deception
- fantasy (e.g. to compensate)
- pseudo-recall (cryptomnesia) and *déjà vu*
- genetic memory
- waking dream or psychodrama
- the collective unconscious
- extra-sensory perception (telepathy or clairvoyance plus identification)
- obsession or possession (inspiration or possession by the souls of the dead).

The first three explanations are empirical, for deception, imagination, and pseudo-recall are familiar phenomena. The fourth is speculation. The fifth is a familiar phenomenon, the sixth is a theory, and the last two are also empirical, although many may find them just as controversial as the reincarnation hypothesis. This book doesn't go further into the extensive literature on the last two hypotheses. Their followers are mainly people who are convinced of the truth of parapsychological phenomena and the soul's existence after death, but at the same time reject reincarnation: spiritualists in the narrow sense of the word.

The explanation of *genetic memory* is merely speculation, as the research into the physical basis of memory does not indicate genetic coding and transfer of memories. Already with the early reptiles brain information transcends genetic information. Carl Sagan points this out in his interesting book about evolution *The Dragons of Eden*: 'Somewhere in the steaming jungles of the Carboniferous period there emerged an organism that for the first time in history had more information in its brains than in its genes' (Sagan 1977: 49). Sagan estimates that the human biography can be stored in a memory of 200 billion bits. With humans the genetic information is about 10 billion bits. Even if nothing of this would be necessary for physical heredity, this would be 20 times too few. It is also unclear how information would go from our brains to our genes. The idea of genetic memory contradicts all empirical data. If memory is transferred genetically, people would convey their memories when they procreate. The seed and the egg can then only have information about the life of the parents up till that point. Apparent memories of a former life simply continue after the reproduction age. Even worse, both spontaneous recall and regression start remarkably often with memories and reliving of a traumatic death in a previous life. Genetic memory only explains this if many people still copulate after death, a proposition as disgusting as it is ridiculous. Furthermore, only in a few instances is a family relationship between the present personality and the personality of the previous life possible. In the majority of cases a family relationship is impossible, for example when somebody born in a small Belgian village recalls an incarnation as a poor black in the south of the United States, two score years back. The genetic memory also fails to explain memories of a series of previous lives with their characteristic intermission periods. As an explanation of apparent past-life recall, we may comfortably discard genetic memory as pure and utter nonsense.

Deception may sometimes be a true explanation, but is ridiculous as a general explanation of past-life memories. Cases of small children apparently remembering previous lives have many witnesses on many occasions. Fantastic conspiracies would be needed to delude serious investigators of such cases. The work of Stevenson shows which checks are used and demonstrates how sensible and careful investigators of such cases may work. With hypnotic regressions at a sufficient level of trance, an experienced hypnotist can use tests and instructions to exclude deception and almost exclude self-deception. One possibility is instructing the subject to traverse various episodes of various previous lives at random. To maintain deception consistently during this playing backwards and forwards, without making mistakes, especially with voice changes, is impossible. Objective indicators of the trance depth – skin resistance, brain waves, and muscle relaxation – also make it difficult to fake. Only paranoid laymen can maintain deception as a general explanation. But such people do indeed exist.

Then there is *imagination*: fantasies people believe themselves. Often this includes compensation. People fantasize interesting and important previous lives to compensate for the boredom, frustration, and insignificance of their present lives. Compensation daydreams are well-known in psychology. Proponents of the hypothesis of compensation believe people remember special and interesting lives, which does indeed happen. People who belong to spiritual movements believing in reincarnation, in particular, may identify with interesting historical personages. Many women seem to have been Mary Magdalene, Joan of Arc, or Mary Queen of Scots, just to mention three popular previous lives. On the European continent, the champion is not Mary Queen of Scots, but Marie Antoinette. Interestingly, people not only compensate but apparently also project present self-pity on to a previous life of a famous person suffering and misunderstood. Such people have few concrete memories, but identify emotionally with recorded events about these persons.

Sensitives and strongly visual people are especially able to fantasize lives during relaxation and light trance, just as authors can write impressive and lively novels about people that never lived. Such visualization easily develops into a waking dream or psychodrama in which the unfolding history has psychological reality, dramatizing problems, desires, or challenges in story form. When somebody knows about previous lives or wants to relive one, such waking dreams can easily acquire historical decor.

Waking dreams are generally rich in archetypes and have continuous happenings without dull or repetitive situations, and lack a clear bodily feeling, but the difference from real memories is sometimes difficult to recognize. The indications of skin resistance, muscle tension, and brain rhythm of dreams, waking dreams, and regressions are the same.

An actual situation may trigger a past-life memory, which thus may have a psychodramatic and therapeutic value, just like a waking dream. Indications for a real previous life lie, then, in obscure historical details that are verified afterwards, in strong and precise bodily experiences that deviate from the present body or an idealized body, in truly novel experiences, and in experiences contradicting existing prejudices. An experienced hypnotist can induce a deeper trance to question the nature of the experience and may redirect the subject to a real regression.

For the cases of spontaneous recall and for most regressions, the hypothesis of imagination is absolutely insufficient. The work of Helen Wambach (1978), notably, killed the idea of compensation. Every person with experience in regression is impressed by the limitation and boredom of most previous lives. There are few past lives in which people were richer, or led more interesting, more varied, or more important lives.

Pseudo-recall or *cryptomnesia* means that somebody thinks he remembers his own experiences, but in fact has heard or read the story or has seen pictures and identifies the events as his own. Cryptomnesia is a real phenomenon. Hypnotic regression easily distinguishes cryptomnesia from real recall. Even a light trance, hardly more than relaxation, can discriminate real recall from cryptomnesia. There is, however, an important exception: when cryptomnesia shields real memories. Somebody identifies with a particular situation because he forgot or refuses to remember a similar real experience. In that case the repressed emotions may be projected in a sham memory, which even physical measurements like the E-meter do not identify.

Checking spontaneous or elicited historical data in a story is often difficult, but in cases where sufficient obscure historical data and previous personalities have been historically verified to make previous exposure to that information extremely unlikely, cryptomnesia becomes an improbable explanation.

Pseudo-recall, especially if it surfaces when visiting places or meeting people, is related to *déjà vu*: the sudden feeling that some situation exactly like this has happened before. For such cases pseudo-recall is a serious possibility. For spontaneous memories cryptomnesia, therefore, is sometimes a realistic explanation, for regression it almost never is.

Other phenomena that we will encounter later, such as birthmarks and the transfer of skills from previous lives, are (after excluding deception and fantasy) strong indicators against pseudo-recall, psychodrama, and the more common forms of telepathy. Holzer gives some good examples of *déjà vu* (1985).

The *collective unconscious* is no phenomenon, but an assumption from Jung to explain the phenomena of what he calls the archetypical material in our psyche. To come up with a collective unconscious is as obscure a justification as explaining mathematicians' acceptance of each others' proofs by a collective mathematical consciousness. When two people are on the phone and understand each other, it is not necessary to account for this by participation in a collective consciousness, and certainly not to place it outside the participants (for example in the telephone exchange). There is a simpler explanation for archetypes: similarity between people in their physical (neurological) and psychological structure. The language of images (probably located in the right half of the brain) has been less explored than verbal and mathematical languages, but it has its own structures and grammar as well.

Another rather frequent explanation is that people don't experience their own experiences but those of other people that have lived at some time, received by *telepathy* or *clairvoyance*. This assumes that people receive experiences of dead people, or that they tap such experiences from some spiritual database, and then identify with these memory-tracks. The usual term for this explanation is 'super-ESP'. Interestingly, this hypothesis is seriously proposed for people who have never demonstrated any paranormal sensitivity at all. It is also interesting that super-ESP is a hypothesis impossible to refute, or, to put it scientifically, it is not falsifiable. Therefore it seems sensible to use this hypothesis very sparingly.

It is rather common for established clairvoyants to identify with lost persons they are searching for, or with the people whose assumed death they are trying to get information about at the request of relatives and sometimes of police investigators. For example, they feel what the victim of a drowning or a rape may have felt. During the investigation they may feel or even demonstrate physical and psychological idiosyncrasies of the victim. Although many examples are known of wrong judgements about the origin of paranormal impressions, clairvoyants and sensitives seldom identify so much with a subject that they can no longer tell the difference (Tenhaeff). Sensitive persons, however, apparently can enter the experience of others, and with previous lives the chances of mistaken identity are obviously greater.

Some regression therapists work with sensitives or trance mediums so that they can quickly identify blocked traumata from previous lives. Therefore the hypothesis of telepathy cannot be refuted. Some sensitive persons can, even in a light trance, pick up the apparent memories of previous lives of others, especially when they know or have known them. It certainly does not happen randomly.

A survey among people attending my lectures on reincarnation strongly indicated that people with spontaneous past-life recall were generally more sensitive than people without. When people do have more than average sensitivity, they may assuredly receive other impressions. The assumption of telepathically reading the memory of another is a simpler explanation than the assumption of reading some general memory database, if only because impersonal clairvoyant impressions will be less likely to lead toward identification. It is easier to identify if there is somebody to identify with. The explanation of telepathy is realistic and has to be accepted as a possibility, especially with people who are known to be sensitive. The explanation of super-ESP, because of its speculative and irrefutable character, had better be discarded.

Most cases of young children with memories of previous lives lack indications for paranormal abilities. Furthermore, regressions exhibit no clear difference between people with and without paranormal skills. It is, emphatically, a misconception that people need specific esoteric schooling, or worse, initiation, to get past-life recall. Nevertheless, the telepathy hypothesis sometimes has to be considered seriously. Particularly sensitive people may identify with others. A genuine interest in or even a real relation with the person involved facilitates this identification. Someone may have lived in the environment of such a person, or admired him or her.

During a regression a remigrant may suddenly find out with deep emotion and intense satisfaction that he has been Beethoven. He experiences himself intensely as the deaf Beethoven conducting a symphony. If such an experience is tracked and experienced several times under the right guidance, he may suddenly dissociate from the person of Beethoven and appear to be an aristocrat on the front row, absorbedly listening and looking. After repeated reliving, he may even dissociate from this person and appear to be a theatre guard standing in the back of the theatre, listening and daydreaming. This rechecking procedure is sometimes called 'seeking bottom'. Schlotterbeck says that, especially in group regressions and in higher-self interventions ('see it all from a distance, from above'), misidentification can occur. He gives an example of somebody seeing herself during a group regression as a German officer who is disenchanted with Hitler and cuts his portrait. Later, in the individual regression, she appeared to be watching this scene approvingly as the unborn child of this officer's wife (Schlotterbeck 1987: 53).

Excluding people who convincingly, but without arguments or evidence, maintain they have lived somewhere or have been somebody else, deception, imagination, and pseudo-recall cannot satisfactorily explain the concrete memories of previous lives in the great majority of cases.

It is a rule of thumb to consider episodic memories as only of provisional value. Whenever the memories are extensive, especially with an overview of the whole life, they may be taken more seriously. Sometimes they may not be personal recollections but telepathic identification. This explanation, however, is only acceptable with people who have already demonstrated psychic sensitivity. During regressions the depth of trance, the technique of guidance, and control equipment like the E-meter are important means to discriminate cases of imagination and identification.

To summarize, the explanation of a genetic memory is nonsensical and the explanation of super-ESP unfounded and worthless. Deception may happen incidentally and is rather simple to check. Cryptomnesia may happen with apparent memory fragments coming up spontaneously, especially when places or people 'seem familiar'. Imagination may sometimes happen with uncritical and frustrated believers. Regressions may include psychodramatic waking dreams (rather easy to discern) and telepathic reception and identification (rather difficult to discern).

An apparent memory of a previous life may sometimes be explained differently, as a memory of an intermission between lives. For most people such an explanation is even more fantastic than an explanation of a previous life. Still, in some instances, maybe around 1 per cent of cases, this may explain experiences in light trance. Indications for this are experiences in which natural laws seem suspended, people have science-fiction or science-fantasy experiences in which mental powers play a great role, and a weak bodily feeling with only vague impressions about their own aspect or sex. Often, these are similar to the discarnate state psychics or mediums report. The difference from the waking dream lies mainly in the absence of emotional psychodramatic material.

Provisional conclusions

Psychic collectivism and psychic transfer, and ideas assuming that the soul is created at birth, can be refuted as speculations unsupported by evidence. Compared with these hypotheses, the materialistic hypothesis is more likely since it is in accordance with general experience. This hypothesis, however, can be maintained only if all the specific experiences mentioned – experiences of dying, psychic and spiritist experiences, prenatal and past-life memories – are refuted, ascribing them all to deception, fantasy, pseudo-recall, etc. For the moment, the only reasons I see for this are prejudice, ignorance, and mental laziness.

These specific experiences make it probable there is a soul, already independent of the body before birth or even conception. The assumption of reincarnation is by far the most probable hypothesis, and of pre-existence only, the least probable. The assumption that the human soul can incarnate in animals or even plants and things gets only meagre support. Chapter 9 will analyse the infrequent memories of non-human incarnations.

With the right guidance many people can recall memories of previous lives with relative ease. In general, to discriminate between imagination and psychodrama, and real memory is rather simple. The distinction between personal experience and the telepathically received experience of others sometimes remains unclear. Particularly in the case of people who have demonstrated paranormal abilities, apparent memories should only be ascribed to the person himself with some reservation.

An empirical vision has primarily to be built from collecting and analysing regressions and spontaneous memories, possibly enlarged by sources consistent with this material. That is what this book will do.

Further reading

The paragraph below mentions some general works on reincarnation. Books on topics that belong to specific chapters can be found at the end of those chapters. Further details on publications cited can be found in the bibliography.

The first general book on reincarnation which treated the subject broadly and with common sense was *The Problem of Rebirth: An enquiry into the basis of the reincarnation hypothesis* by Ralph Shirley (1924). Limited introductions to the subject are *The Power of Karma* by Alexander Cannon (1936) and *Reincarnation: The cycle of necessity* by Manly P. Hall (1939). Another reasonable introduction is *Reincarnation: Key to immortality* by Marcia Moore and Mark Douglas (1968).

Reincarnation, Based on Facts by Karl Muller (1970) gives the most interesting and the most systematic collection of cases. Ruth Reyna (1975) intractably links reincarnation ideas to modern physics. Daniel Cohen (1975) refutes reincarnation. James Bryce (1978) gives an introductory work indebted to Moore and Douglas, and somewhat to Netherton. *Other Lives: The story of reincarnation* (Edmonds 1979), is a fairly easily read book offering a smattering of facts by a badly informed popularizer. A bit more pretentious is *Masks of the Soul: The facts behind reincarnation* (Walker 1981), with arguments for and against reincarnation: an acceptable book, although religious authorities and empirical cases are oddly added up together on both sides of the balance. Even more pretentious, but also a class better, is *Mind Out of Time? Reincarnation Claims Investigated* (Wilson 1981). Wilson takes reincarnation claims apart. To what extent his reasoning is sound and to what extent suggestive the reader should judge for himself. At any rate, Wilson does what his title indicates; he investigates, and that is more than can be said of many pro-reincarnation books. For everyone who plans historical testing of regression material, his work is a must. He did miss Wambach's work, but otherwise he has done his homework thoroughly. His conclusion is: reincarnation does not exist; recollections of past lives are products of the imagination or products of the creativity of the unconscious, similar to multiple personalities.

A recent overview is *Reincarnation: Ancient beliefs and modern evidence* by David Christie-Murray (1981). John Van Auken (1984) published a short, somewhat mystical, treatise which belies its promising subtitle: *How reincarnation occurs, why, and what it means to you!* I had difficulty finding even phrases about the subject.

2 The History and Geographic Distribution of the Belief in Reincarnation

The general assumption that reincarnation is a typically Indian idea is as persistent as it is wrong. Ideas about reincarnation are found in diverse cultures all over the world. Some anthropologists see the reason for this in an original reincarnation belief in an earlier, higher culture since lost, which has left traces all around the world (one thinks of Atlantis). However, this view is difficult to verify and rather unlikely, considering the distribution pattern and the widely divergent character of local ideas. Anthropologically, belief in reincarnation is better conceived as an original category which has arisen independently in separate cultures.

Regions where people believe in reincarnation have more numerous cases of recollection of past lives, especially by young children. Understandably, when things are consistent with the prevailing view they are more easily reported than when in conflict with it. The occurrence of such cases in turn strengthens the belief in reincarnation, although this relationship is more complex than it seems. Presumably, the percentage of children who remember previous lives is about equal in all countries and geographical regions, and the rejection of reincarnation suppresses expression of such memories, and recognition of them, as well as further dissemination. The reverse is not true. A prevailing belief in reincarnation does not stimulate recollection. Most parents do not talk about such subjects with children of three or four, and when children come to them with such memories, parents usually find it troublesome rather than interesting. Stevenson estimates that about 1 in 1,000 children spontaneously remembers a past life. Only among the Druses did he find a frequency of 1 in 500. Another estimate, by the way, is that 1 in 450 children in northern India remembers a past life. Still, it can be argued acceptably that in our culture the percentage is somewhat lower than in more traditional societies. Chapter 14 returns to this.

The regions with cases of spontaneous memories of reincarnation in young children are clearly delineated. One region is in west Africa, roughly encompassing Nigeria, Senegal, Ghana, and surrounding territories. Another region is the home of the Druses in southeast Turkey, Lebanon, and northern Israel. A third region is south and southeast Asia, encompassing India, Sri Lanka, Burma, Thailand, Nepal, Tibet, and Vietnam. The fourth is Japan. The fifth region is an area in southeast Alaska. Finally, there is the general area of the western world, where in Europe as well as in the United States the number of cases is presumably increasing.

The nature of the belief in reincarnation in the various regions and cultures diverges strongly. Some cultures believe that people enter another body immediately after death, others believe in an intermission. Some believe that a person always returns as a human being, some believe that a person can become superhuman and then no longer needs to return, and some believe that a person can return as an animal, because of bad behaviour in this life, or as a change unrelated to reward or punishment for the preceding life.

Then, there are all kinds of views gradually passing into psychic collectivism. Anthropologically, there is a clear relation between views on death and those on sleep, with the notion of the soul usually related to that of the dream. For example, the idea that the soul departs from the body and wanders about during sleep results in the notion that the soul leaves from the nostrils and mouth as a vapour. Upon death, the soul does not return, and floats around. The soul energy may be absorbed by the land, enter the vegetation that people eat, and so end up in semen. Often, the soul is pictured as small and flying. During sleep it departs from the body, for example through the mouth, in the form of a manikin, a snake, a porcupine, a mouse, an insect, a butterfly, or a bird. During the day the soul usually inhabits the head. Therefore head-hunting, decapitating someone to take over the power of his soul, differs from cannibalism, eating flesh. After death the soul is sometimes associated with vultures. The soul wants to repossess the body via the vultures. Finally, there are less unpleasant ideas: the soul will be absorbed in trees and flowers. In primitive cultures especially, the borders between the concepts of reincarnation, metempsychosis, and psychic collectivism are vague. All kinds of modifications and combinations happen.

Margaret Mead compared cultures that believe in reincarnation with cultures that don't. The Eskimos and Balinese, who believe in reincarnation, believe children have prophetic gifts. Early on, they teach their children to do complicated things and trust that they can perform them, because in truth they are adults. Even old people continue to learn, because they trust their efforts will not be wasted. In general, such cultures suffer less from the 'generation gap'. On the other hand, a culture such as the Manus' believes that children are merely products of their parents. After death even the strongest spirits decay slowly into mud and slime. Typically, people in such cultures are written off socially and psychologically once they have reached forty.

These reflections by Margaret Mead are diametrically opposed to the common view that belief in reincarnation fosters indolence and fatalism. Usually people think of Indian culture as passive compared to the activity of western culture with its Christian faith. Every faith, however, including Christianity, can reinforce activity as well as passivity. An individual's personal attitude and response to a belief are decisive, except when the faith in question is basically pessimistic, like that of the Manus. Within such a perspective, considerable strength of mind is needed to retain an active and responsible attitude to life.

Reincarnation can be seen as an inescapable fate or as a triumph of free will. Perceiving reincarnation as inevitable or voluntary is one of the most important distinctions between the various forms of belief in reincarnation. The Hindus generally believe that karma from past lives determines everything in our present life. Hindus do not believe that the returning soul chooses its parents and they do not express any wishes about a coming life. On the other hand, the Tlingits, an Eskimo tribe in Alaska, do believe in choice of parents and often express wishes about their next life. Sometimes they even tell their relatives how they will be able to recognize them in their next life. For them, reincarnation is not a fate but the transcending of death as a choosing and developing human being.

After these introductory reflections, I will briefly review the views on reincarnation of different cultures, dealing first with contemporary primitive cultures, then the eastern religions, and, via the classical cultures, with Judaism, Christianity, and Islam. I will then touch upon the mystic, gnostic, and esoteric views in these religions. Finally, I will look at reincarnation beliefs in modern western history. The chapter ends with references to the literature on this subject.

Primitive cultures

Africa Belief in reincarnation exists in almost 100 black tribes. There are 47 tribes believing in metempsychosis, accepting the possibility of reincarnation into animals; a further 36 tribes believe in reincarnation proper, and 12 tribes believe both are possible. Interestingly enough, the reincarnation idea is probably the older one, and metempsychosis a younger variant.

The Zulus have elaborate notions of reincarnation as a gradual perfection of the individual until return is no longer necessary. They believe a secret tradition exists in all of Africa, originating from ancient Egypt and supported by teachers returning voluntarily.

The belief in reincarnation is strongest in west Africa, where reincarnation is seen as good. People do not desire release from the cycle of birth and death. To incarnate is fine and good for a soul. Childlessness is a pity and polygamy is good because people prefer to return to the same family. After a birth, the medicine man divines who the child was previously. Signs are looked at, and the young child has to pick out objects belonging to the deceased from among other objects. Children receive such names as: Father-has-returned, Mother-has-returned, He-has-returned. In general, grandparents and ancestors are assumed to return in the same family. In the south of Nigeria people believe the soul may return in several persons of different sex (Addison 1933). Like many other tribes, the Yorubas let the witch doctors divine who the child was so they can give it a proper name. During the name-giving ritual they welcome the child with the exclamation 'Thou art come!' (Addison 1933). Their notions about karma are rather vague and conflicting. Good people return as people or as good animals. Bad people become wild animals. Apart from this karmic view, they believe somebody's wishes may have considerable influence on his return. In the Congo, the Bagongo and the Bassongo have children who remember past lives. The view of these tribes is that, after death, the soul descends to the earth's centre and remains there for between two months and two years, depending on the extent of the homesickness for the world above. When the soul returns, it enters a child shortly before birth. Often, a newborn baby bears marks indicating who it was in its previous life. A painful pregnancy is seen as indication of a painful death in a previous life.

Among the Bahumbu in Zaïre, twins and triplets are honoured as reborn chiefs and surrounded with ceremony. The Elgayos of Kenya believe that the soul enters the body after birth during the name-giving ceremony, when the child receives the name of the returning family member. This notion is also found in Uganda (Addison 1933).

Asia Reincarnation beliefs in Asia are no matter of tribal culture, but of religions such as Hinduism and Buddhism. The section on eastern religions below will return to this. The Burmese assume that the recurrence of children who remember past lives is intended to remind people of the truth of reincarnation. Interestingly enough, they believe that individuals return, although the official Buddhist doctrine, anatta, teaches that although people assume characteristics of one or more previous personalities, they are not identical with any previous personality. The Balinese have a strong tradition of reincarnation. They believe people are reborn in the same family again and again. There are some reincarnation views among the Japanese, probably dating from before the advent of Buddhism.

Europe The Celts believed that, after a number of lives, they could attain the 'white heaven' in which they would become aware of God. After every death the soul has a rest period. People who lived badly return as the kind of animal to whom their character corresponded. After purification, they too will ultimately arrive in the white heaven. Teachers who voluntarily return from the white heaven inspire the continuous progress of civilization until everybody will have attained the white heaven. According to some, this is an Atlantic tradition, presumably coming via Ireland.

The ancient Teutons believed that people would reincarnate in the same family with the same name. Reincarnation beliefs of all kinds have been demonstrated among the Danes, the Norse, the Icelanders, the East-Goths, the Lombardians, the Letts, and the Saxons. The Saxons, for example, believed that a person first became a rose or a dove for a while before he could continue on to divine places. The Finns and the Laplanders also had reincarnation ideas.

The Americas The Tlingits inhabit southeastern Alaska and north-western Canada. Until recently, they had elaborate reincarnation views and practices. The Tlingits in particular paid attention to stigmata — body marks at birth indicating the newborn's identity. The returning soul can choose its future mother. Particular atten-tion is paid to dreams of pregnant women about deceased relatives. After death the deceased go to different places, one of which is for those who died violently. There is some belief in metempsychosis.

Neighbouring Indian and Eskimo tribes believe in reincarnation. For example, the western Eskimos believe in five ascending stages after this life. Overlapping reincarnations have been found among the Eskimos, in which someone was reborn before the previous personality had died. In Canada, seven Indian tribes believe in re-incarnation.

In the rest of north America belief in reincarnation was especially deep-rooted and widespread in the east. A common idea was that people of pure heart can remember past lives. Indian tribes with such ideas were the Iroquois, the Algonquins, the Creeks, the Dakotas, the Winnebagos, the Kiowas, the Hopis, and the Mohohavis. The Chip-paways believed that people could relive situations from past lives and even future lives in dreams. The Pueblos believed in the return of young children who had died. They buried the body of such a child underneath the parental home so that the soul could easily find its way back to the family. Many Indian tribes saw the white pioneers as returned generations from the past.

In Mexico and central America, Indian tribes such as the Mayas, the Caribs, and the Peruvians believed in reincarnation. The Mexican Indians believed in a form of metempsychosis. Prominent persons would return as beautiful songbirds and higher animals, while persons of lower rank would return as weasels, beetles, and other lower animal species.

The Incas believed that a person could return to his body if it was correctly mummified. Belief in reincarnation exists among Brazilian Indian tribes such as the Chiriquas. The Brazilian Indians call reincar-nation *lambazap*. Possibly, these reincarnation ideas were introduced by slaves from West Africa. Belief in reincarnation is also found among the Patagonians.

Australia and Oceania It is likely that ideas about reincarnation were originally universal among the Australian aboriginals and later existed especially among the central and northern tribes. After the confrontation with the Europeans, the belief spread among the aboriginals that they would return as white men. Thus, a native who was being executed exclaimed joyfully in his last moments: 'Very good! Me jump up white fellow!'

In the northern Pacific Ocean reincarnation beliefs exist on Okinawa. People there believe that the soul leaves the body 49 days after death. After a varying intermission, never longer than 7 generations (about 200 years), the soul returns in a body with a face and appearance resembling the previous incarnation. They do not believe that people return as animals. Some souls remain discarnate and welcome the recently deceased.

For the rest, belief in reincarnation is found among tribes on Borneo and Celebes, among the Papuans, the Maoris, and Tasmanians, and on Tahiti, Fiji, the Solomon islands, among the Marquesans, and in the southern region of New Caledonia.

Eastern religions

Hinduism Well-educated people and those from the higher castes are particularly familiar with reincarnation and karma ideas such as *punarjanma* (rebirth), *karma* (the law), and *samsara* (the reincarnation cycle). In the rural areas reincarnation ideas are not purely concerned with karma, but are more tied up with rituals and with influences from all kinds of gods and spirits. How you return does not depend on how you lived, but on whether your son has executed the proper burial rites (*antyeshti*) to guarantee a happy birth in the hereafter. Among the lower castes, particularly in the villages, there is little belief in reincarnation. Perhaps this is a collective suppression as the Hindu reincarnation doctrine is rather discouraging for the lower castes. Indian belief in reincarnation has ancient origins. The Vedas never or rarely mention it, but the Upanishads do clearly. Parts of the later Mahabharata and the (incredibly narrow-minded) laws of Manu bring up reincarnation. More cases of recollection are reported in northern India than in southern India.

The general Hindu concept is that human souls originally sprang from the Supreme Being and essentially remain identical with it. Many successive incarnations bring about a gradual involution, making souls forgetful of their origin, confused, and torpid. But gradually, through further experiences in a long succession of incarnations, people begin to realize where they must return to. Then, each life becomes an endeavour to return. Remaining blinded by the fascinations of material life becomes a sin. Man must disengage himself from these and become spiritual, attain *moksha* (see below), and so ultimately find his way back to Brahma.

Another view in Hinduism is that the souls, the *jivas*, begin as the simplest life forms. Via the mineral, the vegetable, and the animal stage they finally reach the human stage, and ultimately become angels, after many more incarnations. Each jiva, each soul, has in it *atman*, the eternal, divine essence. Samsara, the cycle of continually returning lives, leads more or less naturally to growth and ripening. When a soul, however, has attained human self-awareness, it attains freedom of choice and personal responsibility, and its own efforts determine its karma. Opposing views see individual awareness and choice as illusions, and hold that the law of karma continues to operate in the same way. At any rate, man must learn, more or less by himself, through experience or conscious choice, to find release from his imperfections. He must learn that his experiences may continue to attach him to the delusions of material life.

Souls can be differentiated to the extent that they pursue the four universal desires or goals:

Kama, or lust. This is immersing oneself in the pursuit of pleasure and the avoidance of suffering. In this stage the major sin is anger.

Artha, or material advancement. Here the major sin is avarice.

Dharma, or moral and religious virtue and integrity; literally: to fulfil the moral and religious law.

Moksha, or deliverance from physical limitations and from reincarnation.

Some see these four desires as having a natural order: when somebody has sufficiently gratified one desire he will strive for the gratification of the next, higher desire. Others see the transition to a higher desire as the result of an active struggle to destroy the lower desires. These opposing views pertain particularly to the transition between the first three desires. The transition from dharma to moksha is almost always perceived as the result of religious study, asceticism, and conscious contemplation.

There are many views about the karmic relations between lives. The rigorous karmic view is that the consequences of each action manifest themselves with iron necessity in some subsequent life. There is neither providence, nor predestination, but also no reason for fatalism. A second view is that one's thoughts determine the environment after one's death. People end up in various spheres, depending on their mentality in the previous life, with varying intermissions. Finally, there is the view that somebody's last moments in life indicate the coming life, or even that the mood, thoughts, feelings, and contacts of somebody's last moments are decisive for the next life.

The rigorous views on reincarnation and karma are closely related to the caste system, especially through the karma view set down in the laws of Manu, giving elaborate descriptions of the punishments for human imperfections. Sins of the body make a person return as a mineral or plant. Sinful language leads to a life as a bird or an animal, and sins committed in thought only let you return as a low-ranking person. Someone who has lived badly seeks a bad womb: the womb of a dog, a swine, or a pariah. Only those who have behaved themselves end up in a good womb.

The caste system is so vicious, you cannot even escape it spiritually. Only a Brahman, carrier of the holy cord, can attain moksha. Thus, a person who doesn't belong to the highest caste can contemplate and live ascetically until his bones ache, and yet the best he can attain is being born as a Brahman in his next life. A middle position is the belief that people not carrying the holy cord can attain moksha through extremely intense asceticism and heavy penance. Then, some hope is left.

The lower castes have found a practical solution to this oppressive doctrine: in general, they do not believe that their presence in these castes is karmically determined; or they do not believe in karma and reincarnation; or they simply ignore such theories.

A religion with such views also has difficulties with children who recall past lives, since karmic punishments are conspicuously absent in these cases of recollection.

In the sixth century B C two reform movements arose against the gross discrimination of the prevailing faith: Buddhism and Jainism. Outside India Buddhism is widespread, but inside India it has virtually disappeared. Jainism is limited to about two million people in India. They carry some weight, for they enjoy a good reputation and many of them are influential, holding prominent positions.

Buddhism Buddhists prefer to speak of rebirth rather than reincarnation. Hinduism and Buddhism both believe in the workings of karma, and in samsara: the virtually endless repetition of lives with an illusion of personal existence until moksha, the liberation from all this, is attained. Some Buddhists entertain the view that a person's last thoughts strongly influence his next life and, at least, largely determine his surroundings after death, as the Tibetan Book of Death teaches, for example.

The most important difference between the Hindu and the Buddhist views on reincarnation is probably the Buddhist doctrine of *anatta*, which holds that, although characteristics of the deceased are transmitted to the life of a new person, the personal entity itself is discontinued. Thus, the soul lacks a permanent self; there is no atman. Therefore the doctrine is called an-atman or an-atta. The usual analogy is the flame of one candle lighting another candle. There is continuity, but no identity. A modern variant is the analogy of a billiard ball knocking against another billiard ball and passing on its momentum, without the two balls being the same. The anatta doctrine is related to the abolition of the caste system in Buddhism.

Buddhism teaches that Buddha himself was able to remember his previous lives, and instructed those who wanted to remember. The anatta doctrine is found particularly in Theravada Buddhism. As already mentioned, this doctrine is officially adhered to in Burma, while the lay people believe in proper reincarnation, recurrent cases of recollection nourishing this belief. In Buddhist texts the same narrow-minded and infantile horror stories abound as in other religions. If somebody is doing the wrong things, 'he will be born again and again, born either blind, dull-witted, dumb, or as an outcast, always living in misery, always a victim of abuse. He will become a hermaphrodite or a eunuch, or be born in lifelong slavery. He [may also] become a woman, a dog, a pig, an ass, a camel or a poisonous snake, and [thus] be unable to put the Buddha's teachings into practice' (Willson 84: 15). I wonder what happens to a woman who is a victim of abuse, and therefore must be doing wrong things because she cannot put the Buddha's teaching into practice. Note that the list implies metempsychosis. Buddhist ideas are as diverse and inconsistent as in any other religion.

According to some Tibetan Buddhists rebirth occurs immediately. A Tibetan speciality is the reincarnation of lamas, called *sprul-sku*. Here, the entity is preserved because a counterforce is exerted against the disintegration of the personality. This requires will power and physical strength. People with unfinished missions sometimes return in this way. Since the fifteenth century the reincarnations of important lamas have been identified according to fixed oracle and divination procedures.

Probably the best available exposition of reincarnation views in Tibetan Buddhism is the book by Lati Rinbochay and Jeffrey Hopkins (1979). The foreword and the preface state clearly the basic beliefs. It is clear that karma is less important than the attitude just before death. The lucid exposition in plain language reveals how much superstition and shallow psychology the Tibetan belief contains. When less virtuous people die they start to lose warmth from the top of the body, while more virtuous persons start to lose warmth from the feet. If a wish is not granted, people get angry. Apparently nobody is ever just sad and disappointed. If you lost considerable warmth due to your illness, you desire warmth and so you go to a hot hell. Why not to a warm heaven? Because you desired something. A poor unfortunate dying of cold in Bergen-Belsen will end up in a hell, because he or she desired some warmth. What staggering prejudice!

Clericalism in Tibet has also led to a ritualization of views on reincarnation and karma. It is not the quality of the present life which determines the next life, but the fulfilment or neglect of prescribed rituals. Even accidentally forgetting, just once, to give one of the holy statues its bowl of water during the daily water offerings at the family chapel will result in poverty in the next life. When an animal, for example a parrot, repeats the mantra '*Om Mane Padme Hum*', even without understanding its meaning, it will return as a higher form of life (Rato 1977: 9–12).

Mahayana Buddhism This teaches the coming of the Bodhisattvas. Bodhisattvas are people who have attained Nirvana and so are not obliged to return into a body any more but do so anyway out of compassion for still-suffering humanity. The doctrine of the return of great teachers is found in many religions, for example among the Celts, as mentioned before. We will come across other examples. Some Buddhist doctrines elaborate this idea into a whole pantheon of existing and future Bodhisattvas who become Buddha one by one according to a fixed schedule. This turns the highest compassion into a vehicle of superhuman machinery rather than a human experience.

Jainism Like Buddhism and Hinduism, Jainism knows samsara and moksha. The main difference from the other two religions is the view that karma is solely dependent on actual consequences of acts, not on the moral intent. To cause somebody's death unintentionally produces the same karma as to murder him in cold blood or blind passion. Naturally, Jainists are very conscientious. They practise *ahimsa*, complete pacifism, strict vegetarianism, and unremitting service. According to Jainism, before moksha is attained, the soul can only exist in a body. So, after death, it immediately attaches itself to the conception of a child and is reborn after nine months. When people recall past lives with an intermission longer than nine months, this is interpreted as a forgotten in-between life as a child who died young.

Views on reincarnation in Confucianism, Taoism, and Shintoism are rare. Buddhism introduced reincarnation into China, where it became part of folk religion.

The classical cultures

Egypt and Babylon Relatively few historical indications point to a belief in reincarnation in Egypt. According to Herodotus, the Egyptians were the first to believe in an immortal soul. The Egyptians thought that long ago the gods had departed and sinful spirits had remained behind who had to do penance for their sins in human bodies. They believed that after a soul had passed away, it dwelt in all kinds of vegetable and animal incarnations for 3,000 years, and then returned as a human. Preferably, this would be the original body, at least if it had been properly mummified. An intact mummy guaranteed a future domicile and also prevented the need for lower incarnations during the interval.

We have no indications of Babylonian beliefs in reincarnation.

Greece The Greek views on reincarnation originate from the Orphic mysteries which, again according to Herodotus, originally came from Egypt. The Orphic doctrine held that people consist of a small divine element and a large, bad, Titan element. Humans must learn to eliminate the Titan element inside them. This entails many reincarnations from which, ultimately, deliverance is possible. Reward and punishment for a life come in the next human or animal incarnations. The Orphic mysteries inspired the Elysian mysteries, in turn influencing Pindars among others. Pindars adhered to the view that the next incarnation is reward or punishment for the intermission. Reincarnation would take place after eight years.

Some see the myth of Persephone as an allegorical reference to reincarnation. The original Orphic idea of the wheel of birth and death, where the soul is periodically caught in a body and strives towards deliverance, is closer to the classical Indian philosophy than to Egyptian thinking.

A second source of Greek views on reincarnation were the Pythagoreans. Like his teacher Pherecydes, Pythagoras taught reincarnation, following among others, the Phoenicians, the Chaldeans, and the Egyptians. The ability to recall past lives was regarded as a gift from Hermes. Allegedly, Pythagoras recalled his past lives, and therefore was called Mnesarchides. His previous incarnations were, among others, Aethalides, and Euphorbus who fought for Troy.

According to Ovid, Pythagoras taught that good animals may become humans, and humans may become animals. After a long series of animal incarnations, you may return as a human. This differs from the usual metempsychotic supposition that animal and human incarnations may alternate. Heraclitus taught that a human could never reincarnate as an animal or plant, but always incarnated as a human. Empedocles, a pupil of Pythagoras, taught that humans were originally semi-gods who had sinned. During 30,000 seasons they had to wander through all kinds of male and female incarnations.

Plato's *Phaedo* alleges that Socrates, under Orphic and Pythagorean influence, taught reincarnation. Sensuous people would get blemishes on their soul and as a result incarnate more quickly. Plato saw the human capacity to know the truth as evidence for pre-existence, a new argument in views on reincarnation. Further, he pointed to the many cycles in nature. In *Meno*, in particular, Plato accounts for knowledge without previous learning by past lives. *Phaedrus* may be interpreted as containing views on reincarnation and karmic laws. In *The Republic* Plato describes encounters between arriving and departing souls. The arriving souls see the diverse workings of the universal law. Based on these examples and their own previous experience, they choose their life with all the consequences 'before the throne of necessity'. Then, they receive a draught of forgetfulness and enter life.

Aristotle only teaches reincarnation in his early work *Eudemus*. Later he abandons the idea of reincarnation. His writings about the soul only contain indications of a belief in pre-existence.

In the last century before Christ, belief in reincarnation is at its lowest ebb. Stoic and Epicurean views predominate. Cicero, converting from agnosticism to Platonism, re-embraces the belief in reincarnation. He sees life as a punishment for sins in past lives. An interesting new consideration is that important people contribute to society because they unconsciously know that they will personally return to the society of the future. According to the later story, the legendary Apollonius of Tyana learned the reincarnation doctrine from Iarchas in Kashmir. Allegedly, in a previous incarnation as first mate on an Egyptian ship he had refused to deliver the boat into the hands of pirates. Plutarch considers people as beings wandering from life to life. According to him there are higher spirits ('genii') who only incarnate when they have done something wrong, particularly when they have had a bad influence on incarnated people.

The Neoplatonists, especially of the Alexandrian school, again pick up the ideas of reincarnation and elaborate them. There has been an involution: because of pride and a false desire for independence, our souls have ended up in the difficult and evil world we inhabit now. According to Plotinus, our physical world is the least divine, but it is a good place to learn, and essentially good. Carelessness and obduracy get us lost and imprisoned in the sensual limitations of physical existence. We tend to pursue lower desires and to wield power. However, in doing so, we gain experience and give scope to the talents we are only able to develop in our physical form of existence. Ultimately, we return to our original state, but now with all the experience and knowledge we acquired while incarnated. Throughout all the incarnations a part of the soul remains itself, untouched, divine. Our periodic sojourns in the material state make us well aware of the perfection of the spiritual state. Our experiences with evil provide us with better insight into the value of the good. Humans may incarnate as animals. Practising civil virtues (compare with dharma) and becoming humane (compare with artha and dharma) make us return as humans. Living sensually makes us return as animals. Irresponsibility makes us return as a domestic animal. Devotion to evil makes us return as a ferocious animal; devotion to lust or gluttony makes us return as a sensuous or voracious animal. Abuse of the senses makes us return as plants. Specific characteristics, therefore, lead to incarnations as specific kinds of animals. People who devoted themselves too much to music, but otherwise lived purely, return as songbirds. Tyrants return as eagles, and those who speak frivolously of divine subjects return as soaring birds. This is true allegorical thinking, as in many metempsychotic views. Neoplatonists like Proclus of Syria, however, declared that humans always return as humans, and animals always as animals.

Judaism, Christianity, and Islam

Judaism In general, Judaism has few and weak indications for a belief in reincarnation, but, for example in the Old Testament, many and strong indications for a belief in pre-existence of the soul. Reincarnation may often be implied or presumed as a common idea. In the time of Jesus, the Sadducees were strictly materialists, the Essenes believed in pre-existence, and the Pharisees believed that people are either reborn or destroy themselves in the underworld. The Pharisaic notion of reincarnation existed up until the ninth century. Since the eighth century the Karaite Jews have believed in re-incarnation.

According to some Jewish thinkers, the number of incarnations is usually limited to three. Philo Judaeus mixes Platonic and Stoic ideas. He says that souls, staying in a mortal body for some time, pick up terrestrial inclinations such as eagerness to learn. God is necessary for human deliverance. The legendary Simon Magus saw Helen of Troy returned in Mary Magdalene. The Samaritans held the doctrine of Taheb, according to which Adam reincarnated as Seth, Noah, Ab-raham, and Moses. But doctrines that great leaders and teachers may return do not imply that common people normally reincarnate.

Christianity Various passages in the New Testament indicate pre-existence and some appear to indicate reincarnation. The best known example is John the Baptist, who is regarded as the returned Elijah. Such passages are found especially in Mark, but also in Matthew, Luke, and John. John 9: 1–3 and John 17: 24 are seen as indications of a belief in reincarnation. Early Christianity seems to have been divided on the subject. Many church fathers accepted at least pre-existence. Justin the Martyr accepted reincarnation, but did consider recall of past lives impossible. According to him, people who were too unworthy to receive Christ would return as wild animals.

Apparently, Origen considered the gnostic pro-reincarnation argu-ments sound and also pointed to the well-known example of Elijah and John. Further, he made pre-existence of the soul seem plausible. Later propagandists of reincarnation saw his expositions as pro-reincarnation arguments. Because the Council of Constantinople condemned his doctrines in the year 553, some modern gnostics regard this year as the date when the reincarnation doctrine was pushed away from Christian thought. Annie Besant and others propounded this questionable view.

The Second Council of Constantinople in 553 was primarily concerned with the difficulties arising from the Council of Chalcedon in 451, especially with the question of whether Christ consisted of one or two natures. The Council of Constantinople concurred with the imperial politics of Justinian who was trying to gain control over the west, and therefore considered arbitration on the subject necessary to diminish the discord between east and west. For this reason, he put pressure on the Council. On 5 May 553, 165 bishops gathered under the chairmanship of Eutychius, the patriarch of Constantinople. The then Pope, Virgil, was in opposition, and sought refuge in a church. In the Pope's absence, the Council condemned the double nature (one of Origen's doctrines) laid down by the Council of Chalcedon. The Pope continued to resist until 8 December 553, but finally yielded and ratified the Council's resolution on 23 February 554. With this, the unity of the two natures in Christ became the church's official doctrine. A secondary subject of discussion during the Council was the ratification of earlier condemnations of a number of Origen's views. It is impossible to ascertain the views at stake, but likely that the doctrine of pre-existence was among them.

The western church rejected the Second Council of Constantinople. In Africa the imperial troops forced acceptance. The bishops of northern Italy distanced themselves from Rome and refused to acknowledge the Pope's ratification. They found support in Spain and France. The whole Council became irrelevant as the result of the Islamic conquest of most of the provinces of the Monophysitic church.

The long and the short of this is the untenability of the proposition that the church abjured the doctrine of reincarnation in 553. First of all, the condemnation of Origen's opinions was only a secondary subject for discussion. Secondly, the Council was about ratification of earlier condemnations. Thirdly, large portions of the church rejected the Council. Fourthly, it remains unclear which of Origen's doctrines were at stake. Fifthly, Origen's texts defended pre-existence and did not give direct support for reincarnation ideas. Origen taught, for example, that the various circumstances in peoples' lives were the result of sins they had committed during their spiritual pre-existence. The existence of the body was a purification from the sins committed during pre-existence.

In recent times a number of Christian clerics have published tracts arguing that belief in reincarnation is in agreement with the Christian faith. Nevertheless, the doctrine of reincarnation has hardly played a significant role in the historical development of Christianity. According to Guirdham (1970), the Cathars' belief in reincarnation was one of the causes of the Church's enmity toward them.

Islam Islam does not contain explicit belief in reincarnation, although a few Muslim sects believe in it. Several passages in the Koran could be interpreted in this way, but they could as well refer to spiritual rebirth. A number of Muslims think that after death the human soul may pass into an animal or into another person, depending on his state. Because a human soul may end up in an animal after death, the Boras in Hindustan, for example, are vegetarians, and have the custom of buying captive birds to set them free because the souls of dead people could be in them. (This practice has created the bird-catching business.)

Only the Sufis believe in reincarnation, presumably under Persian influence, ultimately from Zoroaster. According to Zoroaster the immortal soul enters this world for a short period, to gain experience. The soul may have descended from higher spheres or may be working its way up from a lower sphere. Contrasting with the Indian ideas such as the tradition of each person having 840,000 incarnations, Persian views of reincarnation assume a small number of lives since they consider progression and retrogression of the soul as self-reinforcing processes. A soul misbehaving in one life creates circumstances in its next life reinforcing the tendency to misbehave. Equally, good behaviour results in the likelihood of good behaviour in the next life. This self-reinforcing acceleration leads after relatively few incarnations to a decisive turn.

The Sufi Jalal-Ud-Den-Rumni taught the well-known evolution doctrine that the human soul originally incarnates in minerals, and develops via plant, animal, and human lives into an angel and upwards.

A partially Islamic sect believing in reincarnation is that of the Druses. They assume immediate rebirth. The Jainists believe that upon death the soul is immediately connected to the conception of a new child and is reborn nine months later. The Druses, however, believe that the soul immediately returns in a child being born. Because of this immediate transition, great importance is attached to the last thoughts of the dying person, since they could have a strong influence on the new beginning. Of course, almost all of the fairly frequent instances of past-life recall have intermission periods. They, too, explain these by forgotten short lives in between. They assume they are a closed incarnation group, and always incarnate as Druses because they are a chosen people (heard somewhere before?). The number of Druse souls is therefore stable. When many people die, by war, famine, or pestilence, the same number are not immediately reborn. They account for this by a waiting place, somewhere in China. The Druses do not discourage recall, but do regard these cases critically.

Gnostic, mystic, and esoteric movements

Christianity and Judaism, as well as Islam, have gnostic movements. In general, they contain elements from the doctrines of Zoroaster, which, via Mithraism and Manicheism, influenced among others such diverse Christian groups as the Paulicians, the Priscillians, the Bogomiles, and the Cathars. Another common source are the ancient Orphic mysteries, which became known as the Hermetic tradition in the Hellenic world through Pythagoras, especially among the Neoplatonists. This tradition indisputably included reincarnation.

According to Irænæus, reincarnation was the central idea of the first gnostics. He refers to Simon Magus and to the strong Zoroastrian traditions in gnosticism. The gist of his rendition of the gnostic views is that repeated incarnations are aimed at gaining rich experience, to compensate guilt and to purify and improve the soul. According to him, the gnostics also taught that people not attaining gnosis would return as animals. It remains difficult, however, to make these two notions agree with each other.

The Ismaelites are a well-known Sufi group. They distinguish *tanasukh*, the normal reincarnation, *rijat*, the return of spiritual leaders, and *hukul* or *burut*, the systematic, periodic return of those who have attained perfection. An important example of hukul would be the return of Krishna as Buddha, and later as Muhammad.

The Kabbala believes in the pre-existence of the soul. The soul chooses its body. If it lives well, it purifies and cleanses itself and, after death, is received into God. For most, one life is sufficient, others will need two, or perhaps three. An idea from the Kabbala is that undesirable characteristics such as stinginess and narrow-mindedness lead to a next life as a woman. Another idea is that whoever forgets even one of the 613 precepts will have to reincarnate. In spite of this narrow-minded view, some hope remains, because

47

ultimately all people end up on high again, apparently even women. Then, it will be the turn of the dark angels to seek purification and cleansing in this world.

The Kabbala has numerous examples of reincarnations of Jewish leaders. Adam allegedly returned as David, and in the future will return as the Mesjicha, the Messiah. Cain reincarnated as Jethro, Abel as Moses, Japhet as Samson, etc.

The Chassidim, a Jewish mystic sect, believe that an untimely death is followed by a supplementary life. There is the further idea that devout Jews are sometimes reborn among the Gentiles in order to instil understanding of the Jews and to help them.

Modern western history

The idea of reincarnation returned to the west with the revival of Platonism and Neoplatonism, succeeding the medieval world-view dominated by Aristotle. In 1439 George Gemisthos Pletho from Mithra visited Cosimo de'Medici in Florence. This resulted in the founding of what became known as the Platonic Academy. The revival of Platonism emanated from this academy, and with it came related Hermetic, Pythagorean, and Kabbalistic ideas. Associated with this Platonic and Neoplatonic revival are names such as Nicholas of Cusa, Trithemius of Spondheim, Paracelsus, and Cornelius Agrippa. An important name in this context is that of the German humanist Reuchlin, who exercised great influence on, among others, Melanchthon.

In the Netherlands, for example, a Neoplatonic offshoot into humanism and the Reformation inspired Van Helmont's discourse in 1690, in which he argued that reincarnation is a maturation and gradual redemption from guilt, which ultimately partakes in the ascension of Christ by building up a spiritual body that liberates the individual from reincarnation. He adds some pungent details, such as that perjurers will be reborn forty times as bastards. What becomes of perjuring bastards remains unclear, but undoubtedly it is extremely unpleasant.

In his monad doctrine Giordano Bruno offers a personal and abstract view on reincarnation. A monad is a microcosmic element, proceeding through all forms of life in an infinite number of worlds in all but endless cycles. Some of these worlds are inhabited, some further developed than ours. The idea of reincarnation on other planets is brought up here for the first time. Bruno's ideas were later to influence Leibniz, who also regarded the soul as a microscopic monad. Death is just a dramatic instance of sleep, leaving behind the heavier body. A portion of the incarnation remains. Thus rebirth entails an only partially new personality. Reincarnation is more metamorphosis than transmigration. Leibniz postulates identity throughout the incarnations, a view diametrically opposed to anatta ideas.

The Enlightenment and its accompanying deism toy with many Greek, Roman, and eastern ideas, probably to ease liberation from the dominant dogmas of the church. Benjamin Franklin believed that no human experience is lost and that, as he said, new editions will keep coming out, with small improvements on the previous ones. Frederick the Great of Prussia was convinced that the better part of a person remains alive. He suspected that he would not return as a king, but was sure he would lead another active life (and hoped he would meet less ingratitude). Following Bruno, Kant toyed with the idea that reincarnation could take place on other planets, via the sun, to ever further and colder planets. Others such as Johann Bode and Louis Figuier believed just the opposite: human souls begin on cold planets and evolve toward ever warmer ones.

During the German Enlightenment in particular, a lot of prominent men, such as Lessing, Von Herder, and Goethe believed in reincarnation. Goethe believed he had lived at least a thousand times before, and was likely to return another thousand times. He regarded death essentially as a recurrent purge. He characterized man as a dialogue between God and Nature, and said that on other planets doubtlessly a higher and more profound dialogue could take place. Goethe believed he had been married to Frau Von Stein in a previous life and was convinced he had lived as a Roman before Emperor Hadrian.

Charles Fourier believed that reincarnation would continue until the end of this earth, and that we would then reincarnate *en masse* on a new planet. Schopenhauer believed that primarily the human will reincarnates. During the intermission the will sleeps. We need to forget our previous lives to start anew clean and refreshed. Only

Buddha had clear recollections of his past lives. Schopenhauer believed in the Buddhist view of karma. Furthermore, he was convinced that we will meet people we know now again in future lives. It is hard to reconcile this with the idea that individuals do not reincarnate and that only the will continues (whatever that may mean).

There are many further names of believers, such as Swedenborg, William Blake, Schiller, Mazzini, Herman Melville, Leo Tolstoy, Paul Gauguin, Arthur Conan Doyle, Gustav Mahler, etc., etc.; then, a large number of Americans from the beginning of the nineteenth century. More recent figures are David Lloyd George, Henry Ford, Rudyard Kipling, Jean Sibelius (who believed that millions of years ago he had been incarnated in swans and wild geese) and General Patton. Books seeking to make reincarnation plausible eagerly quote such people.

Provisional overview

There is no such thing as one system of belief in reincarnation. Ideas about reincarnation are extremely diverse and contradictory, their only common thread being the view that after death people can, or must, or want to return as humans. What are the major differences between ideas about reincarnation? Some see reincarnation in terms of natural laws, others in terms of reward or punishment, others again in terms of development. Return may be punishment for neglecting ritual, church obligations, and so on. Believing in reincarnation may lead to the same kind of fatalism as the belief that someone else has suffered for our (even as yet uncommitted) sins. Reincarnation theories are, like Christian and other religious ideas, susceptible to application in spiritual intimidation and blackmail.

A second difference lies in the magnitude of the number of reincarnations: is it a few, some hundreds, or the Indian number, 840,000? To what extent do past lives influence the present life, and what are the causes of such an influence? Then again, what can be said about intermission? Or is there immediate reincarnation? And, if so, is it at birth or during conception?

This chapter has been a sightseeing tour *à la* 'Europe in five days', my intentions being:

1 To get rid of the idea that reincarnation is an Indian doctrine.
2 To get rid of the idea that reincarnation is a well-defined (and fatalistic) doctrine.
3 To get rid of the idea that reincarnation was originally a Christian doctrine eliminated by a council.
4 To show how reincarnation, like any other general belief, is subject to pedantic righteousness, incoherent associations, incredible prejudice, alarming narrow-mindedness and bottomless speculation, and to show how it may be used as an effective instrument to discipline the flock.

People tend to puzzle and fantasize. Reincarnation is yet another fertile subject. Pointing out that more than half of humanity has believed in it for more than half of recorded human existence is a weak argument. Similarly, name-dropping is a weak argument. After all, what we have here are diverse, contradictory, and often fantastic notions.

Chapter 14 will test the various ideas against the available empirical material.

Further reading

The most important and easily available source book is *Reincarnation: The Phoenix Fire Mystery* by Head and Cranston (1977), which is the main source for this chapter. Originally published in 1961, it is first-rate, extensive and with many exact quotes; the only possible objections are that it is less complete than it suggests, somewhat neglecting non-English sources, and that it overestimates the role of theosophy. Nevertheless, it is heartily recommended!

Another excellent book, unfortunately hardly available, is *La Réincarnation* by Bertholet (1949). His discussion of eastern and classical thought is especially extensive and careful. Bertholet also discusses modern approaches including Kardec and experimental literature such as de Rochas, and other spiritist and parapsychological works. His personal views are apparent only in a sometimes overly serious treatment of relatively unimportant sources. However, the extent of his reading is impressive, his discussion is wide and thorough, and he appears to have had more access to French works than Head and Cranston. For the real student, this work is also a must. Another good French book is *La Réincarnation des Âmes selon les Traditions Orientales et Occidentales* by Des Georges (1966).

Other works are of lesser quality or more limited scope. One of the first books in this area is by E. D. Walker (1888), mostly containing reincarnation thoughts by literary men – witness the broad collection of included poems. Eva Martin's book *The Ring of Return: An anthology of references to reincarnation and spiritual evolution: from prose and poetry of all ages* (1927) has been reprinted and is a valuable predecessor to *The Phoenix Fire Mystery*. Martin quotes widely from poetry and other literature, and in this respect is halfway between Walker, and Head and Cranston.

An extensive survey of German literature is given by Emil Bock (1932). Walker is theosophically inclined, while Bock is a thorough anthroposophist. He seems to give reincarnation a German patent, and all writers are treated as heralding anthroposophy. Still, an informative book.

At the beginning of this century a number of books presented reincarnation as a Christian belief. James Pryse (1900) is one of those who claim that the New Testament teaches reincarnation. His book was reprinted in 1965, and in 1980 translated into German with extensive additions by Agnes Klein. His argument does not convince me, but I am not trained in theology or philology. A less pretentious, friendly, Christian booklet about reincarnation comes from Ernest Wilson (1936).

Many more or less theosophical books contain historical chapters (Atkinson 1908; Van Ginkel 1917). Van Holthe tot Echten (1921), who believes that reincarnation is nonsense, gives a good historical confutation of the claim made by Besant among others that early Christianity taught reincarnation. Eckhart (1937) published a work about reincarnation beliefs among the ancient Germans. Buddhist ideas about reincarnation are discussed by Alexandra David-Neel (1961), who writes many interesting things especially about Tibet, by de Silva (1968), and in the first part of the book by Francis Story (1975). A few interesting remarks about Tibet can be found in Rato (1977). Martin Willson (1984) uses modern reincarnation evidence to correct some scholastic interpretations of Buddhism. He is one of the few religious authors who is well read in the modern literature.

However, he does not seem to realize that this evidence may confirm rebirth, but is at complete variance with the classical Buddhist speculations on the subject. Some historical references are found in Manly P. Hall (1939) and Maria Penkala (1972).

An excellent source of information about ideas in primitive cultures about the soul-body relationship is *Vehicles of Consciousness* by Poortman (1978). The theosophical background of the author does not detract at all from the scientific standing of this work.

3 Esoteric Reincarnation Doctrines: The Views of Theosophy and Anthroposophy

Theosophy

Despite a coherent literature, it is difficult to define the theosophical view on reincarnation. Many of the movement's ideas about reincarnation have been gradually but rather sweepingly modified in the course of its development and some ideas have remained vague and somewhat contradictory. The essence of the theosophical view is made clear in their criticism of Allan Kardec, namely that he neglects the true nature and character of the intermission the theosophists call *Devachan*, does not preach karma, and lacks an explanatory philosophy. Apparently, the theosophists regard the relationship with Devachan, their karma doctrine, and the general background to their occult philosophy as essential to their own vision of reincarnation. The theosophical sources for the following review are given at the end of this chapter.

The concept of monadic evolution Following the classic Indian views, theosophists believe in rhythmic world manifestations, *manvantaras*, alternated with periods of cosmic sleep, *pralayas*. When a manvantara begins, the elementary individual spirits, called monads after Leibniz, awaken. Apparently, many monads are willing to endure the trying exertions of the physical universe. They learn to become creators themselves in matter, ultimately to become co-creators of the next universe. Monads develop gradually. They start with many mineral lives, and they gradually ascend, via plant and animal lives, to human lives. This development is an involution as well as an evolution. The monad begins as a spiritual being, far removed from its physical counterpart. As this physical counterpart gradually evolves into a vehicle of consciousness, and into a human being, the monad gradually involutes to inhabit and to melt into the person with his physical body, and so, finally gains self-consciousness. This human body has evolved from the bodies of the higher animals. Here ends the natural involution of the monad and the natural evolution of its vehicles. Man now continues his development under his own responsibility, ultimately returning to his original spiritual state, but now self-aware and with a fully evolved body.

Before the monad descends for the first time in a human body, it incarnates a few times in one of the highest animals: an elephant, a monkey (actually a degenerate product from cross-breeding between humans and animals), a dog, a cat, or a horse.

Each great manvantara consists of smaller cycles of alternating periods of manifestation and periods of rest. In the beginning of a smaller manvantara, planets come into being as breeding stations for the next step in monadic evolution. Our present mankind went through less dense material conditions in its previous mineral, plant, and animal stages of monadic evolution. Reincarnation is a manvantara-pralaya rhythm of physical and spiritual lives. At the present degree of material density these transitions imply real birth and death. However, the laws of reincarnation and karma are general laws of evolution, applying to all evolving beings in an evolving universe. With our degree of material density, birth means a real threshold, requiring a lot of effort. Why do we exert such effort? What is driving us? The theosophists distinguish five different drives leading to rebirth:

- the attraction of the earth
- attachment to material objects and physical conditions
- karma
- desire for external impressions to reinforce self-awareness
- desire for self-expression in the material world (*trishna*).

Attachment to material objects and physical conditions is a psychological trait, and karma a natural law. The first three drives have material motives, and the last two egocentric motives. Overinvolvement of the ego in itself, and overattachment to matter cloud the real spiritual nature of man, and make him forget his high descent. Still, these conditions make the personality grow, which is the essence of evolution.

In the theosophical vision the total number of lives is virtually immeasurable. On each planetary cycle we have many thousands of incarnations. According to Sinnett (1883: 61) we have had something under 800 incarnations so far on our planet, and we need many more to attain the highest perfection in this world, becoming members of the universal brotherhood, helpers, and teachers for the rest of humanity. Ultimately, we attain Nirvana as a personal pralaya. But the golden thread of individuality remains, and afterwards we will progress further. The most important theme of this monumental development of worlds is the growth of four-dimensional conscious-ness.

The general picture, then, is of a gradual involution of spiritual monads and a simultaneous evolution of the physical bodies the monads use during their incarnations, until both lines merge. After that, the evolution continues under our own responsibility, precari-ously, because of the ever-present risk that the monad overinvolves itself with physical things and with itself: and ensnares itself too much.

Compared to classic Hinduism, theosophy regards the wheel of rebirth less as continuous suffering from which to seek release, and more as planned development under our own responsibility, and thus influenced by our own capriciousness to some extent. But this capriciousness is a cardinal fact of evolution. Opportunities for devi-ation from the plan are essentially included in the plan.

The higher and lower self: individuality and personality The theosophical doctrine speaks of the higher self, the actual monad, the spark of the universal spirit, the unifying principle through all lives; and of the lower self, the emanation or projection of the higher self in its actual vehicle, different in each life. When man forgets his spiritual nature and original descent, the cord between his higher and lower selves becomes thinner. Initiation strengthens and secures the relationship. The lower self has a quasi-independent consciousness, connected with the body. The relationship between the higher self and the lower self is like that of an actor and the role he is playing. When the show is over, only the actor remains.

The higher self, the real individuality, consists of the three highest bodies of the human microcosm: *Atma*, *Buddhi*, and *Manas*. Manas is the real ego, also called the causal body in its manifestation. The personality, the lower self, is the astral soul, deceasing after each incarnation in the astral field of *Kamaloka*. The mental, astral, etheric and physical bodies each contain indestructible elements, the 'permanent atoms'. These atoms always stay with the individuality of the person. The permanent atoms and the aura collect the experience of each life.

In the case of an unnatural death, such as an abortion, an early childhood death, an accident, or a murder, rebirth may occur before the lower self has dissolved in Kamaloka. In Blavatsky's understanding of reincarnation (1886), the lower self also returns in these cases. She considered this an undesirable exception. The earliest literature claims that each personality dissolves completely. On the other hand, life experiences are collected in the permanent atoms and the aura. Blavatsky herself, however, was sure that we, the way we are here and now as living persons, will die and never return. In so far as initiates have strengthened the relationship between their higher and lower selves, they may also retain their personalities.

From death to birth From Buddhi, the second part of the human microcosm, a *Buddhic web* of life threads extends into the etheric body and reaches out from there into the physical body. At death these life threads withdraw and wrap themselves around a core in the heart into a flame of gold and purple. Then they go to the third cerebral cavity and, together with the permanent atom and the life flame, they depart through the top of the head. During this process, the dying person experiences a panoramic review of his sensory life, the retrospect of his whole life in the physical brain. The life panorama later repeats itself in the astral brain. The consciousness of the lower self remains attached to the material brain. When the material body decays, the consciousness of the lower self decays also. Recollection of past lives is therefore impossible.

The remaining astral-etheric portion of the lower self ends up in Kamaloka, the astral field surrounding and permeating the earth. Here, we indulge all our desires, without the administration and detachment of conscience. After the energy of our desires has spent itself, the permanent atom withdraws further into the mental field. The essences of the spent desires remain as astral elements, the *skandhas*. The skandhas are fruits of the finished incarnation and thus seeds for the next one. They are the astral-etheric or etheric-physical carriers of karma. A bad alcoholic leaves a skandha behind made out of astral matter corresponding to this. In a next life, this skandha gives the tendency to return to the same vice. This does not necessarily make this person an alcoholic again, but it gives a renewed confrontation with this tendency. An astral self of particularly bad quality does not dissolve itself at all and may attach itself to the astral body of an animal.

At the end of the Kamaloka period the soul (apparently the higher self) falls asleep and re-awakens in Devachan, the mental world of thoughts. This world also has no causes, only effects. The only action here is indulging one's thoughts. So it is a haven of rest, a world of self-created illusions. On the other hand, one may acquire new knowledge (and thus, it seems, acquire new thoughts). Meeting other people remains a thought projection. Everyone lives alone among ideas. Higher aspirations and higher ideas are expressed here. The wealth of thoughts one had during one's life determines the length of stay in Devachan. Somebody who led his life thoughtlessly, instinctively, reincarnates almost immediately after his vibrations in Kamaloka have ended. When one has finished spending one's thoughts in Devachan, the mental body is discarded and the person arrives in the Manas area, the real home of man, where he is conscious as the higher self in his causal body.

The return to a new incarnation begins with the appearance of a thin golden thread of Buddhic matter with the permanent atoms attached to it out of the higher trinity of Atma, Buddhi and Manas. The permanent atoms are animated one by one, attracting the skandhas left behind at the various planes. The thread continues to branch out into the Buddhic web of life, sustaining and inspiring all bodies.

What determines to what body and what life one returns? The pull of the earth is general and does not lead to a specific life. Attachment to material objects and conditions depends on the state of the permanent atoms and the remaining skandhas. For the greater part, karma operates via the skandhas and, for the rest, via the 'building elemental' and the 'etheric double' (see below). The desire for experience and self-expression in the material world are also non-specific. Next to the condition of the permanent atoms and the skandhas, and the general workings of karma, theosophical literature mentions four other factors shaping a new life:

1 The evolutionary learning potential of the new life.
2 Relations with other people who have been born or are going to be born.
3 Free will, personal preference and insistence (especially of advanced egos).
4 Special missions that have been accepted.

The four or seven 'Lords of Karma', also called the *Lipika*, manage the reincarnation process. They are high cosmic administrators of karma, registering everything in the *Akasha* record and allocating the later karmic lots. They form the 'building elemental' and the 'etheric double' of each physical body. Via this elemental, a well-developed ego may seek contact with the Lords of Karma to declare his willingness to take on more karma than is about to be allocated. The elemental determines the quality mix of the attracted substances. He governs the growth of the body and floats around the mother. He departs at the latest during the seventh year. This elemental is a living being that serves the human evolution, and so evolves itself.

The major influences on the physical body are the elemental and the etheric matrix. Other influences are heredity and the thoughts and feelings of the mother. Some people are interested in the construction of their bodies, others hardly or not at all. Masters always have the same physical appearance. The extent of the similarity between various incarnations is an indication of someone's evolutionary prowess. Advanced egos choose their parents and determine their hour of birth exactly. For common people this is more of a natural process.

How somebody's talents and dispositions develop depends strongly on his environment. The incarnation process continues during three times seven years. A person is not fully incarnated until the age of 21. Before that, his character is a continuation of his previous character, but still easily influenced. The influence of educators is greater than is usually realized. Distinct characteristics, however, clearly come from past lives. The moment of death is not always determined beforehand at birth, is not always determined by karma, and is difficult to foresee.

Intermission and change of sex The normal intermissions between two incarnations grow shorter so consistently during the development of theosophy that it almost dates theosophical literature. In his *Esoteric Buddhism*, Sinnett talks about a normal intermission of more than 8,000 years (1883: 143). He concluded that we are in the body about 1.2 per cent of the time, and for the rest, mostly in Devachan. Consequently, Devachan would be of greater importance. This is inconsistent with the view that in Devachan people merely elaborate and spend their thoughts, and that the length of stay there depends on the wealth of thoughts during life. Soon, the given intermissions change to between 2,000 and 3,000 years as a minimum. A bit later again, intermissions of 700 and 1,200 years are mentioned. People who incarnate in various sub-races require an intermission of 1,200 years, while those who incarnate in the same sub-race have an intermission of 700 years. The 700-year intermission entails a shorter, but more intensive stay in Devachan.

Later still, Leadbeater provides this elaborate classification (1910: 241):

- 1500 to 2,300 years: mature, advanced souls; initiates
- 700 to 1,200 years: those who are going along or nearing the path of initiation; of these, about 5 years in Kamaloka and up to 50 years at the Manas plane
- 600 to 1,000 years: upper class; 20 to 25 years in Kamaloka, short stay in Manas
- about 500 years: upper-middle class; 25 years in Kamaloka, no sojourn in Manas
- 200 to 300 years: lower-middle class; 40 years in Kamaloka
- 100 to 200 years: qualified workers; 40 years in Kamaloka
- 60 to 100 years: non-qualified labourers; 40 to 50 years in Kamaloka
- 40 to 50 years: good-for-nothings and drunks; only in Kamaloka
- about 5 years: the lowest class; only in the lower part of Kamaloka or earth-bound, vegetative.

Presumably, Leadbeater is just indicating the most typical, most frequently occurring divisions. At least, I assume he did not claim that, for example, the higher classes have no good-for-nothings or drunks. The richness of someone's cultural and spiritual life (determining the length of stay in Devachan), and the intensity of his emotional life (determining the length of stay in Kamaloka), and the length and nature of the previous life (for example, an early death, idiocy, or an accident), cause deviations from these averages. In general, the less strength of mind a person has, the more he has left to learn, and the more learning experiences he will have to go through.

Some theosophical writers claim that between three and seven incarnations in the same sex is the rule. Others write that seven male and seven female incarnations alternate. Alcyone (the entity of Krishnamurti) has four to eight consecutive incarnations in the same sex every time (Besant and Leadbeater 1924). Other passages indicate that some people change sex easily, and others with difficulty. After an early death people often reincarnate in the same sub-race, and, where this happens, often change sex.

A strong attachment to particular families or peoples may result in a repeated return to the same place. Jews are supposed often to reincarnate as Jews because they regard themselves as the chosen people. The same could be true for the Druses, and for each other group that, for whatever reason, feels good about itself.

Karma Theosophists firmly believe that karma is the universal law of cause and effect. All of our behaviour both expresses our past, including past lives, and shapes our future, including future lives. Everything falls back on us, but because of *maya*, the illusion created by the sometimes long interval between cause and effect, we usually fail to see things happening to us as results of our own acts.

The theosophic view of karma has three levels:
- as natural law, without providence or release
- as reward or punishment
- as guidance, compensation, evolution and healing.

When we act naturally, according to our nature and responding to the situation, our acts have purely natural consequences. This is the first kind of karma, free from reward and punishment and without guidance. The theosophists also believe that our thoughts and feelings in one life naturally continue in our acts in the next. They regard this second effect – outside-in – as weaker than the first effect – inside-out. Theosophical literature gives few illustrations of natural karmic effects. One example is that cruelty in one life leads to insanity in the next.

Just as thoughts and feelings partially determine acts in a following life, so astral acts may have karmic consequences on the physical plane. An example of guidance and compensation is that undeserved accidents and disasters may be subtracted from somebody's negative karma. In cases without negative karma to be compensated, a miraculous rescue occurs, or compensation is given in the form of positive karma or a reward in Devachan. The managing, compensating character of karma shows also in the idea that races may become sterile and extinct for karmic reasons.

Apparently, the cardinal fact of our evolution is gaining self-awareness and so free choice, and as a karmic result we have become caught in matter and self-centredness. This is mainly because of indulging in sex and so losing the 'third eye' of clairvoyance.

Most theosophical expositions about karma are about the moral, corrective workings of karma. In general, misdeeds are punished and victims recompensed. People may be punished for misdeeds in up to seven future lives. The relation between act and karmic consequence is in accordance with natural law, but is pliable. A murderer is not necessarily murdered in the next life. More likely he may have to save his past victims at the cost of his own life; or he compensates with life-long service and dedication to others. Simple retribution is an exception. The bad luck of a worthy person is the consequence of past evil deeds. The good luck of an unworthy person is the consequence of past good deeds. Nowadays, there are many consequences of bad karma resulting from Atlantic incarnations, because (assuming intermissions of about 1,200 to 1,500 years) people are now in about their seventh life after the time of Atlantis. Bad spirits may induce us to commit evil deeds, but they can only do so by stimulating and profiting from bad karma already present.

Karma is not always specific. Suffering from a disease, for example, is non-specific karma. Generally, 'small karma', karma from unimportant acts, is collected in a broader karmic mass before being released. Our karmic mass may be divided into *sanchita* karma, *prarabdha* karma, and *kryamana* karma. Sanchita karma is the general karmic mass from past lives. Only a part of this is 'ripe' or prarabdha karma, influencing our behaviour in this life. The karmic mass we create in this life is the kryamana karma that will be added to the sanchita karma after this life. However, a portion is settled directly in this life. This is 'small-change' karma. Figure 1 illustrates these forms of karma.

Figure 1 **The forms of karma**

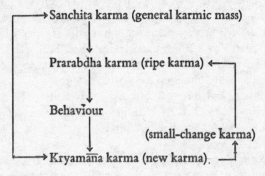

The reanimated permanent atoms and the elemental supervising the formation of the physical body attract the skandhas which largely determine prarabdha karma. Consequently, karma and the related life plan are visible in the physical body in the palm lines among other places. Positive karma, reward for good deeds, results in self-development or in a pleasant environment, depending on whether one considered getting a reward or not. Thus, altruistic deeds result in self-development. Good deeds with a measure of egotism only lead to pleasant surroundings.

Each karma doctrine leads to the question of free will versus predestination. The theosophists answer that the karmic determination of action in situations precludes neither some free choice, nor help from others. Help is always possible, and free will is never absolutely arbitrary, but always a limited free choice. If everything was predestined, then karma, as the consequence of predestined acts, would be meaningless. Karma is precisely the consequence of relatively free choices, plus compensation for undeserved disturbances in life. To be freed *from* karma is nonsense, the point is to be freed *by* karma. To evolve, our acts have to have real consequences. The more developed somebody is, the more subtly and precisely, for example in respect to time and place, his karma works. Finally, karma plays a role in larger groups of people such as cultures, or in institutions such as congregations.

Reincarnations of well-known people The best-known theosophic publications about reincarnations of individual people are *Man: Whence, How and Whither* and its sequel *The Lives of Alcyone*, mapping the incarnations of a large number of masters and prominent theosophists, later centred around the figure of Alcyone, who was recently incarnated as Krishnamurti (Besant and Leadbeater 1913, 1924). Another work about the reincarnations of other theosophists later appeared in four volumes (Leadbeater 1941–50).

Theosophists regard Annie Besant as a reincarnation of Hypatia, an Alexandrian gnostic. Frederick III, the father of Kaiser Wilhelm I of Germany, was a reincarnation of Clovis.

Past-life recall Memories of past lives are extraordinary, since the physical brain containing them vanishes and the astral brain of the lower personality decomposes. Luckily, every experience is not only registered in the physical brain and in the lower self, but also in the higher self, so that via Manas, the causal body, past lives may be recalled. According to Sinnett (1883) general recollection of past lives will therefore only be possible in some faraway future. Van Ginkel (1917) expects that regression by hypnotic or magnetic trance will become the most important way to recollect past lives, but also only in the distant future.

With Buddhic powers the previous lives of others can be perceived. The presence of the other person helps, but is not required. Finally, the records of past lives can be read from the permanent atoms, but this is the most difficult method. Spiritual development, which has made one aware of one's higher self, and, preferably, initiation, are necessary to recall past lives.

In his exposition on the development of clairvoyance, Leadbeater (1899) writes that recalling past lives in normal consciousness is preferable, because this allows taking notes. The surroundings hardly matter, provided the mind is calm, open, and unprejudiced. The emerging pictures of past lives are like film images, that can be speeded up, slowed down, or stopped to look more carefully at the details. One can also position oneself inside one's past, instead of remaining an observer.

Sometimes, you can recognize somebody in a recollection of a past life as somebody you know now, but Leadbeater warns against intuitive identification, which is in general untrustworthy. It is better to take a person in a past life and look into the next incarnations, until you see the present incarnation. Masters are easy to recognize, since their aspect hardly changes.

Karma, reincarnation, and spiritual development If we expose ourselves to many experiences and are sincere in our efforts, we will surely make progress. Karma may be a tool of self-liberation, especially after we understand how it works. We can reach this understanding, because the Masters have revealed the spiritual doctrines. We may learn to serve the Masters through docility, understanding, industry, flexibility, and companionship. We develop these characteristics in life after life. Once we start on the path of spiritual development, we attain the ultimate goal in the seventh life after our first steps. We may acquit the debt we accumulate during this process toward the initiates by helping other people to progress. Only neglect of received insights creates guilt. We may get stuck on the way, but we still remain sensitive to once-acquired truths in following lives. Consequently, many people are sensitive to theosophical doctrines. The only causes of real retrogression are deliberate cruelty and black magic.

Closing remarks The theosophical doctrine of karma and reincarnation has a broad cosmic perspective of simultaneous involution and evolution, with elaborated but abstract views on incarnation and excarnation. It has a number of inconsistencies, as this review may already have demonstrated. The lower self, for example, is placed alternately between the mental, astral, etheric and physical levels. Qualifications like 'astral-etheric' or 'etheric-physical' are ambivalent. Buddhi is the second vehicle of the microcosm, but the Buddhic web permeates the etheric body (sixth vehicle), and at the same time supports all seven bodies. This creates linguistic confusion, at least. I have already pointed out the shrinking intermission periods. Some phenomena, such as the time spent in Devachan, are sometimes defined as cosmic laws, necessarily valid for everybody, and sometimes as dependent on individual circumstances.

Theosophy demonstrates the inspiring but confused and rambling character of gnostic literature, although it compares favourably with most related products. The more independent followers of gnostic movements produce similar, but different, world-views. This has also happened with theosophy. It has led to many individual variants, sometimes carbon copies of the original, and sometimes 'developed' to the point of being unrecognizable. One of the most influential and interesting movements branching off from theosophy in Europe is Rudolf Steiner's anthroposophy.

Anthroposophy

The anthroposophical concept of the evolution of mankind Out of Rudolf Steiner's extensive reflections on the development of mankind, I choose those directly related to his views on karma and reincarnation. During the previous incarnation of our earth, called the Old Moon, the present human souls were at the animal level. The souls then at the human level are now angels. At that earlier stage, a number of these souls, known as the Luciferic spirits, intensified and cultivated their personal consciousness, separating themselves more or less from the mainstream of evolution and consequently they fell behind.

During our development on earth, the inspiration of these Luciferic spirits led to the fall of man, an involution dislodging from the spiritual, falling into the material. Karma entered with this Luciferically inspired fall during the age of Lemuria when the conditions from the Old Moon more or less repeated themselves. During Lemuria, the moon separated itself from the earth (after the sun had already separated itself from the earth in the preceding age of Hyperborea). After the moon's separation, human self-awareness incarnated for the first time. With this began upright walking, which led to reincarnation in our sense. Walking freed our hands, and after that came speech and independent thinking. What somebody does with his hands is connected to his individual karma. What he says is connected to the national karma, and his thoughts are connected to the karma of mankind.

Mankind has an original fund of spiritual power that it gradually consumes in the course of incarnations. We would reach a dead end at the conclusion of this planetary cycle but for Christ, who has broken through the Luciferic inspiration and given us new possibilities. Without Golgotha, reincarnation would ultimately lead to mechanical people with empty souls.

Up until the second post-Atlantic age, the ancient Persian age from 5067 to 2907 B C, people remembered their past lives. In the third age, the period from 2907 to 747 B C encompassing the Egyptian, Babylonian, and Chaldean cultures, past-life recall gradually dwindled. Elsewhere, Steiner claims that knowledge of reincarnation was lost in the Kaliyuga, stretching from 3101 B C to A D 1899. At the time of Christ's appearance, the belief in reincarnation was at an absolute low. Since then, humanity has forgotten all about reincarnation in order to learn to concentrate on this life alone.

Past-life recall was lost when priests started to drink wine. The wedding feast at Cana is symbolic of this. Christ himself forbade the teaching of reincarnation. Reincarnation notions were sometimes familiar to the more esoteric monastic orders; the Trappists' vow of silence was to supply good orators for the church in a next life.

Ideas about reincarnation began to come back during the eighteenth-century Enlightenment, in the work of Lessing among others, but now in a new, Christianized form. These Christianized ideas relate the object to the development of mankind, while the earlier Buddhist idea related the subject to individual development.

In his own lifetime, Steiner says, there is an increasing desire to recall previous incarnations. At the end of the twentieth century, Christ will become the new Lord of Karma and will join a person's individual karma to the karma of mankind. In the future, the karmic consequences of our acts will become ever more directly visible. Resistance to the idea of reincarnation will come particularly from the Anglo-American sub-race, although the mission of this race is precisely to give theories about reincarnation and karma a scientific base.

Between death and birth After death, we feel we are growing out of our body and becoming one with the surrounding world. Then follows a panoramic retrospect of our past life. This retrospect takes as long as we are able to stay awake at one time during our life, a couple of days at most. After that our etheric body dies, so that all our thoughts disappear and only the corresponding emotions remain. An extract from our physical body remains identical for all incarnations. The extract from the etheric body, on the other hand, is different in each life. Then we arrive in the astral world (the Kamaloka of the theosophists). Again, we experience a panorama of our life, but this time backwards, and intensely emotional. The length of this retrospect on life is as long as the time we slept during life, or about a third of the length of our life. During this retrospect we experience as our own feelings how others experienced our acts. This imprints the urge to make up for wrong acts in our astral body.

This retrospect takes place in the moon sphere with the help of moon beings who give our emotional experiences substance, in cooperation with the angels that link one life to the next. In the sphere of Venus we come under the influence of the archangels. Then, we go to the sphere of Mercury where we come under the influence of the Archai. Finally, in the sun sphere, we meet the so-called second hierarchy: the Exusiai, the Dynamis, and the Kyriotetes. Bad karma cannot get through the sun sphere to the Saturn sphere, where we are consecutively subjected to the influences of the Thrones, the Cherubim, and the Seraphim. When we return the energies which went through the sun domain form our predisposition to health, and the energies which did not go through the sun domain, related to procreation and the moon, form our predisposition to illness.

Why do people reincarnate at all? First, to advance their development; second to work out their karma; and third, to contribute to the development of humanity. Steiner's examples of people who reincarnated purely to contribute to the development of humanity are Aristotle, Charlemagne, and Luther.

Karma that originated during a physical life can only be compensated during a physical life. The imperfections of physical life seek out new suffering to become perfect in a new life. Suffering has evolutionary value, it helps us to develop. We cannot work off our karma in only one life, because in each life we have a physical body permitting only certain forms of karma. In general, karma from one life can influence the next seven lives.

Each incarnation is an involution. The mentality, the thoughts of one life imprint themselves on the next life in the astral body with its feelings. The astrality, with its feelings, imprints itself on the next life in the etheric body with its tendencies, habits, and temperament. The tendencies, habits, and temperament of one life imprint themselves upon the physical body and the physical acts of the next life. Our physical acts determine the physical surroundings of our next life. And as our surroundings influence the thoughts with which we grow up, the circle is more or less closed. Unfulfilled drives and interests from previous lives, in particular, determine the body and the environment in which we end up.

Intermission and change of sex Rudolf Steiner, like the theosophical writers, begins with long intermission periods and finishes with shorter ones. Initially, he posited that people reincarnate once in each zodiacal era, every 2,600 years. This seems to be a mistake. A so-called sidereal year is nearly 26,000 years long, or per sidereal sign 2,160 years on the average. (He did use this proper length in his later calculations of the post-Atlantic ages.)

Later, Steiner posits that we incarnate every 1,300 years, to have within each period of 2,600 years one male and one female incarnation. He explains his earlier indications by saying that male and female incarnations are so different that occultists regard such a couple as one incarnation. A male incarnation carries within itself the tendency towards a female incarnation and vice versa. The regular pattern is to alternate between a female and a male life. Exceptionally, consecutive incarnations in the same sex occur. Up to three times in the same sex is still normal, and seven times in the same sex is the maximum.

According to Steiner, those who lived around the beginning of this century had been, as a rule, incarnated between A D 300 and 900. Apparently, he takes a margin of about 300 years around a 1,300-year intermission. Five years later, around 1910, he says that the people living at that time have lived two, three or four times since Palestine, amounting to intermissions averaging 1,000, 700, or 500 years. Apparently, he then thought in terms of a 700-year interval with a margin of about 200 years, which was also the accepted idea in theosophical circles at that time.

Finally, he claims reincarnation in the same culture or nation is rare, with the exception of the 'Middle-European community of nations'. Apparently, this community (undefined, but presumably equal to the German-speaking part of Europe) is something special.

Karmic laws and general relations between lives Steiner's expositions on karma are too diverse to summarize easily. Globally, during the first period of his discourses, his concepts were close to the theosophists, and he continued to use theosophic vocabulary. Most of his audience was theosophically oriented and he himself operated within the Theosophical Association. In the 1920s, towards the end of his life, he constructed a complete anthroposophical world-view of his own, where reincarnation and karma had their specific places. In between, roughly between 1912 and 1918, he came up with ideas about karma which seemed to bear little relation to his thoughts before and after (and to each other).

Steiner characterizes karma as a moral, spiritual, cosmic order alongside the natural, physical order. Physical causality and karmic causality are antipodes and complements. Everything physically accidental is karmically determined, and everything karmically accidental is physically determined. Thus karma is the spiritual law of cause and effect pervading all inner and outward human acts. Knowledge and understanding of karma does not change it; at most it brings about a shift. Karma leaves free will intact. Free will functions in karmically determined situations. (Apparently, free will is a third principle next to karma and physical causality.) Like theosophy, anthroposophy emphasizes that help is always possible.

Another idea is that karma has to do specifically with the consequences of Luciferically inspired human behaviour. Sometimes Steiner claims that karma is mainly valid for a person's acts during his life, and at other times karma is purely spiritual, only active in the spiritual world in between incarnations. However, karmic laws play an important role within an incarnation. Karma from the first half of one's life plays a role during the second half. A lively childhood leads to a spiritually rich old age. Reverence during childhood leads to a beneficent presence in old age, noble wrath leads to loving mildness, and devotion to continued youthfulness. Egoism, and forced development during childhood lead to early ageing.

In 1912 Steiner began a number of discourses on karma as interaction between the microcosm and the macrocosm. By this time, he regards our judgements as the source of our karma. Our imaginative judgements are radiated out to the environment via our bones, our inspirational judgements via our muscles, and our intuitive judgements via our nerves. Everything wrong in our judgement is reflected back to us. That is our karma. Everything correct in these judgements is absorbed by the cosmos to build up the occult Jupiter, the next incarnation of our earth (*GA* 134: I).

Although this is difficult to imagine, his idea two years later is even more complex. He says that the human muscular system is crystallized karma, as the muscles embody the spirit guiding the person to his karmic place. (*GA* 153: I). According to this idea, karma functions mainly by getting us to certain places at certain times. This is an extremely limited view of karma. Besides, our muscular system does not determine where we go, since our muscles obey our nerves.

Later still, Steiner says that the ego inscribes acts into the surrounding ether during life, acts which are read out as karma in the next life (*GA* 157: IV). Then he returns to the concept of karma as based on a spiritual radiation of human judgements continuing to operate after death (*GA* 181: V, VI). Here, the head, the torso, and the limbs differ greatly. The karma of the body creates the karma of the following life, and the head lives from the karma of the previous life. (Oddly enough, this seems to place the muscular system in the head.)

Besides the continuity through different lives – like talents saved – and the transitions from thoughts in one life to feelings in the next, from feelings to habits, from habits to body, and from bodily acts to environment, there is oscillation between opposites. The alternation between male and female incarnations is the most obvious example. Precisely where somebody was talented in one life, he may be awkward in the next. What was innermost feeling in one life may be public behaviour in the next. Family members in one life may be friends in another life, and friends in one life may be relatives again in another life. In the course of our lives we alternate between two groups of people with whom we are related. Another form of oscillation is between ages. During our youth we meet mostly people we knew around middle age in our previous life, and during middle age we meet people we knew during our youth in our previous life. The last part of life has no specific karma or no karma at all.

When a person had a serious attitude to life in a previous life, it shines through in his present incarnation. When the previous life of a person was superficial, it doesn't shine through. This can be recognized because such people laugh and grin a lot.

A common fate may result from a common death in a disaster. In the absence of existing karma, it may create positive karma such as inciting a common undertaking.

Next to individual karma, there is national karma and the karma of mankind. During important historical events individual karma and general karma interconnect.

Examples of karma Steiner gives many examples of specific relations between lives. Materialism and rejection of the spiritual (inspired by Ahriman) leads to a dark intermission, and in the next incarnation to an egoistical intelligence. Egoistical mysticism (inspired by Lucifer) leads to a rudderless intermission and to a defective intelligence in the next life. Deceit in one incarnation leads to flippancy and indifference in the next. Thoughtlessness in one life leads to forgetfulness in the next, and forgetfulness in turn leads to nervousness. Thinking trivially and conventionally leads to greed and gluttony in the next life. A feeble-minded person who experiences hard-heartedness may become generous and benevolent in his next life. Someone who caused others pain will be melancholic in his next life. Facility with languages leads to freedom from prejudice in the next life. Morality without beauty develops the astral without the etheric and leads to a generally weak incarnation, like idiocy, in the next life.

The clearest examples are those where the etheric conditions of a life (the habits) induce physical realities in the next one. Mathematical ability in one life leads to good eyesight in the next; architectural ability in one life to good hearing in the next. Thoughtful people are thin in their next life, those who did little thinking are fat in their next life. People who think a great deal get a beautiful skin with soft lines in their next life, and those who do little thinking get a spotty skin with coarse lines. A dulled life results in a need to sleep a lot in the next life. Those who are active and interested get a low, sharp, powerful forehead in their next life, have strong bones and fast-growing, buoyant hair, and in general express strong spirits. Those who were indolent and uninterested show the opposite physical and psychological characteristics.

People who suffer illness, pain, and hardship patiently, receive physical beauty in their next life. A violent death gives the idealism needed to accomplish important aims in the next life. Infectious diseases lead to beautiful surroundings in a next life, and fatal illness to fortified internal organs. (Apparently, fatal infectious diseases give both.) Diseases have specific karmic origins. The industrial proletarian's hatred expresses itself in the next life as tuberculosis. A weak sense of self leads in the next life to a predisposition to cholera, and an exaggerated sense of self to a predispostion to malaria. People who are prone to emotional outbursts are predisposed to diphtheria in their next life.

Finally, those who think that subsequent lives are all nonsense will have nonsensical subsequent lives! (This explains much of what we see around us. And as far as the future is concerned, dear reader, thou art warned.)

Past-life recall: karma research Normally, the results of past lives only permeate us in dreamless sleep. We cannot simply infer karmic causes and effects from objective acts and events. We can only see karma with the higher levels of awareness that Steiner calls inspiration and intuition. We cannot recall concrete events from past lives, but only the corresponding feelings.

Identifying karmic influences is possible, but requires subtle observation. Steiner calls this karma research. This begins by paying attention to apparent coincidences that influence the course of our life, learning to distinguish karmically predestined acts from free acts. It is important to see our fate as a spiritual reality in which our higher self is active.

In the future we will start to see our past lives through our relation with Christ, which will provide us with the necessary confidence to evolve further. Meanwhile, special exercises can make us aware of karmic workings. Steiner indicated three such methods.

The first method may be called the 'alter-ego exercise'. First, you infuse yourself with the feeling that you yourself actively desired your limitations and sorrows in life, that you procured your own sadness and misfortune. Within you is a more intelligent being who knows better than your normal consciousness what is good for you. Initially, you need to feel strongly that wisdom comes from suffering. Then you have to feel strongly that every pleasure and joy is a grace. You need to feel that in these feelings the world wants to receive you. This develops your responsiveness to this world and your inclination to enter it fully, and so you show you are worthy of this grace. Finally, in case of accidents and nasty incidents, you need to imagine that you have a more intelligent alter-ego bringing about these events. Continuously permeating yourself with these three feelings slowly makes the alter-ego a reality for you. This opens an image from a past life – the fainter it is, the longer ago. Between such an image and yourself are a number of figures. These indicate how many generations there were between the previous and the present life.

We may call the second method 'making transparent'. You imagine somebody without limbs and think away everything done with limbs. This turns him into a floating, non-active creature, making the moon-aspect, the emotional life of a person visible. Next, you imagine this person without senses, making the sun aspect visible, his real heart and temperament. Finally, you imagine the person without thoughts and feelings. Then the Saturn aspect shows his basic mentality and attitude, making the karma visible.

We may call the third method the 'three-day exercise'. You immerse yourself in some event you experienced. Your astral body will work out this experience during the night. The next day you will walk around half aware of this, and the next night your etheric body works out this experience. The day after you feel a strong, but blocked will. On the third night the physical body works out the experience. When you wake up the blocked will turns into an image of the karmic cause of that experience.

Reincarnation and karma in social development According to Steiner, the belief in reincarnation and karma will form the foundation for new social developments and a counterweight to an ever more complex society. The realization that we are building our own future strengthens our feeling of responsibility for the future of our society. He recommends implanting the truths of reincarnation and karma in children's minds so that the soul can integrate these truths. Awareness of reincarnation and karma does not lead to escapism, but rather to acceptance of and love for our allotted position in life.

In his later work, Steiner indicated the previous incarnations of a number of historical figures, mainly thinkers from all ages, and prominent social, cultural, and political figures from his time. Opponents of Germany in the First World War are not shown in a particularly favourable light (perhaps because they did not belong to the Middle-European community of nations).

A specifically anthroposophical doctrine is indirectly related to reincarnation and karma: the doctrine of 'spiritual economy.' In essence the astral and etheric bodies of valuable people can be conserved, and copies transmitted to others. This easily leads the non-initiated investigator astray. He may think that someone is the incarnation of an important soul, while that person only has a copy of an astral or etheric body of an important historical teacher. Steiner gives numerous examples, like the transfer of copies of the astral body of Jesus to Francis of Assisi and Elizabeth of Thüringen.

Concluding remarks: the gnostic paradox Rudolf Steiner is a gnostic *par excellence*. The problem of gnosticism shows clearly in anthroposophy. A cosmic vision such as anthroposophy springs from somebody's desire to ascend to the first-hand knowledge of esoteric subjects, making him independent of existing ideas. A gnostic like Steiner calls on others to gain first-hand knowledge as well, pointing the way. Followers, however, have to start by believing in his revelations, hardly a gnostic attitude. The gnostic student is called to a temporary belief in order ultimately to arrive at his own insights on the basis of this. However, this personal insight may never conflict with the insights of his precursor who, after all, had first-hand knowledge of the truth. At the most, the next generation can elaborate and embroider. A gnostic also does not argue. He paints his intuitions usually abstractly, but full of feeling. Others have to absorb them with little rational judgement and discussion. This basic conflict and eternal paradox of gnosticism, its uneasy marriage between belief and exploration, leads irrevocably to continual separations, since there are always people who have personal interpretations and insights that 'enrich' or 'correct' those of the predecessors. The emancipation of gnostics is always painful, because it implies separation from their own spiritual mother or father. Most of them, then, emancipate themselves only half way, continuing to believe in the value of what was before them, but re-interpreting it. The saddest part of such re-interpretations is their epistemological naivity: they are again presented as 'truth', because the gnostic intellect is embedded in vehement and liberating emotions.

Third-rate followers do not go for truth at all, but for emotional deliverance and intellectual comfort. They often see all of these separations and idiosyncrasies as so many different revelations of the same truth. And since all roads lead to Rome, remaining at home does as well.

If you want to study the ideas of a gnostic, for example on the subject of reincarnation and karma, you are confronted with an impressive collection of concepts full of atmosphere, but abstract, many of them incoherent, a number even contradictory. Next to clarity (at least we can understand what is being said) and consistency (freedom from contradictions without further explanation), correspondence (agreement with actual facts and experiences) remains the third fundamental criterion in evaluating ideas. Chapter 14 compares a number of theosophical and anthroposophical doctrines with the material to date on actual experiences.

Further reading

Theosophical literature has almost no systematic treatment of reincarnation and karma doctrines. *Isis Unveiled* (1877) and *The Secret Doctrine* (1888) by H. P. Blavatsky have brief references, to be found via the index. Sinnett (1883) devotes a few passages to it. An article by H. P. Blavatsky (1886) is concerned with the confusion surrounding the reincarnation concept, and many bits and pieces may be found in the profuse literature from that time. The first book completely devoted to the subject is by E. D. Walker (1888) – informative, but lacking empirical material. Then there are the two books by Anderson (1894) – full of uninformative praise, but with impressive titles. From about 1895 Annie Besant published short essays on the subject (see bibliography). The major writer on the subject is Leadbeater, although his discussions remain limited to short publications, and chapters and passages in other books (see bibliography).

Important and interesting is the work by Arthur E. Powell (1925, 1926, 1927, 1928) who compiled all the theosophical literature about the various bodies. His chapters on karma and reincarnation are informative.

Countless brochures about the subject appeared in the first years of the twentieth century by Snowden-Ward, Irving Steiger Cooper (1917), a reasonable introduction, and Jinarajadssa (1915), among others. Van Ginkel's discussion of the subject (1917) is exceptionally solid and elaborate.

I have already mentioned *Man: Whence, How and Whither* (1913) and *The Lives of Alcyone* (1924) by Besant and Leadbeater and the posthumous publication of Leadbeater's *The Soul's Growth through Reincarnation* (1941–50) as the main theosophical case studies. Another theosophical case is by Challoner (1935), a romantic sketch of Atlantic powers and their consequences, undoubtedly impressing some readers.

Generally, theosophical works trying to give popular introductions to the subject are of low quality: Christmas Humphreys (1943), Geoffrey Hodson (1951), James Perkins (1961), Leoline Wright (1975). Only Virginia Hanson's book about karma (1975) is acceptable. Head and Cranston (1977) are informative about the 'theosophical renaissance'.

For anthroposophical literature, the main source is the Collected Works (*Gesamtausgabe*) of Rudolf Steiner. The twenty-four volumes dealing with reincarnation and karma are listed in the bibliography. The most informative on the subject are volumes 17, 34, and 120, and the 6-volume series, *Esoterische Betrachtungen Karmischer Zusammenhaenge* (*GA* 235–40). There are also small compilation works on this subject by Steiner (for example, 1961). Arenson (1950) gives an entry catalogue for Steiner's first fifty lecture cycles. Other anthroposophical authors on this subject are Rittelmeyer (1931), Bock (1932), Wachsmuth (1933), Husemann (1938), Kolisko (1940), Frieling (1974), Veltman (1974), and Verbrugh (1980). Thea Stanley-Hughes (1976) gives an acceptable popular introduction to reincarnation, with a subdued anthroposophical background. Alan Howard muses anthroposophically about *Sex in the Light of Reincarnation and Freedom* (1980).

4 Psychic Information About Past Lives

Sensitive people often seem able to receive paranormal impressions of past lives; this sometimes happens in a trance. Some sensitives may also give information about the lives of others or about the subject of reincarnation in general. This chapter begins by looking at the relationship between past-life recall and paranormal abilities. Being able to recollect past lives can only partially be regarded as a paranormal ability. Many people can have such memories, but usually only after some trance-induction. Methods that do not induce trance, like those of Netherton, probably work with a trance self-induced by the patient, but this occurs spontaneously and also with people without evidence of previous paranormal gifts; at least the ability to recall unassimilated traumatic occurrences from past lives cannot be regarded as paranormal.

After exploring this relationship, I give examples of people who paranormally obtained information about their own past lives or those of others: first, people with experiences of their own previous lives, then cases of people who were able to perceive something about the previous lives of others, and finally examples of information about reincarnation from discarnates who communicated via mediums. I distinguish:

1 Paranormal impressions: vague extra-sensory impressions during normal consciousness.
2 Clear perception during shifted consciousness as in dreams, trances, and out-of-body experiences.
3 Clairvoyance: clear extra-sensory perception during normal consciousness.

To the extent the material permits, we will come to a few general conclusions about such sources of information. Finally, we will look at the general information about reincarnation from paranormal sources. We will meet some names mentioned previously, such as

Edgar Cayce, Allan Kardec, and Arthur Guirdham. This section also ends with a short commentary.

The relationship between past-life memories and paranormal abilities

This relationship is important for two reasons: first, because a strong relationship makes it difficult to distinguish reincarnation as the explanation for apparent past-life memories from hypotheses such as clairvoyance and telepathy; second, because such a relationship gives indications about the access to and the nature of the past-life memory. Do the memories of people who are paranormally sensitive differ from those of people without such qualities? Interestingly, people who are able to go into trance, or who are clairvoyant, and recollect past lives, are generally well able to distinguish between their own experiences and those of other people. So, identification (or, as Stevenson calls it, personation) does not happen automatically with impressions of past lives. Attributing clearly personal experiences to clairvoyance has no secure basis. Many paranormally gifted people have little or no recollection of past lives, and often these recollections are merely scattered images or episodes. This too makes it unlikely that recollections of past lives are based on paranormal ability. If it were so, then many more paranormally gifted people would have to have past-life recall.

I did a survey among people attending my lectures on reincarnation. The group was too small for general conclusions, but a number

Table 3 Paranormal abilities and types of spontaneous past-life memories

	Inspiration	Healing	Clairvoyance	Telepathy	Prediction
Dreams	80%	98%	95%	90%	80%
General feeling	95%	99%	95%	–	–
Recognizing people	–	98%	80%	–	–
Without clear cause	98%	–	–	–	–
Recognizing places	95%	–	–	–	–

of relationships appeared to be fairly significant. Table 3 shows some results from this survey (TenDam 1980).

In the survey group, people who professed paranormal ability did have more past-life memories. The greatest difference between the 'normal' and 'paranormal' people was that those with paranormal abilities had more memories in dreams. The paranormal abilities most strongly correlated to past-life memories were clear flashes of inspiration, healing hands (magnetism), and clairvoyance. Table 3 gives a summary of the results. The percentages complement the level of significance, indicating the probability that the observed correlation is not due to chance. Figures over 80 per cent only are listed. Indirectly they say something about the strength of the correlation.

People with flashes of inspiration have more memories of past lives, more memories without immediate cause, and recognize places more often (in general, recollection of places is correlated to a greater number of memories). Those with healing hands and clairvoyance tend to recognize people. Interestingly enough, there was no correlation between predicting impressions and recollection of past lives, but there was an emphatic correlation between predictions and the number of memories of past lives. Prognostic abilities may not contribute to crossing the threshold to the past, but facilitate it considerably once the threshold has been crossed. A more straightforward explanation, but just as surprising, would be that people with recollection of past lives get prognostic impressions more easily. Perception of the past in this case leads to easier perception of the future, but the reverse does not hold.

Even if recollection of past lives is possible without paranormal abilities, the memory itself has to be parapsychological or rather paraphysiological, because such memories cannot be stored in the physical body. Esoterically or gnostically oriented clairvoyants indicate three sources of reincarnation memories: the personalities of the past lives, the continually reincarnating soul, also called the higher self, and a kind of general memory fund sometimes described as the memory of nature, or the Akasha record. This Akasha record would be a database storing all the experiences of all people who ever lived, or a database in which all the experiences of each living being are recorded, or a database which stores everything that ever happens.

The last version is debatable, since it presupposes observation without observers or observation equipment, or some kind of recorder co-existing with the universe, registering everything without an observation point.

People with paranormal impressions of their own past lives

During a spiritual seance in 1869 the spirit of a living niece of one of the participants comes through. She recounts that in her previous life during the reign of Louis XIV she had been a nun. A nobleman who tried to elope with a guest of the convent had knocked her down and she had died as a result. She gave some more details and added that at night, while she was asleep, she tended to hang around the old church of the convent in the form of her previous incarnation. She also did this before she incarnated again. To prove her identity, she wrote something down via the medium's hand which only she and the participating uncle knew about. This convinced him, and he asked her during the seance if during the day, while she was awake, she was aware of her past life. She answered that in the daytime she only had the vague notion of a violent death and a dream episode. Later, when the uncle met his niece, he asked her if she ever dreamed she was being murdered. She answered negatively, but said she did have nightmares sometimes about a Roman Catholic priest who was fleeing from a church being chased by armed men. He dictated a few words to her and her handwriting was practically the same as that produced during the seance. (Bertholet 1949: 561; Muller 1970: 172).

Works on spiritualism contain other examples of spirits of living people appearing while the body sleeps, and taking on the identity of a past life.

An example of clairvoyant impressions from one's own past life is *The Boy Who Saw True* edited by Neville Spearman (1953), the diary of a young English boy dating from 1885 to 1887. He discovers only later that what he sees are called auras and other people do not see them. He often receives impressions of people or what is going to happen to them. He sees nature spirits and discarnate people, such as his deceased grandfather and an impressive spirit with a gorgeous aura whom he initially identifies as Jesus. He has the notion that people who fall in love with each other somehow knew each other before. Later, he has a strange dream in which he sees himself in bygone times (compare my survey results!), and subsequently his spiritual teacher, who in the meantime has made it clear he is not Jesus, tells him these impressions are no dreams, but recollections of a past life. It confuses him when his deceased grandfather appears not to believe in reincarnation at all. His guide, however, tells him that some people who have taken off their body change their thoughts just as little as those who have taken off their overcoat. He first gets memories of a life as an Indian, apparently receiving spiritual training. His present guide was also his teacher at that time. Later, memories of other lives come up, chiefly during his voyages abroad.

Further, there is the well-known case of Ivy Beaumont. This schoolteacher from Blackpool, who died in 1961, developed her psychic powers in around 1927. Guided by Frederic Wood, who wrote *This Egyptian Miracle* about her (1955), she developed trances, automatic writing, and clairvoyance. In a semi-trance an entity calling itself Nona appeared and produced more than 4,000 sentences in the Egyptian language of the eighteenth dynasty. Another medium reported in 1930 that Ivy Beaumont herself had lived during this time as Vola, who was well-acquainted with Nona. Later, Ivy got clear recollections herself. She remembered her youth in Syria, the capture and plunder of the city by Egyptian troops, her journey as a hostage to Egypt, the customs of the people there, a number of Egyptians, situations on the Nile, the Pharaoh's palace where she lived for a while under the protection of queen Telita, her connection with the temple of Karnak and her duties as an initiated priestess. She died in a sailing accident along with her royal patroness. In trance, she was able to sing Egyptian hymns and perform the old dances. During a session in which she operated as Vola she suddenly cried 'Stop that!' in Egyptian. When she came out of trance she complained her guide had tugged at her. Since control spirits never feel the physical discomforts of a medium, Vola and Ivy were one and the same.

Ivy also remembered a life in which she died during Nero's persecutions, a life in New England during the seventeenth century, and finally a life as a French girl of noble family who escaped to England during the revolution. However, her Egyptian life was the clearest and most convincing. Initially, her recollections came out only during trance, but later also when awake. Her pronunciation of ancient Egyptian has been recorded (Wood 1955).

Interestingly, her memory was at first accessible only during trance, but later also during normal consciousness. Apparently, some bridge was formed. In Netherton's method (see chapter 16 below) the undigested emotions from the past life form this bridge. This is one of the many examples of the past personality coming to life again. An impersonal akasha is out of the question.

The son of a Brazilian businessman was always able to forecast correctly which of his father's transactions would be successful. He forecasted correctly that he himself would die of rheumatism at the age of 10. When he was 7 he met the wife of the doctor who treated his mother. He ran to her and embraced her, and explained she had been his mother in his previous life, although before this time he had never spoken of past lives. He stated his own name and her name in that life. They sounded Polish. He sensed correctly whenever the doctor's wife became ill (Muller 1970: 165).

Joan Grant is probably the best known example of a person remembering past lives in trance. As she recounts in her autobiography *Time out of Mind* (1956a), her memories began when doing psychometry of a scarab. Her first book about a past life, *Winged Pharaoh* (1937), is generally known. In trance sessions she dictated sections which were pieced together only later. Session transcripts beginning in the middle of a particular situation fitted exactly after session transcripts from a later date. Thus, in trance, she dictated portions which later were put together in the right order to make a whole biography. This seems to imply that the book had been programmed beforehand, and was read out during trance. This makes the book excellent literature, but as an example of a past-life memory rather less convincing. People with recollections of past lives coming up only slowly and fragmentarily, interpersed with the reactions of the present person, are often more convincing in their imperfection (Hondius 1957; Brouwer 1978). Other books by Joan Grant are less known, but well worth reading (see bibliography).

Joan Grant was able to receive information about other people's past lives psychometrically, especially if there was a connection with a present problem (Grant 1956b; Kelsey and Grant 1967). She attributes her paranormal abilities to the training she received in past lives, such as in Egypt. This corresponds with data from regressions. People with paranormal abilities go back to diverse and sometimes obscure forms of temple training in all kinds of periods and places. Egypt is the most frequent. According to some, Tibet is a good second, but Maya- and Inca-type cultures occur more often in regressions with temple training than Tibet, almost as frequently as Egypt.

Memories of past lives may come up during out-of-body experiences, although this is unusual. The three environments which Monroe describes in his book on out-of-body experiences, do not refer to past lives at all (Monroe 1977). Oliver Fox experimented for many years with out-of-body experiences and published articles and a book about it. Once, when he was about 42 years old, he had a past-life experience. He had left his body, and had decided to visit the ruins of some Tibetan temple. He concentrated and expected to feel the usual fast horizontal movement. Rather he felt to his horror the ground beneath him cave in, and himself falling through a tunnel at great speed for a long time. When he stopped and came to his senses, he saw vague, bright colours in which his situation slowly became visible. He was naked and chained to an X-shaped frame, while being tortured to death. Blood gushed from many wounds all over his body, and glowing irons had virtually destroyed his eyes. The pain was more unbearable every second. He heard the voice of a man saying 'Thou art Theseus!' He answered that he wasn't Theseus, but Oliver Fox. At that moment the world imploded, and in the middle of blinding light, enormous sounds, and a raging storm he came back to his bed. He was certain he had relived the last moments of a previous incarnation of himself (Fox 1939).

Paranormal information about past lives of others

A man repeatedly has the strong and unpleasant impression that someone is cracking his skull with an axe, although he has no experience to explain this impression. In a chance encounter a stranger tells him, unsolicited, that he was murdered in his previous life with an axe (Walker 1888: 43).

Freidrich Schwickert (1855–1930), a captain, asked about sightseeing opportunties in the port of Smyrna. He was advised to make a trip to Ephesus with a guide. On the way, everything became so familiar to him that he sent his guide back. Many years later, visiting the court of the Maharaja of Kapurtala, he was involved in a conversation with a Brahman. The Brahman brought him into another state of consciousness and he saw his previous life unreel in front of him like a movie. He was a cavalry commander who died in a battle at Ephesus (Muller 1970: 167). The film character of this experience is striking: he looks at himself as a spectator would do.

Demeter Georgewitz-Wietzer (1873–1949) was an Austrian engineer who wrote books on parapsychological subjects under the pseudonym Surya. When he was 23, a clairvoyant in Vienna told him he saw him in a yellow-white Persian costume. Five years later, a Persian scholar with whom he corresponded told him that in his previous life he had been a Turkoman Persian who had had a relationship with his own order. Seventeen years later, a female psychic in Graz, knowing nothing of these experiences, told him that in his previous life he had been a Persian who was a mystic and studied white magic. One of his acquaintances, an Austrian military leader from the First World War with an interest and experience in parapsychology, told him during their last encounter that perhaps he would consider it a strange thought, but that they had had a good relationship because they had lived together before in Persia, where they had been interested in the same subjects as in this life (Muller 1970: 175).

Augustin Lesage (1876–1954), a French miner, became a psychic painter at 36, and produced more than 700 paintings thereafter. When he was 62, an English clairvoyant gave him a scarab and said that he would visit Egypt. Towards the end of that year, he painted a large canvas called *Egyptian Harvest* and took it with him when he and his friend Alfred visited Egypt the following year. At the temple of Karnak he got the strong impression of knowing the place. He visited the recently discovered grave of the Egyptian painter Mena who had lived in around 1500 BC. On the wall of the grave was a painting resembling his own. In the grave, feelings of such extreme happiness overtook him that he could hardly leave. He received many impressions, but too vague to be sure whether he himself had been Mena. He told another friend he would try to find out after his death. Some time after his death, this friend received the following message via a medium: 'Tell Alfred it is true. I was Mena.' The medium had never met or heard of Lesage. Alfred was absent when the message came through (Muller 1970: 163; Victor 1980).

An older book with mediumistic information about past lives is *Reincarnation: The true chronicles of rebirth of two affinities, recorded by one of them*, edited by Cecil Palmer (1921). Through one of his spiritual guides, 'Cedric, the high priest of Heliopolis', the author received memories of his past lives in the course of three months. They are rather exciting and dramatic tales with a lot of morality and not without vanity: 'I was ushered into the presence of the King. Although I had never had anything to do with royalty, I was cool and self-possessed. His Majesty eyed me with curiosity from head to foot, and told me he had heard of my great abilities as a public speaker and organizer, my profound knowledge of social and political problems, my firmness, and the esteem in which I was held by Government officials as well as by the leaders of the people. He was desirous of adding a few capable men such as myself to his Government, and he at once offered me a fine post amongst his personal councillors on a very liberal income. My first thoughts were for Annetta . . .' (1921: 112).

Another case of someone remembering a previous encounter in a past life with somebody else is that of Gerda Walter, a well-known German parapsychologist. A friend introduced her to a retired captain during a walk in 1930. Immediately, she had the feeling she had met him before, although this seemed improbable. She wondered if it could have been in a previous life, and at once saw a clear image. She was a man riding on a horse through a gloomy forest without paths, surrounded by tree trunks and knowing that somewhere behind him lay a burning or besieged castle or large house. She felt it was a matter of life and death. Then she saw that his horse was being led by a farmer or a charcoal-burner who was walking to the left of him. She immediately sensed that this was the captain to whom she had just been introduced.

A little later, the captain told her that she might think it strange and not worth mentioning, but that he felt that in a past life he had rendered her a great service. How, he did not know, but he had had this feeling from the first moment he saw her (Muller 1970: 118).

Edgar Cayce is the best known and most important example of somebody giving information about the past lives of others when in trance. Joan Grant also received impressions about other people, but usually in connection with existing problems. Interestingly, she seemed to specialize in therapy for the recently deceased and sometimes the less recently deceased, starting from her impressions of traumas from past lives which led to fixations (Grant 1937, 1956a; Kelsey and Grant 1967).

People may communicate clairvoyantly with discarnates, without going into trance. Arthur Guirdham, an English doctor, got involved with reincarnation after studying some dreams and memory fragments of one of his patients. His study sensitized him; he started to receive impressions himself, and gradually learned to perceive them and communicate with them. Sometimes, they gave him information about his past lives, but more often affirmed, clarified, or corrected his own impressions and conclusions (Guirdham (1970, 1974). Later he could explore other past lives. In *The Lake and the Castle* (1976) he describes a life in around 1800, but also lives in early medieval England and in Roman times. *The Island* (1980) describes a life in Greece, in about 1250 BC. All very readable, in an unmistakable Guirdham style, the stories seem reasonably trustworthy, though polished, especially the last one, and it remains partisan literature. It is always about dualism, the basic philosophy Guirdham adheres to throughout his lives.

Another recent book is *Heirs to Eternity: A study of reincarnation with illustrations* by Clarice Toyne (1976). The author has a 'teacher from the beyond' whispering in her ear every now and then, telling her who was who in a previous life, to make reincarnation plausible for the general public. She then collects biographical information on both people to demonstrate the parallels between the two lives. Teilhard de Chardin was Blaise Pascal, Danny Kaye was Hans Christian Andersen, Bernard Shaw was Voltaire, de Gaulle was Joseph II and 'Le Grand Condé' (the most striking similarities, I think). Victor Hugo and Charles Baudelaire are incarnated among her acquaintances. At the end of her book, she compares the book and its expected critical reception with the publication of Darwin's *The Origin of Species*.

General ideas among discarnates about reincarnation

Discarnates often happen to write books via a medium either in trance or fully conscious. For example, Alice Bailey wrote some books in this way, apparently inspired by the theosophical Master who is known as the Tibetan. H. P. Blavatsky apparently wrote *Isis Unveiled* (1877) and *The Secret Doctrine* (1888) under inspiration.

Dr Mona Rolfe lectures in trance. In connection with the coming age of Aquarius, she elucidates the deeper meaning of the book of Genesis in *The Spiral of Life: Cycles of reincarnation*: 'No soul which has progressed beyond the Garden of Rememberance, that is, the seventh plane of the astral plane, can at any time be subject to the law of cause and effect' (Rolfe 1975: 31). However, no longer to be subject to the law of cause and effect because of some progress is a straightforward statement of cause and effect. But she is saying, I don't even want to think about it; life is difficult enough as it is.

Generally, discarnate people give personal rather than general information and advice, preferring to point to our own experience and to stimulate and comment on our own thoughts. However, some discarnates eagerly use the channel of incarnate people to convey their brainchildren to our world. The mediumistic and spiritualistic literature abounds with examples of spirits who, with or without the adornment of the name of a deceased celebrity, pass on edifying sermons and exalted poetry. Identity and style are subject to fashion. In the Victorian age they brought a lot of sentiment. Nowadays, they present themselves rather as messengers from other planets where everything is better, inciting us to stop warring, to be nice to each other, and to develop higher consciousness. Like some kindred incarnates, their presentations do not abound in sound knowledge, practical sense, or good taste. In this way, some frustrated souls satisfy themselves, without doing anybody any harm. It gives many people beautiful feelings and keeps them off the streets. It gets more problematic when the contact persons who channel them (and their audiences) are roused or frightened by prophecies. Some recent examples are depressing. Discarnate entities who approach living people to pass on their messages are usually of limited interest and credibility. Swallowing their stuff is even more stupid than buying goods at the door. Personally, my confidence in colporteur spirits is minimal. Civilized people do not intrude themselves upon others, certainly not when discarnate. They rather limit themselves to persons they know and to subjects people are personally interested in. In general, like normal people, their communication is personal, without any urge or suggestion to publish their statements. But spirits that want to publish apparently want to avoid the trouble of incarnation, or are afraid that, with a body, people are less likely to listen to them. They are quite right. Still, some information is interesting.

Karl Muller gives many examples of personal and general communications by the dead about reincarnation. A spirit told Joachim Winckelman (1885–1956) that they had lived together in the eighteenth century. A group of spirits told him that reincarnation happens faster nowadays than in the past, because human souls can develop faster under the present circumstances. Also, many souls incarnate for the first time. Consequently, the world population grows very fast. Alex Sundien did trance sessions in Denmark from 1943 to 1955. The book he wrote about these contains passages about reincarnation. The ghost of a murdered man says his death was a punishment because he himself had murdered people in a previous life. In many cases guides and helpers have developed to the point where they no longer need to reincarnate. Some souls remain in the lower spheres of the astral worlds after death and can only enter the higher spheres after a few more reincarnations. Sometimes homosexuality is caused by a recent change of sex. These statements all fit the general pattern.

There are too many spiritualist publications with communications from the dead about reincarnation to mention all of them. Many can be found in articles and spiritualist magazines, and many in books. I will review three of the most influential of these books. First, there have been Allan Kardec's informants; second, there has been the well-known spiritualist Arthur Ford who gave his information to Ruth Montgomery and others after his death; and third, there is Jane Roberts, who promulgates the views of one 'Seth' to the world.

Allan Kardec asked and collected answers from discarnates on many questions via mediums. According to Delanne (1894: 7), Kardec did not believe in reincarnation until he began to study spiritual phenomena. The following brief summary of what *The Spirits' Book* (Kardec

1857) says on reincarnation owes much to the compilation by Muller (1970: 35).

Human souls have been evolved from animal souls. Once souls reach the human stage, they do not return to animal bodies. The aim of reincarnation is to continue evolving, nursing one's ills, and redressing errors. Human souls differ greatly in their state of development. The discarnate soul is androgyne. The sex of incarnations changes. Many people have the same sex in a number of consecutive lives. The choice of sex depends strongly on the procured trials and learning experiences. There are no male-female twin souls. Souls are not halves of a higher entity.

Sometimes a person reincarnates almost immediately, but sometimes the interval may take thousands of years. This is partly a question of personal preference. During the intermission a soul may stay in spheres above its own level for some time. This stimulates its desire to develop further. Consecutive lives are often only weakly linked. Circumstances may differ greatly, and talents may remain dormant in a life, enabling other talents to develop better.

Human souls are in different stages of development. Many are on earth for the first time, but in individuals this is difficult to assess. People may incarnate under lower circumstances, even on a lower planet because this fits their development, or to fulfil missions. They retain their capacities, but their possibilities to express themselves are often limited. On every planet a childhood is necessary, although on some planets it is less cramped and clumsy than on others.

To get ahead a soul thinks about its past lives and listens to more advanced souls. This may improve its karma, but it has to test any progress on earth. The soul chooses its general fate and the trials it will be subjected to in its coming life. Not every specific occurrence is planned and determined beforehand. A soul senses the time for a new life drawing near. It can choose its body when it is permitted to do so. A soul which is going to prepare for a new incarnation may ask help from higher souls. If it descends from a good sphere, its friends will accompany it until its birth. When the pregnancy begins, a ribbon of ectoplasm links the soul to the foetus. This ribbon gradually shortens. Slowly, the soul feels itself getting more vague, and then loses its awareness, knowledge, and memory.

Twins may have been friends in a previous life. Family ties often come out from friendships in past lives. Often, we know acquaintances, neighbours, people we work with from a past life, sometimes as family members. Mental similarity between children and parents is caused more by the sympathy between their souls than by heredity. A good or bad upbringing may make a big difference, especially for rather weak souls. A weak soul may ask for good parents. Parents cannot attract a good soul through their thoughts or prayers. An infant who died has had a life contributing little to its development. Sometimes such a short life completes a life cut off early just before, but usually it is the parents' karma. The soul of a mentally deficient person is undergoing punishment and is often aware of this.

Resemblances between incarnations, especially facial resemblance, are due to the ability of the soul to influence the growth of the body. Vague memories and insights from past lives may lead to inborn feelings and thoughts like the notion of divine guidance, or of life after death. Someone's mentality may correspond from one life to the next, but can also develop through inner changes, and be influenced by general and social circumstances.

Reincarnation, as presented in Kardec's book, is not compulsive, except perhaps for lazy or underdeveloped souls. People want to return because they want to develop. Kardec's book is the first statement on reincarnation in agreement with present-day material.

The American medium *Arthur Ford* received impressions of his own past lives and those of others. After his death *Ruth Montgomery* received messages from him through automatic writing (in this case, typing) about the conditions after death, about reincarnation in general, and about the reincarnations of some people in particular (Montgomery 1971). What Ford tells about the conditions after death is consistent with many reports from others. But even after his death, Arthur Ford remains an enthusiast. Descriptions of the discarnate life are filled with impassioned deliberations and sermons. He and his companions describe their state as unity with God, as the most divine state imaginable. What does Ford have to say about reincarnation in his blessed state?

Ford describes the preparations for a new incarnation as an extensive consideration and assimilation of previous lives to select items for compensation, improvement, development, test, or consolidation.

Once we know what we want, we look for suitable circumstances. Our sex is often the same as the one we had in our past few lives. Many of us have a preferred sex. Sometimes, sex alternates for educative purposes. When we can, we may look for parents ourselves. In this choice, we consider the sex of an available embryo, as well as the opportunities offered by our prospective educators, and sometimes the learning experience involved in being born to particular parents. If there are several candidates for one embryo, the candidates are weighed one against the other, resulting almost automatically in the most suitable candidate, as in a kind of computer clearance. Once our parents have been determined, we may hang about in their vicinity for a while, to convince ourselves that this choice fits with our plans. We enter the foetus usually during birth, but sometimes shortly before or after. If we hesitate too long, the child may die. If somebody enters a defective body, he usually does this to work off some karma faster. This is especially true for congenital mental handicaps. Karma is also worked off through serious accidents during childhood. Usually, we unconsciously desired that opportunity. But not all accidents are foreseen, and they may be due to coincidences that are not karmic.

Ford gives an example of a paralysed woman who, as a Roman soldier, had terrorized prisoners to such an extent that from fear they trembled and quaked all over their bodies. Now, she lives through this karma by experiencing a life of helplessness, and weak, convulsive movements (Montgomery 1971: 148).

Ruth Montgomery, always the journalist, asks the deceased Ford about the further vicissitudes of the deceased famous. Abraham Lincoln is living in New Orleans and works together with universities and institutes to find a solution to the race problem. George Washington died as a soldier in Vietnam after leading a platoon on a dangerous mission and being taken prisoner. Rudolph Valentino is happily married and lives in Paris. Napoleon was an ordinary soldier in his next life, and then had two short lives in Portugal and Brazil.

What do we do with such tit-bits? They feed our curiosity without satisfying it, belonging more to a gossip magazine than we would expect from someone living in unity with the divine.

Ford recounts that in Palestine he was once the father of Lazarus, Martha, Maria, and a third sister, Ruth, a previous incarnation of

Ruth Montgomery herself. A later book elaborately describes the fortunes of this Palestinian family (Montgomery 1974). According to the information on the spine, the book is non-fiction, so apparently it purports to be true.

Many accounts have been written about alleged past lives and it is difficult to say anything sensible about such stories. They are most convincing if the lives are not about, or in the direct vicinity of, a famous person, and if they give the reader the feeling of being in a bygone age. The books by Joan Grant and by Arthur Guirdham, and especially the book by Edward Ryall (1974) are good examples of this. About the events in Palestine, however, there are too many competing versions. At least the version by Montgomery's inspirators does not directly contradict the New Testament, although their additions abound in exalted feelings, which would be most appropriate to a noble and sentimental parson's vision of events.

A lot of what Montgomery writes (or Ford says) makes sense, but the distinction between careful reports and enthusiastic embellishments by the communicating discarnates remains fuzzy.

Jane Roberts published a number of books recording information that she received from a discarnate soul who calls himself Seth. Her books are probably the best known publications of channelled spirit messages during the last few years. Seth is a gnostic spirit-philosopher who wants to tell us the real nature of the world and of mankind. His epistemology and metaphysics are elaborately explained in a scientific sounding jargon. They are typically didactic expositions of somebody disseminating the truth, without any trace of dialectic. Vocabulary and exposition seem to embrace logic, but are incoherent and without critical discourse. Doubts are countered by assurance, not by argument.

Of himself, Seth says: 'In the first place I am a teacher, although I was never a scholar. Mainly, I am someone with a message: you create the world you know' (Roberts 1972). His basic message is more or less that our physical surroundings and our physical body originated from our own thoughts and are sustained by them. Apparently, he takes the physical universe for a part of his present discarnate environment. Thus, his philosophy is more or less Platonic. The physical world is only a semi-real reflection of the real mental world. Reminiscent of Christian Science, he summons us to believe in the reality of good, and not in the reality of evil. Experiences which seem to indicate the contrary are merely apparent.

All edifying testimonial literature tends to herald coming redemption. Seth is no exception. Around the year 2075 (still safely far away) people get an intimate contact with their inner being, a being which will mediate between man and the world. I am not sure what this means, but it does not sound encouraging. He continues by heralding new prophets, and to top it all off, 'the third Christ personality' (whatever that may be).

Seth also has some things to say about reincarnation. I will summarize his discourse, although it is rather complex and strongly interwoven with his notion of reality and the human soul. In his philosophy time is not linear, and so incarnations do not take place consecutively. According to him, our incarnations are plays acted next to each other simultaneously. The ostensible causal relationships between lives and the current concept of karma are therefore illusions from which we must free ourselves to become truly creative. To assume that plays can be acted in a world without time, without succession of events, is ridiculous, and it remains unclear how this tallies with the forecast that around 2075 we will all be in contact with our real selves.

Announcements of reincarnations

Some people continue to communicate after death with persons they knew, and some among them manifest themselves to announce their own new incarnation. During a seance in France in May 1924, the name is spelled of the deceased servant of the father of a participant. After a few difficult attempts, communication improves and the spirit says he is going to be born again in the family of some acquaintances of one of those present. He gives the name of these acquaintances, the place where they live, and the composition of the family. He says he will be born again on the morning of 24 September 1924, and may be recognized by his ear. The deceased servant had had a right ear sticking out. The family in question was not informed. At 8 a.m. on the predicted day the doctor who had been present at the seance was told a boy had just been born in that family. When he visited the family three days later with his wife, the baby cried because of the visitors, but immediately calmed down with the doctor's wife. The mother remarked that it was as if he knew her. The baby had a bandage around its head because the right ear stuck out and had to be pressed back (Muller 1970: 192).

During a spiritist seance in Venezuela in 1957, a spirit which had already communicated often, manifested itself with considerable difficulty. It said it was on the point of being born as a woman with a beautiful face but with a crippled leg. It dreaded the birth because it was going to be a difficult life. The mother, who at that moment was in the city hospital, had already been brought to the delivery room twice. Since the birth was difficult, the doctors were preparing for a caesarian operation. The encouragement of the spiritist circle strengthened the spirit. After that, the group received a message from another spirit that the birth had taken place, without a caesarian operation, with the exact time of birth. The group checked the data about the birth and found them correct, right down to the crippled leg (Muller 1970: 190).

Obsessions and reincarnation

An important field of spiritism related to reincarnation is that of obsessions. The Brazilian spiritist hospitals largely receive patients who cannot be cured in other institutions, and they diagnose obsession in about 80 per cent of their cases: a discarnate soul having nestled itself disturbingly in somebody's aura or body. Often there is a karmic relationship.

A farmer who was past 60 had suffered gradually worsening epileptic attacks for eight years. It appeared that an entity called Marie disturbed him. A medium was able to contact Marie after the patient had been magnetized. Marie told her she had been his wife in his previous life. The guides present explained that she had been egoistic and jealous and still clung to him after their deaths. She felt deserted when he was reborn and now she was trying to hasten his death. Bringing Marie round to see her mistake cured the man of his epilepsy within a week. As a kind of atonement, she accepted an incarnation as his child. The patient was not told about this, but the attending medium told him she would like to become godmother if he would have another child. The farmer protested he was already a grandfather and too old. But a year later he had a daughter, a sickly child who died after three months. After the child's death, Marie communicated again via automatic writing, and said she had found it a painful experience but had learned from it.

The same psychic therapist treated three cases of ill-willed obsessive spirits. The spirit of a late doctor who paralysed an 11-year-old boy explained he was acting out of vengeance. After the cure, the obsessor let go, said he wanted to develop himself further, and expected to be reborn in France. A captain had serious digestive problems and swollen veins and it looked as though he was going to have a stroke. It turned out that a male entity was obsessing him. He had known the captain and his wife in a previous life when he had been an opponent who had committed suicide because of them. Another man suffered epileptic attacks at night. The spirit of an easygoing doctor who had done harm to his patients during his life turned out to be the cause of these. In his previous life the patient had denounced the doctor, who subsequently committed suicide and had a bad time after his death. The obsessor said he himself had no idea how he had found the patient (Muller 1970: 196).

A woman of 60 had been mentally disturbed for more than twelve years. She had been in various institutions. Every time, she got better, but when she returned home the problems began anew. A medium diagnosed obsession by the woman's brother-in-law who had died thirteen years before. During his life they got along with difficulty, and after his death he had discovered why. In his previous life he had been the son of a Russian nobleman. The woman, who had been his sister, had him imprisoned so she could get all their inheritance. He had sworn to avenge himself and wanted to imprison her, now in an institution. It was made clear to him that his vengeance was blocking his own well-being and further development. In an emotional scene, brother and sister forgave each other via the medium. From that moment on, the patient was cured and lived another twelve years in excellent mental health (Muller 1970: 199).

Many Brazilian doctors and mediums work with this kind of spiritistic diagnosis and therapy. Doctors who have written about them include Bezerra de Menezes and Ignacio Ferreira (1955). According to Ferreira, who dealt with over 1,000 cases in twenty-five years, passive obsession is the most widespread. In passive obsession the obsessor does not mean to harm anybody, or may even want to protect somebody, and enters the victim's aura in ignorance, but is still disturbing. In his book he describes thirty cases of obsession related to previous lives.

There are also pseudo-obsessions, in which the obsessor is the personality of a past life of the victim. Chapter 13 returns to this.

Provisional conclusions

What may we conclude from this mediumistic and clairvoyant information about previous lives? Sensitive people appear to have more past-life memories. They often remember or see more than one life. Typically, their memories and the information they give about others and about reincarnation in general contain more karmic relations and sex changes. They are usually more interested in understanding causes and effects than in demonstrable proofs of reincarnation. However diverse the sources, the information given is similar. Paranormally sensitive people can usually distinguish clearly between their own and other people's lives. It is therefore rather weak to explain apparent past-life memories by telepathy or ESP.

An important datum is that the past personality seems to be reanimated in apparitions and in pseudo-obsessions. Anatta theories are therefore untenable and the reincarnation idea itself has to be more precisely defined. The surfacing tensions and problems of 'unfinished business' may come either from experiences in this life or from experiences in other lives. The personality from a previous life may apparently influence the preparations for the present life.

Further reading

As the text will have made clear, Karl Muller's *Reincarnation, Based on Facts* (1970) has been the most important source for this chapter. Muller gives references to the spiritistic literature in this area.

The work of Edgar Cayce, possibly deserving a chapter on its own, was hardly considered in this chapter, but will be used in chapters 10, 11, and 12. Besides biographies about him, for example from Sugrue (1942) and Millard (1961), there is an Edgar Cayce series consisting of at least fifteen books with abstracts of his sessions. An example is *Edgar Cayce on Atlantis* by Edgar Evans Cayce (1968). His son Hugh Lynn Cayce published this series with Warner Books and wrote a book himself about his father (1964). New summaries of his thoughts on reincarnation are always appearing. The first and best known of these is by Gina Cerminara (1950), who then wrote two further books on the subject (1963, 1967). There are also books by Langley (1967), Woodward (1972), and Sharma (1975). Using data from Cayce readings, Violet Shelley (1979) concludes that reincarnation may stop. 'Reincarnation unnecessary! This book reveals how the reincarnation cycle can be broken!' promises the cover. Upon closer observation, the whole story boils down to Cayce saying in a few cases that someone did not need to return to earth. Hopefully, this is also true for the designers of such cackling bookcovers.

I have already mentioned the books by Joan Grant (1937–1956), as well as those by Guirdham (1970, 1974, 1976, 1980). There are a number of books by Ruth Montgomery on the subject, including *A World Beyond* (1971). Here too, there is mindless bragging on the cover: 'The first eye-witness account of the hereafter.' Jane Roberts did not stop after the first book: Seth went on speaking.

I have not investigated other spiritistic literature. Probably interesting are *Nyria* by Rosa Caroline Praed (1914) and *The New Nuctemeron* by Marjorie Livingstone (1930). A book with many mediumistic elements is *Initiation* by Elisabeth Haich (1965) in which she writes about her life as an Egyptian initiate. I have no reason to doubt her Egyptian life or her gifts, but her initiation is more interesting for psychologists than for past-life explorers. Compared to this, the little book *The Boy Who Saw True* edited by Neville Spearman (1953) is refreshingly unassuming and open-minded.

General spiritualistic books about reincarnation have been written by Knight (1950), Boswell (1969), and Penkala (1972). Van Holthe tot Echten (1921) writes negatively about reincarnation and explains everything as suggestion, but is intelligent and readable, and bursts some bubbles of false reincarnation arguments.

PART II *Experiences*

5 Spontaneous Recall of Past Lives

Spontaneous recollection of past lives does not occur arbitrarily, but according to fairly fixed patterns. This chapter discusses seven different types of recollection:
- recognition of places at first sight
- recognition of people at first sight
- recollection in dreams
- recollection triggered by objects, pictures, or books
- recollection triggered by similar situations
- recollection cropping up in exceptional physical or emotional circumstances, after accidents, or during illness
- recollection in early childhood.

As this list indicates, recollection of past lives is often triggered by association, apparently conforming to the same storage and retrieval mechanisms as normal recollection. It is independent of previous belief in reincarnation. Out of the 127 cases cited by Lenz (1979), 119 had no previous belief in reincarnation, 5 had no previous opinion, and 3 had a previous belief in reincarnation.

Traces of past lives

Recollection of past lives is only the most explicit form in which they leave their mark. Personal idiosyncrasies may also come from past lives. The full list of traces includes:
- appearance (e.g. face and birth marks)
- behaviour (e.g. curious dressing or eating and drinking habits)
- abilities (e.g. child prodigies)
- intuition
- preferences
- postulates (rigid attitudes to life)
- emotions
- recollection.

Schlotterbeck subsumes all traces before recollection under the correct but vague label of 'patterns', and continues: 'But these patterns and impressions are only appetizers when we are looking for our past lives. We all wish for clearer memories in the form of sensory information' (1987: 13).

Someone sees the landscape of southern Spain in a film and is overwhelmed by an intense, inexplicable feeling of melancholy. Someone hears the name Julius Caesar for the first time and is filled with a sudden, unreasonable hatred. Such emotions without explicable cause in the present life may indicate a past life. Phobias and monosymptomatic neuroses (consisting of one isolated symptom only) without traumatic experiences in this life are also traces from past lives. Chapter 10 and 16 discuss postulates, that is, rigid attitudes to life.

Among the capabilities that may come from past lives is the ability immediately to recognize and assess, usually given the vague label 'intuition'. Much in intuition may, if we go back far enough, be the result of earlier experiences, earlier learning, and long practice (Shirley 1924: 32).

With young children peculiar behaviour may directly indicate a past life. An example is performing rituals for getting up, eating, or greeting which are unknown or unusual in the area but are known elsewhere. A charming example is the little girl who slams her milk mug down on the table and wipes her mouth as if she had just put down a pint of beer with great satisfaction. When her parents reprimand her, she bursts into tears and says it is a tribute to her comrades who she does not want to forget. When the family inquires further, she makes remarks about a past life (Muller 1970: 60; Head and Cranston 1977: 396). The girl also looked markedly different from the rest of her family.

Peculiar, inexplicable preferences are half way between more explicit and more implicit indications. They may be preferences for a particular food, a particular language or country, a particular architectural style, a particular kind of music, and so on. Walter Pater wrote 'Taste is the memory of a culture once known'. Of course, peculiarities develop in this life, but many abilities, emotions, preferences, and idiosyncrasies contain traces of past lives. A strong indication of past lives is extraordinary ability in young children, the child prodigies who have exceptional musical, linguistic, or mathematical talents, or such exotic talents as being able to puppeteer well as a tiny child (Fielding 1898: 336).

The list of eight kinds of traces of past lives helps to actualize traces methodically. Past-life therapy uses emotions and rigid attitudes to awaken recollection, to work off and release these emotions and beliefs. More noncommittal forms of inducing past-life recall can use the other peculiarities as starting points.

Spontaneous recollection in adults

Napoleon used to proclaim that he had been Charlemagne (Head and Cranston 1977: 286). Such statements mean little, even if he himself believed in it. It is an association, intensified to identification, with an obvious historical example. When Charles Emerson says he remembers being with the Greeks before Troy, this is already a less obvious claim, since his role there undoubtedly differed from his life as Emerson (Head and Cranston 1977: 317). But even this statement demonstrates little, since everybody with a classical education is acquainted with the *Iliad*. This too, may be identification with an appealing historical example. Association is even less obvious when Thoreau says he remembers walking in the misty past with Hawthorne along the Scamander in Asia. He also remembered a life 1,800 years before in Judea (where he had never heard of Christ), and a life as a shepherd in Assyria (Head and Cranston 1977: 317). Such statements are not yet convincing without further confirmation, although there is hardly compensation, or identification with historical events. The French writer Gustave Flaubert said he had always lived. His recollection went back to the Pharaohs and he had clear impressions of all kinds of eras, occupations, and circumstances (Head and Cranston 1977: 333). Interestingly, his recollection apparently remained within known history. Rainer Maria Rilke was convinced he had been in Moscow in a past incarnation (Head and Cranston 1977: 371). Such ideas are common, often arising from a strong feeling of recognition when visiting an unknown place for the first time.

Recognition of places at first sight

Guilfoyle asked people if they ever had the feeling they had been at some place before when they were visiting it for the first time. About 35 per cent never had, 50 per cent had one or two times, and 15 per cent more times. Six per cent had had intense experiences apparently from beyond the present life (Muller 1970: 109).

On his first visit to Genoa, Hermann Grundei had the powerful feeling he already knew the old part of the city. On later visits to Italy he had similar impressions in Verona, Bologna, and Florence, but not in Venice, Naples, or Palermo. He slowly recollected a life in the fourteenth or fifteenth century as a monk who performed diplomatic missions for clerical authorities. He recollected clearly his appearance, his name, and his death. On his other voyages he had a similar experience in Constantinople (Muller 1970: 111).

Seabrook tells the story of a young Lebanese who comes to a village during a long voyage and recognizes the place. He remembers his name and gives proofs of his identity. He is able to point out his house and remembers that he had hidden some money. Following his instructions, the money is found. The previous person died shortly before he was born. The village people acknowledge him as the reincarnated villager (Muller 1970: 110).

Recognition of places at first sight is strongly related to the *déjà vu* experience. For this reason, people who believe in reincarnation quickly identify a *déjà vu* experience with people and places as recollection of past lives. Probably, this is justified only in a minority of cases. *Déjà vu* does not necessarily refer to past lives. There is, after all, also *jamais vu*: when a familiar situation suddenly becomes strange and new. Stronger mental short-circuits are, for example, depersonalization (no longer feeling oneself as a person, an I) and derealization (no longer experiencing the environment as real, but rather as if it were cardboard or pastry – as in Sartre's *La Nausée*.

It seems to me that a *déjà vu* experience can only be interpreted as a recollection from a past life when it has more pointers, like knowing objects, houses, or locations yet unseen. Pseudo-recall cannot be precluded in cases of historically or touristically well-known places. Important indications for real recollection are, in particular, clear and specific emotions and feeling or seeing oneself as someone else. Experiences containing discoveries are certainly more than *déjà vu*.

Someone recognizes a landscape and remembers a presently over-grown cliff that had an inscription on it. He goes to the cliff and discovers a mutilated and worn inscription behind the overgrowth. A famous example is the honeymooning Hungarian couple. The woman recognizes the landscape during a boat trip, and wants to go ashore to visit a castle. In the castle she stops at a wall and remembers being murdered behind that wall. The wall is broken and a sealed-off space appears, containing two skeletons (Cannon 1936: 34).

I will give an example of an apparently false memory. A woman is travelling for the first time through Minnesota with her daughter. During a stop at a station she is surprised that the place is completely familiar to her. She recognizes a farm as the place where she once lived. As the stop is long enough to take a walk, she visits the farm with her daughter and the layout and furnishings of the house are exactly as she had described them to her daughter. She recounted this incident to her friends. One of them investigated the matter and discovered that the farm had been built when the woman in question was already adult. At the time of her birth there were as yet no buildings in the area (Cannon 1936: 32).

Clearly this is no reincarnation memory. Identification with someone else can only have been through telepathy with someone who had been living in the house. *Déjà vu* seems to be out of the question because the woman could describe the layout and the furnishings even though she had not been there. Fantasy and pseudo-memory are also out of the question. A psychodrama is impossible because nothing personal or problematic is going on. A strong form of psychometric clairvoyance could be possible, and the hypothesis of a collective memory cannot be precluded. But both interpretations fail to explain why she felt she had lived in the house.

The most likely explanation is a combination of *déjà vu*, imagin-ation, and (self-) deception. The woman may have have had a *déjà vu* experience, a feeling that she recognized the place. She looks for an explanation and imagines she has been there before. During the visit to the farm (perhaps still in a *déjà vu* mood) she has new feelings of recognition and tells her daughter it is exactly how she remembers it. Afterwards she says she had already told her daughter beforehand (imagination or self-deception). Perhaps to pass the time during the wait at the station, she elaborates her experience and makes it more impressive, first for herself and later for others. This is the most likely explanation because it contains the fewest paranormal presuppositions and because alternative explanations are less likely. If there had been telepathic contact with a present or former inhabitant of the farm, then she would have felt familiar with the inhabitants rather than with the furnishings of the house. The hypothesis of a collective memory and psychometric clairvoyance are less plausible because of identification: she feels she has lived there herself. If this woman showed earlier signs of having telepathic or psychometric abilities then these suppositions become more likely.

Out-of-body experiences at night – visiting some place in a dream – may sometimes account for recognition of places. There are examples of people recognizing an existing house from dreams, while the inhabitants had thought the house was haunted, and now seeing the visiting person in real life, they recognize him as the ghost (Shirley 1924: 79). This may also explain the previous example.

In my survey, recognition of places was correlated with flashes of inspiration.

Recognition of people at first sight

The previous chapter gave the example of Gerda Walter. Another case is that of Lanfranco Davito, an Italian policeman. He is on duty, when a stranger comes towards him in the street. At the same moment he remembers this man clubbing him to death during a tribal quarrel, and he goes white with fear. Later, all kinds of recollections of this primitive life come up (Muller 1970: 119).

Recognizing people at first sight is common. Many times it may be *déjà vu* rather than a past-life memory. Faces may seem familiar to us because we associate them with faces we already know; or somebody's acts, or words, seem immediately familiar to us, producing a feeling of recollection. A feeling of immediate intimacy, sympathy, or antipathy is not sufficient reason to assume a past life. The most interesting cases are meetings with mutual recognition, such as Gerda Walter's. Love at first sight, if real, certainly comes from a relationship in a previous life. Strong feelings of recognition may be the starting point for regressions to past lives (Sutphen 1976). About one-third of Lenz's cases were induced by meeting someone, although the recollection seldom came at first sight. The usual first response was one of uncommon familiarity.

In my survey, magnetic abilities, and to a lesser extent clairvoyance, were correlated with recognizing other people.

Recollection in dreams

There are relatively few cases of dreams clearly referring to previous lives. Probably, this is because dreams are usually not remembered well, and if remembered are still hardly convincing evidence. Muller gives three cases confirmed by other evidence. I quote one.

A woman had had a recurrent dream since she was 5 years old. She met a boy, and suddenly they would find themselves in an old house on a flat hilltop. She could see the house in detail. They were playing in a corridor at the top of the stairs. She ran away from her friend and fell through the staircase to the stone floor below. While falling, she saw the black-and-white tiled floor rushing towards her, and everything went blank. Usually, she had this dream when about to take an important decision in her life.

As an adult, she was once asked to visit the troubled inhabitants of a haunted house. To her astonishment, the house appeared to be the house of her dreams. She was told that a few centuries ago, a boy and a girl had fallen to their deaths while playing. When she saw two miniatures, she exclaimed 'My father and my mother!'. These were indeed the parents of the two children (Shirley 1924: 65; Muller 1970: 95).

Lenz had 19 cases, or 15 per cent of his survey, who had memories in dreams, often about several incarnations. He noted the following differences from common dreams (Lenz 1979: 32):
- unusual sensations
- awareness during the dream of seeing scenes from past lives
- uncommon vividness, so details can be described even years later
- a subsequent change of attitude toward death and dying.

These four differences do not seem remarkable to me. The first three only indicate a vivid dream, which is common for dreams that are impressive enough and remembered well enough to be reported later. The fourth is usual for all memories of previous lives.

Holzer states that recurrent dreams are inevitably connected with some sort of reincarnation memory (Holzer 1985: 26). This seems a rather sweeping statement, but could well be true. He states also that the difference between a truly personal memory and one telepathically received is that the dreamer in dreams of the first type feels or sees himself in the scene, while in receiving memories of others, he only watches from the outside. Recurrent dreams are excellent starting points for regressions. Schlotterbeck states the same, but adds that, as in any therapy, dreams just before the start of regression therapy may also be significant. Completing the dream during a session is often a powerful tool, and may release past-life memories. He gives some examples (Schlotterbeck 1987: 23).

In my survey, paranormally gifted people dreamt more about previous lives than others.

Recollection triggered by objects, pictures, or books

When Giuseppe Costa was a child, a small picture of Constantinople and the Bosphorus triggered vague memories of ships and battles, with strong emotions. As a boy of 10, he visited Venice for the first time and recognized it. The following night he dreamt he was 30 years old, and commanding some medieval ships. The flags impressed him particularly. The dream was extensive and chronological. Later he recognized other places, but he only started to believe in a previous life after an out-of-body experience. After visiting the castle of Verres, he identified himself as Ibleto di Challant who lived in the fourteenth century (Costa 1923; Brazzini 1952: 120; Muller 1970: 87).

Francis Lefebvre daydreamed about the sea as a boy. When he was 35 he visited museums in Portugal. Seeing a big drum and a ship's bell, and later a golden object, triggered memories of the life of Vasco da Gama, the Portuguese discoverer. His wife found that a portrait of da Gama looked just like her husband when he was angry. This is one of the few documented examples of recollection of a famous past personality. Lefebvre concedes that his conviction is difficult to prove (Lefebvre 1959: 3–11; Muller 1970: 90).

Joan Grant's memories started when she psychometrically read a scarab that apparently was hers in a previous life (Grant 1956b).

Lenz had 9 cases out of 127 who claimed that memories occurred when hearing a piece of music, seeing a painting, or coming into contact with some object (Lenz 1979: 29).

Recollection triggered by similar situations

Berlin 1943, Sunday: there are bombing raids. As on every Sunday, Hermann Grundei checks the books he keeps in an old safe in a dark corridor. Slowly, he gets the feeling that he has lived exactly the same way before. His impressions become stronger, until he sees clearly the end of his previous life. He sees himself checking his books during a holiday, drawing them out of an old safe in a dark corner. His inspection shows he is bankrupt, embezzled by his bookkeeper. He shoots himself through his right temple.

Grundei thought the incident occurred between 1870 and 1885, probably when he was living in a small seaport and doing something with ships and timber. In 1952 he began to write to seaports and got confirmation of this history from one of them, with the information that the son of the man in question was still alive. In 1956 he visited that son. They both felt as if they were family members meeting after a long time. They looked alike and they spoke alike. People assumed they were brothers. On an old school picture he recognized his two sons, but not his two daughters (Muller 1970: 122).

Interestingly enough, Grundei happened to be born 35 days *before* his previous identity shot himself. Such a 'negative intermission' is rare, but more documented instances are known. Chapter 13 returns to this subject.

Recollection under extraordinary circumstances

An English technician was still under narcosis after an operation, when he began to explain in refined French that he was a French nobleman, describing his life shortly before the revolution and his death by guillotine. His re-experience contained touch and smell. When the technician came round, he remembered everything as a dream. He could still feel a ring on his finger, but he could no longer speak French (Muller 1970: 126).

Hermann Medingen, a German racing motorist, had a serious accident in 1924. After a brief, terrible pain, he was outside his body. He saw various past lives, as a man and as a woman, as if he were looking in different mirrors (Muller 1970: 127).

An interesting example is Charles Lindbergh who, during his flight over the ocean, slept some time with his eyes open. Being dissociated, he felt simultaneously in the past, the present, and the future. He saw people, heard voices, and felt ancient relations and friendships he seemed to know from past lives (Lindbergh 1953; Head and Cranston 1977: 390).

Georg Neidhart, a German coppersmith, lost his wife and child as a young man. After weeks of despair he began to see images and scenes from old times. Later, he had virtually complete recollection of this life and was able to localize and identify it (Neidhart 1959; Muller 1970: 100).

Other experiences may come up under controlled trance, as in yoga or meditation. In 13 per cent of Lenz's cases prayer or meditation triggered recollection. He notes that these people appear to accept their memories more readily than the other cases.

Adult recollection: a summary

With adult recollection the first point is to rule out *déja vu*, pseudo-memory, and imagination. The value of fragmentary recollection is difficult to determine, unless there are verifiable details. The first test is to screen for clarity and concreteness, just as with any normal recollection. A second test is whether the different elements of the recollection are mutually consistent, and consistent with other re-collections. A third test is to compare the contents of our memory with objective, historical facts.

The examples from Hans Holzer indicate that historical testing alone is not enough. Some of his best-researched examples, including one he calls 'the perfect case for reincarnation' (Holzer 1985: 60), are clearly not reincarnations, but obsessions, or rather spirit attachments. Under hypnosis the former personalities state explicitly that they entered only later, during the life of the subject.

Recollection is usually triggered by association: places returned to, people met, objects recognized, and similarities in situations. Recollection also comes up in gradual or acute dissociation: under narcosis, after deep despair, through lack of sleep, in the wake of an accident, in dreams. Furthermore, there can be association with something psychological. The latter can be seen in regressions in which the induction does not indicate the place where the remigrant will land. Often, the emerging life is significant now. A good example of this is Glaskin's first regressions (Glaskin 1974: 21, 207).

A number of visions seem to start like an out-of-body experience, not unlike the experiences of the clinically dead which Moody and others describe. According to Lenz this is the common pattern (Lenz 1979: 47), but this is not confirmed by any other source. He states that 29 out of his 127 cases had some form of tunnel experience (like out-of-body experiences) when *returning*, also a highly unusual finding.

Sometimes memories start to come more easily after the first recollection, and they tend to be less visionary, more like common recollections. 'The rest I have just come to know. It was as if I had amnesia, and after my past-life visions I just started to remember things I had forgotten' (Lenz 1979: 41).

I received the following answers to my survey of the content and circumstances of apparent recollection of past lives:

General feeling of having lived before	30%
Feeling of recognizing people	30%
Dream fragments	27%
Feeling of recognizing places	24%
Recollection without clear cause	21%
When relaxing or visualizing	15%
In the presence of a paranormal person	12%
During illness, accidents, loss of consciousness, etc.	0%
No memory at all.	44%

The survey was only limited and the sample had an overrepresentation of sensitive people and an underrepresentation of older men. It is unlikely that the latter influenced the results. Recollection of older and younger people was alike. If people are going to have recollection of past lives, they usually seem to have it before they are 30.

Apparently, learning about reincarnation via personal contacts is more effective than via lectures or talking. Those who had become acquainted with the subject via personal contacts knew more about the subject and were more convinced of it. Oddly enough, they also had more memories of their own. Perhaps people with past-life recall have a stronger preference for personal contacts, compared with reading literature or attending lectures. People with paranormal gifts were less oriented to existing doctrines in their ideas. Anthroposophically oriented people had learned more via personal contacts and less via lectures than those theosophically oriented, but they had less personal recollection.

A few other results from the survey are shown in Table 4 below:

Table 4

How many past lives do you believe you have impressions of?

One	4
Two	1
Three or Four	4
More than four	4
Unclear	5

Are your impressions generally clear?

Usually very unclear	1
Usually rather unclear	7
Usually somewhat unclear	3
Usually clear	0
Difficult to answer	7

Do you have impressions of place, time, or name of your clearest incarnation(s)?

	No	Vague	Clear
Place or region	7	2	8
Period or century	9	2	7
Name	17	0	1

Wambach's research (1978: 36) also indicates that the name is one of the most difficult aspects of recollection.

Muller found an average intermission of about seventy years in cases of spontaneous reincarnation memories (Muller 1970). Four per cent of the men remembered a female incarnation, and 24 per cent of the women remembered a male incarnation. These percentages are consistent with those of clairvoyants or mediums giving information about past lives.

Spontaneous recollection in children: examples from Ian Stevenson's work

Investigating child cases is expensive and time-consuming. Few people do it, and fewer do it well. The most well-known names are Ian Stevenson, Hemendra Banerjee, Francis Story, and Hernani Andrade. Story worked with Stevenson in India and Andrade works in Brazil, also co-operating with Stevenson. Banerjee worked in India from the 1950s, where he founded the Indian Institute of Parapsychology, and has been living in the United States since 1970. Ian Stevenson, from the Department of Parapsychology of the University of Virginia, is the international authority in the area of child case research. He has collected about 2,000 cases of apparent past-life recall. Of these he has examined more than 200 extensively. He has reported his findings in books and numerous articles. In northern India he examined 105 cases, in Sri Lanka 80, and a few dozen in Turkey, Lebanon, Alaska, Thailand and Burma.

Research into child cases may be compared with legal investigations. It is important to get as many precise and independent testimonies as possible. If a child has never been near the place where the past person lived, and has not met any people from there, it is possible to experiment on the spot.

Banerjee seems to be an enthusiast who is not shy of publicity and works fast. His book *The Once and Future Life* (1979) carries as subtitle *An astonishing twenty-five-year study on reincarnation*. It does not even come close to Stevenson's work. He writes pearls such as: 'It is a scientific fact that a person cannot remember that which he or she has not previously learned' (Banerjee 1979: 17). His concept of reincarnation is definitely religious and not empirical (1979: 24).

Stevenson, who now has data on more than 2,000 cases, takes careful account of all alternative explanations of apparent recollection. He has done solid study of the psychology of recollection and testimony and of the methods to evaluate eye-witness reports. The introduction to his third book (1975) gives a particularly valuable overview of this area. His opponents are less informed. Daniel Cohen (1975) makes sixteen insinuating remarks in eight pages about a particular case, then explains this case as 'wishful thinking' on Stevenson's part, and ends by claiming Stevenson's other cases are less convincing. This is reminiscent of the moronic explanation of paranormal phenomena by 'suggestion', which laymen in the area of the paranormal and, worse, laymen in the area of suggestion have a tendency to use. But if you know that something is nonsense, you do not need to treat it seriously; you just explain it by something ordinary which at the same time is not real – suggestion.

Of the 105 cases Stevenson examined in northern India, 60 were boys and 45 were girls. Of the 80 cases in Sri Lanka, 38 were boys and 42 girls. Usually, the recollection surfaces at the age of 3, when the children begin to speak. Often, their recollection diminishes between the ages of 7 and 9. Some retain their memories as they get older, and with a few the recollection becomes clearer as time goes by. Holzer states that the memories usually fade at school age, but that sometimes the memories return at the age of 17 or 18, even more intensely and in more detail (Holzer 1985: 56).

The scope of recollections differs greatly. Sometimes children remember unconnected fragments, sometimes incidents, such as their death. Sometimes, after finally being able to tell somebody everything about their previous life, they forget it, as if they are released. Hubbard reports such a case of a 5-year-old girl.

Of the many cases Stevenson examined, I will give three examples from his series *Cases of the Reincarnation Type* (1975–83). I give them here as illustrations and leave out the facts, circumstances, and research methods making up the evidence. Chapter 17 will return to research methods. For the rest, I refer to Stevenson's original descriptions.

Laxmi Narain, the 17-year-old son of a rich landowner and tax official, lived in the city of Pilibhit in Uttar Pradesh. His father died and left him a considerable fortune. He was a rather spoiled child who, at the time of his father's death, had not even finished primary school, and spent his money freely on food, drink, clothes, and women. He was also generous, so he ultimately spent all of his fortune. Regularly, after a few weeks of the high life, he would withdraw into his house and devote his time to religious thought. After one or two weeks he would have enough of this and then the *dolce vita* would begin again, in a repetitive cycle.

Like so many spoiled children, he was hot-tempered. Once when he saw a visitor leaving the house of his favourite prostitute, he shot and killed him. He went into hiding and was able, probably by using bribes, to avoid a court case. After this, he moved to another town, where he died within a year at probably the age of 32. That was in December 1918.

In 1921 a boy called Bishen Chand was born in Bareilly, also in Uttar Pradesh. When he was only 10 months old, he spoke the word 'pilivit'. When he began to talk, he talked about his life as Laxmi Narain. The following elements of his recollections were written down before Bishen Chand was accompanied to Pilibhit to check his story:

Laxmi Narain lived in Mohalla in Pilibhit. His father was a rich landowner of the Kayashta caste. His uncle was Har Narain. His school was near the river. He learned Urdu, Hindi, and English. His English teacher in the sixth grade was fat and had a beard. When his father died there was a large crowd at the funeral.

His house had two floors with separate entrances for men and women. His uncle Har Prusad had a green house. He used to have kite races with his neighbour Sunder Lal who had a house with a green fence. He had a short, dark servant, Maikua, of the Kahar caste who was a good cook. He won a lawsuit against some family members. He shot a man who had just left the house of Padma, his favourite prostitute and mistress. He was drunk at the time. After the murder, he hid in his garden, where his mother sent him food. Later, he got some work in Shahjahanpur, where he died at the age of twenty.

Almost all of this proved to be correct. The only incorrect statements were the age of his death, the neighbourhood in Pilibhit, and Har Narain not being the name of his uncle, but of his father. However, there was somebody in Pilibhit whom everybody called Uncle Har Narain. This could explain the confusion. In Pilibhit, Bishen Chand recognized his house and the house of his neighbour, Sunder Lal. In his house he recognized the room where he had hidden some money.

The money was actually found in this room, although not in exactly the place he indicated. He recognized the place where there had formerly been a staircase. He recognized a trader's house, and the place of a former watchmaker's shop.

Most of the recollections began to fade after he turned 7. Emotions related to the previous life were especially feelings for people from that life. He was attached to his previous mother. He refused gifts from some other previous relatives. 'Then you wanted my blood, now you want to placate me with money.' Apparently, he was referring to the family quarrel and the ensuing lawsuit.

With difficulty, he accepted the needy circumstances under which he was now growing up. For example, it irritated him that his father did not buy him silk clothes. As a child, he had the same hot-tempered character as Laxmi Narain had apparently had. He was extraordinarily proud of the story of how he had shot his rival. When he was about 17 his violent tendencies disappeared. He remained hot-tempered until he was middle-aged, although he was more and more repentant after his moods. When he was 23 years old, he met his previous mistress once again, who was now about 52. He embraced her and fainted with emotion. In the evening, he visited her with a bottle of wine (although he was now teetotal) and, in vain, tried to convince her to resume their past relationship. He was bitter that his old house had fallen into disrepair, and scoffed at the news that some merchant had received marks of honour.

As for preferences, he liked meat and fish from childhood, and adored alcohol, although he grew up in a family of vegetarian teetotallers. As a boy of 4 or 5 he used to sneak sips of the medicinal brandy. His preference for meat and fish remained until his middle age. His tendency to drink vanished. When he was an adult, he accepted that he could not indulge his desire for expensive clothes. As a child, he was already interested in music, and this remained, just as with Laxmi Narain. As a child he liked to fly kites, but his present father repressed this tendency. As a 5-year-old boy, he advised his father to get a mistress. Growing up, his sexual preoccupations vanished. Bishen Chand married and led a quiet life in this respect. As for abilities, his knowledge of Urdu was notable, as was his ability to play the *tabla*, a musical instrument. He mastered both, without ever having been taught, and without example in his direct surroundings. When he was 8 he stopped playing the *tabla*.

Between the ages of 3 and 7 his behaviour was distinctly different from that of his family. Every day would witness some comparison with his past life. He was contemptuous of the poverty in the house. 'Even my servant would not eat this.' He took off his clothes and demanded silk garments.

We do not know if Laxmi Narain and Bishen Chand looked alike; presumably, there was no notable resemblance. Interestingly, any eye trouble Bishen Chand had as a child was cured by a medicine Laxmi Narain's mother sent him, with the information that this medicine had helped her son (Stevenson 1975: 176).

Another example is Lalitha Abeyawardena, born in August 1962 near Colombo in Sri Lanka (Stevenson 1977: 117). When she was 2½ years old she began to talk, and almost immediately told of her past life. She said she had been a teacher in Mirigama (about 60 kilometres to the north). Her husband was a teacher as well. She gave the name of the school, the way there from her house, and described the shops. She named a few family members and said she had died of an intestinal disease in a hospital. She was emotional and cried often when she talked about her past life, being worried about the children she had left behind. However, she did not want to return and see her husband again.

The teacher was called Nilanthie, was born in 1914, married in 1939, and died in 1953. She married an assistant teacher who was teaching at the school where her father later became a principal. After a few years of marriage, her husband became interested in other women and perhaps started to drink. He fell in love with someone else and wanted a divorce, and therefore accused his wife of adultery. She denied this and he tried to choke her and threatened her with a knife. In spite of the problems, she remained with her three children. Finally, she did decide to leave. Her husband brought her to her oldest brother. According to her brother, her husband had beaten her and, although she was sick and had a fever, forced her to bathe outside in cold water. Three days later she died of 'non-specific enteritis', perhaps typhus.

Lalitha's recollection of her life as Nilanthie includes about sixty statements. Besides her own name, she remembered the names of her husband and her sons. She knew where her brothers and sisters lived and remembered such incidents as her younger brother biting her finger when she fed him, and much later visiting her on his motor-bike. She listed the classes and the schools in which she had taught, gave information about her direct surroundings and the shops there, and gave the names of a few people and a few villages in the surroundings. Further, she was able to talk about her husband's infidelity, the beatings he gave her, the circumstances leading to her death, and her age at that time. She recognized a number of people from her past, but not all. When she was $5\frac{1}{2}$ and went to school, her recollection had largely faded.

Sometimes Lalitha was aware time had passed, sometimes she spoke in the present and begged for her youngest daughter who was perhaps crying from hunger. When she spoke about her past life she made an almost adult impression. Apparently her emotions were still strong, for she cried a lot. Her hate and fear towards her past husband were strong. She was afraid of sickness in others and in herself. She felt sympathy for her past brothers. Like Nilanthie, Lalitha was pious and interested in religion. She was interested in books and often played teacher. She liked the *kukulala* (a yam-like root) and loved flowers. She was strongly against drinking, and had little interest in housekeeping. Nilanthie had a husband who drank, and a helper who did her housekeeping while she was teaching. A difference was that Lalitha did not like beef, although Nilanthie ate it.

She was 18 months old when she sat in the lotus position, and 2 when she began to sing religious *gathas*. At that age she also took a pencil and immediately held it correctly. She picked flowers for temples and she was fond of bringing offerings in the Buddhist manner. Opinions differed about the physical resemblance of the two women. Lalitha had birthmarks but they were unrelated to her life as Nilanthie (Stevenson 1977: 117).

The third example is Necati Çaylak who was born in 1963 in Karaali near Antakya in Turkey (Stevenson 1980: 229). When he was about 3 he recounted that he had died in a car accident on the bridge near the highway (5 kilometres further on), and named the people who had been in the car with him. Later, when he saw the bridge for the first time, he started to cry and described the accident again. He said the car had not turned over, but had 'climbed up' against the railing. He said he had lost a shoe during the accident. He did not want to cross the bridge.

After that, he began to talk about his previous life. He was called Abdülkerim, had a wife and four children. When he was 3, he named the village where he had lived and almost all the people he could remember. There had been an accident on the bridge about a month before he was born. The widow of Abdülkerim Haddoroglu from Bedirge, the man who had died in this accident in February 1963, visited Necati in the fall of 1966. Necati recognized her and, less clearly, her three escorts.

Abdülkerim Haddoroglu was born in 1934 and lived in Bedirge almost all his life, another village near Antakya. He had a taxi for a few months, but could not drive. Otherwise, he was a farmer all his life. He married and had three children. When he died, his wife was expecting a fourth. He was 29 years old at the time. The accident happened shortly after Ramadan when Abdülkerim and his friends had drunk raki. They asked someone to drive them back in a minibus because they themselves had had too many drinks. Blinded by the lights of an oncoming truck, the car drove into a side wall of the bridge. Abdülkerim died at once and did indeed lose a shoe. The other passengers and the driver were wounded.

Necati remembered many details about this previous life and death correctly: the names of his wife, his children, his father, his mother, and his sister, and the village his wife came from. The information about the accident was correct: the place, the minibus, the fact they came from Antakya after having drunk at a religious festival.

Other details were incorrect: his father's last name, that he had been the driver, and that the car had 'climbed up' the wall. He mixed up the names of the passengers partly with those of other persons involved, like the owner of the car. He recognized his wife, some relatives and acquaintances. However, the accounts of these meetings were unclear and inconsistent in some places.

His fear of the bridge, remaining until he was 10, corresponds with other children's fears of the cause or location of their past death. He was afraid of cars until he was 7, when he became interested in them. When he was 10 he wanted to become a chauffeur. Even as a child he liked raki.

He was the most intelligent child in the family and had a tendency to give his older brothers advice. He suffered from headaches until he was 10. His recollections remained virtually unchanged, including the errors (Stevenson 1980: 299).

Summary of the child cases

In the cases Stevenson examined, the intermission between death in the previous life and birth in the new life is usually between 1 and 4 years. An intermission of more than 12 years hardly ever occurs. Between 25 and 75 per cent of the past lives which children remember can be identified and verified, usually because the deceased personality's family is still alive. He found change of sex in 6 to 16 per cent of his cases. This differs according to region.

Among the Tlingits, reincarnation always takes place within the same family. In Turkey, reincarnation usually takes place in a nearby village. Sri Lanka has greater distances between incarnations, often reaching 75–150 kilometres (Stevenson 1966: 171). In Thailand a child remembered being an American pilot, and another remembered being a Japanese soldier. If somebody is able to remember his past life in early childhood, it usually implies an incomplete death, followed by hanging about and a quick return (see chapters 8 and 9). Stigmata, birthmarks pointing to a previous life, occurred at great variance, from 5 to 50 per cent of cases. In 40 to 50 per cent of the child cases there was a violent death in the past life.

Stevenson found recollection of past lives differed greatly in precision and detail, similar to normal recollection. Particularly problematic are precise dating, the chronology of the occurrences, and the particular circumstances of events. Memory of the names of previous personalities differs strongly, presumably because of different use of names in different cultures. Just as with ordinary recollection, remembering or forgetting depends less on the time that has elapsed than on the intensity of the original experience and of the experiences since.

Sometimes there are multiple cases in one family. In one such family, the father was so tired of hearing his children talk about their previous lives (which they did as soon as they could speak) that he strongly but vainly forbade his youngest child to do so.

Karl Muller found that in child cases 9 per cent returned in the same family (Muller 1970). Ian Stevenson found this in 5 to 10 per cent of his cases. The east and the west hardly differ in this respect. Rebirth may happen as nephew, niece, grandchild, brother, sister, and even as one's own child. Initially, Stevenson found fewer such cases in northern India. Closer inspection found that rebirths in the same family or even the same household were usually kept private. In Sri Lanka only 3 out of 80 cases were in the same family. Perhaps this is related to the usually larger distances between reincarnations in Sri Lanka. Stevenson found that in 46 per cent of the cases in India the previous personality had suffered a violent death. In Sri Lanka this was 42 per cent and was strongly correlated with not being able to identify the past personality. Perhaps this, too, is related to the usually larger distances between two incarnations in Sri Lanka. Other countries have similar percentages. The median age of the previous personality's death was 28 in Sri Lanka, while the median life expectancy of the population was 32. The shorter lifespan is understandable, considering half the cases had violent deaths.

Usually, the present child and previous life have many resemblances in habits, behaviour, idiosyncrasies, and preferences. As mentioned above, karmic relations, in the sense of reward, punishment, retribution, or compensation for the previous life, were not found. Stevenson expected, probably because of his theosophical background, to find indications of karmic relations between the different lives. To his astonishment he found only weak indications of karma in only 4 cases out of 106. Stevenson has made reincarnation plausible with his work, but has made karma, at least in the case of children, implausible. He even claims he found no support for the idea of karma. The interpretation of these cases could well be rationalization.

Muller also found intermissions usually shorter than 12 years in his child cases (Muller 1970). In the east, the average intermission of the child cases is a bit shorter than in the west. Apart from Sri Lanka, deaths are not earlier than average. Stevenson found median intermission periods of 18 months in Sri Lanka, 9 months among the Alevis in Turkey, and 48 months among the Tlingits in Alaska. Among the Alevis, the Tlingits, and in Burma, mothers more often have annunciation dreams about the child going to be born, who the child is, and how people will be able to recognize him.

Stevenson (1966, 1975, 1977, 1980) found 6 cases in Sri Lanka and

6 cases in India with sex changes, respectively 7.5 and 6 per cent. Muller found in his cases that 6 per cent of the boys remembered a female life, while 16 per cent of the girls remembered a male past life.

In Sri Lanka few cases had intermission memories. Such recollections were more common in Thailand and Burma, where there were also more examples of recollection of animal incarnations. In Sri Lanka there was only one case: someone who remembered being a hare in between two human lives. Chapter 9 will return to recollections of animal lives.

Further reading

It has already been said that Stevenson is the international authority on child cases (Stevenson 1966, 1975, 1977, 1980). Information about his approach and research methods is to be found in the general introduction and the introductions to his cases in India (1975), in Sri Lanka (1977), and in Lebanon and Turkey (1980), and especially in the general discussion at the end of these volumes. His latest book is about his cases in Thailand and Burma (1983).

The classic study of the Shanti Devi case deserves mention (Gupta *et al.* 1936). Francis Story, who collaborated with Stevenson, recounts a number of cases in the later edition of his work (1975) which includes his earlier publication (1959). Banerjee published cases. Hernani Andrade published cases from Brazil, some of which are available in English.

Some books about culture and folklore give examples of child recollection, for example those by Hall Fielding about Burma (1898) and by Lafcadio Hearn about Japan (1897). Margot Klausner gives examples from the Druses (1975).

Comparable compilations for the various types of adult recollection are lacking. The best collection we have is by Frederick Lenz (1979). Holzer (1985) is interesting, following up spontaneous cases with regression. Many cases can be found scattered about in the literature. Muller (1970) has a chapter about child cases as well as one about adult cases.

The most famous example of a lasting memory in an adult is the case of Ryall (1974). Further references to exceptional cases are found in the text.

6 Induced Regression to Past Lives

If we have past lives, most of us forget them. We may believe in past lives and still not remember them. The way to recall past lives is the same as to recall lost memories of this life. This way is called age regression. Full regression, originally a hypnotic state, brings back memories, but more intense, more like reliving than remembering. Everything which has happened since may be almost forgotten; we experience the situation just as it happened at the time.

Age regression was probably discovered in 1887 by Colavida in Spain. Six years later, Albert de Rochas rediscovered the technique when experimenting with magnetism and hypnosis in Paris. Soon, past lives appeared in de Rochas' work. He is the great pioneer in this area. His book *Les Vies Successives* (1911) is the first book on this subject, and still worth reading. As mentioned earlier, spiritualists, gnostics, and esoterics criticized de Rochas, because his results conflicted with the gnostic and esoteric teachings, and because he induced trance states. Gnostics, like the theosophists, saw this as an atavistic and questionable method, because it would throw the subject's self-awareness out of action. It was objected that subjects are so open to suggestion during trance that their ostensible memories of past lives would be merely responses to de Rochas' dominant and suggestive presence (Van Holthe tot Echten 1921: 109). The theosophists most kindly disposed saw regression only as a possible way to remember past lives in the distant future (Van Ginkel 1917: 149). That 'distant future' took forty to sixty years. And de Rochas' results agree with all the research since.

Age regression

We may experience the past in different ways and with different degrees of intensity. I distinguish five levels in order of increasing access to the past and decreasing access to the present. Figure 2 below gives an overview of these levels which I will discuss in order.

Experiences

On the first level of *memory* you remain aware of the present surroundings. You know where you are now, you know your own history. You know you are only bringing back information about something that has already passed. If you think about it, or if somebody asks you about it, you can bring back information about the past; for example, where you lived when you were in the sixth form of elementary school, and the name of your teacher. To do this, you do not need to re-experience anything from that time. Facts such as names, dates, and addresses can come up without any image. On the level of memory you are only engaged with facts that come up, sometimes accompanied by fleeting impressions of how it used to be, but these impressions remain vague, in the background. The experience, the awareness remains in the present.

The second level is *recollection*. Here, the past comes back in the form of images and other sensory impressions. You can recall what the street where you lived looked like. You recall the face of a friend at school, and how you fell down on the way home from school and

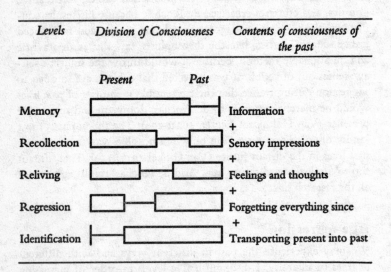

Figure 2 Levels of awareness of the past

how your grazed knee hurt. In recollections images of happenings that impressed you are embedded in a background of vague images blending into each other. You may remember what you heard, what you felt, what you smelled and tasted, although this is more difficult for most people than visual recollection. You can practise recollecting as concretely and completely as possible. Someone else can help you with this by means of direct questions and open suggestions to get your recollections detailed and clear. An open suggestion is, for example: 'You can hear the hum of voices in your classroom again,' or: 'You smell that distasteful cabbage again that has been put on the table.'

A recollection may be so complete that you not only hear the noises again, but also smell the scents and taste how it was to eat spinach as a child or your first ice-cream with whipped cream, and even the feelings and thoughts which you had come up again. This is *reliving*, the third level of recalling the past. Here, not only sensory recollections come up, but your feelings, your thoughts, your mood from that time as well. You feel how you felt, you think what you thought then. This creates a curious split consciousness. You remain who you are now, but at the same time you experience yourself as a 10-year-old boy or a 12-year-old girl. (You may also experience such an 'elliptic consciousness' with two focal points if you stare intensely into the mirror or at an old photograph of yourself). In reliving, your consciousness is divided between the present and the past.

With real *regression* not only do you experience the past again, but everything that has happened between then and now is pushed into the background, and is virtually inaccessible to your consciousness. Reliving still has an uninterrupted connection between the two focal points of consciousness. With real regression, this connection is gone. Regression to the age of 12 means that you live again, feel and think again as this 12-year-old, and that you have lost everything you experienced since then. If your awareness of the present remains intact anyway, then you experience this as if disconnected: it has no influence at all on the awareness of the past. If you are supervised during a hypnotic regression, you may hear yourself answer from your past awareness without your present personality being able to intervene. The temporary loss of memory of everything since applies only to that part of your consciousness that is in regression. Usually, the present awareness continues to exist alongside it.

Someone is brought back to an incarnation in the second half of the last century in England, and is asked the name of the queen. The illiterate slum girl cannot answer this question, although the present personality tries, almost gnashing its teeth, to intervene and say it was Victoria. But it cannot intervene. Everybody present knows the answer and mentally screams it at the person, but to no avail. Such phenomena prove sufficiently the invalidity of the lay argument that someone in trance is open to suggestion and reacts telepathically to those present, especially to the hypnotist. Such things can be accomplished by hypnosis with some people, but only if paranormal abilities are already present, if the trance is deep enough, and if special instructions are given.

Without hypnosis, access to the present personality remains, and questions can be posed in turn to the present and the past personality. Clumsy guidance sometimes can get the past and the present personality mixed up during the regression. Emotional or intellectual blocks may result in interventions from the present personality. Sometimes the present personality answers when, for whatever reason, the past personality cannot answer. In light levels of trance, the difference is often unclear, especially for the amateur therapist.

Regression may deepen into *identification*. In identification any awareness of a separate present vanishes. During regression you will hardly realize that you are lying talking on a bed, you forget pretty much the situation of the moment, you react from the past. With identification you include the present, as far as you are aware of it, in the situation then. You will place the interviewing counsellor in the situation from the past life you are reliving.

This begins with irritation about the stupid questions about things everybody knows (see, for example, Moss and Keeton 1979: 34–5, where a fine example of split consciousness is also given). Feeling suspicious about questions on things that ought to remain a secret may lead to an argument with the interviewer (Dethlefsen 1977: 225; Fiore 1978: 11). Another curious example can be found in Moss and Keeton's epilogue (1979: 190).

The regressions of Nyria (Praed 1914) are a nice example of the identification stage. Nyria is a Roman slavegirl who is constantly afraid she will betray the Christians or her mistress with her indiscreet disclosures to the hypnotist. She keeps asking who the hypnotist is. Why does she meet her in the most unlikely places? Doesn't she have any slaves of her own, that she needs to ask Nyria so many questions? And if she came in a sedan, then what has happened to the sedan? And shouldn't she go and get the sedan for her? (Shirley 1924: 37). In Nyria's case the sessions connected with each other exactly (Shirley 1924: 40), just as with Joan Grant; although in Joan Grant's *Winged Pharaoh* (1937) the sessions came out in non-chronological order, and could only be slotted together afterwards.

At the level of identification it is possible to create new experiences belonging to a particular lifetime. For example, you bring someone back to his eleventh year and bring up a topic he had never heard of at that age. When he comes out of this state, that conversation seems to him to have taken place when he was 11 unless hypnotic instruction erases it again.

Past Lives, Future Lives: Accounts of regressions and progressions through hypnosis by Bruce Goldberg distinguishes the same levels of recall as I do. What I call reliving and regression, he calls pseudo-revivification and revivification (Goldberg 1982: 58). Goldberg gives nice examples of the identification stage (Goldberg 1982: 76, 77, 103). Another recent work also distinguishes five regression levels (Williston and Johnstone 1983: 53). This book, *Soul Search: Spiritual growth through a knowledge of past lifetimes*, gives first-rate examples of regressions and historical tests of regression material, although it is overenthusiastic in places; it offers a better alternative to Marcia Moore's *Hypersentience* (1976).

Reliving and regression to past lives

We forget much in our life. We practically all have amnesia for the period before our birth, our actual birth and the first years of our life. Our first memories may begin at about the end of the third year, sometimes a bit earlier, and often later. Techniques of reliving and regression can bring back repressed and lost memories, and also give access to that first, never remembered part of our life. This demonstrates that we all have a complete and uninterrupted memory of everything we have consciously and unconsciously experienced. For example, in deep regression people may describe surgery they have undergone although they were out cold during the operation. People who practise regression therapy often use the image of a life-tape recorder. The tape can be played back to any moment of our life, although not every moment can be easily reproduced.

De Rochas, the first regression hypnotist, found that if he took people further and further back they could experience their birth, and that he could even go back to the time before they had been born. Surprisingly, if they returned further and were asked about the first concrete experience coming up, a death from a previous life usually emerged. People may describe the prenatal phase in the womb, but this is less common. A third, rather uncommon, experience is of someone recounting a discarnate experience between lives.

Often physical symptoms (somatics) come up in regressions, especially when reliving intense emotional or bodily experiences. Sometimes the somatics are strong. For example, someone is experiencing a thrashing and at that moment red streaks appear on the back or the face. This may happen without hypnosis, as Netherton's work shows (1978: 79). Such phenomena are also found in regressions to the birth experience, another strongly emotional and somatic experience. Breathing often becomes difficult and the subject assumes a foetal position. In reliving experiences of dying in past lives, difficult breathing, temperature changes, and so on, are common. Besides the five levels of awareness of the past, we may distinguish levels of somatic intensity with which the past manifests itself in the present body. When emotionally reliving traumatic episodes, somatics are usual and, in therapy, essential.

Change of language seems to be something else. A strong example of the property in regression of forgetting everything that has happened since is 'xenoglossy', speaking languages forgotten or even never learned in this life, and no longer being able to speak languages spoken now but not spoken at the time of the regression experience.

A 17-year-old French girl is brought back in her life year by year, and in her fifth year speaks in Gascon and can no longer speak French when asked to do so. An Englishwoman is brought back to a past life and does not react to any instructions. A Swedish woman who is present by chance, asks her something in Swedish and immediately she answers in fluent Swedish, although she cannot speak Swedish in this life (Moss and Keeton 1979: 169).

Xenoglossy, subjects speaking foreign languages they cannot normally speak, occurs in less than ·001 per cent of cases (see Wambach 1986). According to Netherton, it can also be attained with his method without using any hypnosis (1978: 79). Dethlefsen believes that this ability can be developed consciously. If true, this would have great implications for foreign language education and linguistic research. Interestingly, selective repression is possible. For example, a hypnotist may instruct the remigrant that he will understand the language spoken to him and will answer in this language. This prevents potential impasses between hypnotist and subject in regressions to infancy, to lives of morons and idiots, and to lives with incomprehensible languages. During the reliving of traumatic experiences during past-life therapy, the therapist often instructs the patient that the intensity of the experience will not be more than he or she can handle, or than is necessary for therapeutic results.

Hypnosis and trance in regressions

So far hypnosis has been the most common method of bringing back memories of past lives in people without spontaneous recollection. A related, but apparently obsolete method is the magnetic induction of trance. Methods working with only a light trance, without classic hypnosis, are spreading fast. Merely finding the right triggers may give access to the memory of past lives. A regression which is beginning then seems to induce a form of self-hypnosis without specific instructions.

The many techniques of hypnotic trance induction are outside the scope of this book. For real regression a rather deep trance is needed, for reliving a shallower one. The trance needed to gain access to the past-life memory differs from the trance needed to keep the regression or reliving experience going. A person may remember an insignificant detail but, yielding to it, the unfolding story absorbs him more and more. The converse also happens: a deep trance may be needed to get into a regression, but the next session is easier, although this time it may be only reliving or even just recollection. The same may happen when reading books. You may gradually get more and more absorbed in a story and become enthralled. Or it can cost you a great effort of concentration to start reading a book and understand it, but it keeps getting easier, until you can easily pick it up again after an interruption. Figures 3a–c sketch some examples of barriers and blocks.

One may compare a barrier with aversion to reading, because one cannot do it well, for example, or finds something sanctimonious about it. Running up against a block can be compared to a chapter or passage you come across in a book or a letter which is difficult or unpleasant for you. Your first reaction is to withdraw, and you can only return by consciously immersing yourself in the text. The figures indicate that to overcome a barrier, the trance needs to be either made deeper or less deep, for the matter to be digested either more intensely or more at a distance. They also indicate that blocks may wear out and vanish after repeated returns and gradual digestion. This is essential in regression therapy.

In later sessions a shallower trance is often sufficient, unless new emotional material crops up. Lighter trances bring reliving rather than regression, or even only recollection. This has the pleasant effect that the participant remains alert, but the unpleasant effect that the experience becomes thin and that the imagination of the participant, which is activated during a regression, easily adds things.

Because the 'participant' sounds official and abstract, and the 'patient', the 'client', and the 'subject' all have drawbacks, I will call everybody who wants to return to his own past for whatever reason a *remigrant*.

Trance depth changes spontaneously during regression (the figures do not indicate this). Being immersed in a book easily leads to further immersion. You may hardly notice a disturbing passage in a book you are reading only superficially, but when you are deeply immersed, it may annoy you enormously. Netherton uses the rule of thumb: 'If it is easy to recall, it is difficult to relive.' Probably, the shallow level indicates a block.

One of the skills of the hypnotist or therapist is choosing the right trance depth, neither going too deep nor remaining too shallow, and following and adapting to spontaneous changes in trance depth. The optimal trance depth depends on the condition of the remigrant, his objective, his past history, and the circumstances. The level of reliving is the basic level, because from here the remigrant may attain easily, sometimes spontaneously, real regression, but also may experience things more easily and freely at a distance as recollection.

(a) Course 1 *Gradual immersion (trance induction relaxation preliminary visualization)*

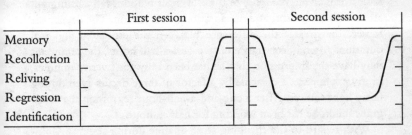

(b) Course 2 *Overcoming barriers (resistance to shift of consciousness)*

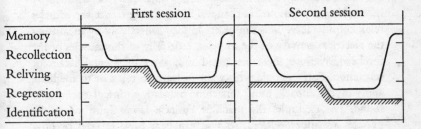

(c) Course 3 *Running up against blocks (reistance to the contents of experiences)*

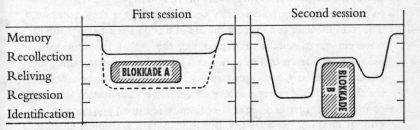

Figure 3 Barriers and blocks

Until now I have discussed trance only as a partial shift of awareness to the past, but more can be said about it. During trance, background noise has hardly any disturbing effect. Another simple and important indicator is an altered sense of time. Almost without fail a remigrant afterwards underestimates the duration of the session. The deeper the trance, the greater the difference between the estimated and real duration. After a deep trance of two-and-a-half hours, the remigrant may have the impression that he has been busy for twenty minutes. In my experience, a decrease by a factor of three occurs even during fairly light trances. After a one-and-a-half-hour regression the remigrant thinks he has been working for half an hour.

With regard to the changing sense of time during sessions, Goldberg reports a subjective lengthening of time, instead of the more common shortening. After twenty minutes, some people feel as if they have been away for more than an hour (Goldberg 1982: 7).

Trance and trance depth can be more objectively determined by monitoring psychosomatic changes. First, during trance the muscles relax considerably. This can be established objectively by measuring the electrical activity of the muscles, especially of the muscles of the forehead, because these are good indicators of mental strain or relaxation. Some people who want to learn to relax or to meditate apply myo-feedback, using a machine translating muscular tension in sound. For example, the machine emits a lower hum when the muscles are more relaxed, so you can hear how relaxed or how strained you are.

A similar, older machine is the E-meter or *emotion-meter* measuring the electric resistance of the skin. The underlying assumption is that, through changes in the sympathetic nerve system, deeper trance leads to decreased sweat-gland activity resulting in higher skin-resistance. The term E-meter comes from the use of this skin-resistance meter to trace emotional tension. For example, the use of an emotionally laden word in front of a subject decreases his skin resistance immediately, without any conscious response. An important application of the skin-resistance meter is as a lie-detector. This application is rather controversial, first because it is politically sensitive, and second because it does not measure lies, but the emotion accompanying lies. People who feel guilty and afraid may react out of fear that they will not be believed, and more hardened characters do not necessarily experience any emotion. Finally, many people have moral objections to this application.

Next to decreased muscle tension and decreased sweat secretion, there is a third physiological change, the altered pattern of brain waves as determined by an electro-encephalogram (EEG). This shows the dominant rhythm of electrical brain activity. For example, someone in a deep sleep has a slow dominant rhythm of 2 to 4 waves per second (delta rhythm). The dream state has about 8 waves per second (theta rhythm). Someone who is awake and alert, especially when strongly involved or concentrated on something, will have a dominant rhythm of more than 15 waves per second (beta rhythm). If people relax but at the same time remain aware, a rhythm of about 12 waves per second results (alpha rhythm). The levels of brain activity are shown in Table 5 in simplified form. There are fairly large individual differences, and the correspondences with normal consciousness and trance may be less stringent in practice than this overview suggests.

There is equipment which analyses the brain activity according to percentage of beta, alpha, theta, and delta rhythms. Usually, the left and the right halves of the brain are measured separately, since they may differ. A 'mind-mirror' shows the subject his state by showing figures or producing sounds. Such equipment is used for learning to relax or meditate.

For undisturbed recollection, alpha-rhythm is usually necessary, for reliving theta-rhythm, and for complete regression delta-rhythm. Under proper supervision many people may reach past-life recollec-

Table 5 Levels of brain activity

Brain rhythm	Typical frequency	Typical consciousness	Remigration stage	Hypnotic trance
β-rhythm	16/second	Alert	Memory	Preparation
α-rhythm	12/second	Calm	Recall	Light
θ-rhythm	8/second	Dream	Reliving	Medium
δ-rhythm	4/second	Sleep	Regression	Deep
δ-rhythm	1/second	Catalepsy	Identification	Complete

tion in alpha. For discarnate recall, at least theta-rhythm is necessary. The more psychic and mediumistic someone is, the more quickly he will enter the deeper stages. In an extreme case a medium may reach identification while still wide awake with a normal beta-rhythm.

The induction of a shift of consciousness usually begins with relaxation, producing alpha-waves. The remigrant becomes calm, clear, and balanced. In classic hypnosis this occurs through verbal instructions and suggestions, but it can be achieved more directly with sensory stimuli. The simplest way to enter deeper levels is to deepen the relaxation. When the subject is connected to an electro-encephalograph, it shows how the brain rhythm slows down.

Depth of hypnotic trance can be estimated according to the hypnotic symptoms during trance. In this way Le Cron and Bordeaux designed a 50-point scale, as follows:

Preparation	1– 5
Light hypnotic stage	6–20
Medium stage	22–30
Deep stage	31–49
Complete trance	50

With conventional hypnotic techniques, about 50 per cent of people would reach medium trance and 20 per cent deep trance. Le Cron and Bordeaux place age regression at level 42, about half-way into the deep stage. In hypnosis, age regression means real regression, not just recall or reliving. During hypnotic regression the voice and the posture change, corresponding to the previous age, or to the previous personality.

When the therapist just wants to determine whether the remigrant is sufficiently relaxed, the myo-feedback meter, indicating muscle relaxation, gives the most direct information. If he wants to keep track of the depth of trance during the session, then the more sensitive E-meter is useful. EEG-data are probably the most reliable, but the use of electrodes on the head may be inconvenient, and some subjects have unpleasant feelings about it.

Among her group of people interested in remembering past lives, Helen Wambach initially found that 70 per cent relived past lives and this percentage increased to 90 per cent when she further improved her methods. In a random sample of the remaining 10 per cent about half could relive past lives under individual supervision. The remaining 5 per cent were resistant to every form of relaxation or abandonment. They remained stressful and neurotically alert. According to Wambach, this tension is related either to fear of death or of losing control (Wambach 1978). Edith Fiore describes a case which seems to support this explanation. A remigrant could not or would not relax. When Fiore finally did succeed, the barrier appeared to be caused by a traumatic death experience in the previous life: bleeding to death as a patient during a lobotomy in a psychiatric hospital (Fiore 1978). My guess is, however, that fear of death is a barrier that can be removed by individual supervision, but that the remaining hard core rather consists of people with strong defences against loss of control. This may be related to guilt rather than to fear.

Netherton discovered that remigrants sometimes seem to block because they enter a situation where secrecy is necessary or extorted. This illustrates the difference between a barrier and a block. What appears to be a barrier turns out to be a block inherent in the experience (as opposed to, for example, emotional blocks). Such a block can be simply removed by asking, 'Does something have to remain a secret?' The difference between a barrier and a block can be found by checking whether the necessary degree of relaxation has been attained, although it is difficult for a therapist to ascertain this with new patients.

Objections to hypnosis

There are four common objections to hypnosis. First, some people are afraid of losing consciousness and control and perhaps never 'returning'. This fear is comparable to fear of out-of-body experiences and is even less well founded. A deep hypnotic trance which is not terminated just passes into a deep sleep and you wake up when you are rested. (Although this may be a long time for someone who lacks sleep). What may arise, however, is a hypnotic tie with the hypnotist (consciously created and reinforced by some hypnotists), which is insufficiently broken at the end of the session. Then you may remain fuzzy, in some cases even for a few weeks. Since it is difficult to ascertain to what extent a bond with the voice or the person of the hypnotist has grown, it is good practice to give an instruction at the end of the session that dissolves any tie which may have grown.

A second fear is that the hypnotist may take advantage of the subject. A hypnotist can give subjects no instructions or post-hypnotic suggestions contrary to the subject's beliefs and values. But a smart and patient hypnotist can mislead a subject in deep trance. You cannot suggest to someone that they should jump out of a window on the fifth floor, but you can suggest it is a door to a beautiful garden.

A third objection is that the hypnotic trance is psychologically or physically damaging. All indications are to the contrary. Hypnosis often eases or solves psychosomatic complaints, even without any suggestions in this direction.

A fourth worry is that frequent hypnosis weakens the will. With normal hypnosis this is out of the question. Only when people want to be hypnotized because of a morbid desire to abandon themselves and surrender to someone else, and if the hypnotist encourages this with powerful post-hypnotic suggestions, may personal independence be weakened.

Mistrust of hypnosis is usually the result of watching stage hypnosis or of reading or hearing scary stories. In stage hypnosis people are bound to the hypnotist by explicit instructions. The hypnotist uses the shift of consciousness to narrow it and direct it towards complete dependence. During stage hypnosis people lose their independence. They do things they would or could never do using their common sense. In part, the success of stage hypnosis is based on ridicule. The subjects of stage hypnotists are usually easy to hypnotize and willing to be manipulated in the presence of an audience. Since in stage hypnosis these two aspects coincide, they are confused. Being easily hypnotized has nothing to do with lack of willpower. Being easy to hypnotize is more related to the ability to immerse oneself deeply in a subject. Good book readers and good music listeners can usually be hypnotized well, as well as those who meditate well. But this does not mean they will respond well to crude suggestions or will trust someone who wants them to do odd things. A remigrant may be hypnotized deeply without any inclination to follow other instructions than those related to the regression.

During a hypnotic regression the remigrant does not need to have a strong relation with the hypnotist. During deep trance the remigrant remains linked to the present through the hypnotist's voice.

However, when no special relation has been evoked, and the hypnotist suggests things the remigrant does not experience or does not want to experience, he just blocks, and if he is further pressed, he simply returns, in spite of any instruction. During a hypnosis without instructions for dependence, suggestions to see things not there don't work, and you cannot be forced to experience things you do not want, and you cannot be forced to say things you do not want to say.

Hypnosis is a psychosomatic shift in consciousness, not a loss of will. In itself hypnotic trance is not harmful but healing. For the rest, everything depends on the competence and the trustworthiness of the hypnotist. For this reason, be supervised by someone you trust.

Past-life recall induced by imagination

Instead of inducing a trance sufficient for regression, the therapist may start on the level of recall, continue at reliving, and eventually reach real regression. Visual images substitute for and trigger initial memories, facilitating the transition to a past life. This is the method of visualization or imagination. Many therapists use relaxation with a mixture of hypnotic and imaginative induction.

The first step in imagination is, just as with hypnosis, physical and mental relaxation. However, the therapist does not attempt to increase this relaxation hypnotically. After some relaxation, the therapist has the remigrant focus his attention on his bodily sensations. He focuses attention on the muscles to relax them more, on breathing, and on heartbeat and pulse. This immersion in one's body draws attention away from the environment, helps one to relax, and stimulates the imaginative powers.

The next step is to let the remigrant imagine a prototypical environment: a garden, a valley, a mountain, a large meadow of flowers, a beach, standing in a cave entrance, cruising down a river, floating in air, etc. The transition to a past life is then pictured by walking down a path or a staircase, ascending a staircase, going through a tunnel, crossing a river, crossing a bridge, or going through a mist. A professional, careful, and elaborate procedure is the Christos experiment described by Glaskin (1974).

On this level of inner imagining, people may express personal problems in an intense and meaningful dream. The experience is real, in that they not only visualize the problem, but may solve it within the same story. This is the technique of the waking dream (*rêve éveillé*), an inner psychodrama that is accompanied and guided by a therapist.

The psychodramatic waking dream is enacted in semi-symbolic images. For example, you see a gentleman on the box of an old farm cart stuck in the mud. When you come closer, the face of the gentleman becomes that of your father. This image shows how you see your father, or how you believe he feels. The therapist may ask you, for example, how you feel, seeing your father in this way. He may ask you to speak to the gentleman, or to go and help him and to see what happens. In this way, the story may unfurl as a fantasy with an intense psychological reality. Waking dreams can be treated like normal dreams, but are more direct and incomparably more effective. 'Gestalt techniques' are well suited to elaborate waking dreams.

However, when someone wants to relive a past life and gets stuck on the imaginative level, the strong expectation of a historical experience may result in a psychodramatic tale enacted against apparently historical scenery. But this scenery will only contain material from normal memory. How, then, do we know the difference between real past-life recall, a psychodramatic waking dream, and just fantasies? The difference between fantasy and the other two is the absence of emotions. Psychodramas include tension which should ultimately lead to relief, insight, and cure. Indications for real recall are seeing new things, having uncommon experiences (like tasting unknown food), and especially a different body (a woman experiencing an erection, a man giving birth to a child). It is also possible, though time-consuming, to check historical details.

What can the therapist do to increase the probability of real past-life recall? First of all, continually ask for feelings. With a false or fantasy regression emotions remain superficial, thin, conventional. In a psychodrama real emotions as well as blocks come up quickly because a waking dream confronts psychological imperfections rather than trivia. Apparently the soul makes use of the opportunity to bring unfinished business into the spotlight and work it out after all.

A second option is to focus on somatic feelings and somatic experiences. Often, after being 'pressed into the bodily feeling', things come up that surprise the remigrant. The most spectacular feeling is to feel oneself in the body of the opposite sex.

An athletic boy who is a health enthusiast and does a lot of training experiences himself as a corpulent middle-aged man, and when asked how this feels says to his own surprise, it feels good. For many remigrants such experiences – going against their own preferences and expectations, and giving answers contrary to their natural tendencies – are the most convincing. These experiences are related to what I have called 'elliptic consciousness', a field of consciousness with two centres.

An advantage of a fairly deep hypnotic trance over a light, imaginatively induced trance, is the possibility of checking whether historical details are coming from the remigrant's ordinary memory. With a sufficiently deep trance, deceit is virtually out of the question. The remigrant may be asked directly if he got any information from books or otherwise, and may answer with finger signals. Also, rewinding and forwarding within a life and between lives is more accurate under hypnosis. Another slight advantage of hypnotic trance is that attendant instructions to retrieve information, such as counting to three or snapping one's fingers, are stronger and more secure.

Regression through magnetism

A magnetist makes passes, that is, he brushes his hands past the body. He may also hold his hands still, or hold one still and make passes with the other. Or he may touch the body with one or both hands. Often he supports the activity of his hands with his eyes and with mental concentration.

The first to write about magnetism was Paracelsus. Later, Mesmer, who introduced the term 'animal magnetism', worked with it, and induced hypnosis mostly with passes. The third important figure in the field of magnetism is Karl Von Reichenbach, a well-known scientist who did pioneer research into the nature of these phenomena in around the middle of the nineteenth century (Von Reichenbach 1849). Eventually it was Albert de Rochas who used magnetism to induce age regression (de Rochas 1911).

De Rochas placed his subject on a chair, held his right hand on the subject's forehead, and made longitudinal passes, along the length of the body, with his left hand. The more passes he made, the further the subject regressed. When he wanted to bring the subject back to the present, he made transversal passes, horizontal movements with both hands in front of the subject, starting from the body's vertical middle line. If he continued these passes, the subject crossed the present, and went into the future.

Opinions differ over whether magnetically and hypnotically induced trances are the same. I believe they are related and that the hypnotic trance, at least of a mediumistic subject, may be directed to a magnetic trance. Hypnosis uses the doors of perception and consciousness, magnetism uses the door of the unconscious psychosomatic processes. Therefore hypnosis is probably a broader and more flexible method than magnetism. An indication for this could be that the scales to measure the depth of a trance, like those of Le Cron and Bordeaux, differ for individual persons. Apparently the depth of the magnetic trance can be measured more uniformly by its symptoms. Table 6 gives an overview of the five levels of magnetic trance and the characteristic symptoms for each level.

The first level of magnetization is lethargy. Besides lethargic symptoms themselves, the limbs and torso becoming heavy and weak, perception of the environment dims, memory decreases, suggestibility increases and the skin sensitivity decreases a little.

The second level of magnetic trance is called somnambulism, because of its resemblance to sleepwalking. Strongly increased suggestibility and lower skin sensitivity characterize this level. If a needle is stuck in the skin the subject feels nothing, like a theatre fakir when he pins a medal on his bare chest with an oversized safety pin at the end of the show.

At the third level, of rapport, the subject takes over the perceptions of the magnetist. When he is pricked in the arm with a needle, he feels nothing, when the magnetist is pricked the subject calls out 'ouch', and a red spot may appear on the corresponding spot on his arm. The memory is accessible, the suggestibility is gone, auras become visible, and the felt skin surface is about 3 centimetres outside the skin.

At the fourth level, of sympathy, the subject identifies with the magnetist and can perceive and express the magnetist's thoughts and feelings, and the perception of auras has vanished again. Finally, in exteriorization the centre of perception can be moved around at will, including to places where the magnetized person has never been before.

Table 6 Levels of magnetic trance

	Lethargy	Recollection	Suggestibility	Skin sensitivity	Perceiving emanations	Perception
Lethargy	+	+	+	+	−	−
Somnambulism	+	+	+ +.	−	−	−
Rapport	+	−	−	3 cm	+	M+
Sympathy	+	−	−	3 cm	−	M+ +
Exteriorization	+	free				

Magnetic trance, therefore, seems to be more specific than hypnotic trance. The symptoms of the first two levels of magnetization are almost the same as those in medium and deep hypnosis, but the symptoms of the other levels can only be induced in very deep hypnosis and only with some people. Presumably, fewer people can be brought into trance through magnetism than through hypnosis. Sympathy, the fourth level of magnetic trance, apparently corresponds to the natural relation between mother and child while the child is still in the womb. The next chapter will return to this.

The magnetic trance creates an intimate relation with the magnetist. In magnetic passes used for healing this will usually remain absent. Although the magnetist's psychosomatic energy goes to the magnetized subject, this does not have to result in blurred identity.

Magnetic trance induction seems to be employed rarely nowadays, as hypnotic and imaginative methods have replaced it. Some hypnotists reinforce induction with magnetic passes or with pseudo-magnetic passes accompanied by appropriate verbal suggestions. All-round practitioners such as Marcia Moore brew apparently effective mixtures of hypnosis, imagination, and magnetism (Moore 1976).

Alternative access to past lives

The Netherton method, which chapter 16 on reincarnation therapy will discuss, uses a person's 'postulates', ingrained programmes, vows, promises, ingrown attitudes, verbally fixed in the mind and sometimes repressed, as triggers for past-life recall. When a patient describes his problems or fears, these postulates come up as repetitive statements. The point is to pick out these ritual formulas, preferably giving them an expressive character. For example: 'I have to get out of this!' or 'Nobody likes me,' or 'I don't need anybody.' Repeating, or having a person repeat these key sentences a few times, elicits their suppressed emotional charge. Directly following this, the remigrant is asked to picture himself in a situation in which the key sentence is literally true or actually spoken, with all its corresponding emotions. For example: 'You are now going to go back to a situation in which you experienced all this for the first time. While I count to five you will go to that situation. On the count of five you will be there. You feel cold and fear. You are in a great hurry. It is dark. You have to get out of this! One, two, three, four, five. What is the first thing you see or feel, the first thing that comes to mind?'

Here, the experience comes directly from the emotion evoked, and crystallizes around the repeated key sentence. Almost always the remigrant arrives in a specific and emotional experience, often in a past life. When he has sufficiently worked through such an experience, the therapist may repeat the procedure with the same key sentence. Usually, a new situation appears, until the postulate complex has lost its charge. If the patient returns to an already relived situation, he had apparently digested that situation insufficiently.

An older method somewhat similar to Netherton's is Ron Hubbard's dianetics (Hubbard 1950), later christened as scientology. Hubbard developed a methodology and terminology completely his own. He used the skin-resistance meter and a stringent procedure to track down and work out mental and emotional problems. This procedure almost invariably leads to past lives. People who spent some time in scientology contributed much to the development of regression therapy. Scientology itself is a strictly organized movement requiring committed participants and discouraging non-committal interest. The set-up is businesslike. If the name of Our Lord had been Ron Hubbard, there would be dozens of copyrights on the Bible by now. Hubbard's books are interesting, but if you order them from his organization, you have to add to the price years of being plagued with brochures and personal invitations.

Another alternative method, probably rare, is the use of drugs. The disadvantage of drugs is that resulting experiences can be given little guidance. Another great disadvantage is the probability of dependence and addiction. Some people disapprove of hypnosis but have no objections to taking drugs. The argument is that under hypnosis you would be dependent on the hypnotist and on drugs you would be dependent on nobody (except your dealer). In my opinion, self-hypnosis and hypnosis with a trustworthy hypnotist are wholesome, and drugs are definitely unhealthy.

Gnostic and esoteric circles object to magnetism and hypnosis as well as to drugs. They normally propose their own prolonged meditation excercises as the only sure and true way. The anthroposophic karma exercises are an example. All such exercises assume that memories of past lives are only accessible for the most serious and devoted students who have to immerse themselves for months or years with abstract deep feelings and abstract high thoughts, with superficial results.

My own survey indicated that people who had come into contact with the subject of reincarnation via a spiritual movement were on the average less sensitive, and had fewer memories of their own. At any rate, spiritual philosophies which instil titbits of abstract reincarnation wisdom, but question and discourage personal experience, are of little value.

Chapter 4 gave examples of paranormal entries to past lives: by mediumistic trance, incidentally by psychometrism, and by clairvoyance. Entry by magnetic passes also borders on the paranormal. Ranking the various methods of entry according to the increasing paranormal sensitivity required from the remigrant or the therapist gives the following list:

- by evoking a strong emotion, preferably anchored in a postulate (as in Netherton's method)
- by imagination
- by hypnotism
- by magnetism
- by psychic trance
- by clairvoyance.

The past-life memory

The evidence from reliving and regression sessions indicates that the memory storing the experiences of our past lives neither ages nor fades. Memories lose none of their brilliance. Many writers, for example Kelsey and Grant (1967), have pointed out that clarity is independent of the time passed. Focus, intensity, and completeness remain intact through time. Apparently our soul registers every experience, conscious as well as unconscious. It stores all our sensory impressions, all our feelings and thoughts, all our semi-conscious and subconscious reactions.

This memory seems to have unlimited capacity and random access. We do not need to rewind a tape until we get the passage we want, but we can go straight to the desired situation or event. Its storage is continuous, precisely dated, and localized, since we can identify the time and place of every event. In addition to this, our memory is structured around associations, as is apparent from, for example, trauma chains. It resembles bookkeeping by double entry: a chronological, continuous registration with random access, and a continuous assimilation and structuring which results in associative patterns, similar to our ordinary memory.

We can experience our memories more or less devoid of feelings. We can experience ourselves inside our past self, as observers of our past self, or from the point of view of others. We can relive a situation and observe our own reactions and those of others, even if we overlooked them then. We can even separate ourselves from our past self and look at situations from a distance, for example from above. Similar to computer-aided design, we can look at situations from various spatial positions, angles, and perspectives. Such transformations are particularly important in reliving disorganized, confusing, or tense circumstances.

All of this is as true for this life as for past lives. Reliving and regression are the same for our present life, with the same possibilities and difficulties. Here too, we can seek out subconscious registers, we can place ourselves outside of ourselves, or put ourselves in the position of others, using complete and unfading memory. Various psychotherapies discovered this, including transactional analysis and therapies which use reliving the birth and prenatal conditions.

Thus there seems to be no special memory for past lives. We reach past lives via the general memory. Lives from further back remain as clear as those of recent lives. By a shift in consciousness, usually called trance, we gain access to this complete memory. An even more direct route is via emotions and postulates: places where our subconscious is only just subliminal. A third entry to this memory is through strong similarity, a strong association between our present life situation and one from a past life.

In reliving experiences and in regressions without a particular aim, eventful situations come up sooner than humdrum ones, and eventful lives sooner than humdrum lives. Emotionally charged situations emerge more easily, the charge depending on the original intensity and the subsequent lack of assimilation, usually because of negative emotions. In conditions of light trance without specific instructions, traumatic death experiences are often the first events to come up.

The situations from past lives seen by clairvoyants often have a relation to the present life situation. The same is true for situations that come up in methods like the Christos experiment, which do not explicitly induce trance, but go fairly deep, and which through their procedures prevent overwhelming experiences. Sometimes the door to someone's memory of past lives is difficult to find, but the memory is seldom completely barred and then only by the person himself. In the absence of strong neurotic barriers or psychotic complications the right key usually gives entry.

We have already encountered examples of specific entry barriers where the therapy situation or the trance condition themselves evoke associations with traumatic experiences, especially death experiences, or where the first experience to emerge is loaded with secrecy. Netherton calls these 'shut-off commands'. When such shut-off commands operate in the circumstances of the therapy, or with relaxation, memory, or trance, they block access until special interventions identify and remove them. Sometimes they may have blocked relaxation in general, so removing them is, in itself, already as important as remembering past lives.

Further reading

The readers of this chapter will mainly be interested in concrete records of reliving and regression. The oldest book is by de Rochas (1911), who worked with magnetism. Another classic is Björkhem's book (1942) probably published only in Swedish. Some of Hubbard's experiences and those of his pupils since 1950 were published in *Have You Lived Before This Life?* (1958). Then there is Bridey Murphy's well-known story (Bernstein 1956). Bloxham published a number of his sessions (1958). Recent records or parts of records were published by Glaskin (1974), Underwood and Wilder (1975), Sutphen (1976, 1978), Dethlefsen (1977), Moss and Keeton (1979) and Langedijk (1980).

Under one hypnosis, a person experienced a complete life as an Egyptian priest. Weden and Spindler's book on this (1978) is readable and interesting, less high-flown and more concrete than some other Egyptian biographies and perhaps even true.

Iverson (1976) and Wambach (1978) present summaries. Short case descriptions can be found in general works such as those by Muller (1970) and Christie-Murray (1981), and in Kelsey and Grant (1967). Netherton and Shiffrin (1978) and Fiore (1978) give examples from therapies.

Most published directions for inducing regressions are in the area of the hypnotic and imaginative methods. Chapter 15 will return to this. Rudolf Steiner's 'karma exercises' originated in 1924 (*Gesamtausgabe* 236). The first real imaginative methods are those of Bennett (1937) and, later, Brennan (1971). Glaskin describes the procedures of the Christos experiment (1974) and Marcia Moore those of her hypersentience technique (1976), and Florence McClain also gives a carefully elaborated procedure (1986).

7 Experiences During and Prior to Birth

For people who believe in reincarnation, pregnancy and childbearing are not only biological processes, but also the somewhat mysterious arrival of an unknown guest. What kind of person will it be? Who will it be? Such prospective parents may worry about whether they will attract 'a good entity'. They may worry about the right attitude during conception or pregnancy to ensure this. Corresponding ideas are that if you do not conceive a child in true love you will not receive a soul that really belongs to you; or, to attract a high entity you must conceive without animal passion; or that it is important to nurture lofty thoughts and feelings during pregnancy so that the foetus will prosper. Serious, well-meaning people who believe in reincarnation are often concerned with such thoughts in producing offspring. Their feelings about this can be quite strong, even if they can hardly imagine how this all works. Are their thoughts justified or not?

The regression material published to date gives a rich picture of how people incarnate, how they experience the prenatal situation during pregnancy, and which consequences this can have. The most informative material is from the past decade. Important authors in this field are Morris Netherton, Helen Wambach, and Joel Whitton. Helen Wambach has brought a total of 1,500 people under hypnotic regression. Of the first 1,100 about 90 per cent had experiences of previous lives. Of the total group 48 per cent had prenatal experiences in the discarnate state and as an unborn child. The other 52 per cent had no impressions or fell asleep during the group regressions (Wambach 1979).

De Rochas found in his experiments that during regression to a previous life in a magnetic trance, the sensitive skin surface of his subjects was located about two inches outside of the physical skin (*l'extériorisation de la sensibilité*). When he brought them back to a period between lives, and they were able to report about this, their 'vehicle of sensitivity' was located in a sphere above the head.

Apparently, there was some kind of out-of-body experience. From the experiences of de Rochas and Wambach I conclude that discarnate experiences are saved in a separate, less accessible memory.

Netherton's therapeutic regressions involve many prenatal experiences in the womb. Wambach looked at how people prepare a new incarnation, how they experience the bond with their new body, and how they experience birth and the situation immediately following birth.

Most of the theological and philosophical literature on this subject is an exposition of convictions rather than a treatment of concrete experiences, and flagrantly contradicts the available empirical material on many points. Authors whose information about the discarnate state and the incarnation process concurs with the empirical material are, among others, Allan Kardec and Joan Grant.

The preparation for an incarnation

How do people experience the situation that they are going to reincarnate again, that another birth is imminent? As with so many other human experiences, the answer is 'very differently'. Helen Wambach asked three questions about the preparation for incarnation. Her first question was whether people chose and prepared their incarnations themselves, or whether they felt compelled or even forced. Her second question was why people were going to incarnate, and, if they did themselves choose, what their main reason or aim was. Her third question was whether people had chosen the sex in which they were born.

Apparently quite a number of people experience nothing during the preparation for their incarnation, or they simply feel that they are sucked towards a foetus. Some compared it to going down a slide or being sucked up by a vacuum cleaner. Similar experiences are also reported by Dethlefsen and others. Other people make elaborate preparations in co-operation with counsellors. Some are resistant or afraid and have to be persuaded. Others again apparently do it themselves, some even too hastily or against advice. The answers Wambach (1979) received, give the following picture:

- 8 per cent felt nothing
- 11 per cent were resistant and more or less afraid

- 55 per cent had at least some hesitation
- 23 per cent prepared themselves actively
- 3 per cent were too hurried or acted against advice.

This means that about 20 per cent were obliged to reincarnate, and about 80 per cent more or less accepted their reincarnation.

There is a gradual transition from feeling pushed into something, to figuring everything out for yourself. Some wait for the inevitable, others regard it as a matter of course, 'something everyone does'. Someone compared it to a completely organized trip recommended to you by a trustworthy travel agency. Some have to be persuaded to incarnate, others are enthusiastic about the prospect of 'going down' again. Others again act on personal initiative, and may make extensive plans. Many people report deliberating with others, mainly friends and close acquaintances who are going to be born again themselves. Apparently, common plans are made, and appointments are made to meet one another later and to do things together. Of the people who reported counsel with others, more than 60 per cent had more than one adviser, some even had a circle of advisers.

Although Wambach found that advice from others was the rule, McClain states that 'Only in very rare, very extreme circumstances does it appear that any type of guidance or suggestion is made from outside sources' (McClain 1986: 22). She probably collected only spontaneous references, while Wambach asked about it directly. Considering the common practice down here to ask professional advice (or less than professional advice) in many matters, I guess that Wambach is right. But perhaps McClain taps a different population of remigrants.

With Wambach, 60 per cent of the people with prenatal memories under regression could answer her question about their aim in life, the reason for coming back. The other 40 per cent were often those people who had not themselves chosen to return. Wambach (1979) divided the answers she received, as follows:

- 27 per cent came to help others and to grow spiritually themselves
- 26 per cent came to acquire new experience as a supplement or correction
- 18 per cent came to become more social

- 18 per cent came to work out personal karmic relationships
- 12 per cent came for miscellaneous reasons.

Some examples of reasons for incarnating were as follows:
- 'I had a lot of work left to do in the relationship with my mother.'
- 'Actually, I didn't have any urgent karma to work out.'
- 'I had to tie together and round off all the loose ends from the life just before.'
- 'I wanted to expose myself to a weak and indulgent life and to overcome this.'
- 'I went back to be able to feel things and to touch them.'
- 'I wanted to come back because I just had died young.'
- 'I knew that my parents needed me because they had lost a 15-month-old girl in a fire.'

Examples of special aims in life were: learning to overcome fear, learning to give leadership, learning humility, leading a political group.

We can apply for special assignments, and request special missions. When people are needed for specially planned developments, and we are able and willing to contribute to them, we can ask the previously mentioned counsellors to consider our application. Karmic considerations will continue, but are not decisive.

Of course our sex is important for our life plan. It still makes a difference whether you are born as a man or a woman. According to Wambach, 76 per cent of the people chose their sex. The other 24 per cent had no choice or paid no attention.

Other literature confirms the impression that a coming life is not fixed in detail, but limits itself to general outlines, general developments, general challenges (Kardec 1857: 325–31). When people remember a prospect, a preview of the coming life, only the most important moments, the great assignments stand out clearly. We elaborate these with our efforts in life. Strongly immoral acts like murder are never predestined. At most it is predestined that we will grow up in such a manner, in such an environment, with such a personality, that there is a great probability something like this will happen. But nobody is forced by destiny to murder (Kardec 1857: 329).

Next to the choice of sex, the choice of parents is important for the life we will lead. People who plan their life also choose their parents. Those who experience their incarnation as something that happens to them, similarly do not know why and how they got their parents. A nice example of a personal choice of parents is the little boy who tells his parents that he had already chosen them 'long ago, when I was still with God'. He was allowed to choose who would be his father. He looked around and finally saw a boy playing the violin during a concert. A string broke, but the boy played on as well as he could. Then he said to himself; 'That will be my father!' The incident with the string had in fact occurred when his father was still in school (Muller 1970: 66). Thus people can be chosen as future father or mother a long time beforehand; this will usually be according to personal bonds from previous lives.

The choice of parents can depend on many considerations. Sometimes they may present special opportunities for the task one has taken upon oneself or, exceptionally, because of appropriate genetic material (Wambach 1979: 164). One woman says that the karmic links with her mother were much more important than the probability of a genetic deficiency (Alzheimer's disease). She was told she should undergo the experience of being raised without a father, and she would be born in the ideal area for meeting the man she was destined to marry (Whitton and Fisher 1986: 42). Sometimes people do not like the prospect of parents with whom they have a karmic relationship. 'Oh no – not her again!' groaned somebody who was told that his personal evolution would be best served by being reborn to a woman he had murdered in a previous life (Whitton and Fisher 1986: 42).

Oddly enough, there are also cases of people who change their minds at the last moment and then are born somewhere else, or who simply err because of haste. Someone wanted so much to return to a body that he approached a foetus even though his friends and acquaintances advised him to wait a little, since he would come into a very large family whereas a small family would suit him better. Another remigrant realized immediately after his birth: 'Wrong time, wrong place, wrong parents, wrong sex!'

Some people remember a strong desire to return because they had previously died young. According to a widespread belief, people who have died very young return quickly. In their following life they use up the remaining life energy, so that they die rather young again. The quick return is generally right, the subsequent youthful death is not.

It also happens that someone incarnates because a previous incarnation attempt failed, for example a few years before with the same parents, possibly even in a body of the other sex. There are very convincing examples of this and I have also come across such cases.

The descent and pregnancy

Prospective parents will be particularly interested in this subject. The first question about pregnancy is the moment of descent: when does the soul enter the foetus? Apparently there is no fixed rule for this. It comes as a surprise, and here I am mainly following Wambach's research which proposes that many people connect themselves with the foetus only shortly before birth, and some even only during or immediately after birth. Only 11 per cent of Wambach's remigrants joined the foetus somewhere in the first six months of the pregnancy, a few at conception. About 12 per cent connected themselves with the foetus at the end of the sixth month, and 39 per cent during the last three months. Finally, 33 per cent descended shortly before birth, and 5 per cent apparently did not want to experience the birth and descended only shortly after birth. That probably means that they hardly influenced the development of the unborn child (Wambach 1979).

Although an unborn child is alive, it is not animated so long as the incarnating person has not descended and connected with it. A child that has just been born, and is already breathing, can be like a house ready for the occupant just before he moves in. Although this is an odd idea, other investigators report similar cases. Hubbard (1950) gives an example of somebody entering a body some minutes after birth.

In a few cases the body is entered even later, but these might imply pushing out the previous occupant. An immediate return in a body already born and inhabited by another makes for an official birth date before the date of death of the previous life, creating a negative intermission period. Stevenson did find such cases. The story of Hermann Grundei in chapter 5 is another case in point.

Hubbard gives an example of a man who is assassinated by two opponents. He is furious and will show them that they cannot get rid of him just like that. He rushes to the nearest maternity ward 'to grab a body'. It is likely that he had to push out another by sheer force. This is probably only possible with people who have little strength of mind, little motivation to start a new life, and little control over their body. When incarnation occurs in the body of a child of, say, three years, this happens usually after a grave illness and results in a marked personality change, as in the case of Jasbir (Stevenson 1966). Langedijk also gives an example (ten Dam 1982).

In even rarer cases, this may happen in adults. *The Boy Who Saw True* (Spearman ed. 1953) gives the example of a man who is replaced by another after shellshock. According to the writer, such things are only possible as the result of negative forms of mediumship in previous lives. Ruth Montgomery has popularized in her later books the idea of 'walk-ins'. I find her ideas far from plausible, but this area is outside the scope of this book.

Asked about their prenatal experiences, 11 per cent of Wambach's remigrants felt themselves to be inside the foetus, 78 per cent outside of the foetus, and 11 per cent felt that they were sometimes inside and sometimes outside of the foetus. Those who descend early often experience a consciousness inside the foetus. Most people, however, float in the proximity of the mother, while connected to the foetus with an etheric cord, presumably the same as the 'silver cord' that plays a role in out-of-body experiences and in dying (Crookall 1961, 1978). As birth approaches, the cord shortens, decreasing mobility. Some people enter the foetus every now and then to inspect it, to see if everything is going well and to adapt the unborn child to themselves. Some report that they could sometimes leave their body after birth. A few could even leave at will during their first year of life.

Further, 86 per cent of the remigrants indicated that they were aware of the moods, the thoughts, and emotions of their mother. From Netherton's work we may conclude that this is probably true for everybody who is closely connected with the foetus. The other 14 per cent presumably all come to the foetus in the last moment. It is a pity that Wambach presents the statistical material in her second book so poorly, making it impossible to correlate the answers between the different questions.

Like many other regression therapists, Netherton found that reliving traumautic experiences in this life is often insufficient to remove the origins of problems and complexes. Things that happen in this life often restimulate the inner wounds and knots caused in previous lives. He found that restimulation during pregnancy or birth always precedes restimulation during life. Dik Van den Heuvel, a Dutch hypnotherapist, concluded that natal or prenatal restimulation is a necessary but not sufficient condition for manifest karmic traumas in life. He compares natal and prenatal restimulation to 'winding up the spring' (TenDam 1982). The trauma register only burst at the first restimulation after birth. There always has to be a trigger event during life.

Netherton found that prenatal restimulation usually comes from the identification of the unborn child with the mother. He gives many examples which show that the unborn child registers the experiences of the mother as its own. An old example is that of an American girl who, under narcosis, goes into a delirium and speaks Spanish, although she does not know that language. The mother, who is called in, is astonished to recognize sentences that her Mexican guide said to her when she was fleeing from a revolutionary situation in Mexico while pregnant with this girl (Muller 1970: 135). The previous chapter compared the relationship of 'sympathy' between a magnetist and his subject with the relationship between a mother and her unborn child.

When a girl tells her boyfriend that she expects his baby, and he yells 'Get out of here! I don't want to see you any more!', the unborn child registers this message as if it were meant for itself. If the child has unfinished business with this theme: being refused, sent away, or cast out, this will be restimulated. According to Netherton, the most sensitive moments are the conception, the discovery of pregnancy, the first communication about the pregnancy, and the birth.

A striking example of the registration of the unborn child and its 'sympathy' with the mother is the case of a woman with sexual problems. During regression she sees her mother, pregnant with her, being visited by her father. She reads him out loud a passage from a book by the Marquis de Sade that had struck her. Although the patient does not know the book, during regression she can cite the whole text verbatim. It becomes evident that this text influences her life as a postulate, because its contents restimulate traumas from previous lives (Netherton and Shiffrin 1978: 84).

Netherton gives examples of repercussions of prenatal and natal experiences in later life. Sometimes the unborn child interprets the pregnant mother's gain in weight as an accomplishment. This may lead later to obesity. Sometimes obesity is caused by something said about the baby during or just after the birth. Any prenatal and newborn experiences which are interpreted as the father being aggressive to the mother, or of strong thoughts by the mother – 'Let him get it over with quick' – may cause impotence and premature ejaculation. A traumatic experience in the time of the 'hormonal bath', when the sex is determined, may confuse the sexual identity. Parents who are very sure about the sex of the child but are mistaken may also contribute to sexual confusion.

Based on Crookall's conclusions about out-of-body and death experiences (1961, 1978), we can expect that the psychic (or astral) body does not immediately enter the foetus, but that there is a link of ether or vitality plasma between them. How this new 'vehicle of vitality' originates is yet unclear. Probably, a core part remains connected to the soul, to which new plasma is attracted. An unborn child which is not yet adopted will then be provided for by the vehicle of vitality of the mother. There may be a temporary fusion or interface between the plasmatic body of the mother and that of the incarnating child. This may explain the 'sympathy' between them.

In all psychosomatic phenomena, in every link between the psychic body and the physical body, including birthmarks and stigmata from previous life, an etheric link is necessary. Each unresolved trauma from a previous life probably still has an etheric charge which is unloaded during catharsis. This explains why every catharsis has concurrent somatics, and why every sure-fire induction includes the use of a somatic.

According to Hubbard (1950), each trauma register contains physical pain or some other somatic. This explains why we cannot resolve karma after the dying processes are completed: we get rid of some ethers, and the rest wait on us until a new incarnation. Restimulation means that old etheric sores or gnarls are opened and connected with our present body.

Netherton claims that registration takes place from the moment of conception. Based on his experience as hypnotist and therapist, Goldberg concludes that the soul is connected to the foetus during the whole pregnancy, but is free to come and go. The definite descent ('the grand entrance') occurs within twenty-four hours before or after the birth (Goldberg 1982: 181). According to Joan Grant, a fertilized egg has to be adopted by an incarnating soul within a few days, or it will be rejected and die (Kelsey and Grant 1967). Wambach's research (1979) shows that few people enter the foetus in the first six months. How can we choose among these conflicting views?

Goldberg found, like Netherton, that during pregnancy the soul apparently enters and leaves the unborn child at will. On the other hand there seems to be an unconscious mind that is in the embryo right after the conception, registering everything that is happening to the embryo and the mother and often identifying with the mother. After the definite incarnation the two experience tracks seem to blend. This may explain a great part of the divergent findings so far. Whitton speaks about soul memory and brain memory, the last functioning from about three months. It seems to me that Schlotterbeck, after first stating that there are two memory tracks (1987: 85), then resolves this problem by identifying three memory tracks (1987: 139). Thus in the final analysis we have:

1 The psychic memory of the discarnate personality entering the body in the last months, during birth or just after birth.
2 The etheric memory which is there right from the beginning, at first indistinguishable from the etheric body of the mother; and during the rest of the pregnancy the immediate link with the psyche of the mother, and so the channel for identification with the mother.
3 The physical brain memory from about three months. (A developed nerve system seems a prerequisite for real incarnation: the psychic body entering the physical body.)

Whitton reports the same findings as Wambach: first awareness of actually being in the body ranges from several months before birth to just after birth. He also finds remigrants who experience that they are hovering over the mother. He reports that they may encourage behaviour that is good for mother and child, and discourage drinking and smoking. In several cases they communicated a name for the child (Whitton and Fisher 1986: 50). Joan Grant explains nausea during pregnancy as inverse 'sympathy'. The child would warn the mother in this way that some aspect of her diet or behaviour is affecting it adversely. But if Wambach finds that only 11 per cent of people descend before the seventh month, then nausea would be an exception during this period. Nausea seems to be a psychosomatic reaction of the mother, not a signal from the incarnating child.

Birthmarks and stigmata are clear examples of the influence of the entering soul on the foetus. People can be born with physical marks such as spots or scratches on the skin, or birth defects corresponding to fatal wounds from the previous life. Chapter 2 mentioned that the Tlingits in Alaska used birthmarks to identify the previous life of the child. With them, as with other groups, some people announce before they die with whom they want to be reborn and by what stigma they can be recognized (Stevenson 1966: 225). Stigmata in the form of skin marks are usually memory aids for the returning person, consciously made after the descent in the new body. Birth defects and real scars have to do with traumatic death experiences which have not been digested, especially with people who return quickly, enter the unborn child quickly, and have a self-image that continues from the previous life (Stevenson 1966: 34; Fiore 1978: 175).

Skin marks can be produced late in pregnancy and early after birth. Defective fingers and toes will have developed much earlier. Stigmata may indicate at what stage of development the soul had already entered the body. An extraordinary case is Wijeratne who had a malformed right arm much shorter than the other, only half as thick, and with only rudimentary fingers. When he started to talk, he explained this by his having stabbed his wife to death with this arm in his previous life. He did not repent, and when he was 15 he said that he would still do the same (Muller 1970: 56).

We apparently do not carry all our traumas with us into a new life. What enters this life depends on choice, possibly also the choice of parents, and on restimulation during pregnancy and birth. We do project a certain self-image when we are going to incarnate. In child cases and cases of birth defects, this seems to be the personality of the last life. But many people can choose the personality of an earlier life as the main determiner of the coming incarnation. We can pick up themes from earlier lives. Joan Grant says that it is not always the 'supra-physical body' of the immediately previous life that enters and influences the unborn child. Chapter 13 will return to these issues.

The birth

Prenatal experiences are less diverse than discarnate experiences. Individual birth experiences are even less so. A child that is just born is fully aware of the situation in the delivery room. He does feel, hear, and see everything that happens, and knows what the people present are saying, feeling, and thinking. The mother, the father, the doctor or midwife, and the nurses regard the newborn child as unaware and ignorant, and have no idea of the presence of a full human awareness. The child feels acutely the gap between his own adult, telepathic awareness, unperceived by the mother and the others present, and his perceived small, helpless body. This experience is sometimes funny, but usually painful, especially if the child is treated roughly or wrongly.

Normally, the birth itself is less painful and traumatic for the child than is commonly believed. A fair number even regard it as a pleasant experience. A normal, uncomplicated birth is not traumatic or even troublesome to the child. The idea that everybody retains, for example, a fear of constriction from this experience is false. Of course, there are many traumatic births: children who begin to breathe before they are well out of the womb and almost choke to death, breech deliveries, etc. The birth itself may restimulate traumas from past lives or reinforce traumas already restimulated in the prenatal phase. Netherton and Fiore conclude that the experience of the birth process is decisive for stress resistance in the rest of life. A good birth leads to strong resistance, and a difficult or complicated birth to stress sensitivity (Netherton and Shiffrin 1978: 133; Fiore 1978: 14).

A few circumstances are unpleasant for almost all newborn children. The first complaint is that the light is often too bright and hurts the eyes, and the second complaint is that it is too cold. A third complaint, already mentioned, is being treated more like a thing than a human being. A fourth, fairly frequent complaint has to do with the newborn's strong desire for physical and emotional contact with its mother. Many remigrants describe their disappointment when they found their mother to be 'away', in other words, unconscious, usually under anaesthetic. Sometimes a woman in labour needs anaesthesia, but, in principle, local anaesthesia is better than loss of consciousness. A welcoming mother is much better and much more pleasant for a child.

All birth regressions are one great plea for the modern, more natural birth care. There is one exception: in a few cases people describe that the amniotic fluid (perhaps under the influence of the atmosphere?) burns and itches on their skin and that they are screaming with misery because they are washed too late. The tendency is not to wash the newborn child, because it would be natural to let the skin soak up this nutritious moisture. But if a child is crying it is better to wash it right away. Furthermore, it requires no spotlights, the warmest possible room, and, especially, a conscious welcome as a full-fledged human being. No evidence yet supports Estelle Myers' claim that a birth in water is better and 'more spiritual'. Future regressions of children born in this way might be interesting.

That children have to cry when they are born because this is good for their breathing is nonsense. A remigrant describes her indignation and rage at being held upside down in the cold and receiving a slap on her bottom to boot, superfluous since she was already breathing, and also insulting. A child may cry because the birth was trying or the reception is disappointing, or as a natural release of emotion as in extreme laughter, great joy, or great exertion. Crying is also an expression of helplessness, evoking a natural desire in adults to receive the child in an attentive, friendly, and helpful manner (Kardec 1857: 156).

The birth can be traumatic for reasons unrelated to the birth process and birth treatment. During regression a patient with an identity problem who had the constant feeling that he had to change his name related that the doctor at his birth kept mixing his mother's name up with the name of a nurse in the presence of the newborn child (Netherton and Shiffrin 1978: 173). Surely, this will only traumatize someone who already has a weak or impaired sense of identity. Interesting birth experiences are also found in Karl Muller's book (1970: 189–93).

The moment of birth and the natal chart: karmic astrology

People who believe in astrology will wonder how the life preparation and life plan are related to the natal chart. Here, the first question is what the astrological moment of birth is. If the moment of birth influences someone's character and life plan, then this moment is probably no coincidence. But what is this exact moment? And do induced and Caesarian births interfere with the fate of the child? Or is everything so well-inspired and well-organized that a person ends up being born at the predestined moment anyway? A German obstetrician, Dr Diehl, instructed an assistant with a chronometer to measure the various moments of birth as exactly as possible in thousands of cases (Dean and Mather 1977: 467). First, they noted the moment the cervix had dilated sufficiently; second, the appearance of the head; third, the first breath; fourth, the first scream; and fifth, the cutting of the umbilical cord. Between the appearance of the head and cutting the cord the interval is sometimes 30 minutes, but usually less than 2 or 3 minutes. The last 4 moments in particular follow each other closely, sometimes within a minute. The first scream often occurs 5 seconds after the body has emerged. In a few hundred cases the 5 times were so far apart that the natal charts of the various times differed greatly. Years later Diehl compared the development of the lives of the children with these natal charts to determine which chart fitted best. He concluded that without exception the chart of the moment of the first breath was the right one. Just as the first breath is the first moment of independent human existence, so in drawing a chart of a marriage, a business, or a country, the moment of becoming independent is also the relevant moment.

What happens with induced births? For this question, the Danish experience is interesting because in Denmark it has long been the practice to induce almost every birth. Research of the charts of thousands of Danish births has led to the conclusion that the chart of the first breath after an induced birth is just as valid as with natural births (Dean and Mather 1977: 171). However, Gauquelin, a French researcher, compared children's charts with those of their parents. The charts of children who had been born naturally resembled those of their parents more closely, especially in corner planets (of proven relevance), than those of children with stimulated births (Dean and Mather 1977: 392). Very likely this means that a stimulated or induced birth upsets the fate of the person to some extent. With induced births people enter the world under an astrological constellation less appropriate than in the case of a natural birth.

Induced births, therefore, are not advisable. Of course, it depends whether an intervention is necessary because of risks attending the birth, or whether the intervention is customary, as in Denmark, because of the working hours of doctors and nurses. Once again recent tendencies toward natural childbirth are supported, this time by astrological studies.

If the right birth moment is important for someone, the people who are involved in inducing the birth may be influenced to make the birth occur at the right moment anyway, I imagine. But this might be true in only the minority of cases. Anyway, there is no point worrying about what you can't control. Natural births are preferable to artificial births, but if an artificial birth is medically unavoidable, go along with it and hope for the best.

Karmic astrology assumes that the natal chart shows the consequences of past lives. The oldest book about the subject is the Chinese *Three Lives* written in around 1600, and translated and edited by Martin Palmer *et al.* (1987). From the hour of birth, it concludes what life you will have, what life you had before, and what your next life will be like. It is the strangest brainless porridge one can imagine. I give some examples. If you were born in a year of the Cock (1 out of every 12 people) in your next life you will be a steward in a large, rich family. Even taking large to mean just 1 wife and 2 children, this claims that more than 8 per cent of all people will be stewards to such families, and more than 33 per cent of all people living will be in rich families. One out of every 12 will be a concubine in the next life, or 1 out of every 6 women. One out of every 12 people will die on a snowy day, an amazing feat for all people living in warm climates. (Palmer *et al.* 1987: 105–9)

Or what about: 'The most appropriate job for you is that of a manager, but you would also be a good butcher'; 'You will have 120 catties of rice, 1 jar of wine, 5 catties of meat, 10 catties of oil and salt, and 200 coins'. Nothing of this seems to be consumed. And what about the number of bank notes, credit cards, or cameras? One out of every 4 people will be extremely lucky, own a farm, and inherit a large fortune (Palmer *et al.* 1987: 171–82).

The editors give an example of a reading: first line: 'You will lose your home and your fortune'; second line: 'You will be wealthy and never suffer financial trouble' (1987: 48). Explanation? None. The editors assert: 'The fusion of Taoist belief, Confucianist ethics, and Buddhist teaching has produced one of the most interesting and flexible systems of divination imaginable. *Three Lives* is without doubt one of the most unusual and interesting of the resulting books' (Palmer *et al.* 1987: 3) The cover promises 'A practical Chinese guide to reincarnation'. Let us move on fast to western works.

Since the works of theosophical writers on astrology, many astrologers have accepted karmic interpretations of natal charts. In 1943 Joan Hodgson published *Wisdom in the Stars*, later reprinted as *Reincarnation Through the Zodiac* (Hodgson 1943). Her book gives general reflections about the karmic background of the twelve zodiacal signs, especially what karmic lessons should be learned from them. Her arguments are based on a notion of karma that is as mechanical as it is lofty, but fortunately leaves our free will intact. Her notions of the zodiacal signs show that she has never heard of the southern hemisphere, as she freely associates the signs with the seasons of the temperate climate in the northern hemisphere, a narrow-mindedness other astrologers are also guilty of (Dean and Mather 1977: 79). Sun sign astrology is, apart from the lucky stars business, the most meaningless and most disproven branch of astrology. Addey says of it: 'I have yet to see a single piece of statistical work (and there have been many now) . . . which gives the slightest indication that the twelve signs, in either zodiac, are valid unities in the sense they are normally thought of' (Dean and Mather 1977: 88). Dean and Mather quote research studies showing that the probability that the zodiac signs are relevant is about 1 in 10 to the twentieth power. Joan Hodgson will be of little help to us.

Martin Schulman's books on karmic astrology are well known. Schulman first points out the moon-knots as astrological indicators of karma. According to him, the southern moon-knot registers the complete history of past lives, and the northern moon-knot is an indicator of the future, the prospective, the not-yet-tried. How an abstract geometric intersection point without any physical reality can register lives of people remains a mystery. Schulman refers to the southern knot as the climax of 100,000 years of people working on themselves. A page later he calls this climax the point in every chart which is inclined to be the weakest point (Schulman 1976). Perhaps Schulman's own southern moon-knot has something to do with logic. Astrologers have diverse ideas about moon-knots (as about almost everything). Besides Schulman's interpretation there are many others. Furthermore, there are two methods for determining moon-knots, the so-called average and real moon-knots. Schulman does not even say which method he uses. In later books (1976; 1977; 1978) Schulman deals with the retrograde planets and the *pars fortunae*. The types of karmic missions related to particular positions remain general. In the cases I am familiar with, I find no relation at all between the contents from regressions and such positions. Such reflections on astrology are gnostic speculations about astrological factors based on abstract views about karma and reincarnation without relation to actual reincarnation processes. Schulman is not too much help either.

Some astrologers are even worse. Some time ago a Dutch astrologer calculated the place and time of birth of past lives using the natal chart of the present life. With this method, degrees of longitude were converted into years at some point, so that the Greenwich meridian received a fantastic cosmic meaning, and intermissions between incarnations varied evenly between nil and 360 years. All utter nonsense.

Another author on karmic astrology is Stephen Arroyo (1978). He looks at all psychic phenomena from a karmic point of view. This adds extra depth, but no new information. Arroyo seems more versatile and more intelligent than the other astrologers mentioned here, but his astrological karma indicators are a lucky bag: squares and opposites; Virgo, Pisces, and Scorpio; the fourth, the eighth, and the twelfth house; the moon, Saturn, and Pluto; the aspects of Saturn, Uranus, Neptune, and Pluto; and the transits. Why the Moon indicates karma, but its aspects do not, why Uranus and Neptune do not indicate karma, but their aspects do, remains one of the riddles in the universe. And nowhere is any relation found with empirical understanding of karma and reincarnation.

The only regression therapist who talks about karmic astrology is Adrian Finkelstein. He maintains that subsequent lives always have the lunar nodes in the same sign, and gives some example and analyses to prove his point. Later, however, he says that it is the same sign because the previous life was not properly completed. This seems to me self-contradictory. Furthermore he gives no data on his statistical findings (Finkelstein 1985: 54). His notions on karmic astrology appear to be copied from the only books on karmic astrology he refers to: Joan Hodgson and the first book of Martin Schulman. It seems that he gets from the material what he first has presupposed.

It appears to me that as a valid discipline karmic astrology has yet to begin. Relationships may be found by correlating the analysed regression contents of a large group of people with an analysis of their natal charts. The present intuitive association and interpretation of nothing into something is meaningless. The best approach is to combine a technique like Wambach's (regression back to the prenatal stage and asking questions about the aim in life and life plan) with aspects of the natal chart which have proven empirical relevance: positions of planets and aspects between planets.

After the birth: early childhood

My discussion of Helen Wambach's research has already indicated that some children can still leave the body during the first year. With most people, this adult consciousness with its paranormal abilities fades fairly quickly after birth, as the experiences in the new body make the soul's self-image conform to the new, infantile body. Normally some time during the third year the new self-awareness which actually belongs to this incarnation starts to remember itself.

The personality of a newborn child is especially clear during the first hours after the birth. Sometimes it stays clear for weeks and months. Often, a baby face shows an adult personality. The personality shown at this time is the personality of a past incarnation, probably the incarnation that is the dominant influence on this life. Joan Grant describes a mean old man she sees looking out of a little face in the child clinic (Kelsey and Grant 1967). Maria Penkala gives another example (1972: 135). The man in Hubbard's example, who immediately entered a new body out of pure rage because his opponents had disposed of him, probably looked out of the eyes of the baby as an energetic and frustrated personality.

Allegedly, the souls of young children often manifest themselves more easily via a medium after birth than before the birth. Many people who are going to be born cannot make themselves known via mediums or more directly, because they need their energy to influence the growing body. After birth, less energy is needed, and the soul can more easily manifest itself to others (Shirley 1924: 165). This may apply only to children who easily leave their body, but is fairly usual in the first year.

Sometimes this possibility remains for a longer period. Eugénie, de Rochas' first subject, felt during regression that she was going to be born again. She felt attracted to a mother who had just become pregnant. She hovered above the mother until the moment the child was born. After that, her consciousness was slowly taken up into the child's body. According to her, she entered the body definitely and completely only at 7 (Shirley 1924: 140).

In any case, the adult awareness of the newborn fades in early childhood. We have to work our way back to self-awareness and responsibility for this life again during our childhood. A sense of our aim in life, of our destination, of the essence of our life plan may accompany us throughout childhood, even though it may be rather unconscious. Actually, our life plan is continually present from birth onwards. Some children have an early sense of destiny, but most of us have to find our direction amidst insecurity and confusion.

Why do we have to go through such a long period of inconvenience each incarnation? Childhood, ideally, is a relaxed period of careless play, as well as a receptive period for careful education. Although people are often more open to education when discarnate, to incorporate the results when incarnating is difficult. When the parents are as wise as their children, childhood is a period of relaxation and carefree existence. If the parents are wiser than their children, childhood offers a particularly good opportunity to develop further. If parents are less wise than their children, childhood is a struggle to come out of an often dangerous swamp, sometimes for karmic reasons, sometimes to gain strength, and sometimes as an inevitable consequence of the social and cultural level of the surrounding society.

Restimulation of karmic misery during childhood is very probable. We have to accept that every time we are again largely dependent on the wisdom and good will of other people. If we refuse this, the only alternative is to become autistic. Some people feel a great resistence to a new long childhood. Helen Wambach found this to be a cause of autism (Wambach 1978). This form of autism is mostly found in intelligent children, often born of intelligent parents. A bad reaction to this may exacerbate the problem considerably, whereas a good reaction (a mixture of patient acceptance, confidence in the future, and, in spite of everything, social stimulation) can prevent a lot of misery.

Barring death through primitive medical conditions, death in the first three years is more often a matter of the parents' karma than that of the child. It may also be the child's own decision. Someone recounts that he realized immediately after his birth that he had chosen the wrong parents and he knew things would go wrong, so he left. Presumably, something like this is rare.

Some esoteric schools see the first 21 or 28 years (3 and 4 times 7 years respectively) as a continued incarnation process. These esoteric schools imagine that at birth the soul floats around the body, and enters the body only slowly during the years. The findings of regression research in no way support this image. We may conclude from birth experiences that almost the opposite is true. The soul is powerfully present in the body, and its self-image usually becomes only gradually entangled in it during the first year. The lowest point of incarnation is in the period between the loss of the adult identity in the first hours, weeks, or months after birth, and the re-attainment of a new identity and self-awareness in around the third year.

The children who retain an uninterrupted memory of their previous life, as discussed in chapter 5, almost always remember the directly preceding life, which has almost always been shortly before. Usually, however, the memories of past lives fade, and only idiosyncrasies remain as silent witnesses of past lives. During adolescence, from about 15 onwards, many people experience the unconscious urge to remember themselves again. Much of the inner confusion and the ostensible romanticism of adolescence is based on the urge to rediscover oneself. Some people have memories, usually before the age of 30, but for most people, regression is necessary. It would be ideal if we could use adolescence to get to know ourselves again, to experience our identity as a soul, and then to 'incarnate' further in the form of active participation in the society around us.

Direct contacts with our own discarnate friends from before may occur in dreams, especially vivid dreams, and in out-of-body experiences. It may also be the other way round: discarnate friends from before our birth helping us by inspiring our feelings and thoughts. I have discussed this subject indirectly in my book about oracles and inspirations (TenDam 1980). Some of Wambach's remigrants reported that the consultants or guides whom they saw in their prenatal regression were people they had dreamed about.

Advice for prospective parents, rape, abortion

The evidence from regressions is important for pregnancy and birth care. The section above on birth has indicated a few practical consequences. The ideal reception of a child is an acceptance of its simultaneous physical helplessness and mental maturity. This means taking care of the child and protecting it, being sweet, kind, and soft to it, and simultaneously accepting the child as an adult. Although you cannot perceive the consciousness of the child, let the child know you believe in it, by talking to the child and welcoming it. No pepped-up feelings, just acceptance of and interest in the child. If you had hoped for a boy, don't pretend you are very glad it is a girl. Probably, the child sees right through you. Better accept the disappointment, perhaps tease yourself about your preference, laugh a bit at yourself, try to get over it, and welcome the child.

Can you attract an entity consciously? For example, can you make sure of getting an appropriate entity, by living in a particular way, by preparing yourself in a particular manner? Or, can you attract a better entity, by having a better way of life? The attraction between prospective parents and an incarnating soul is like any attraction between people. People are attracted to each other because they know each other, because they have something to do with each other, because they have gone through common experiences, or have created a bond between them, often a bond of sympathy, sometimes of antipathy. Temporarily living in a certain way hardly strengthens or weakens a personal attraction. Consciously thinking about a person may attract that person. But you have to be sure who you are dealing with, whether he or she is discarnate, and whether he or she would like to come to you. Discarnate people may have a better overview. At the most, you could send out a thought like, 'Mary, if you want to come to us, you are welcome. We would like to have you.' Sometimes the parents have a reason for this. If they have had a child before, but something went wrong because of a wrong decision, carelessness, lack of self-control, or whatever, the parents can address that child consciously and lovingly and let it know that they want to do things better this time and that it is still welcome. Even then, you have to remain open to whether the child wants to come back or not. You are still the host and hostess: you can tell your guest he is welcome, but you should go no further than to invite him. You do not impose yourself on your guests, let alone overpower them.

Can you attract a better or more aware entity by having a good lifestyle or being nobly disposed during the procreative act? If you talk about levels of entities, you also have to consider your own level: you have created this level during your life (many lives). By living consciously and positively, you are trying to improve that level, although this is usually a long-term business. For the attraction of an appropriate soul, what you do is hardly important. What you are, is. To believe that a particular behaviour before or during the pregnancy attracts better souls is to underestimate the intelligence of the kind of people you want to attract, and to underestimate the spiritual laws that guide incarnation. Noble feelings and noble habits during the conception and the pregnancy are pious deceit. If you expect a respected guest, you clean up your house a bit, and buy a few extras. In this way, you may prepare yourself mentally for somebody's arrival, without 'living above your means'. Be yourself. The procreative act, especially, becomes odd when you think you should have noble feelings during intercourse and above all should limit animal lusts. Asking yourself during intercourse whether you really love the person you are sleeping with also hardly helps. If you want to have children, do not speculate on your own choice, but trust the choice of parents to the children who come to you.

While you are pregnant you can often contact the entity that is going to be born to you. Here too, artificial and natural curiosity differ. As already said, souls connect themselves to the foetus in different stages of the pregnancy, but usually rather late. If you concentrate too strongly on the presumed presence of a soul, you will probably increase the magnetic attraction for souls who are going to incarnate. This makes the foetus an even stronger magnet, increasing the probability of an impersonal advent, rather than the arrival of someone with whom you have a personal relationship. People who pray incessantly to have a child have a greater risk of getting someone certainly inappropriate: a wandering soul. Or perhaps this is appropriate after all: wandering minds attracting wandering souls. But if you feel there is someone with you, you can strengthen and elaborate this feeling. Do not conjure up the first experience, and do not be disquieted when it stays away. Do not be afraid that the wrong person will come to you. This happens only in exceptional, and in themselves karmically determined, cases.

If you have the strong feeling that the child is with you already, then work with feelings and thoughts which come up naturally, especially during the last months of pregnancy. Strengthen these thoughts and feelings, while keeping them open-ended. It is all right to talk about it, but preferably only with your husband or a trusted friend. A mother usually has such impressions before the father does.

What happens if you involuntarily get pregnant because of a mistake or, even worse, as the result of rape? Does this affect the kind of entity attracted? If a woman has been raped and impregnated, then a house is under construction which may, like any other house, be interesting to those looking for a home. For a future dweller, the construction of a house is more important than the reason for construction. How the impregnation happened is less important than what happens later. The reaction of the mother to an undesired pregnancy matters more. If she projects her abhorrence, aversion, and hate for the rapist on to the foetus (and this happens easily), it becomes unpleasant to move into this house. Souls feeling strongly connected to the mother or her circumstances will move in in spite of this. For the rest, attracted souls either have an affinity for the situation based on karmic obligations, or are so unaware that they accept everything indiscriminately. However, the mother's reactions are decisive, not the manner of impregnation. Rape is brutal for the girl or woman, not for the incarnating soul.

But doesn't the quality of the growing body depend on the gene material of the rapist? Perhaps the risk of inferior genetic material is a bit larger with rapists, but probably only seldom is there any relation between genes and rape. Someone can perform such deeds for purely psychological and personal reasons, often with a karmic cause, and have excellent genetic material. Not everyone who lives in a poor and neglected house is a scoundrel, and not everyone who lives in a beautiful, well-kept house is a noble person. This is as true for the inhabitants of bodies as for the inhabitants of houses. The entity about to be born will, often aided by 'incarnation brokers', look at the body, the family, and the circumstances he or she may be born into. Certainly, the consequences of rape will be considered. But this may also lead to sympathy for the mother and provide a stimulus to come.

The mother's behaviour during the pregnancy is certainly important. You must distinguish three consequences of your behaviour: on the biological development of the foetus, on the attraction of a soul, and on the character and life of the person who is going to be born from this foetus. Considering the biological development of the foetus, it is obvious that you can behave more or less sensibly during pregnancy. About the attraction of a particular soul I have already stated my reservations. It is difficult to influence and an attempt is more likely to disturb that to help. As to character and future life, the mother's experiences during pregnancy are etched into the foetus. If these experiences restimulate the connected soul's karmic problems and traumas, these are carried over into the next life.

What does all this mean for the current discussion of abortion? A body is a house someone is stuck with for a whole lifetime. Abortion is destruction of this house while still under construction. Is this bad? First of all, this depends on the moment of destruction. The closer a house is to completion, the more its demolition is destructive and unsympathetic. Second, it depends on whether someone had applied for the house. A prospective inhabitant undoubtedly will dislike the house being knocked down. How serious this is for him or her depends on various personal characteristics and circumstances: to what extent suitable and attractive alternatives are available, to what extent someone had looked forward to a house in this neighbourhood, how much of a hurry someone is in, how sensitive someone is. Third, it depends on the extent of someone's personal involvement in the design and the construction of the house. If someone has concerned himself actively with genetic selection during fertilization, or with making it suitable for him or her personally, then a piece of one's work is destroyed. Looking on while a house you have helped design and construct is torn down is more painful than when you were not personally involved in it. Fourth, and this is the essential point, it depends on whether the prospective inhabitant of the house is already inside the house at the time of the demolition. This would not be demolition, but homicide, and of a crude sort.

People who have an abortion, or want to have an abortion, usually do not know if the foetus is already inhabited and so do not know if, by killing the foetus, they cause a person to go through an awful experience. So the question is whether the soul of the coming person is already connected, notably, whether it has descended (according to Wambach in about 10 per cent cases before the sixth month). When the soul feels a bond with the foetus, but usually hovers around in the vicinity, abortion is like demolition of a house with the prospective inhabitant seeing the house which he has already started to furnish torn from the ground and destroyed by a huge demolition machine. Awful, frustrating, but more melancholic than traumatic, except when it restimulates older traumas, and alas there is a great chance that this is the case. Being inside the house when the demolition machine bears down on you is a really horrible experience.

What are the implications of this for taking a position on abortion? Abortion is only murder when you know there is someone inside. This is seldom the case. Still, tearing down a house without knowing if someone is inside, though short of murderous, is certainly coarse and barbaric. So it should be done only after some hard thinking, especially in this age of reliable contraceptives and morning-after pills. As a policy, abortion should be more easily available up until the sixth month, and after the sixth month only in exceptional cases, such as medical or psychiatric necessity. The child being unwanted should only be a reason when the waiting lists for adoption have been exhausted.

Further, the method of abortion should take into consideration that perhaps the foetus is already human. Anaesthesia of the foetus (if the nervous system is already developed) should be standard practice. Gross mechanical surgery before the foetus is anaesthetized or dead is fundamentally wrong. Finally, specialized abortion clinics are undesirable. Wherever something is done routinely on a large scale feelings are stultified. And in places where human foetuses are destroyed on a large scale shady things may happen.

If you ever consider an abortion, then do it early. Address the person who is perhaps already present, and make your excuses. Compensate for what will be a destructive deed anyway, with constructive attention and care for yourself and the people in your daily life. That never hurts anyway.

Abortion may be a more serious question than I have sketched here, based on my conclusions from regressions. Kardec's informants, who are, on the whole, sober and reasonable, reject abortion as criminal. Only when the choice is between the life of the mother and that of the child do they advise giving the life and health of the mother precedence over that of the child. A life already formed is more important than a life not yet formed.

Further reading

The most important book on this subject is *Life Before Life* by Helen Wambach (1979). Morris Netherton's work is also important (Netherton and Shiffrin 1978). Supplementary information can be found in Joan Grant's work (Kelsey and Grant 1967) and Allan Kardec's work (1857). Muller gives examples of prenatal experiences and announcements (1970). Prenatal experiences are as yet sporadically covered in the regression literature, probably because their therapeutic value is insufficiently realized. Apart from Netherton, Schlotterbeck in particular gives examples (1987). Original work on the experience of the foetus has been done by Thomas Verney (1981).

In addition to the books mentioned above about karmic astrology there is *Karmic Astrology* by Marcia Moore and Mark Douglas. I was unable to get hold of it, but maybe it is better than the rest.

8 The Death Experience and Beyond

The literature about life after death is so extensive and complex that it demands a complete study of its own. For this reason, I limit myself here to material from regressions and to some general works, such as the books by Robert Crookall (1961–78) and Ian Currie (1978). Death experiences from past lives play an important role in regressions, but the best known source of death experiences are the people who were briefly in a state of apparent clinical death and had vivid experiences during this time. Next there are the deceased who report about their world via trance mediums or clairvoyants, and finally there are the clairvoyants who have described their perception of the process of dying. This chapter will show that all these experiences have a clear pattern. The various sources fit together well.

Each account without inconsistencies may in itself be true, but the ample consensus between the accounts of people with accidental experiences is particularly convincing. I will also quote some information that at least does not conflict with this pattern. A few of the examples from regressions are taken from my own experience as a therapist.

What happens when you die? Crookall's work

Robert Crookall's work (1961–78) provides the best insights into the process of dying. Crookall conscientiously collected and worked out a substantial body of empirical material without embroidering it. He is overly repetitive, but he may be forgiven for this because of his painstaking collections and comparisons. He collected and analysed spiritual literature, accounts of out-of-body experiences, and clairvoyant perceptions of dying people, and came to a clear and consistent picture of the dying experiences and events. I summarize briefly in the following paragraphs.

When we have died, we still feel we are present in some kind of body. Crookall calls this the psychic body, roughly equal to the (vaguely and conflictingly defined) astral body of the occultists. The aspect of this psychic body follows the image we have of ourselves. Often, this is how we looked in our recent life, initially how we looked just before death, later usually how we looked at the age when we felt ourselves strongest and best. Our aspect can change, depending on how we feel and whom we meet. Our psychic body is 'ideo-plastic', or, more precisely, 'psycho-plastic'. It shapes itself in accordance with our ideas, or, more broadly, in accordance with how we experience ourselves. Our consciousness in the psychic body is similar to that of lucid dreams: dreams in which we know we are dreaming, are able to influence the course of our dream, and often have vivid and brilliant perception. Our consciousness in the psychic body has paranormal abilities such as telepathy and foresight. With out-of-body experiences and with death our psychic body disengages itself from our physical body.

In the psychic body we move around by imagining, as concretely as we can, the person or the place we want to go to, or by summoning up our feelings about them as concretely as we can. We may create our own surroundings, visit an existing environment in the psychic world, or ideo-plastically decorate an existing environment. The ordinary physical world may be our environment, but usually we need extra effort and an extra vehicle for this, as when someone who wants to go to the bottom of the sea needs a diving suit with an air supply. This 'diving suit' is Crookall's 'vehicle of vitality', and corresponds to the occultist's etheric body.

The vehicle of vitality is an intermediary between our psychic and our physical body, not a vehicle of consciousness. We cannot be conscious in it. It has little structure of its own, but gets its structure largely from the physical body and partly from the psychic body. During out-of-body experiences the psychic body can take a part of this vehicle with it, and be shrouded by it as by a thicker or thinner veil. This dulls the awareness and so gives dull rather than lucid dreams. Frequently one enters twilight states resembling common, chaotic dreams. In this twilight world are mainly deceased people who retain a part of their vehicle of vitality. Often this is the result of a strong attachment to the physical world, sometimes to a certain lifestyle. The following paragraphs will discuss falling asleep, hanging about, wandering about, ghost-walking, and twilight existence, all results of dying processes in which the etheric body is insufficiently cast off. If the psychic body leaves the body while taking some ethers along, the departure is usually via the solar plexus; when it leaves the etheric body behind, it usually departs via the top of the head. When Lenz speaks of the 'etheric body' (1979: 60), he seems to mean the psychic body.

The greater part of the etheric body can accompany one during out-of-body experiences. This usually leaves the physical body cold and stiff, more or less cataleptic. This gives more chance of unpleasant and disturbing experiences in the twilight world. Many regions of this twilight world are populated by petty, narrow-minded, jealous spirits who like to scare the wits out of people who have left their bodies semi-consciously, for example by giving them nightmares. Another complication is that during a complex out-of-body experience where one ends up in the physical world rather than in the twilight world, one can be hampered by the impermeability of materials such as glass, or by the electricity in power lines. And lastly, one may scare ordinary people. The so-called wraiths, silent and pensive grey apparitions, who apparently are seen objectively and sometimes even can be photographed, are separate projections of somebody's vehicle of vitality.

With a natural death in old age, the psychic body departs together with the vehicle of vitality and hovers briefly above the physical body. A cord of vitality plasma (the Indian term is *prana*) remains connected to the physical body – usually at the solar plexus – becomes thinner, and then snaps. This is the moment of irrevocable death. Then the psychic body disengages itself from the etheric copy floating above the body, and gets up into an erect position. When the psychic body is freed from the etheric body the soul becomes aware of its surroundings. Before this, there is a moment when consciousness is lost. If one is already out-of-body, but the cord is still unbroken, one can be simultaneously aware of oneself inside and outside of the body. Sometimes the soul lacks energy to pull the psychic body out of the etheric casing, and one falls asleep. The remnants from the etheric body in the psychic body normally evaporate and after one to three days one wakes up.

When the silver cord is broken, the vehicle of vitality has left the physical body. After the psychic body has left it, the vehicle of vitality in turn decomposes, in a period that may vary from four hours to over sixty days. For many people this may be a period of restful sleep. According to McClain, when she instructs remigrants to go to a point in time about six weeks after death, most people describe a feeling of just being, or just feeling safe, secure, and contented (1986: 120).

People who often have lucid dreams will probably be able to leave their body quickly and without complications when they die. When people die in the flower of life, for example in an accident, the etheric body is so strongly attached to the physical that only a small part of the vehicle of vitality comes along. In such a case, someone is immediately out of the body, fully conscious and, although few ethers have come along, sees the material surroundings because of the unchanged thrust of consciousness. The psychic body may already be out of the physical body, and perhaps has even departed, while the vehicle of vitality still animates the material body. Then, the body is like a deserted machine still running. Dying can look unpleasant, for example, with lengthy rattling, but the soul may be gone already. According to some clairvoyants this can happen years before death, for example with extreme senility, giving a grubby, rundown aura with hardly any colour left (*The Boy Who Saw True*, Spearman ed. 1953: 101).

Sometimes, the moment someone dies other people are suddenly strongly reminded of him. This is known as the 'call'. Paranormally gifted people sometimes see his apparition. This telepathic leave-taking usually happens with people who have prepared themselves for their death. The clarity of the call depends on the spiritual strength of the dying person and the intensity of the relationship. In the case of a sudden death through heart failure or an accident, there is only telepathic contact if the dying person consciously thinks of someone, for example a child calling its mother in its last moments.

The next experience is the retrospect, the life panorama. Apparently we have two retrospects. The first is like a high-speed movie of our whole life, or like a tableau where we oversee all the images simultaneously. This experience is reminiscent of Mozart's, who sometimes saw the complete piece before he began to compose. A subject of Whitton's gives this vivid description: 'It is like climbing right inside a movie of your life. Every moment from every year of your life is played back in complete sensory detail. Total, total recall. And it all happens in an instant.' (Whitton and Fisher 1986: 39).

Next, we experience the departure from our body, giving a sense either of sinking or of rising, depending on how our consciousness is distributed in the moment of transition: in the physical body that is being left behind or in the departing psychic body. Then we have the sensation of going through a door or through a tunnel, or we feel we are rising out of ourselves, usually through the head. The moment the psychic body is free we feel larger and freer. We get impressions of deceased relatives and friends or just of many people, we see our own body and feel the bond through the 'silver cord'. Sometimes we may see two bodies beneath ourselves: our physical body and just above it the etheric copy. We observe impartially the possible death cramps of the body below. Then the silver cord is broken, sometimes with the help of others. Often we fall asleep with a sense of great peace. After some days or some weeks, we wake up and continue on 'up'.

The second, more emotional retrospect is step by step, situation after situation. We experience, too, the feelings of the people we met. McClain implies that the life retrospect will occur after the first rest period of a number of weeks, apparently referring to this second retrospect. After the second retrospect the obvious next step may be learning.

Sometimes, in the case of a violent death, a person loses consciousness only briefly and does not realize that he has died. For example, a dead soldier recounts that he continued to fight for about fifteen minutes before he realized that his acts had no effect and a bullet could go right through him without hurting him. Often a person only realizes his death when recognizing his own physical body. Even more compassion is felt for relatives left behind than in the case of natural death. The dead person frequently desperately tries to make clear to them that although he is dead, he is fine. A deceased person is sensitive to the emotional reactions of his relatives when they hear of his death. Especially in the case of a sudden death, he is sensitive to the feelings and thoughts of the people he is still attached to on earth. A depressing grief is often a great burden for the deceased. Sometimes the deceased try to make themselves known via dreams, via poltergeist activities, and sometimes they queue up for mediums and clairvoyants to give a message.

Many people who die young find it a pity to have to leave behind such a good, healthy body. Apparently, a good, healthy body is a valuable asset one does not have in every life. Many people are shocked about the loss. Others have no feelings of this kind at all. A soldier who was suddenly killed in an attack and mentally kept on running for a while compared it with discarding a warm overcoat while running. Another soldier characterized dying as: 'The soul jumps out of the body like a schoolboy jumps out of the school door: suddenly and with great joy.'

The deceased often describe misty or watery surroundings, indicating that the vehicle of vitality is still present. The physical body, the vehicle of vitality, and the psychic body occupy the same space in a living person. They permeate each other. Yet there is a distance between them in the fourth dimension (perhaps better called the first dimension). The best label for this dimension is 'throughth' (*The Boy Who Saw True*, Spearman ed. 1953). Considering time as the fourth dimension, as, among others, Ouspensky (1934) does in accordance with the physicists, is misleading and fruitless.

Experiences of the temporarily clinically dead

People who were briefly clinically dead have fairly similar experiences. Often, while leaving the body, they hear an unpleasant, crescendoing ringing or buzzing while screeching through a tunnel at accelerating speed. Then they are suddenly out of it and they find themselves outside their physical body floating around in a volatile body, often near the ceiling. The volatile (psychic) body is experienced in various ways, from sensing oneself as transparent and shapeless, via a round or egg- or pear-shaped presence, to a vague outline of a body with a head, hands, and feet, to an outline of the body as it was at the time of death.

They often see or feel the presence of others, sometimes deceased relatives or friends, sometimes someone they recognize as a spiritual teacher during their lifetime. Then there is a light that becomes stronger, and grows into a being emanating love and warmth. Some see an angel in it, some see it as Jesus, others again as the Maitreya, the next Buddha who will appear in the future. This being asks if they are prepared to die. What can they show? What gave them satisfaction? Was life worth the trouble? At the same time the life retrospect appears, not backwards, like some esoterics claim, but starting with birth or the first memory. This quick life retrospect is more or less continuous and laden with feelings. Sometimes they perceive situations through the eyes of other people. The images are clear, life-like, and three-dimensional. The light-being emphasizes themes of love and knowledge in his questions about and comments on these retrospects. 'Was it worth it? What did you learn from it?' Presumably, they can work out this life retrospect sometime later on.

Next they experience a border or barrier, a definite separation, pictured as a stream, a road, a fence, a river, a mist, or just a line. As they approach this border they feel more joyful, loving, and peaceful. However, the border is never crossed, at least not by those who came back and gave these accounts. The whole experience is between an out-of-body experience and a death experience, and most resembles dying.

Different types of dying experiences during regressions

In regressions to past lives it is often important to let the remigrant look back on his life and identify its main themes. This is done after death. Because of the psychoplastic nature of this environment, questions about dying and post-mortem states should never be suggestive. The best questions are ones like: 'What are you experiencing now? What is happening now? How do you feel?' If someone sees a light, the therapist can ask what it means, if it changes, and whether the remigrant recognizes something in the light. He may ask the remigrant what he thinks of his past life looking back on it. Often, he will ask what made the greatest impression, what was the most important, what was the main purpose. Usually, answers are direct and global: apparently the dominant theme from this life surfaces. People can review their whole life remarkably well in such dying regressions.

Life aims are fantastically divergent. For example, one remigrant says that the main purpose of his life was to learn to laugh, because he had been too serious in lives before. Another remigrant had been enormously rich during his life, but died poor as a churchmouse. He simply stated he had to learn that wealth or poverty does not determine humanity. Remigrants seldom mention an extensive life panorama, as the clinically dead do.

The normal pattern of taking a perspective and looking back at your previous life has many exceptions. The most common alternative is somebody realizing he is outside of his body, and remaining in the vicinity of it. Others do not see him and he hangs about his body or hovers around it semi-consciously. When such a remigrant is questioned about his past life, he usually repeats the common feelings and opinions of his last years. If the therapist asks about the meaning of this life, he may receive an answer like: 'Nothing. It did not matter at all. [Pause] I had had this feeling, by the way, for a long time that nothing mattered at all.' Then the remigrant may be regressed to the age just before having this feeling, to proceed to the specific event that imprinted this feeling.

A clerk in an old-fashioned business office, fused with his desk for over 35 years, refuses a promotion because he prefers to stick to his current work. In the retrospect on his life he sees his lifeline in front of him as a thin, glowing thread snapping at some point and become dark grey. When the therapist asks him which situation caused this, the remigrant immediately sees the refusal of the promotion. He renounced a chance to develop and so renounced himself.

Like all human experiences, dying experiences are diverse. Figure 4 distinguishes seven different post-mortem states, differing according to awareness and disengagement. I will characterize and illustrate these seven states with examples from regressions, largely from my experience as a therapist.

The first form of dying is 'passing away'. One remembers nothing, feels nothing, is not aware of any surroundings, at most one feels an undifferentiated 'being around'. This state becomes apparent from the remigrant's simple remark that he cannot see anything. Every question is answered negatively, except when asked whether he has the feeling that he exists. This response can be confused with someone who did experience his death, but cannot relive it on account of some block. In this case, the remigrant becomes irritated because he cannot see anything, or because the therapist's questions bother him. In a true case of passing away the remigrant keeps saying calmly and relaxedly that he experiences nothing. The first description of this state during a regression is from Eugénie, de Rochas' subject. She experienced during regression that she was no longer on a material level, but was floating around in semi-darkness without thoughts or desires and apparently in a subjective state (Shirley 1924: 140).

The next type of dying experience is continuing to 'hang about' the place where one died. One perceives the ordinary physical surroundings vaguely. One may feel attached to places, or even objects, or may feel oneself floating around in the air. Some identify with an animal that comes near. Usually, there is little sense of self. When the hypnotist prods, only a vague, misty presence emerges.

A remigrant relives a life as a servant girl who is sent in to the woods because she is considered useless. After solitary wanderings

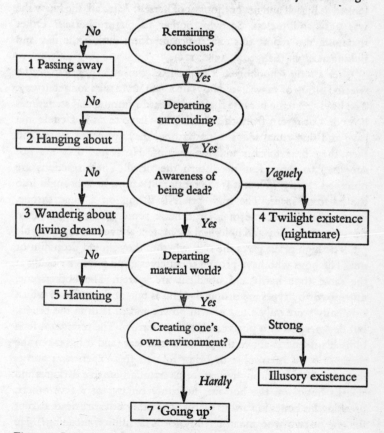

Figure 4 Overview of types of death experiences

she finds a deserted charcoalburner's hut and lives a terribly monotonous and miserable life there for a few decades. When she dies, she is
glad to be out of it, but otherwise little happens to her. During the
day she feels herself hovering above the forest, and when the night
falls, she sinks down among the branches. When light comes again
and it gets warm, she rises a bit again. Apparently, she keeps up this
pattern for quite a number of years, until she incarnates again after an
undefined period of sleep. Further inquiry shows she lacked any self-
image while she was floating around. Asked about her self-image
while she was alive, it appeared that in all those years, she never
looked at herself and never thought of herself. After all, she knew she
was ugly and useless. So why bother to picture herself? Other
therapists also report this experience of rising during the day and
sinking at night (Langedijk 1980: 116).

After a long schooling in a Maya-like community, priests lead a
selected group of 12-year-old boys up a mountain via a long stairway.
The boys feel tense because they have heard rumours that sometimes
boys do not return from this ritual. They have to sit in a circle in a
cave and sing ritual songs. One by one, they are called away, and
then they hear terrible hollow screams. However, they are not
supposed to show fear or disturb the ritual. Their reactions are
observed closely. When it is the remigrant's turn, he is brought into
the adjacent space. The high priest is sitting on a huge throne,
unrecognizable because of a large mask representing a god. Two
priests grab the boy and hold him by his feet above an unfathomable
pit. The high priest gives the sign whether they should drop him or
not. The boys who have proved themselves good pupils by being at
the same time harsh and obedient are spared. The bothersome,
untrustworthy types are dropped. (This is one of those rituals which
originally were only a test of will power and of faith in the priests,
but degenerated into power politics and terror.) The remigrant feels
himself suspended above the pit in mortal fear (and it has taken the
therapist a lot of trouble to bring him to this experience) and is
dropped. He falls through what seems an unfathomable darkness and
smacks down on the bottom, probably on top of a few others,
breaking his bones in various places. The other boys are dead, except
for one or two who moan terribly (or is he himself moaning?). He
remains alive for a few days in a pitch-black world of unbearable

pain and mental derangement. After he dies, he remains surrounded by blackness. After a seemingly endless time (about 700 years) he arrives at the surface of the mountainside, and is struck by the blinding, beautiful lushness of the outside world.

The literature (for example, Hubbard 1958) gives examples of people who are stuck on top of a gate or in a ritual object after their death. In further regression it turns out that these people have been tortured to death, and strong post-hypnotic suggestions have been implanted in their confused and dulled minds, binding their souls to such objects or buildings. Apparently, this is done to make the place more impressive or ominous, or as a sign of warning. The pack of priests performing these hideous acts may be long dead and gone, and the whole cult extinct, while the souls remains bound until the object crashes, the gate caves in, or the walls tumble down.

A Roman dies during the eruption of a volcano. He murders someone in the dining hall, runs out, and a toppling pillar kills him. He sees the sluggish flow of lava cover his dead body. He regards the volcano eruption and the tumbling pillar as punishment for his misdeed and remains bound at the spot. After 1,426 years (scientologists are keen on exact dating) thieves come, looking for treasures. The corpse has been turned to stone, and they throw the pieces in a pit. After 100 more years, grass and flowers grow on this spot, and still later, a little pond has formed. A bird comes, reawakening his perception of living nature. His apathy begins to disappear and the spot starts to bore him. However, he continues to stick around for a while, because he feels terribly guilty and thinks nobody will ever want him (Hubbard 1958).

The last example of hanging about is a woman who experiences an incarnation as a man somewhere in the neighbourhood of lake Aral, just outside of Alexander's empire. He is a solitary hunter who stayed behind alone after the other members of his tribe departed, succumbing to the promise of civilization. His most important experiences are walking in the deserted plain checking his traps, and at night looking at the overwhelming starry sky. After his death, he hangs around in the same area without any contact with humans, more or less sleeping during the day, and during the night looking at the starry sky passing by. This gives him a feeling of majesty, but impersonal and sterile. This death experience is so strongly etched that after each following incarnation the soul keeps hanging about, without contact with other people.

The next type of death experience is 'wandering about', which happens when people do not realize that they have died. They leave the corpse quickly and ignore it, and shut off every further evidence of their real state. They visit the places and people from their past life and dream that they keep on living. It is an innocent and fairly common form of psychopathology, especially in young children who have died in an accident, for example, and who wander around until they find people where they feel accepted.

A little girl is playing on a construction site, up to some mischief. The owner of the construction site, one of two partners, having difficulties because business is going badly, has a particular grudge against the girl. He chases the girl away. The next time, he stalks her and gives her a firm push so she hits her head against a machine and is killed outright. He is shocked and drags the child away to a little mud bank close by, where he quickly buries her and covers the grave with turf. The girl is missed, but the body is never found.

The remigrant who is reliving this initially recounts that a man drags her to a mud bank and leaves her there. She feels strangely lethargic and dulled and does not know what to do. She does not realize she is dead. This becomes clear later on in the regression. Why doesn't anybody come to pick her up? She feels more and more lonely and sad. She cannot answer the question why she does not get up and try to go home. After all, she is not hurt and can move freely. But she feels oddly dull. She just keeps repeating that they do not come and pick her up. She stays there for the rest of the day and the night until people appear on the construction site on Monday morning. Weakly, she tries to attract their attention, but to no avail. She gets weaker and sadder. Why has everybody left her? Since nobody cares about her any more, she wanders around the edges of fields and woods witlessly, and at some point finds a farm. Inconspicuously, she moves into the farm family and dreams she is a part of it. This condition continues for many years, until her mother dies and starts looking for her daughter. The daughter has not aged in the meantime, and looks exactly as she did at the time of her death, only a bit duller. In the regression she describes the joy of the reunion. Her mother takes her with her to what looks like home. Only later does her mother tell her that they are both dead.

A girl of almost 3, the youngest child in a barge family, falls overboard in the strong current without her parents noticing. She is missed only an hour later. She herself has no idea what is happening. She floats through the water and lands in a city park where some boys are playing. One of these, who later turns out to be paranormally gifted, attracts her because of his open aura, and she moves in with him. Forty years later she is still a 3-year-old girl who hugs her doll tightly and sucks her thumb. Only when others see her does she let go of the now older man, feel coddled, and fall asleep.

Neither girl refused to realize she was dead, but was simply not able to understand it. This is probably also the result of the parent's apparent inability to direct concrete thoughts to the children and to attract them. Such children are reversed orphans.

Langedijk gives the example of someone who dies of pneumonia. He leaves a wife and three children behind. He hangs around at home and tries to comfort his wife. His children grow up and have children of their own. His wife gets old and senile. Only then does he have the feeling he can do no more there. Immediately afterwards he has the sensation of coming into a room with a pregnant woman and feels that he is slowly becoming attached to her (Langedijk 1980: 116).

Hanging about can turn into wandering. Katsoguro, a Japanese boy, remembered he used to be called Tozo and had died of smallpox. He was put inside a large earthen pot and buried in a pit at the foot of a mountain. He heard the sound of earth falling on the pot. An old man accompanied him back to his house, flying through the air. After that, he was vaguely 'turning about in the air as if he had wings'. He did not see his environment, it was neither day nor night. He had no clear sense of time. He only heard the vague voices of his living relatives, especially when they prayed for him in front of the family altar. When his mother made a sugar-rice offering to him, he was able to breathe in the hot steam and felt content. Then he floated through the air and came to a village, to the doorstep of a house. An irresistible sensation made him slip in through an open window. He remained sitting next to the fire for three days and suddenly felt the warmth of the fire change into the lovely warmth of a person. It was the 'honourable blood' of his mother. For the rest, he knew nothing (Muller 1970: 41, Penkala 1972: 59).

What is interesting here is the relation between the ritual his family members perform for him and his attachment to a place. Perhaps such a ritual binds, and possibly nourishes, the deceased who hang about. The old man accompanying him seems to indicate that staying close to the parental home does have a positive influence on people like him.

Another category of wandering is people who refuse to realize they have died. This happens with people who are sure that death means the end of everything, or who died intensely dissatisfied, because they cannot accept they have to stop whatever they were doing. Initially, they stay in the body, perhaps they are at their funeral or cremation, then they shake the experience off, regard it as a strange dream, and merrily get cracking again. They go and sit in their study again, continue writing their book, take part in business meetings. Their experiences are an odd mixture of the physical environment they perceive, interwoven with the fantasies they produce themselves. For example, they will sit invisibly in a real meeting and imagine that every now and then someone speaks to them, that everybody listens to them, and that they have an important say in the running of things. This condition is pathological, but disturbs no one and usually is rather innocent for the deceased himself. It becomes serious when the person becomes so wrapped up in it that he more than compensates for his unsatisfying existence, and really keeps at it. His environment may gradually turn into dreamed-up surroundings without any relation to the physical environment and physical events. Then this condition develops into a kind of twilight existence.

Many examples of 'twilight existence' can be found in the literature about spiritism and out-of-body experiences. People end up in a limited, dusky world with capricious and sometimes nightmarish elements. They may wonder if this is the real world, and only vaguely realize that they have died. They just keep on dreaming, half-aware of themselves and of the surroundings. The others they meet in this condition are sometimes subjective projections and sometimes people living in the same half-conscious state. Usually they are too weak to procure lighter surroundings, so they remain in this dusky, half-isolated and half-populated domain. This condition can be compared to a long, fairly structured dream. Joan Grant gives unpleasant examples (1937). The 'vital world' Lenz describes clearly corresponds to the twilight existence: dark, dirty, ugly, and danger-ous, 'like a polluted, run-down city' (Lenz 1979: 106). The other worlds Lenz describes are also recognizable, but seem rather too patterned by religious concepts.

Someone can be well aware he is dead but may still want to stay in the physical world. This is the condition of 'haunting'. One tries to communicate with incarnated people, to manifest oneself via them, and to have experiences which are as earthly as possible. This can result in spiritual contacts, poltergeists, and other mediumistic phen-omena, and sometimes in taking advantage of the mediumistic ac-cessibility of people who are sleeping, drugged, ill, or otherwise. An important subcategory of this death state is described more usually in the esoteric literature: people who are so attached to pleasures and addictions that they haunt and stimulate people who still enjoy these pleasures physically. Typical examples are drunks, gluttons, and the oversexed, and people playing the devil: brutes and sadists. These experiences are uncommon in regressions. Presumably, such people have no interest in regressions and will have fairly large blocks to reliving such experiences. Only rigid methods, like Hubbard's for example, which force people to confront their experiences and feel responsible for them, result in such stories.

A remigrant describes herself as a discarnate who apparently tries to repeat her past pleasures by bringing a married couple to more and more intense perversities. The woman gets pregnant, but she keeps on inciting the couple, so that the foetus is hurt. She wants to kill the child. She enters the body herself, lives for 14 years and then dies while riding a horse wildly. Even after this her fury has not yet spent itself (Hubbard 1958).

People who are fairly self-aware and are able to disengage them-selves well but have picked up strong dogmatic views about life after death can end up in the condition they had expected. They enter a 'dream existence', a state more like a lucid dream than a common dream. As many conditions after death are determined by the human consciousness itself, autism or even solipsism are the ultimate dangers. 'Some spirits get thought-bound like birds get egg-bound' (*The Boy Who Saw True*, Spearman ed. 1953: 105). Devout, narrow-minded spirits and fanatics come into their own little heaven in this way, at best with a few fellow believers (if their images correspond sufficiently and their relationships are strong enough). Once in a while someone's feelings of guilt and fear lead him into a real traditional pitch-and-sulphur Christian hell.

Wambach gives another example of a dream existence. After his death in a prehistoric South American incarnation, someone experiences himself flying in the sky above the jungle. He lived in a culture where it was believed that the soul became a bird after death. Two others reported a death in old Peru, where the spiritual sun was worshipped as a god. Both experienced standing in a golden spray of light after their death (Wambach 1978: 149–50).

Our condition after death, therefore, can contain many dream-like elements. What we experience depends much more on what we want to see and can see than on our life here. The perception of the environment and of ourselves depends predominantly on what we make of it. The mixture of objective and subjective in this 'psycho-plastic' environment is an essential aspect of our discarnate condition.

'Complete awakening' is a calm and liberating experience. You are glad to leave your body, perhaps glance back at it, but your heart goes out to the people you know from the past who have died earlier. With a profound feeling of recognition, home-coming, and happiness you join them in a shining, often park-like environment and depart from this physical world.

A remigrant experiences herself as the wife of a magistrate in a provincial town at the beginning of the French Revolution. An excited crowd drags them out of their home, kills her husband and takes her two children, a boy and a girl, to be put to work as serfs. She herself is put out on the street without anything. She has lost her senses, is incapable of doing anything, and wanders on the road. In the next years she is a tramp, drinks heavily, and is abused until she is too worn out and ugly even for that. Her only human moments are when she thinks of her husband and children, and feels pangs of pain in her heart. Later, she is dying by the side of the road. A man kicks her to see if she is still alive, but she no longer cares. Then, all of a sudden, she feels incredibly relieved and is out. She sees the shining figure of her husband and they embrace each other long and speechlessly, feeling consolation and healing. All her present life, without realizing it, she has worked at a successful synthesis of being a *grande dame* and a simple, hard-working woman.

Crookall's work provides the framework to interpret the differences between death experiences. With complete awakening, the psychic body leaves the etheric shell almost immediately. With passing away, the psychic body is presumably too weak or too underdeveloped to disengage itself from the stronger vehicle of vitality. Self-suggestion can amplify this: you know you are dead and therefore no longer experience anything. All death experiences where somebody remains more or less attached to a place or to the earth, like hanging about, wandering, and haunting, indicate that the vehicle of vitality has not been cast off or only partially so. The same is true for the deceased who end up in the twilight existence. If people wander around, and do not realize they have died, the etheric body may nevertheless be largely disintegrated. Only a minimal 'diving suit' is left to maintain contact with the material world. In conscious awakening, the psychic body is liberated; in passing away, it remains immersed in the vehicle of vitality; and in all dream-like situations, the psychic body perceives its surroundings through the filters of the vehicle of vitality.

The role of intermission in the reincarnation cycle

The different post-mortem and prenatal experiences are related to each other. People who awaken completely make real contact with other deceased. Experiences discussed in the previous chapter, such as deliberating with others and receiving advice from others, presuppose complete awakening. People who dreamed experience birth as an involuntary natural process: they are sucked in, carried in, or feel a wind. Those who have simply passed away and slept do not remember any prenatal existence. People who haunted may be aware of entering a body. Those who wandered will first have to become aware of their condition, or they will get more and more sleepy and observe, with vague surprise, that they are inside a new child. Often, wandering souls instinctively look for a living body, because of their sense of loss.

What implications do these different types of death experiences have for the reincarnation process? The main function of complete awakening is that the past life can be evaluated and the coming life can be prepared for, by conferring with others, receiving counselling, guidance, and sometimes support. According to Whitton (1986), people are helped to evaluate their past life and receive recommendations for their next by a Judgement Board, usually of 3, sometimes of 4 members, and up to 7 judges.

When someone is aware of himself in between lives, he continues to live and to learn and to meet others. Edgar Cayce gives the example of a couple who reincarnated as husband and wife again and again (Cerminara 1950). The man was dominating and the woman servile and submissive. In her most recent intermission, the woman finally developed her independence, so she was able to break out of this vicious circle. Discarnate learning is based on incarnate experiences, and leads to motives and plans for the coming incarnation.

On the other hand, passing away is a natural consequence of a self-awareness still too weak to maintain itself out of a body. Many people can only experience themselves because they feel themselves, see themselves in the mirror, hear themselves speak, and are approached by others. You realize you exist because you bump into things, feel pain somewhere, get tired, are kissed, or receive a tax assessment. All of this is gone when you die. A positive function of passing away lies in the swig of forgetfulness, being able to start afresh.

The conditions in between passing away and awakening are more complex, and usually pathological. The main consequence of hanging about is that nothing is worked off, nothing is prepared, and the next life takes place fairly close to the location of the last death. The dream life, or wandering, can digest the past life to some extent, but provides no preparation and leads to a new incarnation close to a location of the past one, with a fairly large chance of being born in a family related to friends or relatives of the past life. The same is true for the condition I disrespectfully called haunting, but which can be peaceful and comfortable. In this case, choice of parents is conscious.

In the psychodramatic conditions of twilight existence and pseudo-existence psychic peculiarities determine the area of experience. This means that they are close to being solipsistic and, for outsiders, autistic. Pseudo-existence is largely a compensation. People experience what they want to experience, as a gratification. The good side of it is that it helps healing. Someone who was cold feels wonderfully warm. Someone who was destitute is surrounded by comfort and luxury. Someone who was imprisoned roams about freely in beautiful, natural scenery and in interesting, exotic cities. Someone who was sickly and weak feels heroically strong and healthy. The other side of it is avoidance of further development and challenge. A vacation is fine, but after a long vacation it can become more and more difficult to return to work.

Sometimes the twilight existence can be remedial, spontaneous, or planned. Joan Grant provides a few striking examples (Grant 1937). When someone has tortured others in many lives and after his death is still impervious to the misery he caused, a forced rehabilitation is called for. Experience is the best teacher. To experience torture, or to see those dearest to you being tortured, makes it more difficult afterwards to remain indifferent to the suffering of others, to forget to see them as fellow humans. Does this mean that each torturer has to be tortured in his next life? This would cause an endless cycle. Therefore, an alternative is to shut someone in the illusion that he is being tortured during a twilight existence, until the lesson is learned. With stubborn, callous people, this can take a pretty long time: years, decades, or longer. This long duration is because experiences without a body make a shallower and less lasting impression than physical experiences. They work with fine sandpaper and smooth with a fine plane. Such situations remind me of the story by Roald Dahl (one of his few true stories) about the man who found the famous Mildenhall treasure. He does not want to notify the authorities about the enormous treasure, buys a carton of bottles of silver polish, and gets to work on the accumulated oxidation of sixteen centuries. After more than sixteen weeks of polishing one plate, the first glimmer of silver appears. For two years, he spends every evening polishing, but he gets there (Dahl 1977).

One example of such a lengthy, repetitious 'engraving experience' is that of a man who seems to have performed vivisection on babies and infants, sometimes while their mothers had to look on. After his death he finds himself in a grey, volcanic landscape as a screaming, crying child who is dehydrated and starving, thrown on to a hard, uneven stone table and with his own screaming ringing in his ears. He sees a monstrous man with razor-sharp claws bend over him and grin at him sadistically. He feels flames leaking out of the face, and feels the deep cuts of the dagger-like claws slice him to pieces and tear him apart. When he loses consciousness, he finds himself in the arms of his mother again, screaming with thirst and hunger, is torn away and the scene begins anew. Apparently, this surgeon was doing 'research' on the consequences of hunger and dehydration on the tissues of small children. After many years, this situation changes. Now, he experiences himself as the mother. The same scene takes place but in a hot, dry cave without an exit. The mother feels spent, physically and psychically wasted, and has desperately to watch her child being taken away and torn open. Again and again. These two situations together last more than fifteen years, only interrupted by short periods of unconsciousness.

Then he sees himself once again as a man. A spread of heather with a narrow path leads through dark woods. The sky is sombre and oppressive and a low, sallow light gives a surrealistic shine to the scene. A poorly dressed woman walks on the path with a shawl covering her head. Frightened and whimpering, she walks bent over, pressing her young child against her breast. He himself walks behind her, naked and empty-handed. The frightening oppression becomes more and more intense, until a roaring monster attacks the woman and the child. The only thing he can do is to attempt to defend the woman by throwing himself in between the mother and the monster. His attempt is in vain and he is torn apart in terrible pain. He realizes his helplessness and powerlessness until he loses consciousness. Immediately, he feels himself behind the woman again and the frightening oppression increases once more. This is repeated over and over again. Then, after an eternity, as an incomprehensible grace, somebody behind him whom he cannot see, puts a simple cape around his shoulders and gives him a white wooden staff. He has the vague impression that, as time goes on, the staff will harden and his clothes will become more protective, and after another eternity, he will reach the end of this road with the woman and the child.

The duration of the nightmares is not because of punishment, but results from the relation between the hardness and thickness of the cape on his etheric body and the polishing effect of the (purely psychical) experience. Luckily, twilight existence is seldom as extreme as this, but then the preceding deeds are seldom so extreme. I have taken this example precisely because it is so extreme, and the rehabilitating mechanism is so explicit. At the end of his road, the man will have the feeling that he puts his arm around the woman. Then, it seems he becomes one with her, then one with the child, and then he will find himself safe and warm in a new womb.

What happens to the victims of torture? The pain, along with intense feelings of despair, hate, or guilt (for example, if you have betrayed somebody), and a disturbed mind, can make it difficult for a person to come to himself after his death. However, someone who dies with an untouched mind is immediately detached from the fate of the body left behind.

A remigrant experiences being captured along with a group of others suspected of heresy and witchcraft. The prisoners' guard terrorizes them with his fearful appearance and behaviour. She, however, does not feel the least bit of fear or awe, mainly because she has heard from a reliable source that underneath all his showing off he is impotent. In the presence of the other prisoners, she laughs at him and mocks his impotence. Beside himself with fury, he drags her to a separate cell and visits her there at night. While she scorns him again, he throws her down, with her head against the floor, and chops off her arms and legs with an axe, a horrible, but still fruitless substitute for an erection. The remigrant says that standing next to her body she still laughed at this stupid man.

On the other hand, sometimes someone gets stuck in a normal, peaceful death. It turns out that a claustrophobic patient had been buried in her past life, but had identified herself so thoroughly with her body (although she was out of it) that she had the feeling she was buried alive. This can also happen with cremations. Edith Fiore found a cremation experience to be the cause of the complaints of a patient who often felt hot and nervous. Another patient, with a dislike of roses, sees and smells her own body and that of others decompose in a concentration camp, producing a sweet, rose-like scent (Fiore 1978: 230). What does this mean for the old question: burial or cremation? For people who wake up completely what happens to their body is unimportant. With a burial, some leftovers from the vehicle of vitality hover above the grave for some time and slowly disintegrate. With a cremation the connection between the etheric and the material is burned and perhaps a remnant of the etheric shell will roam about more freely. Decomposing polyps still attached to something or floating about hardly matter. However, when a person continues to identify himself with the body and projects himself into it spatially, he will have nasty experiences. However, this will be true in far fewer than 1 per cent of cases.

People who have had a traumatic death are sometimes brought into a healing pseudo-existence by others. In such a renovation a gradual shift to complete awakening is possible. Doubtless they enter their new life with less of a burden after this. Joan Grant gives a few examples of this in her books. A therapist can include this renovation during a session. People who are imprisoned, or who have imprisoned themselves in a nightmare or a negative dream, live in the illusory world of their own consciousness. A true healing environment is at most half illusory, because the growing presence of other people and increasing contact with them are essential for recovery.

Many of the other dream conditions – twilight existence, hanging about, or wandering about – are simply negative. They are forms of 'consciousness degradation', a waste of time and energy. The motley collection of spirits hanging around physical people, objects, or situations, either stupefied, or shuffling around dejectedly, are a despicable and depressing sight.

According to Netherton, a part of the fear of death can be explained because dying brings back associations of all the previous death experiences: 'It triggers replay.' This is particularly unpleasant with traumatic and unexpected deaths. However, many death experiences are so peaceful and liberating (usually dying is more pleasant than being born) that Netherton's explanation can have only partial validity. Maybe he has this impression because relatively more of his patients came up with traumatic death experiences. After all, they may repeat themselves, perhaps through restimulation. One of Netherton's patients always hung around the place of his death until the body had decomposed (Netherton and Shiffrin 1978: 59). I have also come across such repetitions.

An easy or difficult death may be related to an easy or difficult birth. After all, how someone is born is an important indicator for subsequent stress sensitivity. As dying can cause a lot of stress, a difficult and painful birth may increase the chance of a difficult and painful death.

As mentioned in chapter 4, many deceased do not believe in reincarnation. If they have any overview at all, they see a bright world above the twilight world. This world has various gradations of reality and human understanding. They can see the subsequent stages, but not the return. The writer of the diary *The Boy Who Saw True* (Spearman ed. 1953) has a discussion about this with his deceased grandfather.

Further reading

The most important author on this subject is the already frequently mentioned Robert Crookall (1961, 1965, 1966, 1967, 1978). Much has been published in the past years about the temporarily clinically dead. Of the books I am familiar with, I prefer Raymond Moody (1975, 1977) and Dave Wheeler (1977). Spiritualist testimonies on the subject are virtually unlimited. Fairly broad information can be found in Tenhaeff (1936). Other books were mentioned in the references for chapter 4.

Death experiences during regressions can be found scattered in the regression literature. Joan Grant gives many examples of pathological conditions of the deceased and the therapeutic interventions of the living (Grant 1937; Kelsey and Grant 1967). She also gives a nice example of a dream existence in which the person involved only becomes aware of his true condition after a long time (Grant 1947).

9 Unusual Experiences: The Distant Past, the Future, Non-human Experiences

This chapter reviews experiences that are less common, have exceptional contents, and, if real, have great consequences for our views of mankind. They are lower in credibility, but high in interest. If it were to turn out that they are not real memories of past incarnations, they could also lead to alternative explanations for apparent memories of normal lives.

Regressions are most interesting historically when detailing events and living conditions in important times of which we know little. As Wambach's research shows (1978), the further remigrants go back, the more primitive the circumstances. But there are exceptions. A few of her subjects went back to lives in South America in about 2000 B C describing a fairly advanced civilization. There are examples of regressions to lives in a higher civilization, much longer ago, associated with Atlantis. Edgar Cayce, too, mentions Atlantis frequently, often as the first environment in a series of lives. His statements are collected in *Edgar Cayce on Atlantis* (Cayce 1968). Even more interesting are remigrants describing lives on other planets. Next to lives in the far past or on other planets are the experiences of people who describe being an animal, or even a plant. In the same category are experiences of 'lives' as a stone or an object. In scientology even regressions as a robot occur. Then there are quasi-human experiences as a discarnate humanoid, for example as deva or nature spirit. Finally, there is the separate category of impressions of the future. Apparently not only regression but also progression is possible.

Even accepting these exceptional experiences, I have come to the tentative conclusion that a large number of them are not what they appear to be. The reader who does not believe in reincarnation but has managed to get this far anyway will be happy to observe that even my credulity has limits.

My dismissal of some experiences as evidence for past lives may be just as prejudiced as my acceptance of the other experiences. However, my interpretation of regressions is based on their analogy with other parapsychological experiences and my critical treatment is (hopefully) based on empirical and rational considerations.

Memories of the distant past, more advanced civilizations, and other planets

When remigrants regress to ever earlier lives, where do they end up? Accepted evolution theory makes us expect primitive lives, perhaps lives as apes or even less evolved animals. A common theory in spiritual circles holds that people have descended from higher civilizations like Atlantis, which, according to some, may have been colonies from other planets. The material published to date, and the regressions to past lives I am familiar with, give no definite answer. We do find primitive incarnations and indications of previous animal incarnations, as well as indications of higher civilizations, space travel, and other planets.

The theosophical concept is that human souls descended from a spiritual world into the bodies of primates and became entangled in them. Pieter Barten's experiences are interesting in this context (ten Dam 1982). Remigrants reliving their first lives see large, hairy ape-men walking on all fours. Then an etheric human soul descends into them and they walk upright for a short while. When the energy for walking upright has been spent, the soul leaves the body, rises, and has a glorious view of a beautiful landscape. It knows it comes from some higher place. It still has contact with that origin, but cannot return, 'as though there is plexiglass in between'. When it has recharged itself, it returns to the body of the primate, who walks upright for a little while again. In a next reincarnation, maybe many thousands of years later, the human soul still has to leave to recharge. This time, when the soul is out of the body, it gets no higher than the tree-tops, while the ape-man sleeps near a tree or in a cave until the recharged soul returns. The connection between the human soul and the animal body has already become more intimate. These images give us the impression that natural evolution results in bodies that are ready for human souls. Before that we apparently inhabited a spiritual world permanently.

Experiences

When going back further in time, it appears that remigrants may end up in successively more primitive human bodies, and then either seem to emerge from a discarnate state with unknown beginnings or, especially when pursuing trauma origins, with animal lives. Perhaps these are two different preceding developments for souls becoming human: one to evolve out of the spiritual kingdom and one to involve out of the animal kingdom. This presupposes the reincarnation of at least the higher animals. This idea contradicts the group-soul hypothesis of some esoteric schools, but is consistent with mediums and clairvoyants frequently observing deceased pets near their former masters. Apparently mammals dream just as humans do. Since dreams are strongly related to regression experiences and the relation between soul and body, this indirectly indicates that mammals may have individual souls. Birds have dreams lasting only about a second (Sagan 1977). Individualization may start there.

Charles Fourier (1772–1837), believed that we reincarnate on this planet, until we go to another planet en masse (Head and Cranston 1977: 291). Allan Kardec's informants say that we have lived before on other planets and may live later on others. People from advanced planets may descend to our planet to experience simpler challenges or to stimulate our development. We, in turn, may enter more advanced conditions when we have evolved far enough here. Edgar Cayce had a similar conception. Violet Shelley collected statements from eighteen readings that led her to conclude that reincarnation is not necessary. However, most of the readings only indicate that somebody does not have to return to 'this earth'. An example: 'In the present life the existing abilities can only be amplified. It is not necessary, unless the person in question wishes it, to return to this earth for experience.' The title of Shelley's book, *Reincarnation Unnecessary*, is therefore misleading (Shelley 1979).

Many remigrants report experiences in prehistoric advanced civilizations. These experiences are usually identified with Atlantis and, in at least some places and at some times, the Atlantic civilization is seen as having contact with extra-terrestrials. On the other hand, instructions to return to Atlantis lead to diverse situations. Our subconscious also appears to interpret the word 'planet' not only as an astronomical planet but also as a discarnate state or any other parallel reality. Some remigrants may go to such planets as Mars, Venus, or Uranus, but their descriptions make it absolutely clear that these planets are not the astronomical ones. These experiences may have some meaning, but should make us wary to use such names as 'Atlantis' or 'Uranus' in regression inductions, or interpret them as physical environments of past lives.

Pieter Langedijk finds experiences of higher civilizations on other planets when he sends people back to their first incarnation (Langedijk 1980). These experiences often resemble the discarnate state. A world called Uranus, after further questioning, turns out to be a non-physical environment. According to some remigrants, humans incarnated for the first time in the Atlantic age. Others remember lives in colonies of extra-terrestrial origin which stimulated the primitive people on this world in their development, often a difficult task. Barten tells of someone belonging to a space society in an Atlantic incarnation leaving his body when he inspects the development of primitive Lemurians here (TenDam 1982). Netherton assumes that most people who think they remember other planets really remember Atlantis.

Hubbard's remigrants and those of others working with similar methods often come across lives in technologically advanced societies, sometimes on other planets and in science-fiction conditions. Scientology is the earliest and probably largest source of regressions to lives on other planets, often millions or even billions of years back. So far, scientology is the only 'school' familiar with such cases. This is due to the practice of strictly dating the beginning and end of each traumatic experience. The remigrant has to give dates in 'flash-answers', and the therapist checks dates with the E-meter.

Experiences which seem Atlantic, extra-terrestrial, science-fiction-like, or discarnate, are frequent in regressions to lives more than 10,000 years back. Reliving lives in primitive human bodies is less common, but some remigrants regress to ancient primitive conditions with an apparently modern body, to the time of the dinosaurs. Desider Mockry-Meszaros, a Hungarian, painted his prehistoric memories, scenes which went back to the beginning of a barely cooled earth. Before these, he had memories of the underworld of another planet. His paintings were bought by, among others, Maxim Gorki (*New York Times*, 9 February 1930). Goldberg suggests that between 100,000 and 50,000 years ago many souls from other planets began to incarnate here (Goldberg 1982: 45). Another Von Daeniken-like story is someone who experiences himself as a labourer in the construction of a pyramid during regression. He describes the supervisors as people more than six and a half feet tall, with large heads and long fingers. They do not talk, but send out compelling telepathic signals (Goldberg 1982: 90). Regressions to the time of the pyramids seem to differ almost as much as those to the time of Jesus. Sensation seems to make recall slippery indeed.

Monroe encountered three different environments after leaving his body. The first environment was our physical world, but seen and explored without a body. The second environment was like a dream world, corresponding to the astral world of the occultists. A few times Monroe ended up in a third, parallel world. After he had passed some vertical dividing screen, he sped straight through black space for a long time, every time ending up in the same person, in what seemed another life on a somewhat comparable planet. Every time he was disoriented, because he had no idea of the occurrences just before his arrival. When he returned from time to time, he realized that the man whom he entered was getting into difficulties in his personal life and in business because of these odd periods of disorientation. The other world of his 'environment III' was real, physical, and consistent. It almost gives the impression of a parallel incarnation on another planet (Monroe 1977).

Ancient lives in the earliest human development, 'when the world was still young', are remembered just as we remember our own childhood. The regressions get more and more open and full, less and less detailed, until we reach conditions we can hardly enter, as if we have forgotten our early childhood as a human soul, as if we had a first moment in our evolution, too, of being able to hold on to real memories as an ego. Behind this border are only vague impressions and fleeting details which emerge only because of later restimulations. The oldest human incarnations are grand and spacious, but also passionate and childish.

When people go to the future, they sometimes end up in vague, elusive, hardly physical conditions. According to Kardec's informants, our last incarnations gradually turn into a permanent discarnate state. The transition from our last lives and intermissions are gradual, 'like the darkness of the night changing into the breaking of dawn'.

Helen Wambach, Leo Sprinkle and Chet Snow have progressed many hundreds of subjects to the next centuries. The results have only partially been published so far (Snow 1986b).

Non-human incarnations

Historically, one of the greatest disputes between reincarnation believers has been whether or not people return in animal bodies. In other words: is there reincarnation or metempsychosis? Regressions to animal lives are uncommon compared with those to human lives, but there are examples of spontaneous memories as well as regressions. Ian Stevenson found a few examples (1977: 7; 1983: 6, 167). Ron Hubbard gives a few examples of animal incarnations (Hubbard 1958). A psychotic girl remembers being a lion who ate a zoo-keeper. After the customary treatment of these experiences, she was cured. Another example is a remigrant who describes being thrown out of a spacecraft hovering above the ocean. A huge ray eats his body. He then experiences himself as that ray. Morris Netherton, tracking down traumatic chains, normally finds the root problem to be the traumatic injury or death of an animal. However, he found nobody backsliding to animal lives during the traumatic chains (Netherton and Shiffrin 1978: 183). According to Joe Fisher (1985: 136), many of Joe Keeton's subjects regress to animal lives, and Helen Wambach (1978) also had some subjects who found themselves on four legs.

Penkala gives the example of a Chinese slave who walks up to the governor's mother and asks her if, as a little girl, she had had a wild fox as a pet, and wore a yellow petticoat under her red and white striped dress. When she acknowledged this, he told her he had been this fox. He had run away and had lived in an old grave until a hunter killed him. After this, he met the 'Lord of the Other World' who told him he was not a sinner and should take a human body. He was reborn as a beggar and died of hunger and misery when he was twenty. After this, he appeared in front of the same Lord who said he would be a slave in a house of a prominent notable; the term slave was not beautiful, but he would not be hungry and miserable (Penkala 1972: 49).

Langedijk met an American boy who thought he had been a

hippopotamus in a past life. He appeared to have had many lives as a human and he just wanted to be this animal once to experience it (Langedijk 1980: 114). Marcia Moore came across two animal memories among many hundreds of people. One woman thought she had been a cat in a temple, and one man that he had lived as an owl (Moore 1976: 235). Lenz found 6 persons, or 5 per cent of his cases, with animal incarnations before human incarnations. His examples are an owl, another bird, a sea turtle, and a whale. According to Seth, the human soul is simultaneously incarnated in a human body and in one or more animal bodies of different species. Such parallel incarnations have never come up in regressions (although a believer in Seth might produce such impressions) (Roberts 1972).

Margot Klausner describes her oldest memory, from perhaps a 100,000 years ago, as being a kind of flower growing on a rock. It was not yet a real flower, but a more primitive plant without a stem. Instead of leaves it had a kind of moss and the petals were rough and prickly. The heart of the flower form was golden-yellow and the petals were violet. She describes herself amid many such flowers on top of a high mountain. Later, she realizes this is somewhere in Atlantis and she briefly describes the development of mankind on Atlantis. Apparently, she has had human lives in the place where she was first a flower (Klausner 1975). Experiences as plants are rare. Somebody remembered one life as a tree (Pisani 1978).

Oddly enough, 'incarnations' as stones or objects are more common. Someone feels he is a stone statue at the bottom of a stair cut out of the rock. Later, it turns out that priests have killed him in a hypnotic ceremony. He feels himself being stuck inside the stone next to these stairs. He is only freed when earthquakes and erosion burst and pulverize the stairs. A remigrant describes a life as a prominent and lusty Egyptian who dominates many people and liquidates his opponents. The priests seem interested in this forceful personality and manipulate him by hypnotic rituals. During another ritual they kill him and put his soul in a ceremonial lamp with the instruction 'to light forever the gates for the Lord of Darkness'. His consciousness fades inside the lamp. The next thing he knows is the lamp shattering somewhere in sixteenth-century France. Apparently his unconscious state lasted 4,800 years (Hubbard 1958). Scientology also tells of people pulled out of their body with science-fiction-type hypnosis machines and subsequently being put in a bottle or vase, or implanted in a robot.

Some people originally may have been 'devas', angel-like nature spirits who apparently develop parallel to our evolution. They would see people, but hardly notice them. Allegedly, some devas take a human body, perhaps out of interest or sympathy, perhaps even because of a personal relation with somebody. These ideas, popularized by theosophy, appear speculative, but quite a number of regressions seem to indicate pre-existence as a deva. People who may originally have been devas tend to feel differently about life and death. They are less attached to life here and have less fear of death. They are rather idealistic, sensitive to nature and beauty, and with a tendency to clairvoyance, without affinity to things like politics and business. They are the kind of people the Germans call *Schoengeister*. The author of *The Boy Who Saw True* (Spearman ed. 1953) describes seeing a deva in someone's aura, and later his guide tells him he was once a deva himself. However strange, many regressions support this theory. It is possible that there are also more primitive nature spirits that can plug into our evolution. There is sporadic evidence for this.

Finally, there are the interesting examples of 'light people', people who experience themselves before their first life on earth as abstract, geometric energy beings. Pressure is put on them to incarnate on earth (Goldberg 1982: 81). I would refer such things to the land of fairy tales if I didn't know of similar experiences from the practices of colleagues and my own practice. Wambach had similar findings in this direction (Wambach 1979: 50, 58). Some things Goldberg says on the subject hardly seem plausible. It seems to me that here we are at the present borders of our imagination.

Identification instead of incarnation

Once a soul has become human, can it still have animal lives? Such an evolutionary degradation seems unlikely, but experiences as animals are incidentally reported. However, there may be a more likely explanation for this than animal reincarnations. Chapter 8 gave many examples of people remaining stuck in the material environment by etheric or mental bonds. They awake incompletely, which prevents liberation and meeting other people. Such people often hang about or wander around, dimly perceiving the physical world.

Apparently, they can enter, at least spatially, into living people who remain unaware of this. They put themselves in the same spot in three-dimensional space, but a distance remains in the fourth dimension, the 'throughth'. There is no reciprocal contact, as in obsession.

Apparently people may also feel themselves to be in objects, sometimes identifying themselves hypnotically with the object until the object is broken. The example of the man who is plagued by feelings of guilt and rejection indicates that someone may be stuck without a specific material counterpart.

None of this is reincarnation, where one is born into a physical organism with senses, nerves, and everything else; an organism in which one is self-aware and active. A soul stuck in a lamp or a statue is psychotic. Often it got there through some 'black magic', to induce fear and awe in people. Animals also react to such haunted objects. Similarly, someone floating around aimlessly may be attracted to any physical entity seemingly offering shelter. He may attach himself to a fox, a bird, or whatever animal he feels an affinity for, but also a living person. He may follow the animal or person around, identify himself with it and even make some contact ('crawl into the aura'). With animals this is only partially possible, and is often pathological, unless it is a conscious choice as an educational or sometimes therapeutic experience (an extreme form of vacation). The story of the man who falls into the sea and is eaten by a ray proves how pathological this may be. Subsequently, he is the ray. This is no incarnation, but identification.

Interestingly enough people who remember a 'life' as an animal, which clearly was a psychotic identification, are cured of present psychological problems when this experience is worked through and 'erased'. I have already given the example of the psychotic girl who remembers a life as a lion who eats a zoo-keeper. We have to be on our guard against seeing this as the first cause of the psychosis. Presumably she was not the lion, but the zoo-keeper, psychotically trying to come to terms with the experience, like the man with the ray. She had to have a pre-existing aggressive, animal self-image. Through such a self-image, she could have been pulled towards a similar emotional occurrence and subsequently have identified herself with it. Either she hated the zoo-keeper, hung around him, and inspired him to act carelessly, and through the emotion and responsibility identified herself with the lion; or she felt the tension of her own more general hate-guilt feelings and identified herself with these. It may be more specific: perhaps she was torn to pieces by a lion some time before, for example in an arena, and is left with so much hate that she wants to cause it to happen to others. And so on. Anyway, some psychosis was the cause of this identification.

Margot Klausner's experience as a flower-like plant can also be better explained as the identification of a discarnate person who remained attached to the physical world than as a real incarnation. It is a self-hypnosis apparently difficult to rectify. Self-created surroundings are a dime a dozen among the deceased. The only extraordinary thing about the cases here is that they do not create the surroundings themselves but perceive the material environment and imagine themselves to be a part of it as an object, a plant, an animal, or a person.

Progressions to the future

Albert de Rochas, who was the first to reach past lives by means of regression, discovered progression more or less by chance. He sat the remigrant down in front of him, made magnetic passes with his left hand along the length of the body from the head down, while he held his right hand on the forehead. This caused a magnetic trance and, with silent or spoken suggestions, a return in time, age regression. To bring the remigrant back to the present, de Rochas used magnetic passes across the body, where he moved both hands horizontally, from the middle of the body out to the sides. If he continued this long enough, people ended up in the future.

Eugénie, a subject of de Rochas, was the first who was brought into progression. She arrived two years into the future and showed signs of pregnancy, and shortly afterwards, signs of drowning. De Rochas quickly brought her to two years later, and again she was pregnant. When he asked where she was she answered, 'On the water'. De Rochas thought she had started 'tripping' and brought her back. Two years later, she had a child from her lover and shortly afterwards threw herself desperately into the Yser. However, she was rescued in time. In January 1909, she had a second child, on a bridge over the Yser, where she had suddenly gone into labour. She was indeed 'on the water' (Shirley 1924: 140).

In Germany in the 1950s Franz Turni hypnotized people as part of an experiment with reporters. He put the people into a deep trance and let them forecast what they would do in the next few days. These forecasts turned out to be correct, even when unlikely and unexpected (Muller 1970: 146). Of course, this procedure is only valid when the subjects forget what happened during hypnosis, and when post-hypnotic suggestions are ruled out.

Glaskin gives the example of somebody who used the Christos procedure and ultimately ended up in his own life several years hence rather than in a past life (Glaskin 1974: 76). His dress was a mixture of things he possessed at present and things he did not. The season was summer, whereas during the regression it was winter. He said he could see every blade of grass as if it were individually enlarged. He did not recognize the field, but he thought it was somewhere in western Australia, where the experiment took place. He was 21 years old, but in his regression he was 17. He could not climb over the fence around the field and apparently felt unhappy. The counsellor had him visualize going into the sky again and landing anew. This time he landed on the beach and was walking barefoot. He said that he was now 27 years old and that his name was John, although in reality he was called Stephen. He felt himself becoming sadder and sadder, so the therapist let him go into the air again and return for the third time. The third time he landed in the cemetery of a neighbourhood in his own city. Along with about fifty others, he was attending his mother's funeral. He recognized his brother and sisters, his father and his stepfather. The funeral 'had taken place, but not yet'. He said he was 24 years old and was wearing a black suit he had bought in England.

Stephen had never been to England, but was planning to go in the coming year. He was far from happy with the prospect of the funeral. He did actually go to England, and after eighteen months had to return suddenly because his mother had contracted a dangerous spinal disease. Intentionally, he did not buy a black suit. After his return, his mother improved. She recovered and they had a wonderful relationship.

Pieter Barten, a Dutch therapist, has done progressions up to about the year 4040, but warns of the great uncertainty in dating future images (TenDam 1982). Goldberg apparently works regularly with progressions (Goldberg 1982: 152ff.). According to him, the images shift suddenly in progressions to future lives.

In the bulletin of the Association for Past-Life Research and Therapy (May/June 1982), Dion Dolphin writes that during her past years as a therapist she has asked many people to go to the twenty-first century to see how things are going. They do this in what she calls a 'slightly altered consciousness'. She concludes that people can see their future as easily as their past and that the images of the future correspond with each other. Based on this, she knows what the twenty-first century will be like. I will give you the picture. Hold on to your hats.

People will have learned to stop fighting. There is no money in the way we know it now. There will no longer be separate nations, although there is still a great number of separate cultures. Most cities are much smaller. People move around in amphibic minibuses, perhaps in the air. Groups of people and children travel around the planet and stop for a while at specific cultures to learn from them. When such a group stops travelling for a while, they land on a farm and run the farm while those who have run the farm up until then, can travel. Of course, there is space-travel in space-ferries to space-cities, but the most important thing remains that people tend the earth, garden and restore our Earth to its original purpose. There may be some difficult times towards the end of the twentieth century, but immediately afterwards a golden age of love, peace, joy and harmony begins.

The author of all this beautiful prose does this as part of a research programme in the context of her academic (!) studies. Besides this, and this explains more, she is an initiated priestess in some 'Order of Melchizedek'.

De Rochas' and Glaskin's experiments are interesting because they indicate that progressions may be meaningful without being an accurate picture of future occurrences. In *Winged Pharaoh* Joan Grant writes an analogy consistent with this notion:

The past is fixed, that which has happened cannot be changed. But every action changes a future which is fluid and can be modified in a past that is lasting. Your next day, or the next life you will be born in, is like your mirrored image in a pool. At any moment you can check what the pool of your future looks like, but through your own free will you can make storms rage over it or make waves on its peaceful surface. That is why so few forecasts bear out.

Just look at the gardener with his watering can. I can foretell that he is going to cross the courtyard without spilling anything because that is the future that his present acts are making. But if he trips, or throws down the can of his own free will, then his present future has been changed, because through his act he has brought about a different effect, and so, my forecast will not bear out. But this is an image that only few people are allowed to see, because you could then influence someone's deeds (Grant 1937: 130).

Now, just as with the gardener who begins to walk through the garden with his watering can, there may be patterns in the development of mankind which have been designed and will be worked out in more detail on the way. For this reason, people can have impressions of the future of society. Perhaps they have even designed their own personal future in it. However, Wambach's research makes it clear that many people do not even plan their coming life, let alone have they already made preparations for lives in the further future. It is questionable whether they are at all able to pick up images of this future. Dolphin's sugar-sweet twenty-first century is exceptionally nonsensical. The details of her picture show the people involved belonged to the New Age subculture after the 1960s, and probably lived in California. The picture says more about the 'Order of Melchizedek' than about the twenty-first century.

When you can look forward as well as back, then you can look back to a moment where you looked forward to the moment you looked back, or you look forward to the moment you will look back to this moment where you are looking forward. Then, time appears as a folded dimension. I have not found this in the literature, although one thing comes close. Edward Ryall is one of the few people who has a complete memory of a past life (Ryall 1974). He remembers that on the coast a gypsy woman foretells him that later he will come back sometime and will be surprised how many changes time has wrought. It is 301 years later when he returns to this same place and indeed is astounded by the difference.

Provisional conclusions

This chapter has discussed extremely interesting empirical material, but it is hardly sufficient in quality and quantity to warrant important theoretical consequences. The preliminary conclusions, taking experiences other than reincarnation memories into consideration, are more or less as follows:

1 When somebody goes further and further back in time he ends up in primitive conditions, in more advanced civilizations, or in less physical states. Some therapists find the initial trauma of a series to be the injury or death of an animal. Obviously this happens with people who end up in more primitive conditions when they go further back.

   Perhaps there are multiple lines of evolving into humans. If there is only one line, then the most likely hypothesis is that there has been evolution as well as involution, and that discarnate souls incarnated in ape-like bodies. The second most likely hypothesis is that human souls are metamorphoses of souls who have gone through a large number of animal incarnations.

2 Therapists should avoid instructions to go to Atlantis or Lemuria, or to other planets, since such indications are probably open to multiple interpretations in the subconscious. Each label not corresponding to the concrete experience of the remigrant is risky. For example, when asking someone to go to the 'twenty-first century', the subconscious could interpret this as the twenty-first century from now, or the twenty-first century according to a different calendar.

   Although special states of consciousness generate valuable and highly interesting information, and may give us confidence in the seemingly unbounded potential of man, it remains a field which is neither transparent nor familiar. The experiences of the human subconscious (and conscious) teach us that you have to instruct it just as carefully as a computer, otherwise unintended leaps can occur.

3 It is difficult using the literature available, to form an opinion about the value and the reliability of science-fiction-like experiences. They occur too frequently to dismiss them as imagination; but they occur too frequently in a light trance via imagination and visualization, and too seldom in deeper trances via hypnosis, to convince readily. Probably many people have unconscious memories of a civilization with space travel. However, the protocols published to date are still too weak to consider such an important conclusion as confirmed.

4 It seems that non-human incarnations may simply be identifications of people who died incompletely. As working through and erasing such experiences often has therapeutic value, such identifications are probably undesirable and often pathological.

5 Impressions of the future seem possible, but apparently these impressions are based on a total extrapolation of the past, considering people's tendencies, resolutions, and plans. These impressions are more like those of an architect who knows what a building is going to be like than an actual observation of the future of that house. Probably the future is only fixed to the extent that the past determines it and our plans designate it. Next to individual life plans, there is probably an overall plan for human development.

Further reading

Hubbard's book (1958) is riddled with extraordinary experiences: in the ancient past, on other planets, in pure science-fiction conditions, in animal lives, in attachment to objects. Perhaps this results from his selection (although his examples vary considerably in quality and are summed up carelessly, hardly implying selection), perhaps it results from the method, perhaps also from expectations within scientology. Finally, people with such experiences may be attracted to scientology.

Other examples are scattered in the literature, although Marcia Moore (1976) and Pieter Langedijk (1980) mention a relatively large number. Perhaps such stories are less common under deep hypnosis, or other authors are more critical or more afraid of criticism. Finally, there are Edgar Cayce's books (especially 1968), cited earlier.

PART III   *Conclusions*

10 Causal Connections Between Lives

Even when we have no direct recollection of a past life, we still exhibit memory of past incarnations in our idiosyncrasies, our preferences, and our characteristics (Van Ginkel 1917: 60). The same is true for our relationships: 'Love is an eloquent witness.' And I add, 'so is hate'. Our past lives stir especially in our emotions, our fears, our habitual reactions and problems, barely beneath the surface of consciousness. And with most people, hardly anything except the right mental and emotional key is needed to make these past lives surface.

This and the next two chapters analyse the connections between lives, based on the available experiences. These connections are normally loosely described as karma. Karma is a difficult topic. The speculations about it are rather diverse and usually abstract, providing no individual examples. The empirical material presents a confusing picture. Edgar Cayce hardly ever gave information about past lives without pointing out the karmic relations As chapter 4 illustrated, most sensitives and psychics give information containing a lot of karma. On the other hand, Ian Stevenson found, to his surprise, hardly any indications for karmic relations in the spontaneous memories of children (Stevenson 1975: 34, 65). Helen Wambach found karmic obligations in 30 per cent of her group. Another 30 per cent felt they had been free in the design of their life, and the rest were unclear or somewhere in between (Wambach 1979: 42, 75).

These differences probably result from the different groups of people Cayce, Stevenson, and Wambach worked with. Stevenson researched children who had ended a life – often prematurely – with only a few years intermission, and a fairly short distance from their present birthplace. Cayce advised people with psychic and physical problems. He moved into past lives when someone's present fate and present suffering remained incomprehensible within the framework of the present life. Wambach's subjects were people interested in reincarnation and curious as to whether they would be able to remember. I will analyse these differences later.

I distinguish three kinds of connections between lives: causal patterns, educative and therapeutic patterns, and free patterns. These three kinds of relation are not necessarily mutually exclusive, but the difference between them is fundamental for an understanding of the transition between lives. This chapter begins with a reflection on the concept of karma. Chapter 12 discusses the relationship between the three connections.

The natural and moral interpretations of karma

In the current views of karma there are three fundamental antitheses:
- determination versus influence
- natural law versus jurisdiction
- decisiveness of actual deed versus moral intent.

The first fundamental antithesis is that between karma as determining everything versus karma as one influence among others, such as heredity, astrological constellations, extra-sensory influences, coincidence, and free will. We come across the deterministic view of karma mainly in the early theosophical literature where karma is praised in mystical and abstract prose (Anderson 1894). Anderson is ecstatic about karma because it frees us from indigestible theological notions about original sin, or the Redeemer, or the crucifixion, and gives us a spiritual law permeating everything and makes all ostentatious injustice comprehensible.

Karmic justice means reaping what we sow, picking the fruits of our own efforts. However, this is only meaningful when we ourselves have some responsibility and some choice. A deterministic view of karma gets us into the wheel of predestination, reducing human history to a heaven-and-hell show in a puppet disco. A real difference remains between views seeing karma as a major influence on one's fate and those seeing it as a minor influence.

The second fundamental antithesis is that between karma as a spiritual law of nature versus karma as evaluation or jurisdiction. An intermediate position is that the consequences of our acts naturally form a karma fund, but that allocation of karma in our future lives depends on evaluation or even free will. We can postpone or roll the debt over, but we cannot cancel it. Which karma is worked out in which order depends on the evaluation of the karmic judges (among whom we ourselves always are) and the karmic administrators. The theosophical view remains in a roughly half-way position: karma is regulated by the Lipika, or Lords of Karma, beings so powerful and objective that they work as a spiritual natural law. Concrete conceptualization of such views is difficult. Adherents of such thoughts assume that this is because the nature of the subject is beyond our natural understanding. Such an argument can never be disproved, is self-sufficient, and therefore should be regarded with the greatest reserve. For a non-believer the assumption of a Lipika is identical with the classical mythological personifications of natural powers and natural laws.

The third fundamental antithesis lies in the views about what determines the karmic result: the actual act, as the Jainists believe, or the intent. According to the Jainists, it makes no difference whether, by opening the window, you have caused someone to fall off the ladder and die by accident, or out of vengeance, or to lay your hands on the inheritance. Most views on karma put greater emphasis on the intent behind an act. For many, karma is itself reward or punishment for good or bad intentions, for well-meant or ill-meant effort, or for laziness. According to Rudolf Steiner, karma is a moral, spiritual world order, complementary to the causal, physical world order. He therefore believes in the moral position. The question of how much of the intent should be included in the evaluation of an act is naturally as old as the question of ethics. For example, Abelard became famous because of his interest in intention in the moral evaluation of an act. If the actual act is decisive for karma, then it is a law of nature as well, albeit via a paranormal link.

A deterministic view of karma will coincide with the notion of karma as a natural law, and may coincide with the factual as well as the moral view. After all, moral reactions are natural to us. If somebody pushes you over by accident, this may irritate you, but you react differently when you realize it was done on purpose. To the extent that our acts have consequences for other people, there may be a natural law even while moral aspects play a part, since to make moral judgements is part of human nature. On the other hand, the view of karma as jurisdiction can only correspond with a non-deterministic view and a view where intention is more decisive.

Conclusions

The classical Greeks had a nuanced view of the determination of fate. They had three goddesses of fate who wove peoples' destinies: Adrasteia, Nemesis, and Themis. Adrasteia decreed the natural consequences of acts. With her, there were neither providence nor redemption. Adrasteia corresponds to karma as natural law. Nemesis decreed the rewards for good deeds and the punishment for bad ones. In our terms, she corresponds to the jurisdictive view of karma. Third was Themis who decreed the correction of consequences of acts. She constantly tried to restore order and harmony, to heal, and to educate. She corresponds to karma viewed as a corrective and therapeutic force.

The karmic repercussions of an immoral act have Adrasteia putting the burden of the immediate consequences on us. We then may have to undergo Nemesis' karmic punishment, and Themis arouses the desire in us to make up for this act. Our capacity to place ourselves more or less under the influence of either Nemesis or Themis is consistent with this subtle Greek view. If we want to compensate for our imperfect deeds, we place ourselves under Themis as it were, and Nemesis' force is less necessary. When Themis is busier, Nemesis gets more of a rest. They work in a kind of job-share system. Adrasteia stays constant, she has full tenure.

Chapter 2 saw various reincarnation philosophies distinguishing between people who have to come back for karmic reasons, and the reincarnation of those who do not have to return but do so of their own free will. The Ismaelites for example, distinguish *tanasukh*, the average reincarnation, and *rijat*, the return of spiritual leaders. To assume that reincarnation may be more or less obligatory or voluntary is consistent with Wambach's results.

I distinguish four levels in the reasons given for reincarnation (a particular incarnation may contain a mixture of levels):

1 *Natural*: Incarnating according to the laws of nature. The reincarnating soul does not communicate with counsellors and guides and cannot influence his return. This may happen when someone falls asleep after his death and experiences nothing before his birth except the 'vacuum cleaner sensation'. Without guidance this is a wholly natural process.

2 *Educational*: Incarnation based on karmic obligations and a desire for lessons in life. Here, people receive guidance, sometimes force-

ful, and to some extent have a life plan. A person's say in the matter varies from little ('detention work') to substantial ('choice of essay subject').

3 *Volitional*: Incarnation on the basis of personal interests and resolutions, with a personal life plan. The individual has complete say in the matter and chooses his own guides if he wants them ('promotion research').

4 *Mission*: Incarnation based on a greater or lesser contribution to the development of society. Here, the life plan contributes to a larger plan. The classic Buddhistic notion on this score is the existence of the Bodhisattvas, the Lords of Compassion who return to help advance mankind out of free will. According to Mahayana Buddhism the Bodhisattvas appear as world teachers according to a fixed schedule. The Ismaelites share this notion. They use the terms *hukul* or *burut*: the periodic return of the perfected. Among Wambach's subjects, mission considerations are sometimes dominant in ordinary active and well-meaning people who lack the aureole of a world teacher. Apparently voluntary return is less of an exception and less of a sacrifice than suffering would-be world escapists believe.

Examples of karma within the present life

The following examples illustrate the difference between causal relations, educational relations, and voluntary relations. I divide causal patterns, that is, relations according to natural law, into retention, repercussion, and fruition. *Retention* or persistence is merely continuity. If we have a fat nose, we will have it for the rest of our life unless we undergo plastic surgery or are involved in an accident. Once we can read French, this ability stays with us as long as we read French every so often, do not experience brain damage, or become senile. Examples of *repercussion* are youth traumas: experiences from our childhood continuing to play an 'underground' role for the rest of our life. Unlike retention, these experiences undergo important metamorphoses. If a child catches his parents in a sado-masochistic act, he will not keep catching them at it. Neither does it imply that he will imitate their behaviour; this is no simple retention. The consequences of the experience may be diverse: a thwarted desire to live because he sees the society in which he has to grow up as a capricious, inhumane, and frightening puppet show; a tendency to introversion or vulnerability; he may exhibit sadism by twisting the legs off spiders and flies. The reactions to traumas differ greatly. A typical repercussion is like a piece of the past lying in one's stomach undigested. A 'hangover' is an example of a temporary repercussion.

Fruition is like the relation between sowing and reaping. The fruition of experiences produces a new result. If you subject yourself to an authoritative father, you may remain submissive as an adult, even to your deceased father. This is retention or persistence. If the father's authority resulted in fear, and this in turn to an inferiority complex and psychosomatic problems, then this is a repercussion. Fruition here could mean that you had an authoritative father, internalized this authority, and transformed it into your own authority. Fruition entails ripening and metamorphosis.

Put differently: retention or persistence takes experiences and abilities along unchanged, repercussion is based on carrying undigested, haunting experiences along, and fruition is based on digesting and transforming experiences. Retention, repercussion, and fruition are three causal relationships in human lives.

Next to this are the 'educational patterns', which include the influences of guidance, upbringing, therapy, and correction. If someone has to change schools because of his behaviour, is sent to a youth custody centre, is banned, or put in jail, then these are not simple cause-and-effect relationships, but interventions from evaluating second or third parties, intended to punish or reward someone, to advance his development, or to bring him around to different views. We may also do such things to ourselves. We may punish ourselves and educate ourselves. Every experience we consciously seek, all changes we make growing up, are also educational. Educational relationships include all the ordeals, tests, and masterpieces others require of us or we require of ourselves.

Free patterns include all choices in our life where we choose according to our own preferences and interests. As these choices are seldom completely arbitrary but related to what we have done before, I use the word 'patterns'. Apparently, causal, educational, and free patterns also play a role in between our lives. The rest of this chapter will limit itself to causal relationships: retention, repercussion, and fruition between lives.

Retention: continuity through lives

I will give examples of retention from the literature and from experiences with regressions in four areas: abilities, tendencies, looks, and relations.

People may take talents with them from one life to the next. Arbitrary examples from the literature are: organization skills, debating, singing (see the nice example in Penkala 1972: 176), and being a good puppeteer (Fielding 1898: 336; Muller 1970: 44). A less common but notable retention of an ability is glossolalia, speaking a language from a past life. Examples of this are Shanti Devi who could speak the Muttra dialect without learning it, an American woman speaking Coptic, an English sports instructor speaking ancient Egyptian, and Therese Neumann (known for the appearance of blood on her hands and feet on Good Friday) who spoke a few sentences of Armenian. The Armenian may have been (pious) deceit, since it is possible easily to memorize a few sentences.

Child prodigies are examples of particular intellectual and musical ability. Intelligence and intellectual abilities develop in the course of lives, although there may be considerable differences between one life and the next. An exceptional intellect does not appear out of the blue and it grows out of the brain mass inherited from the parents just as little as a fantastic command of the violin grows out of a violin received from the parents. Undoubtedly such gifts stimulate, especially when the parents play the violin well themselves, but there is no substitute for practice.

Probably without exception paranormal abilities are the result of temple training in past lives. Meditation, imagination, out-of-body experiences, clairvoyance, telepathy, every form of sensitivity, mediumship, or any other paranormal gift, can be traced back in regression to one or more lives with lengthy training.

A second area of retention is that of tendencies. Emotions and emotional attitudes may be carried over from one life to the next. Self-confidence and feelings of inferiority, extroversion or introversion, mystic tendencies or common sense, may be brought along from past lives; so may all kinds of special preferences and interests, such as a strong desire for particular kinds of food (Fiore 1978: 6), an interest in architecture, or a predilection for natural gardens, etc.

Also, we may take important aspects of our mentality with us from past lives. One man became more tolerant after the Crusades, when he discovered those 'heathens' to be more civilized than the heavily armed, half-organized ragamuffins that came to devastate the Holy Land. That experience created a tolerance that lasted in subsequent lives. Another, after a similar experience, was left with a healthy distrust of external religious display as a measure for inner religious quality.

Less pleasant tendencies, too, continue to have influence. A Samaritan is maltreated by Jews and develops a hatred of them. He takes his anti-Semitism with him to a following reincarnation. Someone with a hatred of blacks turns out to have been taken prisoner as a Phoenician sailor, and to have suffered for a long time as a galley slave under brutal, dark-skinned overseers. Some authors carry things too far, explaining anti-Semitism and the like as always resulting from past lives. Just one step further and the Nazi concentration camps are a karmic correction for stubborn and arrogant Jews who considered themselves the chosen people. Sociological and socio-psychological explanations are more likely when it comes to mass events. These examples indicate only that at least some events have specific causes from past lives.

Routines, too, may come from past lives: food preparation, housekeeping, religious acts (Stevenson 1966). The same is true of trivial habits: scratching one's head, twining one's hair around one's fingers, plucking at a shoulder, biting nails, rubbing one's nose, and such. I cannot explain how and why such inane habits sometimes persist throughout lives.

The last example of tendencies continuing throughout lives is even more unpleasant than that of prejudices, namely addictions. We have a fair number of cases of alcoholism and opium addiction (for example, see Netherton and Shiffrin 1978: 94). One man takes drugs and ultimately is addicted to morphine. In his last life he was an opium addict. In the preceding life he was a child of rich Chinese parents, the servants continually giving him opium to keep him quiet. Although this situation may have karmic reasons of its own, the addiction others inflicted on the infant was carried on through subsequent lives. The behaviour of junkies or dealers recruiting other junkies may or may not have origins in past lives, but will certainly have consequences in next ones. An alcoholic patient had had in a past life a wife who locked him up in an asylum after she discovered that he was having an affair. He is shut off from everything, is terribly bored, and his only diversion is brandy. He is so efficiently turned into an alcoholic that he dies a wreck. This event probably did not come out of the blue, but again, once an addiction has started, it continues as if it were a purely natural law. Interestingly, both Joan Grant and Florence McClain give examples of addiction that started because of an insufficient dose of alcohol or morphine: Soldiers dying in great pain, craving for more alcohol or morphine (Kelsey and Grant 1967; McClain 1986).

Besides abilities and tendencies, physical features may continue. I have already given the example of birth stigmata. Racial characteristics may also be carried on to some extent, through incarnations in other races. The most susceptible part of the body is the face. I mentioned the example of Francis Lefebvre who began to remember the life of Vasco da Gama. His wife cried out immediately when she saw a painted portrait that it looked exactly like him when he was angry.

Alexandrina was the reincarnation of a sister who had died before her. Except for the hair and the eyes, which were both a bit lighter, the second Alexandrina looked exactly like the first one. There were considerable physical similarities, like hyperaemia of the left eye, eczema behind the right ear, and a slight asymmetry of the face. Naturally, there were also strong psychological similarities (Shirley 1924: 46).

Doctors are unable to discover the cause of the stomach cramps of a 49-year-old man. After concentrating for a week on the reasons for his pain, he has a lively regression with sounds and scents. He has been sentenced as a heretic and his intestines are being pulled out with glowing irons. While being sentenced he hears his name: Jan van Leyden. He is exhibited in an iron cage, still alive. His stomach cramps began after he had been looking at the monkey cage in a zoo for a long time, fascinated. He finds a portrait of Jan van Leyden and sees, among other details, the same beard he himself had when he was younger (Muller 1970: 161).

Sigurd Trier, a well-known Danish spiritualist, conducted many seances about reincarnation. He concluded that the reincarnating soul forms the face from the parental material. The result depends on the strength and the willpower of the incarnating soul (Muller 1970: 247).

The experiences of many people after death and before birth may assure us that true relationships carry over beyond birth and death. Sometimes two people are married their whole adult lives but after they have died have nothing left to say to each other and may part, never to meet again. However, people who mean something to us, to whom we feel related, whom we trust, are often people we know from past lives. Naturally, sympathy may come from agreements in opinions, preferences, and character. A sympathetic or antipathetic first impression says even less. Such impressions easily occur because of unconscious association with people we knew earlier in our life.

Homosexuality is sometimes seen as a consequence of a recent change of sex after a number of lives in the other sex. This may lead to sexual confusion and trans-sexuality: a man feeling he is a woman trapped in a male body, or a woman feeling she is a man trapped in a female body. A pertinent case is that of Paulo, the reincarnation of his sister Emilia who had taken a dose of cyanide one and a half years before Paulo was born. She was very dissatisfied with being a girl. She announced her return as a boy during a spiritist seance. The boy, however, was confused about his sex. He refused boy's clothing until he was 5, when a pair of trousers was made from a skirt of the deceased Emilia. He started to accept his sexual role, but retained a feminine identification. As an adult he did not marry and avoided the company of women (Steiger 1967: 78). Such maladaptation to the present sex may facilitate latent homosexuality but is never a cause of homosexuality. I will discuss homosexuality in the next chapter.

Repercussions: undigested experiences from past lives

This chapter will only go into this subject briefly. Chapter 16 will return to it extensively, as it is important in past-life therapy. Here we deal with general experiences of pain, fright, chronic misery, much of which is not understood or is misunderstood, and which, partially because of an untimely death, has been insufficiently worked out. Experiences remain undigested because the experience itself was wounding and overpowering, and assimilation afterwards was difficult or impossible. Insufficient digestion leads to repression or ostensible pseudo-digestion and rigid patterns of response: explanations and other semantic reactions engraved so deeply that they instantly become a character trait (Korzybski 1933). After Hubbard (1950), we call such fixed semantic reactions 'postulates'. Examples are: 'I have already tried everything. It is hopeless.'; or: 'I will never show my feelings again.'; or: 'Not me.'; or: 'I am going mad with loneliness.'

The basic trauma mechanism works the same whether the cause is in this life or a previous life. Stutterers are often afraid to be punished because of what they say. Netherton at times finds physical abuse during childhood to be the cause, and at other times punishments in past lives. Traumatic death experiences, in particular, have repercussions. First, because dying may be the end of a traumatic sequence, and second, because it often obstructs the digestion of the experience, especially in the case of incomplete dying experiences, from falling asleep up to haunting. Even when someone works out his experiences to some extent after his death, a portion may remain and be taken on to a next life. As chapter 8 has already shown, this probably has to do with substance remaining from the vehicle of vitality. Incomplete dying experiences themselves may have repercussions: agoraphobia may often be the result of a wandering soul.

The repercussions of traumatic experiences reveal themselves in psychosomatic complaints, in phobias, in complexes, in nightmares, in compulsions, and in pseudo-obsessions. The last usually happens when a whole life has remained undigested. Chapters 13 and 16 will return to pseudo-obsessions. Real obsessions also occur: the disturbing presence of a deceased person whom we may or may not have known in past lives. Obsessions and their treatment are outside the scope of this book.

I will give some examples of psychosomatic and psychological repercussions. Drowning or seeing a person drown may result in a fear of water. A woman who was a nomad and died in a sand storm is now afraid of wind. A sentinel, falling asleep and thus causing the deaths of himself and his comrades, is now a woman with amnesia. An overweight man starved to death in his last life. A teenage girl is afraid of meeting new people. Every time she meets a new person, her nose starts to hurt. Two centuries ago she was a girl who spent three weeks in a French hospital. Every time a visitor came the nurse washed her face roughly, the soap getting into her eyes and nose (Goldberg 1982: 56).

Sexual traumas may cause menstruation problems or frigidity in this life. This may be traced to abuse or maltreatment, or to chronic and degrading discomforts such as chastity belts. Often, chronic headaches can be traced back in regression to decapitation, being guillotined, shot through the head, hanged, or scalped. Such traumas have a particular repercussion if the pain was mentally as well as physically intense. A woman with migraine experiences in regression that her life ends when three men club her on the head, rape her, and leave her dying (similar experiences are common enough to make any sane man a feminist). After a few repetitions of this experience, she can look back on it calmly, but the headaches stay. After some further digging, it turns out that she feels guilty because she had cheapened herself in this life. She saw this death as a well-deserved punishment. Only when she was able to see this life more in terms of choice and responsibility, and less in terms of guilt and punishment, did the headaches stop (Fiore 1978: 16).

A girl with phobias remembers a life as a male beggar. He is imprisoned and beaten to a pulp with a metal ball with iron spikes. Subsequently rats nibble at him, and he dies. She can only disengage herself from this experience when she realizes that the killer's anger and hatred was a reaction to her previous persistent harassing (Cladder 1983); not that such a terrible death is an even remotely justifiable or understandable punishment for harassment. Apparently, comprehension liberates and incomprehension fixates. People reliving concentration camp experiences show that comprehension or incomprehension have an effect in so far as they have a bearing upon oneself. People who ask themselves emotionally how all of this could ever have happened when they see this happening to people around them often digest these experiences. People who get stuck in the question: 'But why did it have to happen to *me*?' do not (as yet) experience catharsis.

Fear of the dark is an unconscious memory of terrible experiences that we once had in the dark. Being overweight is often the result of a previous starvation. Edith Fiore found that people who were more than five kilos overweight had, almost without exception, starved to death in a past life (Fiore 1978: 6). Amply endowed girls are often subject to constant remarks about their weight while being sexually harassed or molested. As with other sexual traumas the symptoms of related anxieties, such as anorexia, usually appear with puberty (Fiore 1978: 33).

Homosexuality is an ordinary retention when a remigrant ties into a previous life as a homosexual and associates this homosexuality with an interesting and gratifying life. In some cases homosexuality vanishes as the result of past-life therapy. This shows that homosexuality at least sometimes has a traumatic cause (Kelsey and Grant 1967: 138). Problematic repercussions of homosexuality are likely when this disposition leads to an unhappy and unsatisfying life here. A homosexual who leads a happy, gratified life may have to deal with a bit of social stigmatization, but otherwise is just as little a case for therapy or reincarnation therapy as is a heterosexual. And if the social stigmatization runs amok, then society should be in therapy.

Fruition: the fruits of experiences and activities in next lives.

Experiences that have been digested result in personal characteristics. Lengthy exertion leads to ability. Gratifying digested experiences lead to preferences and character traits. Interactions with others lead to relationships.

First, preferences: a life which on the whole has been gratifying or ungratifying may lead to associations with the country or the time in which one lived, with the sex, or with the trade of that life. A happy life in Greece gives happy associations with Greece in subsequent lives, a preference for Greek music or Greek food. A difficult life as an Irish land labourer in the last century may lead to a dislike of potatoes; not because of a potato trauma, but because of association. A life as a land labourer might have its own karmic background, and someone could get through this life splendidly while still disliking potatoes now because of unconscious associations with weariness and ultimate starvation. Many degrading experiences as a woman may lead to a rejection of men, and to a predilection for purely female company.

Conclusions

A second example of fruition is that of developing relationships while working and living together with others. A relationship in this life with a strong spontaneous acceptance or rejection may be a retention from the same relationship in a past life, but may also be the fruition of specific occurrences in a past life. A lengthy and good business relationship with someone new may lead to feelings of intimacy and trust in a following life.

The most explicit form of fruition is the development of abilities. Exertions in one life may result in capabilities in the next. Practice leads to development, neglect leads to atrophy, to backsliding. Practising incorrectly leads to incorrect development. Lives in which somebody did little wrong, but also little right, lives in which somebody buried his talents, are worthless. Inactive lives, even under the motto of ascetism or contemplation weaken the spiritual muscles. Someone who had deeply experienced how easily words can wound and be interpreted incorrectly resolved to say nothing in his next life. Such isolation and silence does not lead to phenomenal oratorical talent (as Steiner claimed that he and esoteric clergymen believed) but are more likely to result in stammering, stuttering, and poor speech. Unsociable lives lead rather to isolation even amidst people than to social wonders. An active life, struggling with one's talents, leads to practice of willpower and faculties, and with this to independence and individuality. Passive lives accomplish the opposite. Perhaps this will go down wrongly with spiritually oriented readers. Many great teachers, from Buddha to Aristotle, taught that contemplation stands above action, but ultimately this implies only a preference for the discarnate over the incarnate condition. Contemplation is introspection in between actions, but sustained long enough it is just a beautiful, noble, and inconspicuous form of suicide.

People can have been engaged in spiritual disciplines in which they subjected themselves to others, and perhaps actively practised being passively open-minded. Such dubious temple training or magic leads to negative mediumship in later lives and to hypersensitivity for (especially paranormal) influences. Susceptibility to obsessions and some forms of mental illness can probably be traced back to this. Someone is taken over by another person after shell-shock (*The Boy Who Saw True*, Spearman ed. 1953: 231).

This brings us to the next subject: a form of fruition in which the psychological reality of one life becomes a psychosomatic or somatic reality in the next; or: a reality of the psychic body becomes a reality of the etheric and the psychic bodies. Examples of direct psychosomatic consequences are weak intestines because of gluttony in a past life, or being plagued by obsessions as the result of a weakening of the will in past lives. The more indirect psychosomatic consequences reveal themselves less specifically. Surrender to negative emotions may lead to lymphatic diseases and diseases of the nervous system in a next life. The excessive sexual abuse of one's body may lead to feeble-mindedness in a next life. The sexual abuse of others, especially where there is strong domination and aggression, as in sadism, may lead to epilepsy in a following life. These may be ordinary repercussions. Surrender to physical pleasure and other emotions with a strongly physical component involves the vehicle of vitality, and this may attract etheric parasites. When such parasites, or a disposition for such parasites, are transmitted to a next life, this may upset the development of the nervous and the endocrine systems from the beginning, sometimes even during the pregnancy.

Listing the causal connections

Retention, repercussion, and fruition, as illustrated in this chapter, are connections between lives having two important characteristics: they are identical to processes occurring within a life; they are free from any kind of evaluation, influence, or intervention from the outside. One exception to the first point is Marianne de Jong's observation that agoraphobia may be the consequence of wandering after death. An observation from Ian Stevenson could be a second exception (Stevenson 1966). He found in most child cases a person who knew the family from the past life as well as the family from the present life, but who was usually not informed about the birth of a child with memories of a past life. Considering the experiences with hanging around, wandering, and haunting, it could be that, consciously or not, the deceased moves from the environment of one living person to another. Here, the relation between both lives is not karmic, but results from natural inclinations until one finds a pregnant woman. This is consistent with the experiences mentioned in chapter 8 and the wandering soul's needs for identification mentioned in chapter 9. It also explains the short intermissions of a few years, the relatively small distance between the place of death and the place of birth, and the absence of indications for karma.

I will conclude with an overview of the relationships discussed, pointing out the gradual transition from fruition to retention. If personal experiences lead to a personal relationship (fruition) then the personal relationship continues to exist (retention). If practice makes perfect (fruition) then this state of perfection may be taken further (retention). If someone has a natural gift for playing the piano, then this may be the result of an ability already existing in the previous life (retention), but also the result of persevering practice in the past life, even if it did not then lead to a satisfying result (fruition). For some people, this conviction is the basis for incessant perseverance even if they know they will not make it in this life.

Retention

1 Abilities
   Intellectual and musical talents (child prodigies)
   Glossolalia (speaking foreign languages spontaneously)
   Paranormal talents (through temple training)
   Other special talents (among others, puppeteering, organization skills).
2 Tendencies
   Interests
   Emotional attitudes
   Mentality
   Addictions.
3 Appearance
   Facial build and facial expression
   Racial characteristics (skin colour).
4 Relationships
   Self-evident friendship
   Self-evident animosity.

Repercussion

1 Physical idiosyncrasies (like birth stigmata).
2 Psychosomatic complaints (epilepsy, anorexia, frigidity, migraine, phantom pains, allergies, asthma, hyper-activity).

3 Phobias (fear of heights, agoraphobia, fear of strangers, fear of snakes).
4 Postulates (engraved semantic reactions, among others, prejudices, character neuroses).
5 Obsessions and pseudo-obsessions.

These repercussions are the consequence of physically and mentally extremely painful experiences remaining undigested because they have never been understood, were misunderstood, or were repressed. The largest category is the experience of a traumatic death caused by others. How traumatic experiences from previous lives affect following lives has scarcely been discussed. Chapter 16 will return to this.

Fruition

1 Experiences lead to interests and preferences.
2 Interactions lead to relationships.
3 Exertion leads to abilities
    Practice leads to development
    Neglect leads to atrophy
    Dubious exertions lead to dubious characteristics (culminating in psychic susceptibility through negative mental training and the practices which proceed from it).
4 Perversion may lead to psychosomatic complaints.

Retention, repercussion, and fruition: stumblingly, we become dancers.

Further reading

The literature available contains general reflections on karma but rarely addresses the specific subject of this chapter. In the esoteric schools reincarnation and karma are closely connected. For this reason, theosophy and anthroposophy contain many reflections about karma. The end of chapter 3 gives references. Relatively speaking, the best book is Virginia Hanson's work (1975).

The first attempt to refine the concept of karma using concrete cases is Gina Cerminara's book (1950) based on Cayce's readings. I will return to this in chapter 12. Clarice Toyne describes the past lives of a number of famous people such as Winston Churchill and Charles de Gaulle (Toyne 1976). She heard these past lives from a personal guide. Their value is hard to judge – at the least there is remarkable parallelism. If it concerns real past lives then it would indicate substantial retention.

Like Rudolf Steiner, Douglas Baker (1977) concentrates on the karmic causes of disease. Baker may have some understanding of karmic laws, but he seems to lack understanding of the laws of argument. His pieces of wisdom are shaky and incomplete; nor do his other books about reincarnation (1978, 1981) inspire confidence. He throws around his incoherent and irrelevant quotations just as liberally as his titles and memberships.

Finally, there are the writers on karmic astrology: the astrological relationship between the past and the present life. As I have already said in chapter 7, these writers have apparently not heard of the results of astrological or of reincarnation research. Almost everything is intuitive musing. Time will tell whether there is any value in it. The prize for the most nonsensical book ever written about reincarnation undoubtedly goes to the book about karmic astrology written by Gervée Baronti, *Your Previous Life on Earth: Reincarnation simplified* (1938). According to an article in *Prediction* (1937), a saddhu in India, apparently a member of some unspecified order of which Ms Baronti said she was a member, taught her real knowledge. If you were born between 1 and 8 January, then you lived in England during the reigns of Henry VIII and Elizabeth; between 15 and 21 January in India in about 300 BC. I myself, between 25 March and 1 April, in fifteenth-century Russia. And so on. Thus 2 per cent of the present world population lived in England during the reigns of Henry and Elizabeth. Think of it! Where did all the people go who lived in other places at different times from the fifty-two historic hotspots she specifies? The mind boggles.

Reasonable, albeit short and dispersed remarks about karma and relationships between lives can be found in Muller (1970).

11 Educational and Therapeutic Connections Between Lives

This chapter presents a summary of the relationships between lives that belong to the realm of developmental psychology. The regression experiences portray a rich picture of psychological and pedagogical human development throughout lives. Apparently, three kinds of processes often mix with each other: evolution, education, and self-development.

Evolution, education, and self-development

I understand *evolution* to be the natural development that comes from continuous experience in challenging circumstances. We are not spectators looking at our lives from the point of view of a film in a cinema. We have to make decisions, exert ourselves, take risks. We learn from our experiences, even when we are unaware of it. We seem to have an inborn drive to gain experience. When circumstances remain the same we get bored and look for new stimuli. Although this may lead to passive consumption reactions such as addiction, there is a general powerful drive pushing us on to new experiences. Curiosity, restlessness, and a desire for variation are evolutionary drives.

We may try to close ourselves off from this learning, this evolution, if we like. We may flee our experiences, we may shield ourselves from new experiences with prejudices and ideologies, we may try to repeat experiences. The postulates mentioned earlier, the ingrained agreements with ourselves, arrest our personal evolution by working with fixed formulas. But there is no escape from experience: avoidance, flight, repetition, and shielding in themselves lead to more experience. Even suicide provides experience. Experience is the source, the engine, and the destiny of our evolution.

A second process is *education*, comprising all forms of support and influence from more developed people, our fellow *évolues*. Education

231

as an influence through lives includes help in evaluating the past life and in preparing the new life with a life plan. Education may vary from noncommittal suggestions to powerful interventions you can hardly withstand. Evolution is a natural mechanism proceeding from human nature; education is conscious interaction between people, confirming our essentially social nature. The stronger help the weaker, the more advanced help the less advanced. Our development is a social reality, because we help others and because we are helped in turn.

The third process is *self-development*. All freedom begins with the possibility of making mistakes. Self-development begins primitively, in the form of uncontrolled personal responses such as incarnating in a hurry, or disregarding advice. It continues with isolated intentions based on partial insight, and culminates in the fully conscious, masterly control of destiny. Shaping your destiny begins with self-development, and sooner or later, gradually or suddenly, includes contributions to the development of others and of society. Human development is emancipation under the appropriate conditions: namely, self-awareness, freedom of choice, and responsibility. The engines of our development are our own nature, other people, and our free choice.

Development objectives: wisdom, love, competence

In what direction are we developing? What are the aims of our development? In the muddle of individual goals, and pedagogic, therapeutic, and correctional karmic processes, three fundamental and two conditional aims play a role in human education and self-education, and are the basis of life plans. The most fundamental aims of development apparently lie in the direction of intelligence, morality and competence. Concrete life goals in various lives are related to these three general goals.

Much of development, during as well as in between lives, has to do with the development of knowledge and cognitive faculties, powers of judgement, insight, ability to see the whole picture (the helicopter view), and discernment. Think, for example, of the presence of light in the experiences of the clinically dead: it points to the past life and discusses this with the deceased; it puts particular emphasis on aspects of knowledge and love. A deep, comprehensive, and realistic insight is wisdom, practical rather than theoretical wisdom. The second general aim could be described as morality. It encompasses the development of attentiveness, friendliness and good will towards other people, and to some extent, towards nature. It concerns feelings of empathy, solidarity, and sympathy. Ultimately this grows into love. It develops voluntary bonds with the reality around us, especially the reality of our fellow *évolués*. The third aspect is the collection of diverse abilities, skills, and faculties, which differ for each person. I call the wide and effective repertoire of abilities and talents built in the course of lives 'competence'.

Adaptation, correction, and therapy

Two conditional aims belong to the planning of a particular life. The first type of conditional aim is adapting the life to character, circumstances, and karma. The second type is the necessary correction and therapy after stagnation or a development in the wrong direction: not to develop intelligence, but to heal self-inflicted stupidity; not to develop moral sense, but to heal immorality; not to develop abilities, but to correct disease and weakness.

According to Allan Kardec (1857), the main business of our evolution is the development of intelligence and moral sense, with intelligence generally being developed before moral sense. This is obvious: love without understanding remains a smothering and autistic sentiment. Love easily makes blind unless some distance is maintained. Love is often blind because you do not want distance. Some people like to see themselves as emotional types versus others who are 'only' rational. Alfred Adler showed that people often used the so-called primacy of emotions to manipulate others and to shirk responsibility. It is a deception because feelings can be elicited or dampened by mental images. People who say they just cannot help feeling in some particular way suppress their prejudices and images. They cheat. People are only turned on if they turn themselves on. Those who see themselves as characters with willpower and action underestimate the role of the images and notions driving them, and besides that underestimate the emotions they suppress. Their blindness is similarly self-inflicted.

Along with the development of the intelligence and talents there is the strong temptation to neglect emotions, especially empathy. The whole of morality is based on seeing other people as fellow beings and accepting them as such. Morality without empathy and intelligence is just a good habit, turning into a bad habit when circumstances and people change. Traditional morality can strangle, even lacerate.

The effect of immorality, the 'bad things' in a previous life, depends much on the 'good things' we did. Just as one light in a dark night makes a great difference, one constructive act can change the effects of many destructive acts. Lenz gives a nice example (1979: 70).

Wisdom without love is sterile, wisdom without competence is impotent. Intelligence with competence but without morality leads to guilt, karma, and so forces us to develop our moral sense. There is no moral indignation about pollution without scientific ecological insight. Interestingly enough, technical developments lead to challenges which can only be solved morally rather than technically. Gordon Hardin wrote a famous article about technical and moral problems in society, *The Tragedy of the Commons* (1969). This is all part of the game: it triggers further evolution.

Development stages and disorders

As mentioned in chapter 2, the Hindus have developed a nice categorization for general stages of development: kama, artha, dharma, and moksha. According to Huston Smith (1958), the four phases have the following characteristics.

Kama is a state in which we consciously or unconsciously strive for pleasure and avoid displeasure. Here evolution operates via the experiences of pleasure and displeasure, and education via reward and punishment. Self-development is scanty. Kama at its best is a fine sensitivity to the physical and erotic pleasures in life.

The second state is *artha*, in which we strive for a personally optimal position in life in terms of, for example, possessions, influence, respect, and fame. Artha at its best is a well-ordered and controlled life with great success in all these areas. Here, the concept of the art of living is already considerably enriched.

The third phase is *dharma*: social and religious virtue and righteousness. Besides running our business well, we try to be a responsible citizen, a tender mother, a good family man, an honest merchant, etc. We try to make something of our own life and to contribute to society. We look back on our life in terms of what we have meant to others, whether we have left the world a little better than we found it.

On the artha level the effects vary more from person to person than on the kama level, and on the dharma level they vary more than on the artha level. It makes a big difference whether someone has been a hard-working village grocer or the founder of an international company. There is an even greater difference between people who did their best in the community council and those who helped to advance humanity.

The fourth level is *moksha*. The most practical and probably the original meaning of the word is rising above the limitations of being incarnate. This does not at all imply renouncing the world, but rather partaking consciously of the world of the discarnates while possessing all the faculties of incarnate existence.

Chapter 2 has already mentioned that people may advance from one level of goals to the next in various ways. The optimistic view is based on the operation of evolution. The experiences on one level lead to a natural wealth of experience driving someone to want new experiences on the next level. This thought is comparable to Maslow's hierarchy of needs: when the fundamental needs have been satisfied, the higher ones emerge. When we are sufficiently satisfied in our need for pleasure and comfort, we automatically move to the level of a personal career, and later to the level of social activity and moral criteria. And when we have satisfied these needs, the need for moksha emerges: for a spiritual life.

In the pessimistic vision we can stay an interminable time on the lowest level, and falling down from a higher level is all but impossible. The exertions of the souls who are already liberated, the atavars, Bodhisattvas, and Buddhas push us forward, fighting against the odds. This vision emphasizes human free will, in particular our capacity for fixation, regression, and perversion. In the disciplinary vision a well-organized and civilized society stimulates people to go on to higher levels. The most difficult step is that from dharma to moksha, requiring renunciation of the world and stringent religious discipline. Moksha means that someone is freed from this world. The more positive view of moksha as the state of a fully conscious person who combines the discarnate and the incarnate states does not contradict the disciplinary vision. In the latter, exercises to accomplish moksha are only more psychological, and may take place in the middle of everyday life or in a merely temporary retreat from active life.

How are the four stages of development related to the three primary goals of development? Surrendering to kama develops animal-like intelligence: one has to become clever to find pleasure and avoid displeasure. Artha develops intelligence further because the acquisition of possessions, influence, respect, and fame makes demands on energy and intelligence. With dharma, the scale tips over to moral sense. Dharma actually means law, and I take this to mean voluntary obeisance to moral, human, and social patterns. The two golden rules of dharma are: 'Do not unto others what you will not have them do unto you,' and 'Do unto others, what you will have them do unto you'.

Human evolution and human experience stimulate the further development of intelligence, moral sense, and competence, but free will remains. The most primitive form of free will is laziness. 'Too much sitting, *the* disease against the Holy Ghost!' Nietzsche called it (1889). The numerous forms of unwillingness, combined with incapability (usually a lot of unwillingness and little incapability, while convinced of the opposite) give rise to four fundamental development disorders:

1 *Fixation*: wanting to stay in one place, getting stuck.
2 *Regression* (in the sense of development psychology): wanting to return to the past.
3 *Extortion*: forcing oneself to skip intermediate stages of development.
4 *Perversion*: not developing as a human, but as a beast, a plant, a thing, or a god (the first three are evolutionary regressions and the fourth is an evolutionary extortion).

The development from kama to moksha resembles a decreasing natural evolution and an increasing self-development, with education and therapy probably playing an important role all along. Education stimulates others in their development; therapy and correction help others to overcome fixation, regression, forcing, and perversion.

Specific psychological and educational connections between lives

The list below reviews four psychological and educational relationships between lives, each subdivided into more specific ones. I will give examples of all of these.

1 Carrying over good things
     Positive inversion (externalization)
     Somatic precipitation.

2 Intentions resulting from the life retrospect
     Go through experiences again
     Do things differently, experience them differently
     Make up for things
     Experience things oneself.

3 Delayed assimilation
     Replay, second chance
     Inversion of negative experiences (internalization or 'boomerang karma')
     Indirect inversion.

4 Retention and fruition of fixed will or desire
     Conscious retention of postulates
     Discharge of fixed intentions.

Carrying over good things When we meet consideration we tend to be considerate as well. If we receive love we tend to give love. This also happens between lives. When we look back on a life as an invalid and realize how much love and care we received, this may arouse care for others in our next life. Positive inversion or externalization is wanting to do good to others because others did good to us.

We call psychic experiences in one life leading to a physical condition in the next life 'somatic precipitation'. Edgar Cayce gives a number of examples of women who devote themselves to beauty in music, dance, and bodily care, and were themselves beautiful in their next life. Apparently this is not a reward from a karma authority, but rather a natural, purely interior reaction. If we have developed ourselves aesthetically in one life, we may use this aesthetic attention and perceptiveness to look for a foetus which will give a beautiful body or which we may influence. Whatever the mechanism, attention to beauty in one life gives beauty in the next life.

Apparently, patient endurance of an undeserved fate (one not in the life plan) may lead to a surplus of energy in the next life, a kind of spiritual encouragement premium. According to various authors a conscientious lifestyle could lead to health and beauty in a next life. According to Rudolf Steiner, patiently enduring lengthy physical suffering leads to beauty in the next life. Edgar Cayce's examples are consistent with this idea.

Reactions to the life retrospect When we look back on our past life after death, with or without a guide, we may want to experience things again or to experience or do things differently. We may want to make up for things or experience them ourselves. Wanting to do things differently, or wanting to experience them differently, may lead to a change of sex. One person regarded his main task in this life as tying up the loose ends from his past life after he had suffered an untimely death (Wambach 1979: 48).

Another looks back in shame on a life of primitive atheism, and the next time he becomes a fanatic Muslim (Van Ginkel 1917: 93). This is a good example of a psychological rather than a natural connection. A primitive and non-religious life does not automatically lead to a fanatical next life. An automatic relationship would be retention: the next life is primitive and non-religious as well. This man's reaction is a personal response to a personal evaluation. Because the evaluation is tainted with a negative emotion (shame), he tends to overreact (fanaticism).

Another example is of an overly protective father who had deserted his family in two past lives. In a regression a workaholic experiences that a few centuries ago in Greece his family had starved to death because he was unable to feed them (Goldberg 1982: 56). When soldiers look back at their lives, they are not ashamed of the violence they committed or the deaths they caused but of fanaticism and cruelty, especially if they have enjoyed it. Kardec also indicated this.

McClain found that some of the young protesters of the late 1960s and the 1970s were casualties of the Second World War and Korea, while others of that time had come back eager to return to the military. A couple of the more militant of the anti-nuclear protesters were casualties of Hiroshima and Nagasaki (McClain 1986: 131).

Homosexuality seems often to fall into this category. Netherton found that homosexuals usually have several previous lives in which they have been homosexual or had homosexual episodes – freely, reluctantly, or forced. The key lies in the life immediately preceding the first homosexual life. It is usually about very aggressive sex with women. For example, men raid a village, kill the men, rape the women, and then kill them too. While being raped besides a dying child a woman gets a knife and kills the man. Now sexual intercourse with a woman is associated with pain, bloodshed, and death. The deceased man is ashamed of himself and vows he will never do that to a woman again, or rather have it happen to himself. Homosexuality thus begins as a defence mechanism Williston and Johnstone (1983) give comparable examples from men watching how their wives are bleeding to death in great pain while trying to give birth. As in the previous example, the woman involved may scream and curse the cause of her misery. The man vows he will never do this to any woman again. In the first instance the guilt is never about sex itself but about the violence. In the second instance guilt is associated with perplexity and helplessness. In both cases the women involved may make similar vows, possibly resulting in lesbianism in the next life. Impotence and frigidity may have the same origin.

Delayed assimilation Delayed assimilation usually leads to a repetition or a second chance, but often enough it may lead to inversions and negative experiences in the form of internalizations. 'Repetition' may occur after a suicide when that person enters a similar state of isolation and loneliness in a next life, either to learn that his suicide did not get him any further, or as a second chance to manage it better this time. Here too, the repetition is no natural law but a psychological or educational fact which may come about for different reasons, and so may lead to different results. The new situation restimulates the predisposition or 'set' which triggers the tendency for repetition. A suicide with honourable motives, for example to prevent treason, does not have a repercussion. According to Edith Fiore (1978: 164), suicide may lead to an optimal desire to live in the next life. Although this may be true, I do not think it is a rule.

The inversions from negative reactions via internalization are well known. Gina Cerminara (1950) calls it 'boomerang karma'. Someone who was quick to condemn others' behaviour gets a next life in which his own behaviour is quickly condemned. Someone who frequently mocked others is frequently mocked by others in his next life. Someone who was deceptive is deceived. Someone who provoked jealousy is made jealous. Someone who exploited others is exploited. Someone who killed another person's child experiences the death of his own child. Someone who made other people dependent on him is dependent in his next life. A man who made his wife wear a chastity belt while he was on the Crusades became impotent in his next life (Cerminara 1967: 107). A man who had gouged out people's eyes became blind in his next life.

Such inversions are so common that they are almost synonymous with karma. But they are not a natural law. The unlikeliness of this is clear from the consequence: it would never end. If someone has to be mocked now to make up for his own mocking in a previous life, the others who mock him now have to be mocked in their next life, *ad infinitum*. In my opinion, this is the common educational principle, 'he that will not be advised must suffer'. If you refuse to deal with the effects of your acts on others, then you need to feel these effects yourself sometimes. The remedial twilight existence, of which chapter 8 gave examples, is based on the same principle.

I find 'boomerang karma' an unhappy phrase to denote this relationship. A boomerang only comes back if it misses its mark. Here, karma bounces back precisely because it hits other people. Besides that, the mirror is far from perfect, and what returns often differs. If somebody's child died because of your carelessness, your child will not necessarily die from carelessness in the next round, let alone from the same kind of carelessness, or from the same other person. First of all, this death may deeply affect you during your life, changing your reactions completely, leading to care, too much care, wanting to make it up to other children. Or, if you close yourself off to such an extent during your life and after your death that the principle 'he that will not be advised must suffer' is called for in order to prevent further degradation (dehumanization), then your child may die in many different ways, for example through somebody else's carelessness, or, again, through your own carelessness. This is a case neither of mirror-image nor of jurisdiction. Somebody goes through an experience curing him of immoral behaviour, which also naturally obstructed his own development.

Why do people accept educational interventions, willingly or unwillingly? Ultimately, because something inside human beings, the soul or a higher self, wants to undo, to overcome the limitations, the damage, and the imperfections of a personality. Apparently we have an original drive to develop and emancipate ourselves. As long as this evolutionary drive is intact, the person will take negative karma upon himself. This karma appears negative, but is a positive reaction to previous negative psychological acts. In the example of the child dying, it might be less your carelessness and more your subsequent indifference which was negative, self-denouncing, dehumanizing. Every effective education ties in with the evolutionary drive and the effective evolutionary mechanisms of human beings.

Indirect inverse reactions are often symbolic. Again, this is not a natural relation but a semantic, psychological one, meaningful at least to the person involved. Maltreatment and cruelty, or enjoyment of maltreatment and cruelty without repentance, often lead to physical inferiority (such as multiple sclerosis and polio) or physical deformation in a new life. Edgar Cayce gives many examples of this. Chapter 4 gave a comparable example from Ruth Montgomery's work. Precipitated somatic traits are possible in repetitions and inversion experiences. Someone partially blind turned out to have made improper use of his eyes in hypnosis in a past life. Cayce gives examples of asthma as a karmic consequence of squeezing the life out of a lot of others through torture, of anaemia after spilling blood oneself, and of bed-wetting as a reaction to the immersion of so-called witches during the witch hunts. Such indirect, symbolic inversions are less effective, and indicate such resistance to karma that direct, constructive, effective compensation or therapy was impossible. The indirect inversions clearly illustrate that compensation is not necessarily personal. If someone mocks another, this does not mean he will be mocked by the same person in a next life. This would also lead to a vicious circle.

Cayce provides examples of people who suffer because of their great size as a consequence of pride, superiority, and contempt of others in a past life (Cerminara 1967: 53). These same characteristics may lead to being painfully small in the present life. The same cause may lead to opposite reactions, depending on what is the most educational. And that, in turn, depends on who is involved. Someone who is ashamed of his pride will be more willing to accept a small body. Someone who refuses this may end up in a large body and realize only later how unpleasant this is. The incarnation contractors and incarnation brokers undoubtedly possess a great pedagogical imagination.

Retention and fruition of fixed will or desire If someone comes to the intense resolve, during or after a sweeping event, that he will never show his feelings again, it may continue to operate in following lives, even if highly inappropriate. The consequences of postulates depend on their formulation. A man who experiences his wife dying in childbirth bearing a dead child, resolves 'never to go through this again'. In his present life he is impotent (Goldberg 1982: 71). Impotence may have more obscure causes. An impotent man experiences during a regression that he is out hunting with a friend. By accident, he shoots his friend. His friend dies, calling him an imbecile, wishing he had never met him, and refusing to be touched by him. In this life the deceased friend is the man's wife, and his reluctance to touch his wife translates into impotence (Goldberg 1982: 79). This is an example of somebody else's words creating a postulate. Another example of such a postulate is the girl who is murdered while being told that, as a woman, she is just a stupid, irresponsible being (Hubbard 1958).

Frigidity and impotence can be found among people who have sworn to celibacy in a past life, as well as in people who broke this vow. Either the vow remains effective, or breaking the vow causes such shame or such fear of breaking the vow again, that people put themselves into a state which prevents this. Women may have had such awful experiences in labour or with a primitive abortion that they want to quit the propagation business altogether. This may lead to impotence and frigidity, but also to homosexuality in a next life, even as a male. Here, too, the important thing is to look for the particular psychological or pedagogical mechanism in each individual case, and to avoid thinking along apparently fixed laws of natural relations.

The diversity and unexpectedness of the effects of karmic causes is clear from the following example, from Joan Grant (Kelsey and Grant 1967: 63). During the First World War, she is nursing a soldier who has been terribly wounded in the foot. The wound is months old and refuses to heal. She has an impression of the soldier's previous life. He is a Catholic priest who prays incessantly to receive the holy stigmata (the bleeding hands and feet as a sign that one has attained a mystic union with Christ's suffering). His subconscious took the wound in his foot to be an answer to his prayers.

Most postulates function linearly, others antithetically. Linear postulates are, for example: never showing your feelings any more, doing everything that is asked of you etc. They lead to the recurrence of particular situations. Antithetical postulates result in a pendular reaction. Gina Cerminara devoted a chapter to this subject which she entitled 'Balance: the pendulum' (Cerminara 1967: 174). Antithetical postulates are resolutions to do the opposite from now on. Warriors storm a valley, kill the men, and take the women prisoner. One warrior has several women, but their eternal quarrels get on his nerves, so he resolves firmly to have only one woman in his next life (Cerminara 1967: 176). Now, he may have such exaggerated expectations that, out of disappointment, he will try one after another next time. The pendulum swings back and forth, until the oscillations get smaller and smaller.

A small, weak, and fairly unattractive woman in Palestine prays for strength and beauty. During the Crusades she was a powerful man, and in the American colonies an attractive woman. However, as a beautiful woman she was so vain and proud that in this life she is small and weak again, with strong feelings of inferiority (Cerminara 1967: 178).

People may also overreact to the life retrospective, especially when looking back unguided. Whitton and Fisher give a good example. A man finds out that in his last ten lives he alternated between extremes of sanctimonious and licentious behaviour. Watching himself fluctuate from one extreme to the other, he became annoyed and perplexed to the point of dismissing physical life. Suddenly there appeared an 'incredibly vivid woman's face' explaining that eroticism is a rudimentary force, provoking interaction and intimate involvement, and so may develop conscience, altruism, benevolent concern. Up until then he saw sex and spirituality as separate worlds, and did not know how to choose between them (Whitton and Fisher 1986: 73).

The art of living

On the basis of the last two chapters, we can come to a number of important conclusions:

Karma is not computerized jurisdiction. It is partially subject to natural law, and in this respect no compensation for or counterpart to causality but just one form of the causality of our human nature (see chapter 10). It is also in part a reality of psychological development, consisting of the warp of our own reactions and the woof of educational advice and other people's interventions.

A good birth and a good death are important. A complete awakening and a good retrospect on this life, preferably with others (see chapter 8), and good preparations for the new life, preferably with others (see chapter 7), may prevent a great deal of unnecessary misery and disorientation.

There are the two golden rules of dharma: 'Do not unto others what you will not have them do unto you', and 'do unto others what you will have them do unto you'. In spite of the apparent simplicity of these two rules, I subscribe to their golden character. See other people as human and treat them accordingly. It does not mean treating everybody the same, namely, as yourself. After all you, too, want to be treated as an individual.

Neither let positive emotions carry you away nor let negative emotions overflow in feelings, thoughts, and actions.

Accept your fate, but remain active.

Be extremely careful about fixing your will or judgement in a particular notion. Apparently, firm intentions and rigid judgements may operate throughout incarnations. Be sparing with 'oaths' and make only those which avoid fixation and promote development, such as the strong resolve to be attentive and open during the retrospect on your past life and the preparation for your future life, or the resolve to get the most insight from it, and search seriously for people who are close to you or may teach you a lot.

Be neither too ambitious nor too humble in your life plan. When making a new life plan, first consider the attitudes and abilities you have been developing, and the obvious further goals of development. Next comes the heritage of traumas and postulates. Often you do not find a combination of parents, sex, and living conditions ideal in every way. Consider your desire to incarnate, your own motivation to live. Besides what you yourself want and can handle, the actual living conditions usually set limits to competence development and karma settlement. You try to find prenatal and postnatal conditions that stimulate selected traumas, without stimulating the others. Further, you will look for adequate and instructive circumstances. You can only work at so many problems accumulated in your lives. To want to settle all accounts in one life is a noble, but usually foolish ambition. Be a little less ambitious, work off a little less personal karma and contribute a bit more to other people and the world. When settling accounts, consider that you are only a minuscule particle in the chaotic and grubby business of mankind. This may simultaneously intensify and moderate our desires to settle the accounts. It gives us a longer time span.

Never base your actions on the provocation of negative feelings in other people. Sometimes you cannot avoid negative feelings in other people. Others, too, have their own responsibility in this, but never base your actions on it. Apparently, it is a moral (and therefore political) constitutional principle that actions and institutions based on inciting worry, fear, horror, hate, jealousy, shame, and guilt, are wrong. And what is wrong easily leads to what is evil.

Further reading

As with the previous and the following chapter, literature explicitly on the subject discussed in this chapter is lacking. The most informative work is still that by Edgar Cayce and the analyses made of it, especially by Gina Cerminara. Some things can be found in Helen Wambach and the books by the past-life therapists Denys Kelsey and Joan Grant, Thorwald Dethlefsen, Morris Netherton and Nancy Shiffrin, Edith Fiore, and Bruce Goldberg.

12 Free Connections Between Lives

Our character and career may in some ways be connected with our previous lives without any involvement from retention, repercussion, or fruition (chapter 10), or from psychological reactions and educational interventions (chapter 11). The connection may be based on our own voluntary deliberations and choices. This chapter discusses undetermined relations which leave things open and susceptible to free choice. To clarify the transactions from and combinations with causal and educational connections, I will conclude the chapter with a summary of the whole area of connections between lives, at the same time giving a better definition of the concepts of karma and dharma.

Indeterminism

As mentioned above, Ian Stevenson found many similarities between the past and present personalities of the child cases he examined. However, he rarely found karmic connections. The new family and new living conditions appeared without relation to the past life. The apparent reason for this is the absence of a life plan in falling asleep, hanging about, wandering, and haunting. No reflection, no self-education, no teaching. When planning is absent, coherence will be weak. Characteristics simply continue, and there are some repercussions and some fruition in a life simply unconnected to the previous life.

Partial intervention, if there is any at all, may only lead to some line in life, or merely determine where someone will be born. As mentioned before, the Chinese man who remembered a life as a fox, remembered the 'Lord of the Other World', saying to him: 'You are not a sinner, take a human body.' After a life as a beggar he died when he was 20. The same lord said to him: 'You will be a slave. The denomination is not beautiful, but you will not suffer hunger and misery' (Penkala 1972: 49).

Wijeratne's case is an example of negative somatic precipitation in a child (Stevenson 1966: 149). Wijeratne was a boy with deformations on the right side of the chest and his right arm. Between the ages of $2\frac{1}{2}$ and $5\frac{1}{2}$ he talked a lot to himself about a past life and said that his malformed arm was a punishment because in his past life he had stabbed his wife to death with his right arm. Francis Story correctly notes that this case is different from most birth stigmata because it appears to be a punishment. Most stigmata are what he calls psycho-kinetic consequences of people having thoroughly internalized their physical wounds after their death (Story 1975: 277). This relates to the psycho-plastic character of the psychic body (see chapter 8). Linked to a strong postulate like 'this is how I am' or 'this is how I have become', the image can be engraved in the growing foetus of the new body.

Thiang San Kla is a Siamese sergeant, claiming to be his uncle Phoh reborn. He was born three months after Phoh died, but had a large birthmark which corresponded exactly to the knife wound Phoh died from. Phoh had a festering wound on his right big toe. Thiang's right big toe was slightly deformed. Phoh had been tattooed on both hands and feet. Thiang was born with tattoo-like markings on hands and feet. This last detail is interesting because it indicates that the self-image is decisive.

Skin marks, therefore, do not imply that the body has been entered early in its development. Ravi Shankar's mother noticed his stigma (a 'cut' in the neck) only when he was three or four months old. (Stevenson 1966: 92). A Brazilian girl got high fever and red stripes all over her body a few days after birth. She was run over by a train as a girl of twelve a few years before that. Child cases show a lot of retention, some aspects of repercussion, and incidental somatic precipitation or some other psychological or psychosomatic reaction, and much that is undefined, accidental. The same is true for every life without a life plan.

A second indeterminism comes from making choices. Once a choice has been made for the particular life of a particular foetus, this choice entails consequences unrelated to past lives. If someone incarnates mostly because of karmic relations with others and these others are in a particular culture in a particular social class for reasons of their own, then a birth in their vicinity can entail the same culture

247

and the same social class: living conditions unrelated to your own past lives. Each culture, each situation has its own openings and limitations for our development. This is a natural consequence of social development and not of our personal past lives. Even well-considered incarnation choices have consequences unrelated to our own direction.

Levels of free choice: suspension, selection, preference, and mission.

The second level of freedom, next to indeterminism, is the possibility of suspending karma. Nobody can do everything at once, and each life has only so many opportunities to work off karma. That is the difference between the general karmic fund of repercussions, complications in relationships, and moral obligations and the karmic package for the coming life. This package is also called 'ripe karma', an unfortunate expression, because it implies a purely natural process. Besides maturing, other psychological and educational factors play a role, as well as adaptation to the particular body and the circumstances of the coming life. Postponement may produce a calm and easy life, as when one allows oneself a period of rest to relax and regain peace of mind every now and again in life. Suspension or postponement gradually changes into selection of karma, the third level of freedom. This is simply setting educational priorities. In education, overload is well known: wanting to teach children too much at once, pointing out too many things to them, starting up too many activities with too many goals all at once. The geography project has to teach the children geography, accuracy, group work, composition, awareness of the problems in the Third World, newspaper reading, and improvement of the pupil/teacher relationship. This is like teaching a wounded person to use his right arm while his left leg is being amputated, his headwound is still fresh, and his blood production needs stimulation.

Netherton describes karma as 'a debt to ourselves, to be repaid by us at a time we choose and in a way we choose ourselves' (Netherton and Shiffrin 1978: 184). This description is correct, but underestimates the degrees of relative dependence in educational conditions, and underestimates the social aspect. We may well feel a debt to another although it remains our debt to ourselves. In real relations with true reciprocity, working off accumulated tensions, frictions, and short-coming is a social process. But the basis of Netherton's description holds here as well.

The fourth level of freedom entails the possibility of choosing on the basis of your own wants and preferences. You can let your feelings of affinity with people, circumstances, activities, peoples, or cultures guide you. You do not start from what you need to do, but choose from your inventory, your fund of experience, relations, and capabilities. You choose what you want to associate yourself with and by whom you want to be guided.

The fifth level of freedom is that of not choosing something on the basis of considerations about yourself, but because of a 'mission': a calling or task that contributes to a wider development.

The life aims playing a role in the preparation of an incarnation, such as those mentioned by Wambach's respondents (see Table 7), illustrate the relations between the consequences of causal, psychological, and free connections. Less than half Wambach's respondents were able to answer her question about their aim in life. Obviously, those able to answer this question were mostly on the levels of education and therapy, self-realization, and missions. The causal processes of retention, repercussion, and fruition also affect them, but do not decide the coming life. Retention, repercussion, and fruition determine the material and tools with which they can work and from which they can choose. However, this is a final not a causal arrangement. Evolution gradually changes into education. Education gradually changes into self-development. Self-realization

Table 7 The relation between life aims and the three connections between lives

Evolution	Education	Freedom	Spiritual growth and helping others	27%
			Special developments	12%
			Learning love and compassion	18%
			Karmic relations and obligations	18%
			Supplementary experience	25%

Source: Helen Wambach, *Life Before Life* (1979)

gradually changes to contributing to the evolution, education, and self-development of others. Unfortunately, the way Wambach published her material prevents analysis of interrelations between, for example, self-development and helping others as a goal, or planning and actively preparing the coming incarnation. They probably correlate strongly.

I suppose most of the people who could not answer the question about aims, were unable to because their life was more causally determined. The 18 per cent who responded to this question, who said they had to work on karmic obligations and relations, probably have educational or self-educational exercises. Their karma will not be a simple repercussion of traumas in relationships, because direct repercussions do not lead to meeting the people who are connected with these traumas. Phobias and postulates are surprisingly impersonal.

However, 23 per cent of Wambach's group did not feel any imposed aims, but could themselves plan. They functioned on the fourth or fifth level of freedom. Some reported they could choose a mission and apply for particular tasks. The fifth level of freedom, then, is fairly common and is not limited to exclusive leaders. If this were true, it would imply a remarkable chasm between the incarnate and discarnate state in one of the most central dimensions of being human: the development of one's own freedom and responsibility.

Builders of grand systems and pragmatic craftsmen

Enthusiastic therapists and researchers who often meet guides in regressions before birth and after death, and learn to communicate with them during sessions, have a tendency to forget this central aspect of the development of free will and responsibility, perhaps out of enthusiasm and perhaps because of an attitude that is more religious than scientific. This results in curious reflections, like this one of Goldberg's:

We are aided in making these [reincarnation] decisions by our Masters and Guides. These highly evolved entities have completed their karmic cycles and their purpose is simply to help and advise us as to our next lives. They do not moralize or pass judgment. They simply counsel us and try to help as best they can. The individual soul always has free will to ignore their advice. Many of our decisions are poorly made for this very reason. These Masters and Guides also receive advice from even higher entities with higher vibrational rates in the seven higher planes. These much more advanced entities receive their advice from even more evolved sources, the ultimate authority being God or ALL THAT IS (as many parapsychologists refer to God). The final result is, of course, excellent guidance (Goldberg 1982: 39).

This reminds me of a group of facilitators who, for all their proficiency in communication and co-operation failed to accomplish anything together, and concluded that this was because they had no super-facilitator. The troubles in life sometimes! Nietzsche exclaimed: 'To educate educators! But they first must educate themselves!' Goldberg's pyramid of super-counselling looks as though it gives a basis to human development, but it takes the ground from under our feet. In his view, freedom consists of being able to accept or refuse the wisdom of others. Moreover, Goldberg puts the cart before the horse: the ultimate result is fantastic counselling. The result of all our building efforts is, as it were, ever better scaffolding. To put up the scaffolding, we need even better scaffolding, which is put up with even better scaffolding, *ad infinitum*, *ad absurdum*. More than this, this unending absurdity has a name. Development in his view amounts to going to ever higher teachers presiding over ever higher kinder-gartens: 'Life as pudding.'

Many people benefit greatly from coaches and tutors themselves performing less than their pupils. I may teach past-life therapy to people who may teach others, doing it much better than I ever did. Daily life really does become enigmatic when one's eyes are full of pudding. But that is the way it goes if we would put the universe and humanity in a system continuing from the beginning to the end of time, rather than helping our fellow man take one step, and taking one step ourselves.

Goldberg seems to be an active and practical therapist. However, like many others, he yields to his desire for a cosmic, comprehensive perspective. Freud would doubtlessly diagnose it as an oceanic need.

Sometimes, reincarnation therapists seem to pose themselves as frustrated high priests and initiates with the irresistible urge to pass their wisdom on to suffering humanity. There are such enthusiasts all over the world. Thorwald Dethlefsen, a German past-life counsellor apparently feels the need to use regressions as a springboard for metaphysics. His first book about reincarnation (1974) contains the protocols of some sessions and the next ninety pages explain the workings of the world and mankind. His second book contains a large number of protocols and sensible comments on them (1976). However his third book leaves experience far behind with the ominous sub-title (translated into English) *Esoteric Psychology – the ultimate knowledge of the perfection of humanity* (1979). His book discusses the 'ultimate principles of reality' and provides such blinding insights as 'life is rhythm', or even:

Breathing is the basic human experience. We can study the laws of polarity in the light of breathing. They can be applied to the whole universe. For so below, so above. When we breathe in, then, without further ado and with absolute certainty, breathing out follows as the opposite pole (Dethlefsen 1979: 69).

I doubt whether Dethlefsen has any knowledge and understanding of the physiology of breathing. Also, apparently he has never heard of respiratory problems. And why the universe should be studied in the light of respiration also remains unclear. Why not in the light of daily motions, or of Friday afternoon traffic congestion?

Dethlefsen also provides sensible and pertinent psychological insights, undoubtedly partly because of his practical experience, but they vanish into the blue when he starts his cosmic bubble-blowing. Every now and then he becomes ostentatiously practical, as with his example of someone who crashes into a tree at 120 miles an hour. According to him, the driver gained his understanding of the principles of energy (120 mph) and resistance (tree) from this experience. This is clearly no example from a regression. People learn the most incredible things from life, but I have never heard anything in a life retrospect as abstract as this. Also, equating constant speed with energy warrants pessimism about the author's knowledge of physics.

His astrological reflections, too, lack any evidence of knowledge of the empirical work in this area. Perhaps he can do without such things, since he works more fundamentally.

Helen Wambach asked her subjects, among others, why they had been born in the twentieth century. One of them answered: 'I chose the twentieth century because of the historical transition from a religious to a scientific vision, and at the end of this period, a spiritual awakening' (Wambach 1979: 69). Others also reported a feeling of liberation after the shift from a religious to a scientific orientation. We should go forwards, not backwards. The scientific world view may need to be drastically enriched and transformed, but rebirth differs from returning to the womb, as attentive readers of the New Testament should know. Science is not the be all and end all either, and science is more complex and uncertain than dogmatic scientists believe. Scientific procedure itself is subject to the shuffling and fumbling of analysis and the draughts of scepticism. But, fumbling, we come along; shuffling, we learn to walk; stumbling and picking ourselves up we emancipate ourselves.

Freedom and arbitrariness

Indeterminism, the first level of freedom, manifests itself in people incarnating unplanned, unprepared, in an unguarded moment, on the spur of the moment, or without supervision. This makes the new life have little connection with the previous life, not through sleep, the power of natural processes and chance circumstances, but because of a sudden impulse. This may lead to odd, usually drab, and chaotic lives, and sometimes to lives with challenges greater than people can handle. This also happens to pigheaded people who, in spite of all advice, still want to tackle the big fish. And if they do not want to be advised, well then they must suffer, and that means a life of fantastic failure, all strings attached. However, the will of a stubborn pupil is a human will and must be respected. Breaking someone's will is worse than letting someone fail, even with all the psychological wounds and scars this involves. This a decent incarnation counsellor will never do, because this takes the breath out of the reincarnation cycle, takes the meaning out of human evolution.

During the preparations of an incarnation based on our own

affinities and preferences, deep and lasting wishes and resolves from the previous life are retained, but supplemented and often supplanted by choices and preferences built up during the intermission. Edgar Cayce gives an example of a diseased relationship between a dominant man and an oppressed woman. This relationship was repeated throughout a number of lives and kept getting worse. 'Not only did her weak subjectiveness cause her misery, but it made her husband a monster of egoism. There was cowardliness under the mask of patient and gentle suffering.' In the present life she was able to break this vicious circle because she had developed more during her intermission than her husband had. Thus education during the intermission may decrease our attachment to our past. Apparently, we may learn to plan our own coming life better during the intermission. An archdeacon who had believed a bit in reincarnation during his life was hardly surprised to find out, after his death, that he had already lived many times before and would live many times again. What did surprise him, were special training courses for this subject. There, people learned to analyse their past lives, to arrive at conclusions on the basis of this, and to make plans (Shirley 1924: 161).

When planning a coming life, our preferences influence the choice of development aims, the kind of work we want to do, the role we want to fulfil and, especially, the kind of people we want to meet and with whom we want to live and work. Past experiences strengthen these preferences. We want to do something again, or to experience it from a different side. Social developments too, influence our preferences, at least inasmuch as we as discarnates can keep track of them. Some bide their time until they can make the contribution they want and can have the role they want. Moreover, we often have preferences for peoples or cultures.

Similar considerations apply to the choice of sex. For most people, the choice of sex is derivative. In cases of spontaneous memories (seldom with a life plan) 13 per cent have sex changes, 4 per cent of the men remember a previous life as a woman, and 24 per cent of the women remember a previous life as a man. In regression cases (usually with a retrospect and preparation for this life) 80 per cent of remigrants appear to have changed sex at least once. Here, too, the main conclusion is: patterns, but no fixed rules. A few of Wambach's examples are as follows (1979: 75–7):

- 'I did not choose my sex. It was just time to go back, so I took what was available.'
- 'My sex was not important for my purpose.'
- 'I chose to be a man because that would make it easier to participate in the advance of science.'
- 'I preferred to become a woman, but I chose to be a man anyway because the trials would be greater.'
- 'I wanted to be a woman because my female half is better able to love, is more expressive, and has a better sense of herself.'
- 'I wanted to be a woman, so I would be better able to give.'
- 'I chose to be a woman because my parents would accept that more easily.'
- 'I chose to be a woman because my partner wanted us to have the same sex as we had in 1503.'

A strong, existing preference is retained (see chapter 10). However, a preference may also be the result of free choice, a free consideration. Some people are so faithful to a sex or country or trade that they hardly choose. They may become doctors one life after another, or may have the same sex for many lives. As mentioned, 20 per cent of remigrants only experience lives of the same sex.

A Jewish life may lead to more Jewish lives, a Japanese life to more Japanese lives. One strange observation from Wambach is that of many Americans suddenly having a life in, for example, Asia in the penultimate incarnation before this one, after a whole series of European and American lives (Wambach 1978: 131).

People who fall asleep after their death hang around, wander or haunt, and often incarnate in the vicinity of where they died, even if it was far from their place of birth in a land where they had only stayed temporarily, and outside of personal considerations. Think of the examples of the Burmese children who remember dying in the Second World War as an American pilot and a Japanese soldier. Incomplete dying often makes a reincarnation in the country of death natural. However, with complete dying the desire to return to the same country or the same people is a question of personal preference and 'faithfulness'. If someone considers it important or pleasant to be Jewish, the chance is greater that he will be Jewish in his next life. This may be a rational and at the same time instinctive choice.

People's needs for continuity and change probably differ greatly. Some people, after being a scientist, want to bring out a different aspect of themselves the next time, want to do something different, for example become a rock star or a jet pilot.

Three reincarnation patterns

Based on the published regression literature, and on the experiences of myself and my colleagues, I think there are three patterns of reincarnation. The pattern that makes up the greater part of the reincarnation sessions is one of people who are fairly aware of their condition after their death, look back on their past life with this awareness, and may continue to learn. Usually they prepare their new life in consultation with others and using others' advice. Capabilities, attitudes, preferences and so on continue, traumas and postulates leave repercussions, and the influence of psychological reactions with more or less drastic educational interventions continues. The length of the intermission differs considerably, but is seldom less than a few years and averages about 60 years. Helen Wambach found a 52-year average, and Karl Muller, using a smaller and more diverse sample, slightly under 80 years (Wambach 1978; Muller 1970).

An incarnation process likely to be much more common, but relatively rarely found in regressions, is of people with little or no awareness of their intermission: of sleep, hanging about, or wandering. The best examples of this are the child cases Ian Stevenson researched. They experience being born as being connected to a foetus, or more indirectly, as suddenly sliding off something, or being sucked up into something. The intermissions of these incarnations are usually shorter, varying from a few months to almost ten years. They hardly have karma in the usual sense of the word because psychological or educational considerations to prepare the new life are lacking. Evolution is the general pattern: gaining experience, condensing this into a slowly growing understanding, humanity, and competence, and sometimes the repercussions of traumatic experiences. This kind of reincarnation will be the most common. Ultimately, experience leads to more awareness, until people remain more and more awake between lives and more receptive to contacts with other people. Then, the reincarnation process changes into the first type mentioned.

The first type gradually changes into another type as people become more independent in their learning and development. Many people get the urge to do some real work: contributing to the development of others, incarnate or discarnate. This may be more or less compared to gradually finishing school, and building up a real circle of colleagues through practical experience (although there is permanent education here). To this state belongs also the ability, acquired in between incarnations, actively to assist other people with their reincarnation and the evaluation of their past lives. This means a decreased urge to reincarnate and a more selective choice of a new life. I suspect, but the scant data make this no more than an educated guess, that the average intermission between these incarnations is a little under 250 years, with big differences within the intermissions of the lives of one person, as well as between persons. The people who belong in this third category constitute a growing evolutionary network with, most likely, strong individual specialization tracks. Some people will reincarnate more often, others less, and this division changes depending on the circumstances on earth and what kind of people are needed.

So, there are three populations as far as reincarnation is concerned:

1 *Population I:* General evolution; no individual life plan; undirected and short intermission; a new life close to the old in time and distance.

2 *Population II:* Personal development; a personal life plan with mainly personal development goals and personal settlement of karmic relations; some retrospect; some consultation and some foresight in the intermission; awareness of the intermission; personal ties with other people.

3 *Population III:* Personal contribution to greater developments; personal learning and working objectives; conscious deliberation in the intermission; at times a guide for incarnates; a new life linked to those of friends and associates; reincarnation as a free choice.

Figure 5 gives the approximate distribution of intermissions. In practice, there may be exceptions, various shades and combinations between these three patterns. Still, the differences are clear, real, and important. Say you divide sporting into three categories; recreational (just for fun), amateur, and professional. These categories clearly differ in training, in amount of time spent on it, and in the money it costs (or yields). None the less, there are many shades and combinations. Sometimes professional soccer players just have fun with the game, or amateur players, who earn nothing with the sport, may be members of a sponsored club, etc. The same goes for the three groups. Someone from population II or III may hang around after his or her death and be reborn within a few years. Someone from population I may receive personal help and some preparation for his new life, as the example of the Chinese slave shows.

Life plan and life course

What happens when you plan your life consciously and want to contribute to social developments? And how does this influence the actual course of your life? You think about your coming life and make a life plan. This life plan contains aims you want to realize in society and goals for your own development. In these personal goals you will consider the repercussions of traumas, postulates, and karmic relations. I categorize traumas, postulates, complicated relationships, negative psychological reactions, and remedial interventions all together under the classic heading 'karma'. Karma, then, is nothing more or less than the liabilities of past lives that we carry with us. On the asset side are: developed intelligence, moral sense and competence; and relations consisting of respect, acceptance, and trust. Together, I call these assets 'dharma'.

Thus you have a general karma-dharma balance made up after the profits and losses of each life are calculated (at least, with people in populations II and III). The life plan may contain global or detailed indications of when karmic items will come up, and when particular abilities will be cleared. We have, then a karma-dharma clock as a part of our life plan. I know only one example that describes this mechanism as such. A man preparing a life as an amorous female finds himself working on the things he wanted to change. He was setting up this change by working with a piece of machinery, 'a sort of clockwork instrument into which you could insert certain parts in order for specific consequences to follow', planning his forthcoming life on earth (Whitton and Fisher 1986: 43).

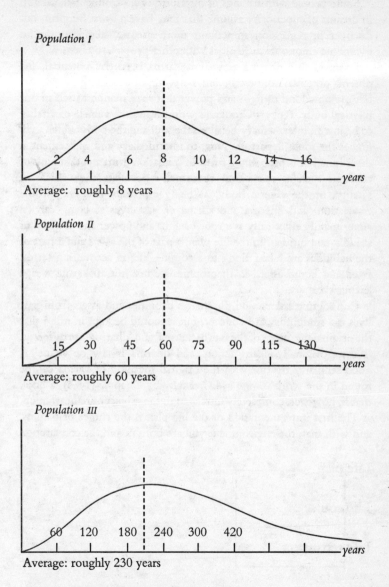

Figure 5 The distribution of intermissions

Some people with feelings of inferiority who compensate for this in dreams of superiority assume that they have a great life plan, but discover in regression something more prosaic, like 'learning to overcome emotional difficulties with other people'.

I suspect that dharma as well as karma is etheric potential, the dharma potential not obstructing, delaying, or obscuring the psyche, but giving a kind of light and power that may manifest itself in our physical body. Robert Crookall's work shows the vehicle of vitality to be just an intermediary between the soul and the body which may hinder the soul's departure. Next to intermediary and encasement, a third function is probably a form of 'radiation armament'. Think of concepts such as mana and charisma. I postulate the vehicle of vitality, or the etheric body, as being especially decisive for the association, and dharma and karma of past lives as being carried along mainly etherically as a robe of light and power and as a veil of shadow and burden. In the life plan, a part of the assets and a part of the liabilities are taken along to a coming life; in accounting terms: fixed and liquid assets; in theosophical terms: not all karma is ripe karma.

Considering karma and dharma as liabilities and assets from past lives is a straighforward concept, but it should be kept in mind that the original meanings of the words 'karma' and 'dharma' are different. 'Karma' originally means 'action', and 'dharma' is 'law' or 'virtue'. A good scholarly treatment of the original meaning of karma can be found in the work *Karma and Creativity* by Chapple (1986), a book that is, however, completely unrelated to the subject of reincarnation.

The first implementation of the life plan is the choice of parents, and with that, the environment you are born in and the constitution

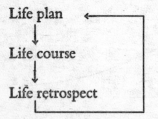

Figure 6 The incarnation cycle (basic figure)

you are born with. The course of the whole pregnancy or the rest of the pregnancy and the birth also influence the birth situation and the talents one has. Environment and talents determine the course of life directly, but also indirectly: in the extent to which one is able to make independent choices during one's life which will themselves influence the course of life. Figures 7–9 give overviews of the planning cycle.

The relation between the life plan and the course of life may be specified as in Figure 7. The diagonal line shows that choice of parents may happen before conception but may be postponed until birth. The later the choice of parents, the more the elapsed period of pregnancy will influence the choice.

Figure 8 shows the overview of the total life–planning cycle. The double arrows indicate personal freedom and responsibility.

1 Consideration of the coming life contains many options. The

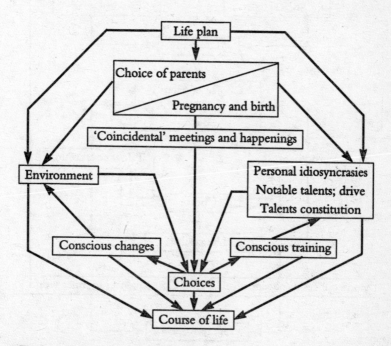

Figure 7 Planning the Course of Life

existing dharma and karma may be selected and worked out personally (except for karmic repercussions of lives without a digestive retrospect).

2 Choices made in the course of life; whether we do something, how we do it, and also how we react to things.

3 The retrospect determines how we work out our life and so what consequences this life has for us. It makes a big difference whether a difficult life is ended in hate, with a shrug, or with compassion.

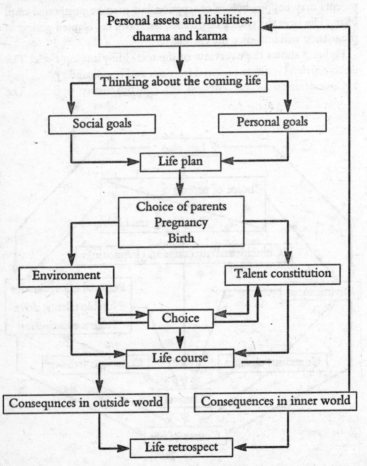

Figure 8 The incarnation cycle of population III

This planning cycle applies to people from population III. People in population I have neither a life plan nor a retrospective. There is no choice of parents, but a choice of foetus based on the vicinity of an available foetus and the suitability of the psychic and etheric conditions of the mother and her direct environment. Figure 9 shows the more simple incarnation cycle of population I.

The incarnation cycle of population II may be directly compared to population III, but social purpose is seldom involved, and the incarnation guides do much of the thinking and planning. In the absence of guides, in emotional or intellectual seclusion, a one-sided, impulsive and unfinished life plan is normally made, with many direct reactions to an often one-sided, impulsive, and unfinished retrospective. The previous chapter gave examples of this. The most important differences among the people in population II are the quality and the effectiveness of the incarnation guides or incarnation educators, the weight of the karmic burden, and the energy of the dharmic potential.

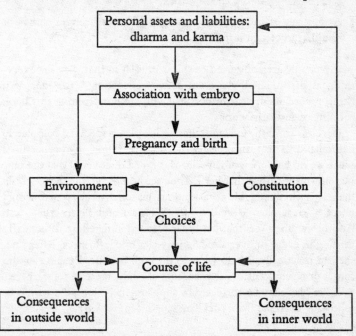

Figure 9 The incarnation cycle of population I

Conclusions

Whitton and Fisher (1986: 45) say that people firmly committed to their own evolution, study and prepare themselves. People devoid of ambition will often fall asleep after their previous life has been judged. 'Materialistic' souls (population I) often rush back to a body when they realize their discarnate state.

Finally, our help from guides, colleagues, or friends may continue during life as inspiration and spiritual guidance. When we deviate from the planned course of life, they may inform us telepathically about our life plan. More spectacular protecting interventions have led to the notion of guardian angels, guiding spirits, and spiritual guides. Thus, our life plan affects us during our life in three ways:

1 As a series of forgotten prenatal post-hypnotic suggestions urging us to do something or avoid something in reaction to particular signals.
2 As a series of meaningful 'coincidences' of meeting people, arriving somewhere, or finding books which are going to play an important role in our lives.
3 As a series of inspirations making us think of certain things or resulting in certain impulses.

Many people are convinced of this, so much so that they see everything as preordained. An unattractive conception – the idea of it being preordained, dear reader, that you are now reading this book robs me of any satisfaction.

It is clear from the evidence that no life plan is specified completely beforehand. The plan consists of patterns, filling in the details is what we do here. A woman who was raped discovered that the rape was not planned but that her karmic script indicated that she would make herself vulnerable to a random personal tragedy that would effect a great change in her life (Whitton and Fisher 1986: 47). Another woman sees that her life is planned in detail up to her early thirties, in order to overcome negative karmic influences. After that, she can practically decide what to do with her life. People can also forget or refuse to plan, often because of a reluctance to reincarnate.

A life plan may be corrected or supplemented along the way. The following example from McClain (1986: 129) is clear:

I originally planned to be a doctor. I started in that direction but I did something very different. I've always felt a little guilty about it. But I see now that being a doctor was not the best choice for growing into my blueprint. Somewhere along the line my subconscious must have realized it wasn't the best route for me to take.

A man gets a father who had done him wrong in several lifetimes. In a situation in which he can easily let his father die he decides to get help. Later he himself had an accident and was lucky to survive. However, his life plan had assumed he would let his father die and that the accident would kill him. After the accident the plan was at an end. He learned that 'sketchy plans for future lives had been brought forward to operate in the current life' (Whitton and Fisher 1986: 45). According to Whitton and Fisher this happens more often than not (1986: 99). They further claim: 'There are also people who appear to be placed precariously between destiny and fate, between scripting their lives and taking the stage as impromptu players. They have a plan, but the plan is open to an inordinate amount of improvisation' (1986: 99).

Using dharma and avoiding karma is excellent work. But producing dharma and settling karma is the real thing. Apparently evolution throughout incarnations leads rather to fertile contribution than to sterile contemplation. And remember, sensing that you have a life plan may be calming and comforting in the vicissitudes of life, but never prevents the necessity of making real choices sometimes.

Further reading

Helen Wambach's material (1979) was an important source for this chapter, as were the results of regression protocols, especially when they contained part of the retrospect and the preview of the life. Whitton and Fisher (1986) give a number of important examples. The experience of colleagues and myself as therapists has contributed a lot. Ian Stevenson's work has also been important, especially for the insights into the incarnation process of population I.

13 The Soul and its Personalities

Belief in reincarnation has pleasant aspects. Our goodbye to this world is not final. We will meet again the people to whom we feel related, we have more than one chance, etc. But to what extent is it we who will have subsequent lives? This is a question about the transience or intransience of our identity, our sense of I, a subject with many opportunities for conceptual confusion.

Identification, identity as self-image

Sometimes we are ourselves, sometimes we are not, sometimes we are not sure. How we experience ourselves depends on our thoughts and feelings, our physical condition, other people, the circumstances, our age. How we see ourselves changes all the time. Sometimes we are quick-tempered, sometimes calmness personified. One moment we may say, 'I am cheerful. I am hungry.' The next moment, 'I do not want any more. I am dead tired.'

Sometimes our self-image changes considerably. We thought we were terribly clumsy and now it turns out we are dexterous. We thought we were misunderstood loners, and suddenly it turns out we are popular. We thought we were lucky, and suddenly we have a streak of bad luck. We thought we were clumsy with girls, and now we know we are homosexual.

To say 'I' now differs from saying it ten years ago. In another ten years we will have changed again. Ten years ago, we could say: 'I am insecure. I have adolescent pimples. I am good in French. I do not have a boyfriend yet. I love my father.' In ten years time we might say: 'I am divorced. I have two children. I love my job. I have contact lenses. I have fallen in love again.'

Stage hypnotists can make people believe they are chickens or famous singers. Similarly, our day-to-day identity, our normal self-image may become interspersed with virtually hypnotic suggestions by others and ourselves. Many people see themselves quite differently than those around them do. This may involve conceit or self-deceit, and in serious cases megalomania and paranoia. Psychiatrists and psychologists know all about identity problems (I do not mean their own identity problems). The old adage 'know thyself' points out that our present self-image may contain much mystification. Identifications with parents, brothers, sisters, and many others can be woven into our self-image. Our identification also changes quickly with our experience of success or failure (a basic theme in individual psychology), with our experiences of satisfaction and frustration (a basic theme in psychoanalysis), with the growth of understanding or perplexity, with our physical condition, with our being satiated or hungry, with our being warm or cold.

We integrate all these different self-perceptions, reasonably so, because they all share the same experience track and memory fund: one memory of experiences in one body, connected by many elements of continuity. In general, our sex and many other physical traits remain the same, and past experiences remain the same for the rest of our life. With most of us, a number of characteristics and idiosyncrasies remain more or less the same, as well as such qualities as intelligence.

However, the picture is more complicated. Our identity shifts in the course of our life and in the course of every day, but we also have differing and sometimes conflicting identities at the same time. Faust's lament, *'Zwei Seelen, ach, wohnen in meiner Brust!'* ('Two souls, alas, live in my breast!'), is the classic example of this. We may feel conflicting emotions simultaneously, as though we are divided, as though we are being torn apart. Psychology works with various self-concepts. Transactional analysis speaks of the Parent, the Adult, and the Child, in each of us, as three sides of our 'I'. In the Parent, we encounter identification with others whom we see or saw as our superiors. When breaking away from our parents to become independent of them, we may idolize other examples, and identify ourselves with heroes, whether from the past, from the silver screen, or living around the corner. We may identify ourselves with Florence Nightingale or John Travolta. We may do this for a short while or a long time, all the time, or only on special occasions. Woody Allen tries to identify himself with Humphrey Bogart in *Play it again, Sam*. Others only go as far as imagining themselves in the movies.

Identifications may get out of hand. Psychiatric patients who fancy they are Napoleon have been speaking to the imagination for almost two centuries. And next door may live somebody who knows he is Christ and is being crucified again.

Some regressions produce identification with interesting or satisfying lives from the past. Although I pointed out in chapter 1 that the compensation hypothesis does not fit the majority of cases, there is pathology in this area as well. For example, volume one of *Reincarnation Report* contained the following account:

If the Guinness Book of Records had a past-life category, Patricia Diegel might be a top contender. A past-life counsellor, Patricia recently told us that she can remember 927 past lives of her own. She started with 27, including Mary Queen of Scots. When she later met a client who also had Mary Queen of Scots, she said 'I gave her that life. I didn't need it any more.'

Patricia Diegel advertises in *Paradise Neighbourhood News* that she teaches the Master Sciences from an Esoteric Viewpoint (Evolutionary). Moreover, she has collected these sciences in *The Cosmic Mandate*: a blueprint for immortality. She has given more than 25,000 readings of past lives (which she calls immortality consultations) and has taught hundreds of people to look into their past lives through the 'trinity-process'. Her specialities are the Initiations, the Rays, the Hierarchy of the White Brotherhood, and the evolutionary path. The pamphlet's motto is: 'The Christ in me greets the Christ in you.' Every identity can be smothered in such luminescent slush.

Our identity has three other complications. The first complication is that besides normative ego states and constructed self-images, there is our great unknown: our subconscious. The subconscious is a chapter, or rather a library, in itself. The second complication is that the course of a life can split into different strands of experience within different sub-personalities. A famous and relatively recent book about an extreme case is *Sybil* (Schreiber 1973). To some extent everybody's personality is a community of relatively independent parts. We may be aggressive where competition plays a role, and in our role as father be patience and friendliness themselves. Or we may reveal any other combination. Psychotherapy makes successful use of this in 'ego-state therapy' (Watkins 1979; Edelstein 1981). Psychosynthesis, too, is familiar with the term 'sub-personality'. However, the examples I have seen from this field seem rather to mythologize undesirable traits than discover the existing personality structure.

A related complication is that of selective loss of memory. Many people cannot recall large chunks of their past life. For example, someone cannot, for all the world, remember instances when he was angry or had to endure scorn. Parts of the personality remain underground as it were. When these sub-personalities have partial or complete loss of memory, we come near psychosis.

Our personality is like a family living in close quarters, members of which may consolidate and furcate. There are the sensitive and insensitive members, older, younger, conceited wiseacres, vague copies of other people, black sheep and criminals who are seldom there (at least, in most of us). That a soul is an individual, an indivisible entity, may ultimately be true. It is certainly true for our body. That our identity, our 'I', is indivisible is a myth of people who parrot what they have been told by people who have pinched their eyes tightly shut.

The pathology of self-images

We have a healthy identity when our sub-personalities live together as a harmonious and considerate family; when we are parent, child and adult simultaneously; when our male and female sides are balanced (preferably a man in the lead in a male body, and a woman in a female body). Our self-image becomes pathological when the various family members dominate one another, ignore each other, or even forget each other (for example in the case of Sybil). Suppressed identities may break into the parental home every now and then. Even without obsession we may legally be psychotic; 'unaccountable'. When we identify ourselves with a strong and schematic ideal-projection, this self-image creates a tyrannical pseudo-identity. Freud would call this an overly powerful super-ego, Harris a tyrannical parent.

Many spiritual people see their 'higher self' as their perfect self, able only to reveal itself partially. Such people populate churches, sects, and noble world views. Their ideal of humanity is to lay off the all too human and become a kind of angel. To me this is evolutionary extortion: not wanting to be who you are, but who you think you ought to be. An angel image is a shining robot identity, a mechanical and infantile attempt to rise above the reality of humanity and the world. Successful identification leads to inhuman robots, unapproachable people caught in their self-righteousness, play-acting exaltedly in their own decorated little heaven. I am not the first to point out the bad taste and the tediousness of such ideal images.

During their lifetime people may build up an illusory existence (see chapter 8). The inherent morbidity shows in the suffocating atmosphere of their angel world, and in the way they see the real world. For those with the strongest self-hypnosis, the environment is light. Pain, sickness, doubt, misery, meanness, and hopelessness are absent or unreal, imaginations of the as yet unawakened soul. They walk around as innocent as plants or, protected by perfect habits, as robots. When the self-delusion is a bit less potent, the exterior world is dangerous: full of the traps of tempters, false Messiahs (of the other clubs), cynics, blockheads, and sleepwalkers. The outside world may also be dark: the outside world is a hell. With even weaker self-hypnosis we have to acknowledge our own imperfections. Then we become actors in the classic melodrama 'oh, woe is me', yearning for the angel in us (or outside us) and eternally struggling with the beast or devil in us. An overview of the types of ego inflation is given in Table 8.

The quality of the self-image can be most easily recognized from how someone lives with the animal in himself. In a healthy person the animal is present as friendly pets in the family of sub-personalities. In all forms of 'ego inflation' (identifying yourself with something higher, perfect) the incompletely suppressed animal deteriorates into aggressive animals of prey, false dogs and cats and underground vermin in the house of our consciousness. Many people fight with raging wolves that they fail to kill because these are parts of themselves, rather than calming them down, taming and making them faithful and watchful dogs. This fight is worse in powerful personalities who deny the sub-personalities they are ashamed of entrance to the house. These transform and deteriorate from black sheep and crude criminals into sulking sadists and burning devils. Wanting to escape into a heaven creates the suction power of hell. I associate the character of Mephistopheles, the inner scorner, with the cynic.

Of course we have to distinguish between people in ordinary situations and in horrible and violent situations. Someone in a concentration camp may naturally think of his wife back home as an angel. Someone who is tortured justifiably experiences the world as a hell. Only self-made heavens and hells are pathological. Much may be said on this central topic of psychology. All kinds of projections, shifts, reaction mechanisms happen, for example, in the case of boys who are in love with angelic girls and feel themselves to be masturbating beasts. Life is difficult. But apparently that is just what makes us grow up. The perfected grows out of the imperfect, the permanent out of the transient, peace from war, health from sickness, calm from nervousness, wisdom from stupidity.

Next to disassociation and inflation the most important identity diseases are: depersonalization, derealization, and, what I will call in the same terminology, 'deseparation'. Depersonalization means losing your sense of I while staying fully conscious, no longer feeling an identity, a personality. The memory of 'having been around' does not bring back the feeling of 'being there'. You are an empty bottle of fleeting thoughts and colourful shadows. Derealization works the other way round. You experience yourself as surrounded by, trapped in, unreality. This existential experience is lethal: everything is decor, cardboard, grey paste with the bewildering, disgusting, wholly impossible pretension that it is real! As noted above, a well-known description of this experience may be found in Jean-Paul Sartre's

Table 8 Types of ego-inflation

Self and world view	Suppression successful	Suppression doubtful	Suppression unsuccessful	
			Ordinary energy	Strong energy
Beautiful (heavenly)	Angel-plant (1)		Angel-beast (4)	
Neutral	Angel-robot (2)		Angel-beast (5)	Angel-devil (8)
Dangerous		Angel-cynic (3)	Angel-beast (6)	Angel-devil (9)
Dark (hellish)			Angel-beast (7)	Angel-devil (10)

book *La Nausée*. Solipsism, the doctrine that only I exist and that others are only apparitions of my own consciousness, is the intellectual dummy of derealization.

Mysticism strives for experiences, states of consciousness going beyond the limits of the present self-image, through identification with things outside the body: an object, another person, other living things, a landscape. A further experience can be no longer to sense any separation between oneself and the environment, the sense of 'pouring oneself out over the world', becoming one with all (thus, with God), the *unio mystica*, the mystic unity. Clinically speaking, such a state of consciousness can be compared directly with depersonalization or derealization. In the first state we no longer experience our own reality, in the second we no longer experience the reality of the other, and in the third we no longer experience any separation between ourselves and the other. A clinical translation of the *unio mystica* is 'deseparation': the disappearance of separateness. Propagandists of deseparation always have a preference for becoming one with the world, with God, or with 'all people', and seldom with their wife, their neighbour, or the cat across the street. A tree or another being or object without danger of responding to your passion for oneness is more acceptable.

In deep and intimate human relationships moments of healthy deseparation may occur as episodes having value merely because the partners are not completely and consistently unified. It is one of the most attractive ingredients of sexual intercourse. Or rather, it may be. In the world of soft sex and porn, people are more interested in losing themselves than in finding another. Anyway, sex may be pleasant even without deseparation.

Our identity, our being ourselves, our 'I', then, is not a fixed and indivisible fact, but rather a collection of results of identification processes open to influences and arbitrariness. Identification is a natural and apparently essential characteristic of human consciousness with its own morphology and therewith its own pathology. The identification process may even remain in a zero state for a shorter or longer period while our body and consciousness remain intact – witness depersonalization.

In practice our physical sense primarily determines our sense of self. For example, we experience ourselves spatially in our body with the focus of our sense of self in our head, behind our eyes. Hereafter, 'personality' means the identity tied into the continuity of our physical sense in our total fund of experience, beginning with our first memories.

The identity of the discarnate person, higher self and life plan

The descriptions of the discarnate state in chapter 8, largely based on Crookall's work and on regression experiences, show that we can be more ourselves and less restricted in between lives. After a complete dying, we are free from confusion, inhibition, and defect, but not all-knowing and infallible. The deceased who report their state admit this, but often in giving their descriptions, speeches, and answers clearly forget their limitations. Feeling free easily leads to forgetting limitations but, fortunately, not to loss of limitations. Discarnate people, through their feeling of freedom and the easy availability of much information, tend to be overenthusiastic – witness much of the literature they convey (Ruth Montgomery and Jane Roberts, for example).

Completely awakened discarnates are usually similar to when they were most themselves in the incarnate state, allowing for the subjects they consider and the people they meet. These in turn depend largely on their state. Immediately after their death most people take on the appearance of the life they have just finished, to begin with, that of the last time they felt good, and later of the age and the condition in which they felt best. Only later do they acquire an aspect less tied to their past life. In general they appear to others in the form most familiar to them. When interested in subjects that particularly concerned them in a particular life, they often take on the personality of that incarnation. Thus, the self-image of a discarnate is both more flexible and more stable than that when incarnate. The personality remains untrammelled. People who get stuck in the etheric intermediate area are rather uninhibited, indulging in their pet emotions and pet thoughts.

Someone who has become himself has a free personality. Theosophists do speak of the higher self, but the disadvantage of this term is the implication of being a separate entity from our ordinary or lower self. For example, people talk about 'my higher self' and 'my lower self'. Like the expression 'my self', these are blunt and misleading indications because they suggest identity in terms of 'having' rather than 'being'.

Many see the higher self as all-knowing, all-wise, and never changing from the beginning to the end of incarnations. This is only partially true. Of course there is a continuity of entity. I will call this entity the 'soul' from here on. I call 'spirit' all the phenomena of consciousness, including self-consciousness. The content and structure of this self-consciousness, the self-image, grows out of our experiences in the body. Physical, incarnate experience, and not psychical, discarnate experience leads to awareness and self-awareness. Once we have self-awareness it can awaken and blossom in the discarnate state. The soul awakens and focuses itself in its incarnations. Ultimately, this is spiritualization, and the body is the vehicle for spiritualization. Initially the soul only has an awareness thanks to the organism it inhabits, and after death it sinks into forgetfulness (falling asleep). Gradually it learns to dream after death, the dreams become more vivid, and subsequently the soul awakens in meeting other real discarnate people. Full self-awareness, then, is triggered, leading to, in pedagogic terminology, growing 'self-responsible self-determination'.

Discarnate people do not normally experience themselves as an abstract being, but in their own image. Their personality, their reflected self, therefore changes almost at will. The personality of the discarnate person can be best characterized as the personality he was in his most optimal incarnation, but now without physical limitations, and with access to all his other personalities with whom he feels identity. The various personalities of the different lives may be compared to the various sub-personalities we know during one life. When someone dies he continues the personality of the past life, but soon enough he can gain access to past personalities, and thus after his death he grows into this larger personality, usually after the digestion of his past life, focusing around the most aware and the ripest incarnation. This comprehensive sense of self disappears during each incarnation, similar to sleep: we experience a break of consciousness but not a break in personality.

We see the opportunity of a future life from the vantage-point of our broader personality and design the new life based on our experiences, characteristics, development needs, and preferences. At least that is the usual state of population III after a complete death experience. We know we will lose a large part of our awareness and will be able to express only a part of our abilities. In making our life plan, we draw from all the personalities of past lives. In each new life one past incarnation provides the dominant, feeding personality, usually decisive for the character, the capabilities, and often the looks of the new incarnation. Without a conscious intermission, personal formation, or choice, as in population I, the dominant personality is simply the personality of the past life. With a conscious choice this may be quite different. We can reach personalities from quite a few lives back. We do have less choice in lives and episodes which carry unreleased tensions, have karma.

The consciousness we have in our larger personality is the consciousness of our psychic body, which Crookall calls 'psychic consciousness'. When we are shrouded in ethers we more or less have a dream consciousness. Apparently there is one stage of consciousness above the 'psychic consciousness' called 'cosmic consciousness'. Everybody who deals with the discarnate state needs to characterize its consciousness. Whitton uses the terms 'dissociative consciousness', 'affective consciousness', and 'metaconsciousness' (Whitton and Fisher 1986: 7). His definitions do not seem very apt to me. His dissociative consciousness is, as he rightly defines it himself, more a state of being than a state of consciousness. He mixes dissociate states with the corresponding consciousness. Out-of-body experiences may be a dissociative state, but they may have a dissociative (what I called 'elliptic') consciousness only at the moment of exit or entry. Out of the body one may have either dream consciousness or psychic consciousness. To imply that the sleeping body has a sleep consciousness is stretching the concept of consciousness until it becomes meaningless. In sleep we are unconscious, just as subliminal perceptions may be called subconscious. Further, Whitton's definitions of affective consciousness and metaconsciousness overlap. Affective consciousness may have 'oneness with the universe' and in metaconsciousness we lose all sense of personal identity. This is unclear terminology. I suggest, therefore, using the following terms:

- unconsciousness (sleep, loss of consciousness, catalepsis)

- dream consciousness (dreams, incomplete awakening outside the body)
- consciousness (physical perception)
- self-consciousness (physical self-perception)
- psychic consciousness (complete awakening outside the body, lucid and vivid dreams, higher self-consciousness, spiritual self-perception)
- cosmic consciousness (permeable boundary of the self-notself, perception of larger, cosmic whole of which we are a part, without loss of personal identity.

When we choose a previous personality as the prominent 'root' of the coming personality, we automatically take all the traumas and postulates attached to it as well. The dominant or root personality functions as a matrix for a number of secondary personalities, usually two or three, sometimes up to six or seven. The reason for involving these other personalities in secondary roles like side-roots in the coming life, may be because of special capabilities from these lives which are pertinent now, or because of contacts they had with people we are going to see again now, or because such lives carry a number of undigested general feelings or have specific traumatic experiences of which we consciously want to rid ourselves, or that we take along involuntarily.

Thus our present personality is often only in a small part determined by our genetic, more general, physical predisposition and our environment. First of all, for the most part we have chosen this predisposition and environment ourselves with our relationships and our development in mind. Second, we have a life plan we designed or accepted, and a fund of capabilities and characteristics compiled from our past personalities. At any given moment in our life we have, besides our personality developed so far, the yet unrealized potential of the life plan. Our personality is not only what we are, but also what we want to be according to our life line. Thus, we have:

- the as yet unexplored potential of our soul
- the discarnate part of our larger personality
- the unrealized personality potential of this life
- our present personality (with a number of sub-personalities)

- our traumas and postulates (often related to problematic sub-personalities).

Therefore, our development entails:

- resolving traumas and postulates
- liberating and incorporating problematic sub-personalities
- harmonizing and connecting the other sub-personalities
- realization of our life line
- contacting our larger personality
- always developing more knowledge, understanding, and wisdom; more morality, empathy, and love; more independence, competence, and creativity.

The reality of personalities from past lives, pseudo-obsessions and obsessions

Apparently, past lives are not mere memories, but the personalities from past lives continue to exist as such. According to Pieter Barten: 'Each personality we have been, still exists now. In a complete regression we relive them again with all their feelings, all their thoughts, and all their emotions. They see not only the reality from their past around them, but also the present reality' (cited in ten Dam 1982). Thus a regression to a past life is more or less an animation of the past personality. With a life directly related to the present life you experience this past personality simply as an aspect of yourself. A life that is less related is experienced roughly like a lucid dream. You are as easily inside as outside.

The past personalities exist in different ways. Some are sleeping structures as it were, empty balloons which you have to give energy and consciousness to bring them back to life. After that, they return into the fold of the wider personality because their lives have been completely worked out. They have become free roles of the larger personality. Other past personalities retain their own charge of un-digested experiences or of dammed-up capabilities that they could not fully express in their life.

Dagmar O'Connor, author of *The First Pharaoh* (1956), recounts that during a session with a medium a guide said to her: 'Mercia wants to talk to you.' She could not believe this because Mercia was the name of a previous incarnation of herself. But the guide said, 'Why not? She is just as real as the other parts of your own self.' He compared the consecutive lives with a mother soul's 'tentacles' sent out to gather knowledge and experience. These personalities contact each other just as they do other people. Then, through the medium, Mercia said that she was not the mother soul but another 'tentacle' living in the spiritual sphere and still being a part of herself (Muller 1970: 221). Apparently this personality was not a feeding incarnation, but was aware and had access to the soul. A past personality, then, may live outside our present incarnate personality, from the energy of the larger personality. The soul it seems, does incarnate incompletely and, alongside the current incarnation, may be conscious in discarnate personalities from past lives. A complete incarnation of a soul seems to be uncommon, if possible at all.

Phobias and complexes in the present personality may become fused with the problems of past personalities. Less circumscribed, but sometimes stronger, are connections with postulates from past lives: rigid, almost compulsive ideas and attitudes so fused with ourselves that we hardly perceive them. In personality disturbances and fixations such as phobias, complexes and postulates, in particular, our past personalities are like Siamese twins. In this limited sense, we may speak of a return of the same personality. This is one of the most important empirical qualifications of the reincarnation concept: personalities retain their separate identity, at least when a person retains self-awareness after death.

In our daily lives these past personalities may come up at different moments and in different ways. Some people may have a different face in different circumstances, or start behaving differently in different phases of life. Many such changes come from the choreography of sub-personalities, but some may come from past lives. The exploration of past lives related to the present life elicits a recognition of themes in the present life, sometimes coinciding with sub-personalities.

The accounts from spiritistic mediums and clairvoyants, too, demonstrate that personalities of past lives can clearly stand on their own. Chapter 2 mentioned a nice example: the African who had a pleasant and easy life because he was always advised by his best friend, the personality from a past life. During seances contacting the dead, people sometimes announce that they are the past personality of somebody who is now living, and they want to give an explanation or advice to help the life of the actual personality. This occurs without the latter knowing anything about it.

Chapter 4 mentioned the example of the spirit who appeared during a seance and said that she was the previous incarnation of a woman who at that moment was sleeping peacefully in another country. She said she often wandered around in a nunnery where she had died in a previous life. When asked whether the ordinary personality knew about this, she answered it was just a vague dream and a certain feeling (Muller 1970: 172). Here, we see an example of a previous personality that can only appear when the present personality is asleep. The past personality is integrated in the matrix of the subconscious and can only have a consciousness of its own when the consciousness of the ordinary personality is under cover, as the stars appear after sunset.

The negative example of barely integrated personalities is that of 'pseudo-obsession', where someone carries the personality of a past personality in his body or his aura, and not integrated into the larger personality. Often it was a traumatic life, sometimes short, which never arrived at full self-awareness or in which self-awareness was lost, crippled, or stultified. Pseudo-obsessions are usually attended by shifting psychosomatic complaints. The Brazilian spiritualist doctors regard autism as a symptom of pseudo-obsession. I would add to this anorexia nervosa, bulimia, persistent migraines, and phantom pains, together with emotional instability.

In past-life therapy we start with a regression to that traumatic life, and then the therapist leads the haunting, restless personality through a complete dying experience, guided by the present personality or, if necessary, the therapist. After that, the pseudo-obsessor becomes an integrated 'family member', either in the present life or in the larger self. Healing a pseudo-obsession is interesting, satisfying, and has spectacular results: a revolution in general well-being and a dramatic disappearance of the psychosomatic complaints.

Such unintegrated, haunting past personalities may sporadically disturb ordinary age regressions, when a different personality suddenly appears to manifest itself. This may scare the wits out of the inexperienced therapist because he may be reminded of an obsession.

The treatment is easiest with hypnosis, because the therapist can imprint beforehand that contact with the larger self can be made at all times, for example by finger signals. Then he immediately sees whether the intervening personality is from a past life or from a different person. Anyway, the appearance is a positive sign, suddenly opening up a whole field of healing. When an obsessor or pseudo-obsessor can tell his life story it may be extremely relieving, and sometimes leads to spontaneous healing.

Let me give a few examples of pseudo-obsessions and obsessions. Muller gives the example of a Brazilian who has worked hard for his family all his life and has put everything aside for it. When he was 63 years old, after an accident, he started to get nervous and to reproach his wife for adultery. The family laughed about it since they found it a silly assumption. However, he became more and more agitated and finally psychotic. He became aggressive towards his wife and later also to other people, and had to be kept under constant surveillance. Finally, he was put into an asylum. After a few days of agitation he was calm and friendly to everybody again. After three months, he was sent home healed. But there all the symptoms returned immediately. He wanted to beat his wife and screamed day and night. He was brought back to the asylum where he became calm and happy again for two months.

A psychic reading said that in his previous life he was a rich Spanish merchant. He was a widower with a number of older children when he got married to a young girl who had lived a carefree life as an embroiderer for the bullfighters. He caught her during adultery and sent her out of the house. Later, he met her in the company of one of his sons, while she mocked him. This resulted in a fight with the son, who was seriously wounded. He forgave the son, took him home, but the son died of his wounds. Thereupon, the father committed suicide. Apparently, as he got older and weaker, the personality of the past life was freed and produced the shadows of the past along with its feelings of distrust and hatred. Here we see someone acquiring a pseudo-obsession at a later age through the personality of his own previous incarnation. It seems that a weakened constitution and a strong emotional charge in the past personality may suffice for this to happen (Muller 1970: 210).

Bruce Goldberg provides the example of a young American

woman on holiday in Germany who is planning to depart for Belgium. She runs into a twenty-four-hour delay. To pass the time, she visits a castle turned into a museum. In the castle she sees the portrait of an inhabitant from the thirteenth century. She goes into spontaneous regression and relives the woman's complete life. She is unable to move a muscle during the experience, which lasts about forty-five minutes. Later she goes to a therapist to confirm a few details (Goldberg 1982: 66). Goldberg justly says that this is not classic *déjà vu*. Here we have a temporary obsession where the deceased tries to catch someone's attention, either through the woman's accessibility or because a personal relationship exists. This may also be a previous incarnation of herself, and so a temporary pseudo-obsession. Anyway, it is clearly a case of a separate personality intervening. The rigidity, and maybe even the twenty-four-hour delay, are clear interventions.

Another possible obsession case is that of an intelligent and attractive anorexia nervosa patient experiencing herself in a past life as a fat and extraordinarily unpleasant man who likes to keep attractive little girlfriends and abuse them (Goldberg 1982: 127). The difference between these two lives is so extreme that I wonder if the patient might be a previous girlfriend who is obsessed by this boor. It would fit in much better with other anorexia cases. If this is true, the regression therapy has ingrained this obsession further, and the author's conclusions are prematurely optimistic, although the anorexia virtually disappeared. Some past-life therapists, like Louise Ireland-Frey (1986), always check first and treat attachments and obsessions before entering into regression therapy, in order to prevent reliving the lives of others and creating more confusion than is resolved.

Muller gives the example of a medium who is treating an obsession receiving the message that in this case the disturbing personality should not be removed, since this was a past personality of the same person and is to be integrated (Muller 1970: 213). The previous example from Goldberg appears to be the reverse: an obsessing personality which should not be integrated but separated. Past-life therapy without insight into obsession and pseudo-obsession may be counterproductive. Another reason for laymen to refrain from it.

The appearance of personalities during regressions

Someone regressing to a past life feels these experiences as his own in spite of large differences in body, habits, emotions, and opinions. During a regression he can be his present and his past personality simultaneously. Apparently Joe Keeton's regression technique results in the double existence of the past personality, who is in contact with the counsellor, and the present personality, who is present as a powerless but conscious observer. I have characterized this as an 'elliptic' consciousness, a consciousness with two focal points. And this is precisely what a personality is: a focal point of our consciousness, a sense of self connecting and centring a string of experiences.

All recollection, reliving, and regression experiences contain some elliptic consciousness. You can remember being beaten when you were 6. You remember it, you re-experience it, and at the same time, you feel sorry for the 6-year-old from the vantage-point of your present age. Many forms of self-reflection dissociate the focus of awareness somewhat: self-pity, self-judgement, narcissism, and so on.

Colin Wilson has often remarked that in people with multiple personalities (such as Sybil) these have a hierarchy. I have used the analogy of a family structure. The hierarchical structure is complicated. First of all, some sub-personalities know about other sub-personalities. 'Carla' can talk about 'Jenny's' character but 'Jenny' knows nothing of 'Carla's' existence: a who-knows-about-who hierarchy. In the regressions Joe Keeton induced, the present consciousness knew about the past consciousness, but not vice versa. Still, the present consciousness was powerless. This indicates another hierarchy: personalities who have access to the body's 'driver's seat', personalities who have temporarily lost access, and those who never have access. Third is the genetic hierarchy: who begot who. For example, all Sybil's personalities were furcations outside her knowledge and control. Sybil was the weakest personality although she was the original, the root personality. Furcation may be compared to a mother who faints every now and again, not realizing that she is bearing children who each take a piece of her energy from her. I believe that the same is true for personalities from past lives. Some have access to the larger self and, consequently, to all the other personalities. Others are introverted or isolated, some of them imprisoned in an undigested life.

When regressing people to past lives we enter an area with a definite but as yet hardly charted structure. Each life plan has connections to a limited number of previous lives (usually between 3 and 6). When we leave our present personality, we probably enter one of the feeding incarnations, most likely the central feeding incarnation, the main root of this life. When we are preoccupied consciously or unconsciously, we end up in the incarnation most strongly connected to this preoccupation. When we are preoccupied with questions of death, our first experience may be a traumatic death. If we feel fear, or another negative emotion, or if we are stuck, we enter situations which created traumas or postulates. Consequently, we only enter lives connected to our karma or dharma. Other lives are only accessible via the larger self. Indications of contact with this larger self are the ability to relive positive post-mortem or prenatal experiences, and the ability to leave our selves and experience the same situation from within others.

During regression the personality of a past life may be so strongly present that it is possible to talk with it directly. Short-circuits may also occur. Chapter 6 gave examples of 'identification'. Here, the past personality sits squarely in the driver's seat. The opposite can also happen: the present personality may enter a situation relating to the past personality. Shirley gives an amusing, but disturbing example of this (1924: 58). It seems to be a short-circuit after an experience of the larger self, with an insightful overview of all past lives and the present one. Robert Monroe had a similar experience, just as amusing and just as disturbing. His experiences take place in what he calls 'environment III', and give the impression of a parallel incarnation in another planet (Monroe 1977).

Often, contact with the larger personality speeds up a therapy. Sometimes it is just a question of passing the buck. This happens when the therapist doubts whether a regression to a particular episode is desirable, and asks the larger self or a guide for advice. But the therapist has to judge the value of the advice, and remains responsible. Sometimes, the remigrant is reluctant to relive something and wants to experience it from a more stable, a more objective point of view. Contacts with the larger self are helpful as intermissions which stimulate the experiencing and working out of traumas and postulates, not when they replace doing so.

The chance that an alien personality will come up during a regression apparently scares some people. They associate regression with trance, and trance with getting lost, with a risky form of passivity. Only obsessors and pseudo-obsessors may come up, either unobtrusively or demonstratively. A regression to the experiences inducing the obsession may be liberating, especially when the obsessor is treated as a full person. The probability that an obsessor will enter during a regression is very slight indeed. Mediumistic people who regress with somatic effects such as stiffness, cooling down, and staring, or returning to tense situations where they were psychic, might rouse past adversaries or similar souls. However, a therapist who remains calm and self-assured can easily prevent this. Incidental or permanent physical contact and the right verbal contact with the right instructions are sufficient. If a psychic remigrant has less control of the driver's seat than there should be, this seat is still protected when the therapist remains in control. An insecure or scared therapist should let the remigrant return.

Spiritual sensitivity and ability in a therapist are helpful, but not necessary. Calmness and professional skill are more important. The remigrant may go by a simple rule: if you really trust the therapist he is probably good enough.

Dissociation techniques, that is, communicating directly with separate sub-personalities and personalities in the consciousness of the remigrant, give good therapeutic results. The therapist may ask the present personality to intervene in a traumatic episode. People can comfort themselves as a newborn baby. They can rescue themselves from the hands of henchmen. They can provide the comfort, understanding, love, security, and relief that was once profoundly lacking. They don't rewrite history but change its psychological repercussions. Whole personalities can be imprisoned in undigested experiences and totalitarian postulates blocking psychic energy. Technically, this resembles the static twilight existence described in chapter 8. Chapters 15 and 16 say more about dissociation techniques.

The possibility of parallel personalities

We can clarify a part of the relation between the soul and its personalities with some exceptional cases found in the regression literature: overlapping incarnations, simultaneous incarnations, and furcating incarnations. When the last personality died after the present personality was born the intermission is negative. This may be from a few days to three months, and, in rare cases, up to three years. During a regression into this life, a break may occur at the age of eighteen months, and suddenly the remigrant is in the dying experience of the previous incarnation. Apparently people sometimes withdraw after birth. This does not always lead to the child's death, but perhaps only to a change of personality. The person who enters the body is usually someone who has just died rather near by; in other words, someone who remained earthbound. This may happen rather directly, and the memories may cease on the same day as the previous personality died. Sometimes a confused soul has been wandering about for some time, looking instinctively for a body. Almost always it finds a growing foetus, but on rare occasions it apparently finds a living body just being abandoned by the inhabitant. Pieter Langedijk (1980) writes of a remigrant who remembers sitting and eating in a high chair when she was 2 years old. When he asks her to go back to the age of 1, her reaction is: 'There is nothing. I am not 1 year old.' Every time he brings her back to the age of 2 she has experiences, but at the age of 1 there is nothing. Then, instead of telling her to go back to age 1, he tells her to go one year back. 'Now where are you? You are somewhere, aren't you?' 'Yes, I am in a concentration camp in Germany and I am being shot.' A few weeks later she entered an eighteen-month-old child. Langedijk reports, too, about a dead woman. She was looking for a new family when she saw a mother with a beautiful daughter. Her desire for beauty was so strong that she hung around until illness exhausted the girl, then she pushed her out and crawled into the body herself. After that, her life was difficult because she did not fit in with the family at all. The beautiful body entranced her and she did not realize that her mother and father had a terrible relationship (TenDam 1982). Apparently this is not karma but what Rousseau called 'natural punishment'. Such cases only look like overlapping incarnations. They overlap in terms of the registrar's office, not in terms of psychological life histories.

Such negative intermissions or apparent overlaps also occur in spontaneous child cases. Stevenson found a few cases and investigated them. The example of Jasbir is the most well known (Stevenson (1966: 34). Jasbir died when he was $3\frac{1}{2}$. Immediately after that, he came back to life, like someone who has been temporarily clinically dead. However, it turned out that there was a new personality in the body who remembered his previous life. Another well-documented case is that of Hermann Grundei (Muller 1970: 122). His previous life ended thirty-five days after the birth of this life. The striking resemblance is interesting. Perhaps here there really is an overlapping incarnation. Anyway, negative intermissions have been demonstrated. They usually occur when the young child is weak or ill, or has little will to live. The entering personality normally has a strong drive to incarnate quickly. Change of personality may also happen after, for example, shell-shock. According to the *The Boy Who Saw True* this only happens to people who have practised dubious forms of magic in their past lives, and have taught themselves to be open to the will of others (Spearman ed. 1953: 231).

Can we have simultaneous incarnations? I have found some indications of this in regressions but it remains a tricky field. The only example I know from the literature is Pat Roberts (Moss and Keeton 1979: 171). Pat describes the life of a woman who lived in Liverpool in around 1900. Many obscure data were later verified in the archives and from gravestones. Even the names and the birth dates were correct. The only problem was that many facts, though true, appeared to be in conflict. Further investigation showed that two women with almost the same name had lived rather close together. Facts from these two lives had been mixed up in the regression. This could be a parallel incarnation or perhaps an obsession. The case of a pair of English twins who were infamous criminals supports the idea that a soul can incarnate in several bodies simultaneously. It looked as though the two women had the same personality and the same consciousness. Rather than a split personality in one body – as with obsession – it looked as though this was one personality in a split body. An alternative explanation may be a common obsessor. Bruce Goldberg speaks of 'simultaneous multiple incarnations', but does not give examples from his regression practice (Goldberg 1982: 43).

Wambach's material on regressions to prenatal conditions (1979) contains some mysterious cases. One remigrant says she 'had to find her other half to make a whole.' She says she was a small girl with long hair before she was born (Wambach 1979: 53). Another re-migrant says that she and her mother were the same person until her awareness entered the foetus. At this point, they separated. She herself remained virtually unchanged, whereas her mother changed considerably. She felt as though she was in control, while her mother felt helpless (Wambach 1979: 119). This could indicate that the mother's personality split, the strongest aspects of her personality going to her daughter where they became a separate personality.

Strange as it seems, this is far from impossible. Cases like Eva and Sybil show us how sub-personalities can function independently. We could also ourselves be a sub-personality of the larger self, a sub-personality able to furcate parts of itself in our subconscious, where they may lead a more or less independent existence. Of course, a sub-personality which is only psychologically different differs greatly from a sub-personality which has separately incarnated. Simultaneous incarnated personalities may exist unknown to each other.

A preliminary summary

We need to distinguish between the soul, an entity which exists either aware or unaware of itself, and the spirit of self-reflecting awareness or self-awareness, growing from the experience in a body. Our self-awareness is the product of a 'radiant' soul, and a 'reflecting' body. The more the soul's reflection is focused, the more self-awareness there is. Different physical experiences lead to different foci and, consequently, to different identities. Sooner or later, self-awareness can be retained after death. In the course of its incarnations the soul collects more and more personalities in which to experience itself. Each personality is continually developing (sometimes temporarily stagnating or degenerating) until it finds peace, well-anchored in the larger self, has found its place in the large house of the field of consciousness, in the light of the soul. A person is only relatively an individual (literally: indivisible).

In one of the first reasonable books on reincarnation, Ralph Shirley says that it is difficult to determine just how much individuality exists in a human or animal life (1924: 35). Perhaps a rudimentary form exists even among the simplest forms of animal life, although this is speculation. We have but few leads. Among even the most developed people, individuality is less constant than we like to believe, and it may be broken in extreme circumstances. I believe a fairly good indication for individuality is the evolution of the nervous system. Without a nervous system there is no physical vehicle for reflection. Without a cortex there is no physical vehicle for self-awareness.

The much-used terminology of the higher and lower self is misleading, especially the frequently used comparison of the higher self as the actor and the lower self as the present role. In this view each life is a play. When the play is finished, the role is finished, but the same actor will return to play a different role for a different audience tomorrow. If we compare subsequent lives with an actor's subsequent parts, then at least we are actors who identify so much with our part that we forget we are acting it. This results in rather poor theatre. Good actors are able to empathize with their character and at the same time remain aware that it is a role. Furthermore, we lack an audience in front of the stage, unless we assume that some cosmic beings are manipulating us. As this assumption cannot be disproven, it is more suitable to science fiction and paranoia. Third, we never repeat lives. We do not rehearse and perform the same life a number of times. A successful performance is not re-run. On the contrary, we are more likely to repeat the bad performances and the early exits. Rehearsal, if any, is done a little just before life, and then we are sent on the stage with a good smack of amnesia, a clumsy little body, and the prospect of a lengthy dependence on older actors who have been sweating on the stage for a bit longer than we. Finally, and most importantly, an actor plays characters that have nothing to do with each other on consecutive evenings, whilst our lives are clearly related, although less strictly than the adherents of karma as an all-powerful law of nature like to believe. The demonstrable relations were discussed in the previous three chapters.

We are more than just our present personality: 'behind, above, and below' our present personality we find a larger self, usually remaining latent during our lives and, with most people, probably lacking a separate awareness, existing rather as a forming and feeding matrix or womb. Psychologists, with their adroit topology, would locate it in 'the subconscious'.

Normally, we have an individual consciousness, and an unrealized personality located in the subconscious as part of the matrix of the larger self. We also have a primary feeding personality, and a number of other past personalities, selected on purpose, or simply as retention. All these personalities live in the subconscious or unconscious. Besides all this, traumas or postulates from other lives have often become linked to this life through restimulation. Because there are often traumatic chains, whole series of lives may connect in this way to the present life. The primary feeding personality is the most interwoven with the present personality. Usually, the secondary personalities are easier to identify separately because they are more distinct. They normally have a clear relation to specific moods, attitudes, and aptitudes.

Further reading

The little that has been written about the subject of this chapter is theosophical, gnostic, or mystic. Little work has been done on personality theory using regression material. The most advanced, as far as this subject is concerned, are the spiritist reincarnation therapists in Brazil, cited by Karl Muller (1970). The Kardec spiritists have ideas about the relationship between the reincarnating soul and its incarnate personalities, as do those with mediumistic talents. Some familiarity with the discarnate condition is necessary to have such ideas. Joan Grant offers a few indications (1937, 1952; Kelsey and Grant 1967). An interesting and extensive treatment is *The Meaning of Personal Existence, in the Light of Paranormal Phenomena; The Doctrine of Reincarnation and Mystical States of Consciousness* by Arthur W. Osborn (1966).

14 An Empirical Understanding of Reincarnation

The first four chapters of this work discussed ideas about reincarnation. The following chapters were about memories: the research on spontaneous memories and a review of the results from regressions. They were based on the empirical literature, the practical experiences of counsellors and therapists, and my own experience as a counsellor and therapist. Several chapters have referred to preliminary or provisional conclusions. I have used these words, not out of insecurity or false modesty, but because reincarnation is still a relatively new field of research. Nevertheless, existing ideas can be disproven more conclusively on the basis of existing evidence and new ideas can be formulated. This chapter compares traditional ideas about reincarnation with the empirical evidence and the conclusions based on this evidence. This chapter will not need revision as quickly as the previous ones.

General ideas about reincarnation

What reincarnates? The soul. But what exactly is that? The Tlingits, West African tribes, the Burmese, and many other peoples, believe that reincarnation is the return of a person who lived before, with all his preferences and peculiarities. He has a preferred spot in which to be born, he sometimes announces his new birth, and he usually resembles his past personality. The Hindus believe rather that the soul is divine and always stays the same. Leibniz's monad doctrine and theosophy contain similar ideas. Each life is like a character in a play (lower self) in which the actor (higher self) loses himself.

Reincarnation beliefs may diffuse into pre-existence beliefs, and are sometimes mixed with psychic transference, such as the belief that people bear the traces of the lives of past people without having been one of them. Thus ideas vary from the notion that the same personality returns to the idea that the personality is lost at the end of a life and only the higher self carries some memory of it.

The evidence from past-life therapy, especially with pseudo-obsessions, shows that the reality is more complex. The previous chapter introduced 'the larger self', 'feeding personalities', 'furcation', etc. Significantly, past personalities are usually quite independent, even if entangled in the present personality. Past personalities continue to exist, sleeping, dreaming or awake. They may stimulate or inhibit the present personality. When somebody has vivid memories of a past life while his self-image is still weak, as in Stevenson's child cases, a considerable portion of the past personality can apparently become interwoven with this life. How much it fades as time goes on and how much is incorporated in the new life depends on the person as well as the circumstances.

Why do we go on reincarnating? One concept is that souls evolve from unconscious, passive, and primitive stages into conscious, creative stages. Human souls were once animal souls, and perhaps had plant and mineral stages before that. Superhuman stages are often assumed, going from angels to gods. An alternative concept is that humans were originally spiritual, incorporeal beings, developing particular proficiency during incarnations, becoming creative in the physical world, and perhaps developing more qualities too. In this view, the incarnate state is basically educational.

Many schools of thought emphasize that this education is tenuous since people are wont to forget their descent, get wrapped up in themselves, in karmic complications, or in physical pleasures, pains, and limitations. 'You are a lost son before you know it.' Others view the incarnate condition as the result of succumbing to temptation, the fall of man, or the punishment for misdeeds in the discarnate state. Diverse, often paradoxical philosophies are superimposed on these thoughts: humans attain self-awareness through incarnations with the aim of losing it again, or they leave God with the aim of finding Him again, etc.

The empirical evidence is less high-flown. Many remigrants end up in primitive conditions when they go further and further back in time, making reincarnation look like a slow and volatile process of becoming more human, more civilized, more cultural, and more aware. Other remigrants end up in more advanced civilizations and in discarnate states when they go a long way back. The reasons they give for reincarnation here are more vague and more diverse. Often, they talk about helping the less gifted primitive folk down here.

McClain rightly looks critically at the 'old soul' business, in which people make differences between old and young souls, usually placing themselves in the old-soul category, looking more or less benevolently on the primitive, still materialistic, extrovert (and often more successful) young souls around. She says instead: 'Regression evidence (our own as well as that of other researchers) indicates that all souls were created at the same time – a very long time ago' (1976: 8). Yet thinking of the very different origins we find in regressions – animals, devas, 'light people', other planets – this seems a bold statement. Her paragraph on the 'Origin of man' (1986: 132) remains unsatisfactorily general. McClain should tell us more about that evidence, and about those other researchers.

Incarnation gives particular abilities and learning opportunities, different from those of the discarnate state. The cardinal difference seems to be that a discarnate person lives in a psycho-plastic world: he can make his body and his environment correspond to his inner state. In the discarnate state the mind is its own place. Incarnation means entering a world of more objective things and events. An imaginative glass of water does not quench your objective thirst. It may help you feel less thirsty, even depressing your body's need for water, but in the end you may still die of thirst. Wishing for your lover to be just around the corner does not make that happen. (It may even make you miss that possibly more interesting person that actually comes around the corner.) Your piano playing is only fantastic after fantastic practice. The real is what makes a difference. In the physical body, in the physical world, perception and imagination differ much more. This also enhances the reality of other people.

Consequently, incarnation is anti-solipsistic: it forces us to have experiences, to learn, and to develop. And our physical structure triggers self-perception (seeing, feeling, and hearing yourself) and so makes self-consciousness unavoidable. We take the self-image of the incarnation with us into the discarnate state and this enables us to remain aware of ourselves after death. Our body, our nervous system, our brain are the incredibly complex scaffolding around our growing self-awareness. At some point, this self-awareness is so strong that it does not dissolve when it leaves the scaffolding after death. That is our real spiritual birth: the existence of 'I' outside the womb of the incarnate state. We alternate between the initially sleepy and later lucid existence of discarnate citizens, and the simultaneously wakeful and drugged existence on the incarnate front.

Each incarnation tests our insight, our compassion, our competence. The goals of recurrent lives appear to be continual evolution and emancipation:

- developing our intellectual capacity: intelligence, knowledge, understanding, insight, and wisdom
- developing our emotional capacity: sympathy, compassion, joy, peace, and love
- developing our capacity for independence, freedom, and responsibility
- developing our capacity for action: doing, making, and creating.

Recurrent incarnations with interim periods of reflection enormously increase our potential for growth compared with one life only. Therefore, goals can be more ambitious. The advantages of reincarnation compared with a single incarnation are:

- an enormous increase in time for experience, including repetition of the phases of growing up
- an enormous increase in variation: sex, health, family, position, culture, and circumstances
- an enormous increase in recuperation: refreshing, recharging, or recreational intermissions
- an enormous increase in justice. This argument is so obvious and well known, that it needs no elaboration.

Visions warning about the dangers of the incarnate condition certainly have a point. People with active, balanced, and fulfilled lives, with fruitful and meaningful work, all too commonly then go through all kinds of difficulties and end up in lives of confusion, misery, and even degeneration. It then takes a lot of time to get back on top of things. However, the empirical evidence shows clearly that human relations and compassion play an enormous part in our lives and in the relation between lives. The traditional reincarnation philosophies are remarkably weak on social themes, although life aims such as individual religious or spiritual development are far less common than social themes.

Conclusions

What do the traditional views say about the number of incarnations and about intermissions? The number of incarnations varies from just a couple in Persian-type views, to hundreds of thousands in Indian-type views. Persian thought sees a good life as increasing the chances for an even better next life, and a bad life as increasing the chances for an even worse life. In other words, it sees positive and negative developments as self-reinforcing. Consequently, in a few lives the person will either elevate himself above human status or sink below it. Indian thought presumes that it may take a long time for a person to attain the full experience needed to develop from simple, limited feelings to the realization that the main reason for being here is to get out of here, as a process through lives from kama via artha and dharma to moksha.

And what does the empirical evidence say? The evidence confirms both mechanisms of slow, gradual development and self-reinforcing development at the same time, and therefore refutes both extreme positions. Anyway, it refutes completely the idea that people usually have only a couple of lives. A problem during therapy can normally be followed through a great number of lives. About 90 per cent of regressions take place in the past 3,000 years, and the rest in undatable primitive circumstances or in cultures reminiscent of Atlantis. Virtually everyone who has some experience with regressions believes in at least dozens of lives, and probably hundreds. Higher estimations are speculative because of difficulty in dating old lives. According to Goldberg, if people go back more than 10,000 years they usually end up in discarnate states (among others, as 'light people') or in more or less science-fiction-like environments, apparently in Atlantis or on other planets. Such thoughts are reasonable but not commonly accepted, and they presently lack a firm underpinning. Besides, there were men on earth before then anyway.

According to the Druses a person is reborn the moment he dies. According to the Jainists, a person is immediately attached to a new foetus after death, so the period between dying and being born again is about nine months. In Africa intermissions of 1 to 3 years are assumed. Allan Kardec (1857) indicates intermissions varying from a few hours to many thousands of years. The theosophists started out with intermissions of more than 8,000 years and ended up with Leadbeater's classification where intermissions vary from 5 to more than 2,000 years. Rudolf Steiner began with an incarnation cycle of 2,600 years and ended with an intermission of about 700 years.

Based on the empirical evidence, we can be fairly precise about intermissions. The diverse cases of Karl Muller (1970) ranged from immediate incarnation (and even negative intermission) to a number of centuries, with an average intermission of 70 years. Helen Wambach's work (1978) is more exact and more reliable. She found intermissions varying from 4 months to more than 2 centuries, with an average of 52 years. Joel Whitton (1986) found intermissions ranging from 10 months to more than 800 years, with an average of about 40 years. Stevenson (1966) normally found intermissions of a few years, and a maximum of 12, in child cases. Thus the Africans are basically right. Chapter 12 gives a possible explanation for the discrepancy between regression and child cases. The population explosion is often explained by a drastic reduction of intermission times. Whitton says that intermissions have been steadily diminishing over the past several hundred years. I tend to agree, but as yet we lack statistics. If intermissions are *not* shorter, then many souls are incarnating for the first time. To date, indications for this are also lacking.

At any rate, both regression and child cases refute the Druse and the Jainist ideas about immediate reincarnation. The Druses have invented a temporary reincarnation country 'somewhere in China' where children can live for a few years and then die prematurely to return as real Druses. Poor China! This is a familiar kind of argument: impossible to refute. The general theosophist and anthroposophist ideas are also at complete variance with the empirical data, and are apparently based on such abstract considerations as an astrological age lasting 2,160 years, and 700 being a beautiful number.

Other theories claim that incarnations follow cycles. For example, everyone is born once (or twice) in each astrological age (the age of Pisces, the age of Aquarius, etc.). Further astrological speculations are that you are born first as Aries, then as Taurus, then as Gemini, etc. Most regressions are weak in that kind of information, but existing data do not support this claim. Naturally, it always remains possible to claim that between an incarnation as Taurus and an incarnation as Virgo you died three times as a young child. Whoever believes such unfounded claims, please return as a Druse!

Independent evidence that the natal chart of one life is connected with that of the next is lacking. If we look at regressions, and at the indications of how a new life is prepared and how a choice of parents is made, such a connection seems unlikely. Helen Wambach's inventory of birth experiences is either a grand con-trick, or a refutation of these astrological theories. As uncertain and unclear as Wambach's material may be, the regressions of 750 people are an incomparably better foundation than the speculations of 75 astrologists.

Chapters 10, 11 and 12 above, collected patterns of relations based on empirical evidence. This material flagrantly contradicts the idea of cosmic clocks relating the place and the moment of birth of one life directly to the place and date of birth of another life. Finally, in Stevenson's cases the birth date of the present life and that of the past life could often be verified. I am afraid little connection was found. Seeking patterns in regressions and child cases is more realistic than inventing connections.

Finally, there are the ideas about incarnations from other planets to earth, or from earth to other planets. This does seem possible. In therapy, cases with apparent problems of a choice of planet are rather common. Some people seem unable to accept they have landed on such a backward planet as ours. (As a character in a science-fiction-film says, 'I never expected to die on a third-rate planet in a third-rate galaxy', — and I would add, in a third-rate movie.) Although I find many of these regressions convincing, these problems possibly obscure a general unwillingness to incarnate, or a feeling of general superiority. This subject would profit considerably from the standard registration of regressions and research as used by Wambach.

Similarities and differences between lives

The first subject is change of sex. The views of Hindus, Buddhists, and some Cabbalists on sex change are among the most extreme, as chapter 2 mentioned. They warn men not to be petty or stingy, otherwise they may return as women. Theosophy and anthroposophy believe in cyclical alternation and allow only limited deviations. According to Van Ginkel, the average person alternates 7 male lives with 7 female lives (Van Ginkel 1917: 71). These ideas are unsubstantiated. Some people even do not care about their sex. On average, the probability of a sex change between two subsequent incarnations is from 15 to 25 per cent. The probability of any sex change in a series of lives approaches 80 per cent, as only 20 per cent of remigrants report no sex change (which does not disprove that there ever was a sex change). Anyway, some people seem strongly to favour one sex rather than the other. Which sex a person is born depends on diverse factors and considerations. Population I people, for example, have a fair chance of being born the same sex as before.

Another subject is that of physical similarity. According to the theosophists, the more somebody approaches the level of Master, the more his appearances resemble each other, especially the face. If this is true there are many more Masters in the world than the theosophists have realized until now. How much two incarnations look alike differs greatly. Probably, the similarity is greatest when the soul has been in contact with the foetus from the moment of conception. People may carry particular features with them, for example in the face, for a number of incarnations. The central feeding incarnation has the greatest effect here.

The idea of return into the same family, nation, culture, and race is common. Druses return as Druses; Jews would prefer to return as Jews. Rudolf Steiner claimed that people never return in the same nation and the same culture, with the exception of the Middle Europeans. There are also theories that a whole nation may reincarnate *en masse* in another nation. For example, the ancient Greeks would have reincarnated in the French, and the ancient Romans in the British. These tunes have all kinds of variations. Where families are important, ideas about return in the family prevail; when nationality is important, people believe they return in the same nationality. There are apparently no fixed rules here either. Certainly in population I people tend to be reborn close to the place of death of the last incarnation. The two Burmese children who remembered being a Japanese and an American respectively, both of whom died in Burma during the Second World War, illustrate that, with this type of death and rebirth process, proximity is more important than national or cultural identity.

More than half the regressed Americans lived in the United States in the one, two, or three immediately preceding incarnations. The British have often lived in England before, and the French in France. In my practice in the Netherlands I have come across people who lived in the Netherlands at around the turn of the century fairly often. There were also a few cases of lives in the Netherlands in the sixteenth and seventeenth centuries. Most past lives were somewhere else, but a random sample of a hundred Dutchmen will contain more people with past lives in the Netherlands than a random sample of a hundred Swedes.

Attaching importance to a birth in a particular family, country, or religion, or in a particular region or city, increases the chances of being born there. Regional, national, religious, and cultural identifications increase the chances of return. Jews may certainly return as Jews, especially if this is important to them. Also the converse: a person who lived in Italy and was terribly bored all his life by the same view of the Apennines is unlikely to be reborn with the same view.

There are no huge reincarnation waves through nations and cultures. Reincarnation is personal, guided by individual preferences and by personal relations such as intense working or living relationships which created a strong bond in a past life. People with such relationships have a strong tendency to meet again the next time, because of karmic entanglements, reciprocal feelings of sympathy and trust, or being kindred spirits or sharing some task.

Someone from population II or III is rarely born among people with whom he has no relation at all. In each life we meet a few people we know from past lives. Apparently, strong feelings of sympathy and antipathy continue throughout lives. Such feelings, especially entanglements, are stronger dharmic or karmic connections rather than correction for misconduct or compensation for good conduct in a past life. The widespread idea that people who recognize each other at first sight, or who fall in love at first sight, may know each other from past lives is true.

A thought coming up every now and then is the twin-soul idea. It presumably originates from Plato's idea that male-female souls were separated and went to earth temporarily to reunify themselves again in our well-known pairing rituals. The idea of a twin soul fascinates some people, especially when they feel lonely, are tired of their partner, or are sentimentally romantic. It gives some people the same glow in their eyes as others have when claiming Jesus is in love with them.

The empirical evidence does not support the idea of a twin soul, but people may become so attached to each other that they continue an intimate relationship life after life. In some instances, two people may have been married to each other in more than half their past lives. In others, they may have been brother and sister, father and daughter, or business partners. Lenz found examples of twin souls in 15 per cent of his cases, but he defines twin souls as 'persons who have similar interests, capacities and attitudes', which seems to me to stretch the concept to meaninglessness (Lenz 1979). The idea that most of us have soul-mates, people to whom we have grown close in our lives, with whom we can be at ease (especially outside the restrictions of the body), is an idea as stimulating as it is true. Still, people who have the same type of origin, the same type of 'roots', may have a deep affinity even independently of shared experiences.

Holzer has a different understanding again of the word soul-mate. According to him we may have several 'potential' soul-mates, but they are always of the opposite sex. This invalidates the first syllable of 'soul-mate'. It seems to me necessary to establish a clear terminology. I propose the following: *twin souls* – souls which have the same origin, which began their individual existence at the same moment, which normally are together when discarnate, and which often share experiences when incarnate; *soul-mates* – discarnate friends who have shared many incarnate experiences. A twin soul is thus an original sibling, and a soul-mate a friend of many lives. Twin souls went out together and soul-mates have come together. Just as your sister may be your best friend, a twin soul may be a soul-mate. Of course, people are especially fascinated by the idea of meeting a twin soul or soul-mate of the opposite sex (or of the same sex, if they are homosexual). But it is immediate familiarity and mutual confidence that counts, not immediate sexual attraction.

A 'reincarnation wave' is a large group of kindred spirits continually reincarnating close together. Some talk about a 'group soul', but this implies one animating entity (similar to an entire bee population or ant hill) and that is certainly not intended. Arthur Guirdham's books (1970, 1974, 1976) point out the crystallization of a group of people remembering Cathar incarnations. Reality is often difficult to distinguish from illusion here, but the idea seems acceptable. The common misfortune of the Cathars probably considerably strengthened their cohesion. The process in which people begin to realize that they once all lived together is called 'ingathering'. Any spiritually powerful person who knows or claims to know a little bit about his past incarnations can use his sensitivity, charisma, and good will to convince all the nice people he meets and immediately finds sympathetic that they belong to the same circle. Many enthusiastic testimonies will continue to come from people who found their real friends before they found themselves. I myself agree with Groucho Marx: 'I would not think of becoming a member of a club that would want me as a member.' But I am reasonably happily married, have reasonably nice children, reasonably gratifying work, and meet a reasonable number of reasonably interesting people as it is.

What about metempsychosis, or animal incarnations? We have only limited indications of metempsychosis and these are more likely to be identifications than animal incarnations. Some people believe they see animal characteristics in some of their fellow humans, or point out what they see as a pathological love of animals. There may be more obvious explanations for men with a thick neck and little eyes, for example, than previous pig lives. Besides, would any pig with an ounce of common sense like to become human after going a few times through the destruction camps called slaughterhouses? Or are the slaughterhouse experiences precisely what confused him? Victims of torture and terror sometimes begin to identify themselves with their persecutors. And this in turn is a nice explanation for the underhand tricks the man with the thick neck and the little eyes plays on his environment. Which brings us neatly to the next subject: karma.

Karma

Views of karma are rather diverse. Chapter 10 contrasted the deterministic with the voluntaristic view, contrasted karma as a natural law with karma as jurisdiction, and contrasted karma as the consequence of actual deeds with dependence on moral intent. Finally, karma as natural law (without evolutionary motives but with evolutionary results) differs from karma as intervention through reward, punishment, and correction, and from karma as guidance, compensation, evolution, and healing. What does the evidence show?

There appear to be no direct karmic relations between lives, in the sense of immediate connections between past and present events. Specific karmic relations do exist, not as natural laws, but as psychological and educational patterns. Undigested traumatic experiences cause phobias, problems, and complexes in subsequent lives. A past life can also cause deeply rooted, rigid attitudes and views. Chapters 10, 11, and 12 gave an inventory of connections between lives and classified them. It shows many views of karma to be untrue, and puts others in perspective and gives them more nuances.

We can discard the deterministic views. Clearly, occurrences and deeds from past lives are neither unequivocally ingrained nor have an unequivocal effect. On the contrary, a deterministic view where action *A* always has karmic repercussion *B* is nonsense, much as it may satisfy people who like to feel themselves embedded in a computerized superhuman order. We can also discard the view that the actual deed, regardless of the intent, determines karma. Our psychological reaction determines what we take with us to a next life. After all, our soul is what goes from one life to the next, and psychic reactions are semantic, that is, the effect of an experience is never direct, but always depends on our interpretation.

All other ideas about karma seem to be more or less true. There is jurisdiction to the extent that we ourselves, alone or with others, judge our past lives and sit in judgement on ourselves. The mind is its own place and with that a higher court of law is superfluous. People only appear in front of Moses or Our Lord God when they create such a thing. We judge ourselves from our own narrow point of view. A person can only conquer himself if he accepts himself. Sometimes, powerful judgements force people to look in an impartial mirror, or remedial interventions may imprison people in a pseudo-existence after their death, or make a birth or life plan for them which is difficult to avoid. But nobody is coerced.

As suggested in chapter 12, I prefer to use the word 'karma' colloquially, as a collective term for every liability we take with us from past lives. This is why I want to stress the concept of 'dharma' also, to indicate the assets: the light, warmth, and strength that we take with us. The notion that karma can be postponed appears to be true, as well as other notions that have a human perspective on karma. Karmic mechanisms work just like the mechanisms within our life. The only difference is that the life retrospect and the life prospect are more powerful than the reflections and plans during our life. Still, each day we can look back on our life, and every day we can prepare the rest of our life. We are less at liberty because we have more or less forgotten our life plan. But we can digest karmic repercussions, and take decisions supplementing or deviating from our life plan. Supplements are not always improvements, because we normally have a better overview and better advisers before our birth. However, we may have made our decisions before birth too hastily in overreaction to an experience from a previous life. We may come to our senses during our life. This is particularly true for people who reincarnated fairly quickly under fairly emotional circumstances. We may always go beyond our incarnation preparations: 'Today is the first day of the rest of your life.' Would you kindly check your agenda? And check the time? In spite of the whole gamut of reincarnations, now is now.

Previous chapters contain examples of how karma works. Karma and dharma are probably etheric, part of the vehicle of vitality. In our psychic body we are free, we are ourselves, except when we have a narrow-minded perception of ourselves, which is more or less our own choice as well. At any rate, it contains nothing inhibiting change. Reorientation automatically and immediately changes our psychic body. But we are confronted with the vehicle of vitality and our physical body, although they are part of us, as an external reality, because we cannot change them immediately and at will. Karma and dharma are the burdens and the strengths within us. Meeting someone who is familiar is neither karmic nor dharmic by itself. The karmic factor is in the charge within ourselves, related to the other. And the other has such a charge for us. These charges may be positive (dharma) or negative (karma), or mixed. They may be inactive or active. They may be located in the body or in the aura. Catharsis during therapy heals a karmic wound or dissolves a karmic gnarl. Every moment of acceptance and liberation resolves karma. It is questionable whether a sullen sense of duty inciting us to do our best for someone we may have harmed in a past life resolves karma. In our next retrospect, we may feel less guilt at best, and when the other sees us benevolently in his life retrospect it is yet easier for us to release our negative feelings. As our relationships with others grow, we take ever more of them into us, and doubtlessly the part of our wife or our child that we carry interacts with the part of ourself our wife or our child carries. But whatever the character of this interaction, it is subject to how we each manage within our soul. Karma and dharma are within us, 'nearer than hands and feet'.

A number of beliefs, especially religious ones, contain the idea that the kind of last thoughts, the kind of death, or the kind of funeral or cremation influences the condition after death, and sometimes the next incarnation. Here too 'the mind is its own place'. Someone intensely convinced that he will go to hell, may go there, at least as a phase of the illusory existence. Being convinced that you are doomed to eternal wandering because your children failed to give you the correct burial does not promote your peace of mind. A thorough conviction that you will return quickly doubtlessly increases the chances you will do so. Nevertheless, the real effects of thoughts and feelings are easily misjudged. A seemingly strong conviction may be discarded right after death like an ill-suited jacket. Or a seemingly unimportant idea may after death have a great influence. The better you know yourself, the smaller the chance of surprises after death. Ideas about the importance of last thoughts and such are usually religious and clerical intimidations. Doubtless some people panic when they die without having received the extreme unction, and many more couldn't care less.

An Italian woman living in the sixteenth century is known to the people of the surrounding villages as a witch. Indeed she performs rather disgusting rituals with the blood of animals, and exceptionally of a child, in order to retain her youth. These bloody rituals only make her older and uglier. Ultimately, she panics and goes to a chaplain to ask for remission of her sins. The chaplain refuses to absolve her because she is a child of darkness, a servant of Satan, eternally doomed. The woman dies in great fear and convinced of her own darkness. Although she does not go to hell, her fear leads her into darkness and causes her to lose consciousness. Although she is properly reborn again later, this whole life remains undigested. In a regression her experiences resurface, and she finally receives absolution.

The idea that a failure to perform rituals and duties to a T dooms you to an unpleasant next life is just narrow-mindedness and terrorism. Some Cabbalist and Tibetan ideas are less sadistic, but just as totalitarian as the old-fashioned preachers of hell-and-damnation.

Rituals can fill your life with peace and regularity, can make you more conscientious, and foster feelings that are easily lost in the wear and tear of daily strife. They can also be an expression of spiritual loyalty. Life is often so chaotic, tough, harsh, or depressing that rituals giving a sense of peace are important. But they may as a consequence also act as powerful tools. Power used with the best intentions for the benefit of everybody is especially free from common sense and the normal human inhibitions, and, sooner or later, may turn into totalitarianism and finally into exploitation, extortion, inquisition, and terror. Some burn you alive and tell you this is the last remaining way to bring you to Christ, others only shave your hair and besmirch you and declare that after death the hellish fire awaits you.

Gruesome and cruel practices continue up to the present day by fanatics, just for kicks, as a sport, and even as part of research. After all, you may torture people just to find out how people react to torture. Many people die in circumstances making it impossible to think and feel properly. What a mess it would be if a mother who was gassed with her children received a bad next life just because she was terrified. The gas chambers were brutal. Some ideas about what happens to people after death are brutal, too.

I am making a detour here because there are many nonsensical, totalitarian, and even cruel twists in religious and spiritual thought. 'If you do not convert and become an active member of the right club you will have to start a new cycle of perhaps thousands of incarnations.' I have heard such statements from well-meaning, even noble people. This is not giving stones for bread, but poison for air, clouding, enslaving, and imprisoning the spirit even while singing Hosanna and burning incense.

An example comes from Van Helmont's conviction that a perjurer will be reborn forty times as a bastard (Van Ginkel 1917). We no longer fall for this crazy idea because it is out of fashion. But some people still seriously declare the annihilation of millions of Jews to be the karma of the Jewish people. Well, we can similarly consider it our karma to be incarnated on a planet among people fostering such thoughts. Most people with such distorted ideas would never commit such extermination themselves. But the line from these ideas to the concentration camps is straighter than the line from the past lives of the victims to the concentration camps. I do not claim that all that was mere coincidence. There are sufficient indications that people who feel an intense personal hatred for a particular group had extremely nasty experiences with that group in a past life. Think of the example of the anti-Semite who was disparaged and treated as an inferior by Jews in his past life as a Samaritan. Spending long years as a galley slave with sadistic Negro overseers may easily make you a Negro-hater. Certainly the hatred of many feminists for males is not without reason, either. But it is dangerous to extend individual explanations to mass phenomena. Mass phenomena do not result from personal karmic knots. Understandably, someone who has been maltreated by men in several lives becomes a man-hater in a next life. None the less, it is a primitive reaction, indicating lack of insight and mental health. If somebody with a wart on his nose beats people up, it is still not true that all people with warts on their noses do the same. This is as true for warts, as for sex, race, or membership of any group or culture. I hope my preliminary classification of karmic relations in the past chapters will not lead to such rash generalizations.

Some esoteric writers, like Rudolf Steiner and Douglas Baker (1977), see illness as karma from past lives. Baker describes the karmic origins of psoriasis, anorexia, breast cancer, mongolism, etc. Such ideas stimulate the notion of particular reasons for having particular diseases, and from here the next thought could easily be that it is a person's own fault if he has a particular disease and that diseases are karmic necessities. 'Feeling bad is good for you.' This thought, though unsympathetic, may be true. Research in this area is possible by regressing people who have had a particular disease, preferably with non-suggestive questioning, and checking the similarities between the victims of a disease (and the differences with a control group). Even if significant relationships are found, they will only be indirect.

It is improbable that the hatred of industrial proletarians results in something as specific as tuberculosis in a next life, as Steiner tells us. People may harbour and digest feelings of hatred in many different ways. Particular karmic charges may dispose us to particular psychosomatic complaints, or may increase the susceptibility to infectious diseases, but research remains necessary.

Finally, the notion of carrying positive results from past lives into following lives is less widespread and elaborated, and is usually limited to talents. There is nothing wrong with this notion.

The process of incarnation

The religious views of reincarnation say little on this subject. The main differences are to be found in views on the moment when the soul actually descends. According to some this happens during conception, according to others during the birth, and according to a third group when the name is given. The latter is common especially in Africa. Name-giving is therefore an important ritual there.

The regression material presents a rich picture. Souls may be attached to the foetus from conception, and may even provoke a conception. Something important to one person, for example, the choice of parents or the choice of sex, may be unimportant to someone else. People differ in the extent of their life plans, as in the aspects that are important to them. The widespread belief that birthmarks and prophetic dreams can identify the soul of a newborn child is generally true, but it is easy to see things which are not there. The identification procedures for newborns like the ones in Africa and Tibet, for example, do seem unreliable to me. Identification at a later age, when a young child has to select objects belonging to his previous incarnation from among many other objects seems more reliable.

Another common belief is that children who remember a past life will die young. This is one of the reasons why children's memories meet with reservation, even in cultures believing in reincarnation. When the child wants to return to his previous family, continually making comparisons with his previous life, and rejecting the limitations of being a child, it is just awkward.

Why do fewer children in the west remember a past life than in the east? In areas where such cases do occur in the east, about 1 in 500 up to 1 in 1,000 children have such memories. A rough estimate is that in western society this percentage is about half as large. The main reason is probably that neither the materialistic, nor the agnostic, nor the Christian views in the west encourage parents to accept these memories, and so make ignoring or repressing the child's recollections more likely. A second reason may be that incarnations of the population I type are relatively more common in non-western countries.

The children Stevenson investigated had a shorter intermission and were born closer to the place where they died in their past life than people in regressions. Children with spontaneous memories frequently died young in their previous life, often in accidents or by violence. Apparently, most of them belong to population I. They hardly realize they are dead, they barely remain aware, and their personality enters the new incarnation virtually unchanged. This explains why child cases have fewer memories of the intermission. About 50 per cent of remigrants have such memories (following Wambach's results), while in child cases the number is less than 25 per cent.

Many collected statements from small children indicate prenatal memories. Some of these statements indicate a sense of a pre-existence and a sense of reincarnation, even without personal memories of the past life. Karl Muller collected cases of children with general insights into the prenatal state and reincarnation (Muller 1970: 70).

Memories and regressions

Is it common or uncommon to have memories of past lives? Spontaneous explicit memories of a past life are certainly uncommon: most people do not have them. But are past-life regressions commonly attainable? Between 70 and 90 per cent of those interested in remember- ing past lives are simply able to do so, as many have found out to their surprise. Esoteric circles caution against an easy and gullible road to incarnation memories and argue in favour of a solid esoteric schooling, because the experiences of the past personalities can only be reached via the immortal part of the soul, which is, of course, quite something. The previous chapter discussed the relation between individuality and personality, and sketched a personality theory concurrent with the regression experiences. Esoteric schools object because of their concept of the higher and lower self and (I suspect) because lay regressions topple their precarious monopoly on the only right way to develop.

Theosophic and anthroposophic circles tend to react ambivalently toward people who remember past lives, partly because people with memories of their own have shorter intermissions and less karma than these doctrines postulate, and partly because these circles fear imagination. Finally, as chapter 5 discussed, they object to hypnosis. What is especially scary and unfair about hypnosis is that it is incomparably faster and more effective than their meditation and concentration exercises. It is wrong being so easy.

This reminds me of Henry Ford's rejection of the automatic starter. He said it would corrupt the masculine character of the American male.

'Cranking up that car in the morning is good for you.' And so, countless people drive out of the present with the automatic hypnotic starter (or with the newer, more effective non-hypnotic starters), and leave regular members standing next to their cars, because starting with a manual crank is tiring and seldom works if you do it half-heartedly, or if the crank is made of rubber. Of course, the garage drivers deny that the others really went anywhere. Besides, the hypnotic drivers are not members of the Automobile Association and cannot drive at all and are a menace to themselves and others. A real automobile driver stays in his driveway.

Another idea about remembering past incarnations is that the historical decline and resurgence of the belief in reincarnation and of past-life memories are providentially determined. The esoteric schools claim their advent to hail the new age. Some time in the future, which Rudolf Steiner saw as being the end of this century and the theosophists later, more and more people will remember past lives. Doubtless, this coincides with the expectation that these schools will grow and will gain considerable influence.

Steiner's ideas about historic planning are self-contradictory and historically incorrect. Steiner says that reincarnation was lost in the Kaliyuga (from 3101 BC to AD 1899). But everything we know about reincarnation ideas is from this period. His statement implies that all of that is false knowledge. Only after 1899 comes real knowledge about reincarnation, a date which perfectly separates out the founding spiritist and theosophist publications (before 1899) and Steiner's own publications (after 1899). Further, Steiner claims there was an absolute low in the knowledge of reincarnation during Christ's time. This is certainly incorrect for Africa and Asia. For Europe and the Middle East it is inaccurate because the actual low was almost a century earlier, when a resurgence of Platonism brought a return to reincarnation ideas.

Elsewhere Steiner claims that concrete memories of past lives were gradually lost in the third post-Atlantic age (from 2907 to 747 BC). Historically, nothing backs this up. Further, regressions of people who remember lives in which they remembered past lives or were aware of reincarnation indeed usually return to a period fairly long ago, but seldom more than 2,000 years ago. Steiner's notion that memories of past reincarnations were lost because the priests drank too much wine attributes a staggering influence to wine and to priests (both serious misconceptions, especially the second). To take the wedding at Cana as a symbol for this is a little difficult to imagine.

Steiner believed that reincarnation ideas returned during the eighteenth century Enlightenment in a Christianized form, that is to say, in the light of the development of humanity, whereas the earlier Buddhist ideas had concentrated on individual development. This is rather an odd idea considering that the Buddhist anatta doctrine can hardly be interpreted as individual development, and also considering that reincarnation thoughts re-emerged precisely because the ancient Indian culture became more known. In the eighteenth century, Christianized ideas come up that are a kind of preparation for the new age beginning after 1899. The only conclusion is that Christ revealed a secret that only Steiner could tell in public, after proper preparation by the German Enlightenment and less proper (Buddhist-inspired) preparation by the theosophists. This view is inconsistent and does not correspond with historical facts.

Summary

A breakdown of views about reincarnation reasonably consistent with the present evidence is as follows:

1 Everybody probably reincarnates dozens or hundreds of times, or even more.
2 Intermissions vary greatly, and usually vary from a few months to several centuries. A few years to a few decades are most common.
3 At least 80 per cent of people change sex, with varying frequency, and without fixed rules.
4 Many people have some form of a life plan, which is never a 100 per cent blueprint.
5 Memories of past lives can be healing, and may be part of a life plan.

Of those who are interested in experiencing a past life, for example via regression, about 70 per cent do so, given the right counselling. An able and experienced reincarnation therapist can raise this percentage to 90 to 95 per cent. Wambach and Finkelstein give the same percentages. Blocks are usually connected with fear of death and resistance to all forms of psychological analysis, for example random association.

The present empirical evidence contradicts many religious and esoteric views. The intermissions are normally shorter than believed.

Related ideas such as the anatta doctrine and metempsychosis can be discarded. The workings of karma are far from universal and mainly psychological. The relation between a transcending individuality and ever new personalities is viewed too rigidly and schematically, resulting in the idea that reincarnation memories can only be found through esoteric exercises or initiation. Fulfilling religious duties is not half as important as some would like it to be. The main differences between regressions and classic esoteric or pseudo-esoteric ideas are: the workings of karma are less fixed by laws; the intermissions are shorter; there is no fixed rule for change of sex; and no special education or initiation is needed to remember past lives.

I should mention, however, that some practising regression counsellors and therapists see a great similarity between the regression evidence and religious or gnostic authorities. Although there are always some correspondences, the differences are so abundant that I doubt the intellectual honesty of the authors involved. There are even people who consider the Tibetan Book of the Dead a good guide, confirmed by regression evidence. You must close more than one eye to be able to say that.

Further reading

There are as yet few attempts to form a comprehensive empirical vision. The first book tending in this direction is by Allan Kardec (1857). Broad, reasonable treatises on reincarnation have since been published by Van Ginkel (1917), Ralph Shirley (1924), and, above all, Karl Muller (1970). The general discussions in Stevenson's research are excellent, but are limited to cases of spontaneous memories in young children. The two books by Helen Wambach (1978, 1979) are an important first step towards a statistical framework. A reasonable summary can be found in David Christie-Murray's book (1981). Gina Cerminara (1950) tries to build a theory on the basis of Edgar Cayce's work. Together, these books give the best overview of reincarnation, but contain little summarizing and analytical work on regressions and regression therapy. This book tries to fill this gap, although writing about a rapidly developing field like regression makes additions and revisions necessary every few years. Muller introduces his book with Allan Kardec's epitaph: 'Being born, dying, being reborn and always advancing, that is the law.' The same law holds true for the development of knowledge.

PART IV *Applications*

15 Counselling Techniques for Past-life Recall

This chapter provides an overview of the techniques for conducting regressions. It is closely connected to the next chapter about past-life therapy. The transition from counselling to therapy is gradual. Remigrants who begin out of curiosity may encounter difficult or traumatic material. Using the practical tips in this chapter, a prospective counsellor can come a long way, but it remains a profession where one learns by observation and supervised practice. It is tempting the gods to go ahead with explorative regressions thinking the incidental therapy case will solve itself.

Most therapists, especially those with a professional psychological background, are scared by laymen carrying out regression. On the other hand, Florence McClain says: 'The only thing you need . . . is this book . . . time, and a friend who can read.' 'Over a period of almost twenty years, involving over 2,000 regressions, I have never had a situation which developed in a traumatic experience . . . Seldom, if ever, will you encounter any situation of undue distress in a regression experience.' (1986). Few counsellors would agree. But in any case her built-in safeguards are important: avoid words and phrases that may trigger negative responses; emphasize the regression as only an exercise in remembering; close with positive statements.

Regression goals and regression paths

Why do people want to regress? For the same reason that people want to recall lost memories from this life. Technically speaking, the main function of regression is to remove loss of memory, whether of early youth, of an emotional episode, or of a past life. The most likely reason for doing this is to satisfy curiosity: curiosity awakened by the possibility of remembering past lives, curiosity about what this experience is like, curiosity about historical circumstances, curiosity about oneself. Besides this, there are other reasons for regression similar to reasons for simple regression in this life: finding the roots of problems and understanding and removing them through cathartic and liberating re-experience of the original traumas. A well-directed regression can provide insight about the course of this life, the aim of this life, and the life plan. Regressions can stimulate self-knowledge, insight, and self-realization. Like simple regressions, regressions to past lives, to the prenatal period in the womb, and to the period in between lives may be carried out for educational and therapeutic reasons.

There are several ways to help a remigrant return to past lives. The simplest is the 'chronological path'. We start with a few recollections within the present life which we gradually deepen into reliving. For example, we ask the remigrant to remember a situation when he was 20. Asking concrete questions, we have him elaborate this situation. We help the remigrant see what he saw then, we help him go back to his feelings and thoughts, possibly supplemented with the things he heard, touched, and otherwise experienced. Then we go back to something that happened a few years earlier. In this way, we work through a number of experiences, reliving each as vividly as possible, sometimes resulting in real regression. With this method we can go back to the first years of childhood, the first months after birth, the birth itself. Finally we ask the remigrant to go back in time until he finds a concrete memory. If this succeeds, he is often in his previous incarnation, usually around the time of his death.

This procedure takes time, but has advantages. We see how deeply the remigrant relives, and whether he remembers experiences from a time hitherto inaccessible. It also gives the remigrant self-confidence when he remembers something from his earliest childhood that he can later verify. Another advantage of this procedure is that its only pretension is that it possibly leads to a past life.

After relaxation and visualization, or after initial reliving within this life, and without special instructions to go back to a particular life or a particular type of life, the remigrant usually enters a life directly related to the present life or containing experiences relevant to the present life. Some counsellors give instructions like, 'Go to the life most strongly related to your present life,' or they may suggest that you return to the most convincing past life, or the most instructive, or the one most telling for your present self. Such instructions can be useful, but probably are rarely necessary.

Particular interests are useful to direct the remigration. In reincarnation therapy there are the phobias, complexes or other problems, and the therapy will concentrate on the relevant incarnations and situations. But a person could also be interested in tracing a relation with a relative or partner, or in finding a life where a particular talent was developed, or in the life just before this one, or in a life as the opposite sex. Any peculiar preference, hobby, or skill may be used as a departure point (Fiore 1978: 10). Paranormally gifted people are able to trace this gift to some form of temple training in past lives.

Once we have the first concrete experience of a past life, usually the dying experience, we can take a few episodes further and further backwards. When we get back to the birth, we continue backwards to the life before, from there again back to a childhood experience, and so on. Or we may go from the first experience right back to an early childhood memory, and then take a chronological sequence to death. For example, we can bring a remigrant back to the moment when he was a child in the past life, already aware of his surroundings (McClain prefers the age of 12). We may ask the remigrant to describe a situation typical of the society of the time, for example. Once this situation has been well-described, our next question could be to ask the remigrant to go back to a situation where his life was different. Or we could ask about the next occurrence which had a great influence on the remigrant's life. We may also ask about a situation where the remigrant became acquainted with someone who was later important to him. Such questions direct the regression to the most important events and encounters in a life.

The 'problem path' starts with a problem like fear of heights. We instruct the remigrant to go back to the last time this fear was acute. We let the remigrant describe the situation in detail and have him relive it. Then, we return to a situation causing the fear. Often, the remigrant returns to a past life. When the trance is deep enough, we may ask the remigrant if he needs more experiences to get rid of the problem. This question may be answered with finger signals. Causal experiences do not necessarily come up in chronological order. Sometimes the first experience is from an older incarnation and the second experience from a more recent incarnation. The experiences are worked out in order of appearance, connected by association and restimulation (the re-activation of an undigested problem through later similar circumstances triggering the emotional heritage, thereby affirming and often reinforcing it). Sometimes a whole 'chain' of experiences is worked through. The next chapter will give concrete examples. Regressions done for reasons of therapy are always problem-oriented, never chronological.

When a remigrant is just curious about the origin of particular characteristics or idiosyncrasies, the 'question path' should be used. For example, a person could wonder about the origin of his musical talent, or his fancy for horses, or his sensitivity to Japanese music. The first instruction is to go back to the situation where this characteristic originated or developed. To diminish uncertainties about projections and prejudices, we suggest that the first impressions do not yet give clues. We do not instruct to go back to a certain time in this life or in a previous life. The emerging experience is relived as fully as possible. Next, we instruct the remigrant to go back to another situation. With a relatively deep trance the counsellor may use finger signals to ask the remigrant if there are any further situations and how many, but asking the remigrant directly is also often effective. It increases the efficiency and the accuracy of the session, although it remains unclear why and how.

The counsellor may give open instructions about particular 'exploration paths': self-knowledge, peace, balance, learning. The remigrant will usually find experiences that were impressive or important, that changed a life, or that still influence this life.

Finally, we may leave everything open, as in the Christos experiment. The only instruction the counsellor gives is that the remigrant will experience something in some past life, emphasizing that the remigrant will be himself. Fiore, for example uses: 'It will be somebody in another time, another place, but it will be you.'

Besides the chronological 'path of reality', there are eight different paths to finding traces of the past:

Problem paths (usually in therapy):

    Tying into perplexities and emotional problems

    Tying into postulates.

Question paths:

    Tying into special preferences and relations

Tying into special talents
Tying into special behaviour
Tying into physical peculiarities.
Exploration paths:
   Direction to criteria such as self-knowledge, learning, etc.
   Open.

Induction techniques

Induction means conducting a person into trance, here to the first impression from a past life. A typical example of an induction technique is the Christos experiment (Glaskin 1974). A remigrant lies on the floor with his eyes closed. One person massages his ankles and another rotates the knuckles of his fingers over the remigrant's forehead. This divides the remigrant's attention over two points far apart and makes him pleasantly dizzy. The Christos experiment simulates an out-of-body experience to dim external sensory awareness.

The counsellor asks the remigrant to imagine his feet growing out of his physical feet. Then, he pulls them back again. The same is done with the head, and both experiences are repeated a number of times. Finally, the remigrant imagines himself swelling out of his body on all sides until he feels like a balloon that practically fills the whole room. Then the counsellor asks the remigrant to imagine his own front door. This is where visualization begins. He has the remigrant describe this front door minutely. He has him rise along the wall of his house to the rooftop and asks him to describe the surroundings from the top of the roof. Next, the remigrant imagines himself going straight up about thirty yards and describes his surroundings again. The counsellor brings him higher and higher until he cannot or will not go any further. Usually, this is in the stratosphere where the horizon is vaguely bent. Some remigrants end up in space and see the earth as a ball. The counsellor then has the remigrant imagine night falling and seeing the stars, and then it becomes day and the sun is shining. The counsellor asks: 'Who made it night and then day again?' If the remigrant answers: 'I did', this indicates that he is 'visualizing lucidly'; he is acting consciously in his world of images, as when someone having a vivid dream is consciously present and acting in his dream. Then he returns to earth, to another time and place. The remigrant describes the landscape and the place where he is about to land. When landing he has to feel ground under his feet. He describes his feet and the rest of his body, and usually turns out to be in another body. From here, he describes the environment and enters another life.

The Christos experiment, then, is a step-by-step virtual out-of-body experience after an initial relaxation, supported by visualization and with two built-in safety devices: the ascent (which sometimes fails); the remigrant making his own day and night.

There are other induction techniques. Most counsellors use relaxation (often supported by hypnosis), visualization, and virtual out-of-body inductions. A quiet environment, without distractions such as ringing telephones, helps. The remigrant does not need to believe in reincarnation, but he has to accept a possibly interesting experience. It helps if he trusts the counsellor. The first step in the most common induction technique is physical and psychical relaxation. When someone wants to relive something from a past life, he will need complete concentration. Attention has to be steered clear from daily worries and preoccupations. The first time, curiosity and insecurity may disturb the relaxation. Bodily, we want to attain decreased muscular tension, increased skin resistance, and a calmer brain-wave pattern, going from beta to alpha and then to theta.

Get the client into a relaxed position, usually lying down. Some counsellors and some remigrants prefer sitting. Lying down is more relaxed, but some people associate lying with passivity and subjugation, and prefer to remain seated. The sitting position shows the depth of relaxation and trance more easily. With deeper forms of trance, there is less chance of tongue problems if the remigrant is sitting. I prefer remigrants to lie down, but they may remain seated if they prefer to do so. The induction below assumes the lying position, but can be used in the sitting position as well. The basis for relaxation is a calm environment, a pleasant dreaminess, and concentration on the body: breathing, physical sensation, and heartbeat. The attention of the remigrant has to turn inward, free from his daily worries and preoccupations. When the remigrant focuses his attention on his body, he increases its relaxation.

Some counsellors use a soft, pleasant background music. McClain advises against this, because it may 'trigger associations and emotions which have nothing to do with the particular lifetime under scrutiny and can therefore muddy the waters' (1986: 34). Every counsellor has his own preferences. Many of his techniques are intended also to relax himself. The greater the counsellor's experience, the less aids and preambles he requires, until his presence and voice are sufficient without any hypnotic amplification.

Ask the remigrant to focus on the quiet rhythm of his breathing. Have him imagine each inhalation bringing in a calm and fresh vitality and each exhalation taking out tensions and 'whatever does not belong to him'. Have him relax each part of his body by imagining a warm light passing through his whole body starting from the top of the head. Use words that affirm it is the remigrant himself who sends this warm light through his body, and even that the remigrant himself is this warm light. Associate the relaxation continuously with becoming more oneself, rather than with passive surrender. The counsellor simultaneously reinforces relaxation, openness, and a sense of self. The remigrant descends into himself, turns inward. Most counsellors begin with the top of the head and work down the body to the feet. Usually I suggest working with the order of the 'sensory homunculus' in the cerebral cortex:

● toes	● wrists
● feet	● hands
● calves	● little fingers, and through the fingers to thumbs
● knees	● eyes
● legs	● nose
● hips	● temples
● torso	● cheeks
● neck	● lips
● head	● jaw
● shoulders	● tongue
● upper arms	● throat
● elbows	● stomach
● lower arms	● abdomen.

The remigrant ends with the warm, relaxing light completely

surrounding and permeating him. It is particularly important that he visualizes the light streaming from his fingertips and eyes. McClain afterwards has remigrants become unaware of their feet, their legs, 'as if they do not belong to your body'. This is exactly the method Morrell used to exteriorize (Morrell 1974). Interestingly enough, McClain does not include the head in this. This seems to be just as well. I would not recommend an inexperienced counsellor to use this technique.

Finally, ask the remigrant to feel his heartbeat, and his blood pulse in diverse parts of his body: especially in the neck, temples, hands and feet. Focusing on breathing and heartbeat probably touches parts of the brain that evolved before the cerebral cortex.

Transpose this relaxed feeling on to some visualization. Have the remigrant imagine that he is pleasantly floating on air, or is lazily reposed in a gently rocking little boat or on a raft, or have any other pleasant association with mild, warm air and murmuring, fresh water. When the remigrant needs to stay close to you, you have him imagine that you row the boat or punt the raft. Denys Kelsey uses the image of crossing a wide river, where the remigrant leans back in the boat with his hands hanging in the water.

I myself have often used a technique related to the Christos experiment; you have the remigrant feel lighter and lighter, until he is floating in summer air, surrounded by sun and mild breezes. He becomes lighter and lighter until he feels himself coming to rest. Then suggest that the remigrant goes down to a place where he can be himself. He experiences this as slowly getting heavier and waking up in a breeze carrying him to a landscape that slowly comes to him as he is descending. Repeat a few times that the remigrant is coming to a place where he can be himself, a place that is his own. He descends until he feels the ground beneath his feet. Then he takes a good look around him and describes everything he sees, turning a complete circle. This experience deepens the trance, and functions as a safety device. Only if the remigrant reaches that place will he go into regression.

Leaving this place, the remigrant goes on a journey. Ask him if he is ready for the journey or if he yet needs something. These preparations may consist of visualizing someone or something to accompany him on his journey to a past life. Say, for example: 'You see something you would like to take with you on your journey. Pick it up, feel it and describe it.' If the remigrant wants further assurance, somebody whom he trusts and who supports him may arrive. This is another safety device. Then he starts his journey. For example, he may go to a place with an extraordinary mark on the ground. He stands on top of it holding his object tightly or having his guide close to him. A white mist arises around him and then the sun filters through it, surrounding him in a gorgeous golden-white light. All impressions around him fade. He experiences himself in this mist and feels the mist beneath his feet. Suggest that he sees the mist move with increasing speed, while he himself remains where he is, and that he is now going back in time and space, to another time where he will experience himself as another person who is still himself. He feels the ground beneath his feet again, and the mist lifts. He looks at his feet, and the rest of his body. The mist lifts away further and the situation becomes clear.

Instead of suggesting a mist, you may suggest a path ascending to a pass which gives access to another landscape, or a beautiful butterfly landing on the remigrant's outstretched hand. Let him describe the butterfly. Then let it flit away and the remigrant follow it down one path and up another, and at the end of the path find a passage or crossing – a gate, a door, a tunnel, some steps, a little bridge, or the like – and then he enters a past life. If he is in a boat, being ferried, there is a sun-drenched mist over the middle of the river. He goes through the mist to the opposite bank. When he gets out of the boat and walks up the bank, he is in a past life.

Some counsellors seek guides to protect or lead the way, or even have the remigrant ask for permission to go on a voyage. This is a form of spiritism: the idea is that a discarnate person will accompany the person to his past lives. There is some sense in that idea. I prefer it to prayer, but I have reservations about it.

1 This method implies that guides are necessary because regression could be dangerous. Calling for protection may incite the idea that protection may be necessary, which may arouse insecurity.
2 It ignores the remigrant's own inner steering ability.
3 It seems to be more for the protection of the counsellor than that of the remigrant. You may ask yourself what is making you waver. Probably you are not sure of what you are doing. Calling for guides is fine, but not as a compensation for shortcomings.

4 It looks like taking a step from thin ice on to even thinner ice. If you lack sufficient insight into what happens during a regression, can you discern and evaluate the presence of discarnate guides? Can you judge whether they are really present, or just figments of the remigrant's unconscious (or even your own)?

5 This course of action gives you an undeserved emotional satisfaction. After all, you can flatter yourself with the idea that you are co-operating with exalted spiritual presences.

A balanced and objective appraisal of this method is difficult, but I think you only need to use the method with psychotic patients. The procedure I have described leaves room for a guide to present himself. If you believe such guides may exist and may help, leave it to them to appear. Watch for them, do not call them.

Counsellors who like to call for guides also tend to work with rather exalted images during the introductory visualization: temples, rainbows, pyramids, holy mountains, esoteric and occult symbols. Marcia Moore exemplifies this style (Moore 1976). For example, she uses the procedure of walking in ever higher meadows, with flowers that are successively red, orange, yellow, green, blue, purple and white. This road would take you from the lower chakras (flower-like centres of energy and perception in the human aura) to the upper. The image is acceptable, but rather farfetched. The assumption that there are seven chakras with fixed colours is at least arguable, and chakras are more whirlpools than springboards into past lives.

Another tendency such counsellors have is to send the remigrant on long trips: to their most important incarnation, to their most spiritual incarnation, to incarnations on Atlantis or earlier, to their first incarnation, to incarnations on other planets, and on other special trips in the 'Famous European Cities in Five Days' style. I prefer simplicity and substance. If you are confident and the remigrant is relaxed you do not need other input.

If the remigrant turns out to be mediumistic (the body cools quickly and communication decreases), simple body contact and continuous verbal contact, sometimes supplemented with a few suggestions to return, is sufficient. Other safety devices may be built into the induction and the support of the counsellor.

Stick to a limited induction repertoire. This gives in-depth experience with people's reactions, and sensitivity to individual details and nuances. When a remigrant blocks during the induction this is meaningful and can be used as a point of departure in further counselling. For example, a remigrant cannot float in summer air because she feels a chill making her heavy and restless. In answer to the question about the cause of this chill, she sees an unpleasant eye. This eye turns out to be the entry into two past lives. Another remigrant lands in a place supposedly all his own, and is annoyed when he finds this place so full of people that he cannot find room for himself. Have him describe this feeling and then simply ask him to go back to the first situation that caused it. Sometimes this is in the present life, sometimes in a past life. Another person lands in a pretty meadow with trees, but while he is landing he has the feeling the trees are coming at him, to shut him in and cast a dark shadow over him. The counsellor asks him to intensify this feeling and the remigrant is in regression almost at once. *Each disturbance in the induction is the best introduction to a regression.*

Respect whatever the remigrant's psyche chooses. Do not muffle or fight, but evoke and intensify. Does a remigrant feel as though he cannot relax at all, as though he is lying on top of his couch? Ask him to describe that feeling, to specify and intensify it. 'As if I cannot move. As if people are looking at me in a large room.' The regression follows effortlessly.

A completed induction indicates easy access to past lives. But sometimes you are obliged to run through something else first. This is more effective and gratifying than trying to force the issue with exalted visualizations and helpful guides.

Counselling techniques

Before discussing counselling techniques I will give an example of the beginning of a session (C = counsellor, R = remigrant):

C: [after the induction] You are now in a different place, in a different time. Your situation becomes clear. What is the first thing you see or feel?
R: The sand is warm.
C: How do you feel that?

R: With my feet.

C: Are you sitting or standing?

R: I am standing and looking.

C: What are you looking at?

R: At something in the distance. I can't make it out.

C: It becomes clear to you. You see what it is.

R: A boat.

C: You see a boat. You see and understand more about the situation. Tell me what happens and what you are doing there.

R: They are my friends. They are fixing the boat. I think something was broken. I have taken a walk along the beach until they are ready. They don't need me there [suddenly a bit more emotional].

C: Why not?

R: They think I'm too young. I don't count at all yet. Though I caught the biggest fish yesterday! Boran boasted about the fish we had caught. But I had caught it!

C: How do you feel now?

R: Rotten. I can't stand it.

C: Now, you are standing, looking at the boat in the distance. They are fixing it. You can't stand it. The sand is warm on your feet. Look at your feet. What do they look like? What are you wearing? Feel your body and tell me what it looks like.

R: Light-brown feet. Ugly nails. One is broken. Wide, ragged shorts. No, a kind of skirt. I'm not wearing anything underneath it. It feels strange. I am wearing some kind of necklace. It is light and smooth. Some kind of small shells or light, smooth little stones. My sister made it. She is handy. She has beautiful hands. She is pretty. When she marries, I will be alone. I think they are calling me from the boat.

C: While you walk back to the boat, think about your sister and the way you live at home. You see clear images of your life at home, the way you grew up, and why you are going fishing now. You think about your life. Tell me about it. What is your name?

R: I have impressions of a hut. Playing in the sand. There is a younger brother. My name is . . . Rom . . . Rob . . .

C: You are near the hut and your sister is calling you. You hear her calling. What is she saying?

R: Robur! I don't see my father and mother. Just an old woman. She scolds a lot, but she is good to us.

This fragment illustrates a number of techniques:

1 The counsellor speaks in the present tense. He does not speak of memories, but of impressions.
2 He follows the remigrant's impressions closely and ties into what the remigrant tells him.
3 Every now and then he repeats and summarizes.
4 No matter how strongly he suggests or instructs, the suggestions and instructions are open. The only closed suggestion is that the remigrant is walking towards the boat. Although this is a reasonable assumption, the remigrant may answer, 'I walk away', or 'I just stand and pretend I don't see anything'. This divergence disturbs the flow. Or the remigrant wants to please the counsellor and starts to imagine himself walking towards the boat. The experience then fades and the remigrant is out of it.
5 The counsellor anchors the impressions by asking for details, by amplifying feelings, physical sensations, asking the remigrant's name. After sufficient anchoring, he goes further on to other background information.
6 He neither examines nor interrogates. He avoids questions that may satisfy his own curiosity but are removed from the remigrant's experience.

A question about age, for example, would have fitted perfectly after the remigrant said that they thought him too young. At this stage questions about dates and geography are wrong. The counsellor's questions and open instructions steer the experience and help to work it out and specify it. His mere presence helps, because verbalizing helps. Even if someone is able to remember past lives without counselling (usually on the level of recollection or reliving, and rarely on the level of a real regression), it is more difficult to do this alone and silently. Verbalizing prevents mental staring, fogging, and fixation.

Elaboration questions focus the remigrant's attention. If the remigrant just skims his experiences or gets stuck in them, anchor him with the right questions and instructions. Using the right instructions you can have a remigrant jump back and forth in his life, bring him to a standstill, accelerate occurrences and slow them down, and skip parts. The counsellor can bring the remigrant to his sixteenth year, back to his third, and forward again to his thirtieth.

What kind of counselling techniques exist? First, the basic interview technique, a combination of non-directive counselling and directive suggestions:

1 *Open questions:* What is your first impression? What is happening? What are you doing? What do you look like? How do you feel? [Usually, the counsellor asks multiple questions, preferably overlapping, allowing the remigrant to choose the most relevant.]
2 *Elaboration questions:* Why didn't they need you? How did you feel when that happened? Did that happen before? How did that go, exactly?
3 *Repeating and summarizing* [using the remigrant's words].
4 *Open suggestions:* You get a first impression. You see what is happening. You see what you look like.
5 *Elaboration suggestions:* You walk to the hut and hear your sister calling. She is calling your name.

Elaboration makes the recall more complete, more concrete, more real, moves it into a real reliving experience. At any time when it is necessary to cross the border between recollection and reliving again you need an 'anchoring technique'. Once a person is reliving, he normally only comes out of it when he reaches a block or is counselled badly.

Anchoring techniques are:
1 *Impressing body sensations:* Look at your hands and feet. What do they look like? How do you feel? Strong or weak? Young or old? Male or female? How do you feel when you walk? Are you stiff or nimble? Tall or short? What does your skin look like? Do you feel hot or cold? Do you feel pain or discomfort? Are you sitting, standing, walking, lying down?
2 *Impressing observations:* What colour is it? You see it more clearly now. What do you hear? Do you smell it? How is the weather? Do you feel wind or rain? Can you taste it? Is it heavy? Go over it with your hands. What does it feel like? What do you notice? [Make the images precise and add other sense qualities.]

3 *Impressing feelings:* How do you feel? What mood are you in? Do you have any feelings? Let your sadness grow, it is all there again. Are there other times when you cannot stand it? Go to a moment when this feeling is particularly strong. Are you afraid of something? Are there things or people you care about? [Schlotterbeck (1987: 16) uses as a key question: What does that do to you?]

After anchoring, work things out. The elaboration techniques are:
1 *Identity:* Who are you there? How old are you? What do you usually do during the day? What is your role? Look in the mirror.
2 *Orientation:* What time of day is it? What season is it? Are you inside or outside? What is closest to you? In what direction is your house? Where does that path lead?
3 *Relationships:* Are you married? Do you have brothers and sisters? Whom do you usually work with? Who is your best friend? Are there people who are obstructing you? How is that other person related to you?
4 *Meaning:* What does this man mean to you? How did that happen? How did you get into that situation? What impresses you most? What do you like best? What are you doing there, and why? What are you trying to attain? Go to a situation that illustrates what came out of this.

Because a remigrant may have doubts about the reality content of his memories, it is usually beneficial to start the regression with something trivial. Anchor the remigrant in his body, his perceptions and feelings, before going on. You may feel that something trivial is about to lead to something more important. I call these 'entry situations'. A movie would provide a crescendo in the background music. During a regression, there may be a growing pleasant or unpleasant anticipation. Give a good summary of an entry situation before the regression continues. A remigrant gives her age, describes what kind of person she is, and says she is walking home. You summarize: 'You are a girl, about 16 years old, who feels a bit depressed and is taking a detour home. You walk around the large puddles in the road, but there is mud on your shoes anyway, and you know your mother will be displeased. You feel vague anticipation, as if you might be leaving home, or someone will come and something will happen.'

Applications

Limit the exploration of a whole life to well-selected episodes, just as a movie shows us well-selected episodes of a whole story. How do you choose episodes? Often the first experience is a death, so if you want a complete picture of the life, you will have to go back. But first finish the dying experience, until the person has left the body and has had the global retrospect. Ask what were the most important goals or lessons in this life. Better yet (because it is more open) ask about the most important themes of this life. The remigrant may answer with a few words about basic feelings, repeated difficulties, lessons, or goals. Then, go through the life chronologically. A few suggestions for a choice of episodes:

1 The birth.
2 The first moment of self-awareness as a small child.
3 A typical growing-up experience.
4 The most important or profound childhood experience.
5 A situation typical of the environment in which the remigrant grew up.
6 The first time the remigrant made an independent decision.
7 A situation typical for the remigrant's relationship with the opposite sex.
8 A situation clearly indicating what the remigrant's work is.
9 A situation showing the remigrant's own family (engagement, marriage, moving into his house, the first pregnancy, etc.).
10 A typical situation in middle age.
11 A typical situation in old age.
12 Again: the death.

Other moments besides death that often come up first are those in adolescence or early adulthood when the remigrant thinks deeply about himself and his life, and intense childhood experiences. The remigrant may also enter a situation resembling his present life situation. Naturally, this may be explained as a psychodrama, rather than a reincarnation memory. Chapter 17 gives arguments pro and con. Anyway, psychological association is also relevant for memories of past lives. A person's present interest in going back to a past life does not come out of a psychic vacuum. The attitude or mental set influences the unconscious choice of memories from past lives.

At any time you may go forwards or backwards. You may flash

forward to consequences, or flash back to causes. Once a remigrant is walking through a landscape, is aware of his mood, and knows what he looks like, ask him what his destination is, and suggest that he is approaching it. If something important has happened before his arrival he sees this incident. When asking abstract questions, make sure to phrase it in concrete terms. Rather than 'what is important to you in this life?', suggest 'now you will experience a situation that makes clear what is important to you in this life'.

Sometimes a remigrant is so engrossed in an experience that his memories and descriptions start to overflow, without making progress. Ask him then what was most important in this experience, what was its main consequence, and what he learned from it.

The most common flash-forward is: 'Go to the next impressive or important or informative situation.' You make bigger jumps with: 'You are older and your situation is different. You see an event illustrating your new life situation.' If the new situation contains something inexplicable, the remigrant being suddenly rich for example, ask how this happened. If the remigrant remains silent, bring him back to a situation explaining this wealth. When this confuses or arouses emotions in the remigrant, this is an indication to go back to the situation causing this confusion or emotion. When an episode seems to be 'loaded' with emotion or meaning, do not jump right into it, but go back to a moment just before the beginning of it. Have the remigrant go through the whole episode clearly and chronologically. If either you or the remigrant are dissatisfied at the end of this, traverse it again, as in past-life therapy.

A regression to a past life is only finished when the death has been experienced. If this dying experience remains vague or unsatisfactory, it usually helps to go back to the experiences just before and during birth. Ask about the discarnate experiences. This leads to a level of broader consciousness, to the larger self. You can use this dissociation technique to go through confusing or burdening experiences with greater distance and overview. (I will return to dissociation techniques later.)

A painful or tragic death requires extra effort from us. The more realistically the remigrant experiences his death, the better. The examples of death experiences in chapter 8 indicate the kind of questions to ask. If the remigrant is detached from his body, and feels more or less balanced, ask him to look back on his life and to say what was most important in this life. What was the most joyous, what was the saddest event? What did he learn particularly? Where did he fail? Usually, the answers are surprisingly to the point, and the remigrant does see the main lines of his life clearly. Sometimes there are indications for returning to particular situations, to take a look at feelings of dissatisfaction or satisfaction. If the remigrant does not have a good life retrospect, does not meet any friends, kindred spirits, or helpers, and does not enter peace and light, we ask him to find the experiences or characteristics blocking this. If the impressions remain vague, we ask the remigrant to go back to the experiences that caused his incomplete liberation. Sometimes you end up in the birth experience, finding reluctance, unwillingness, or doubtfulness about the coming life.

Bring the remigrant to a sense of completion and peacefulness after a dying experience, evaluate briefly, and then perhaps go back to another life with him. The most important exception to this is tracing 'chains': consecutive, similar, more or less repetitive, pregnant experiences, linked throughout various lives by restimulation. Often they concern fundamental life aims, difficulties and life attitudes. The last two are usually found in past-life therapy.

Questions about abstract information such as names, dates, and facts, tend to fade the regression. This kind of information is usually located in the 'data memory' (first level, see chapter 6), apparently a different register from the experience register. Names, dates, and facts seem to be stored in a different part of the memory than the visual and emotional. When asking about names and facts before the reliving experience is anchored, the remigrant often blocks. You need more elaboration first.

Counsellors usually ask for factual information to check the historical reality of the experience, to convince the remigrant (and themselves) of the authenticity of the regression. Otherwise they do it to gain interesting conversation material for cocktail parties, or to talk more convincingly about their work. New counsellors especially, have a strong need for historical confirmation, and are so enthusiastic about having crossed the border into another life that they immediately want to know the remigrant's first and last name, the birth date, the area and country and all kinds of historical details. Although some remigrants easily provide this information, it often obstructs the development of the life story (which is more interesting anyway). Develop the concrete life story and the most important events first, and 'arm' it only afterwards with historical facts, unless the remigrant himself, with his mixed emotions of doubt and enthusiasm, needs historical details. But ask questions that lead to concrete experiences. If the remigrant fails to remember his name, bring him to a moment when he is called unexpectedly, or to the moment when he writes his name down for the first time. Another point of orientation is the name of the nearest town. Ask if the remigrant ever went to the nearest town. If he did, evoke the image of the town when the remigrant arrived there, and ask the name of the town. Or, if the remigrant never went there, ask him to go to some conversation that mentioned the town, and to catch the name of it. Ask for such information within concrete memories. This works more surely and precisely. Do not ask directly in which century and in which town the remigrant lived, but ask about clothing, food, important traditions, and so on. Ask rather 'What age are you living in?' than 'what century are you living in?' The second question presupposes our calendar, which may differ from the calendar of the past life. It creates a link with the present and may call the remigrant back. When the remigrant is sufficiently anchored, this may not be disturbing, but do avoid it if the reliving is shallow.

A good moment for asking for objective information is during the restrospect after death. You may ask the remigrant to see a map with a little white light where he lived most of his life. You may even ask for specific years. You will have to regard even quick and concrete responses ('flash answers') with reservation, because mistakes are made easily. Many indirect indications are usually better than asking for names, birth date, date of death, and place names. Sometimes, during the retrospect, a remigrant may even answer questions which can be historically verified. Paranormally gifted remigrants are sometimes able to receive names of places, graveyards, or libraries containing historically verifiable material.

Guidance techniques

The best known guidance techniques are counting and flash answers.

A remigrant relives an encounter and feels that he knows the other person without knowing who it is or what he is doing here. Say, for example, 'I will count to three and on the third count you will remember what the other has come for, and what his relation is to you'. Counting is effective with forwarding and rewinding as well: 'On the third count you are in the next important situation.' The counting instruction can be supported visually: 'I will count to five and on each count you will take a step (up or down) towards the situation. On the fifth count you will go through a gateway (door, curtain) and you immediately receive new impressions.'

Counting and flash answers lubricate the regression. Using them sparingly and successfully increases the remigrant's trust in you. They will be less and less necessary during the regression. If continual 'lubrication' is necessary, it is better to find the cause. You may snap your fingers on the final count: 'On the fifth count I will snap my fingers and you will immediately have an impression of the reason why you are having difficulty staying in the experiences.' The answers are often informative: 'I prefer sitting to lying down.' 'Something is eating my leg.' 'I need something in front of my eyes.' 'I keep thinking of my brother. Strange, I had not realized that.'

Open selection criteria, such as going to typical, instructive, meaningful, important, or impressive situations, or situations with many repercussions, are suitable to open exploration. Often they lead to more specific explorations. For example, a female remigrant remembers a life as a woman. In the middle of the description of a typical scene from her marriage, she says in a tight voice that she did not want to marry at all. This is a lead to go back to the moment when the marriage was decided. Ask, for example, what she did not like about this man. If she answers with difficulty, bring her back to a situation where she clearly sees what she did not like about the man. During the life retrospect, ask her what the marriage meant to her, how it fitted into her life, and so on.

The two basic principles for the order of the 'shots' taken, are the 'chronological path' and the 'thematic path', following an emotional or existential theme. Leads can be induced from peculiar words or expressions, surfacing feelings, hesitations, and pregnant details. Regression experiences should be meaningful for the remigrant's present life. Ask about this after the retrospect, or at the beginning of the regression. The remigrant often sees connections in the discussion afterwards, and sometimes during the regression.

Good guidance is mainly a question of dealing adequately with barriers and blocks, with rush, with stress, and with associations. The three main barriers are: not getting into the regression, going in too deeply, and coming out of it. Usually, failing to regress results from a weak induction, coming out of it from bad counselling (for example, asking too many abstract questions too soon), and going in too deeply results from an induction that was too heavy. What looks like a barrier may also be a block to avoid particular contents. Blocks occur with experiences of fear, repulsion, reluctance, or heaviness. The remigrant walks with leaden feet: the images come to a virtual standstill; or flies with winged feet: the images pass quickly, become impersonal, and fade.

A whole volume could be written on blocks and responding to blocks. The most important thing is not to see barriers and blocks as disturbances, but as leads. Sometimes a barrier indicates that the remigrant is looking for more support and would like to consolidate his self-confidence as well as his relation with you before he proceeds. You may ask for the cause or the reason for a barrier or block and take it from there. A barrier is usually caused by something neglected during the induction.

Barriers are often blocks resulting from the whole setting of the regression. For example, a remigrant associates lying down with subjugation, especially if the life closest to the surface is associated with, for example, being forced to lie down for a long period, or in a sickbed or in other negative situations. Such negative associations are easily prevented by a sitting position. More difficult barriers are, for example, negative associations with doctors. For example, in this life or a past life, a remigrant had a traumatic experience with a treatment, and associates the counsellor with the doctor, and the regression with the treatment. Or the remigrant blocks through associations with a father, mother, or other authority figure. Sometimes a regression is easier with a person of the opposite sex. The most common barrier is that the remigrant associates the regression setting with letting go, opening up to another person, dependence, and that these feelings arouse blocks. Helen Wambach found that fundamental barriers had to do with fear of death and a resistance to every form of psychological analysis, even free association, in the presence of another person. Fear of death usually blocks because of an unpleasant dying experience just beneath the surface of consciousness, or because of superstitious fears. The best preparation is to practise relaxation and visualization regularly, with or without the aid of a cassette. When there is progress there, chances for regression are good.

You can give a remigrant wings on his leaden feet: 'Look at it as if it were happening to somebody else in a movie. You are interested, but you feel comfortable lying here, looking at it.' Or ask him to look at it all from above, as a floating observer, keeping to a distance where he feels safe. A virtual out-of-body experience creates a virtual observer. Reserve finger signals for direct questions to the unconscious. If hypnotic instructions were absent in the induction, return to the life retrospect after death, or to the point in the visual induction where the remigrant was his complete self, or the highest point where he floated bodilessly. You may often introduce finger signals here. Simply ask the remigrant to raise one finger to mean yes, and another to mean no, and tell him that the questions are directed to the real, higher, or deeper self. The remigrant has to react directly, without thinking. Many remigrants are surprised to feel a particular finger itching or raising itself, even when they had a different answer in mind. Counsellors who use hypnosis, use finger signals at the beginning of the session, asking the remigrant whether he is ready to go to a past life, and to check possible leads. Deal with initial blocks, like blocks during the induction. Use them as leads for an 'excursion'. A block during an otherwise smooth regression may be the consequence of having skipped an important element in the preceding experiences: 'If you have skipped an important experience or an important part of an experience, then go back to it now.'

Another initial block may be that the remigrant feels that he is somewhere, but fails to get a clear image of it, while anchoring techniques do not work. Possibly, the remigrant has landed in a situation where he was blind or deaf, or had to keep things secret. Ask him if the trouble is with his ears, or his eyes. Or ask him if he has to keep something secret, or what he is doing there in the black of night. If such a question is correct, the block dissolves.

Some blocks look like just the opposite. With 'rush', the remigrant chatters on and on, going through one experience after the other, and listens poorly. Often, this is paired with fleeting impressions of background information, making the experience more like story-telling than movie-watching. The most obvious deblocking tech-nique for a rush is to stop the film and examine the resulting photograph. Then ask the remigrant to describe the picture carefully. If necessary, focus the picture in on details. Have the remigrant concentrate on one detail of the experience, have him pin that detail down and enlarge it.

A man enters. He seems to be an old friend. He says something. The remigrant gets excited, runs out of the house, and has all sorts of vague adventures. Then instruct the remigrant to go back to the man who enters, to stop the image, and ask for details. Often, after a rush, there is a resistance to looking at details. Insist on the most trivial detail if need be, and, from this detail (still motionless) work the image outwards. The man who enters wears a ring on his left hand. Ask for a close-up of the ring. Is it gold or silver? Broad or narrow? Does it have a stone? Then the remigrant looks at the hand. Is it rough or delicate? White or tanned? Etc.

In principle, 'rush' is caused by insufficient anchoring. When standstill and analysis of the details are successful, look at the three anchoring points. Does the remigrant have enough body awareness? Are his feelings sufficiently strong? Rush is most common with hurried or intellectual people. The intellectual rush is less one of speeding through experiences, but more immediately building a world of thoughts around each image. For example, a remigrant sees a town in the distance. Before he has any clear notion of what he is going to do, before he feels or sees anything, he is telling you this is an old harbour road, maybe in France, that there was fighting in the city council recently, and that a new prefect from the capital has just arrived. The whole superstructure consists of interesting but abstract information, built on a minimal substructure of concrete experience. This quickly brings the remigrant back into memory and recol-lection, and the experience changes into storytelling while lying on the couch. When the rush happens suddenly, the remigrant skims an important, but for some reason threatening situation. It may be an escape from an experience the remigrant wants to get out of as fast as he can, but it may also be a running start to gloss quickly over an approaching sensitive point.

Applications

Encountering difficult emotional situations without liberation creates stress. Situations of pain and disorientation, in particular, gives rise to somatics, physical reactions like sweating, heart palpitations, shortage of breath, restless movement, ect. Some remigrants smell terrible during a difficult dying experience attended by strong emotions. Strong somatics indicate that something is being worked out, a spontaneous transition to therapy. We have to help the remigrant through the experience rather than call him back just when he is on the verge of healing. Calling him back would be just as wrong as pushing a baby being born back into the womb because the midwife has not arrived yet. The remigrant has to face the death, has to relive the agony of his last moments. If necessary, we suggest that the experience will make the remigrant understand, without feeling real pain and with subdued emotions. Experiencing fully, and understanding what is happening is more important than experiencing all the emotions.

The extent of catharsis when a death is relived depends on 'coming up' well after leaving the body. When a remigrant dies incompletely, comes up badly, and continues to feel restless, then bring him to a state of light and peace, 'rewriting' the dying experience to include complete catharsis. For example, a person experiences that he is pushed into a swamp, already half-choked. After that, he feels as if he is floating in a dark, cold atmosphere, with a pressing weight on his throat. Suggest, for example: 'Now you slowly drift away from the place where this happened. Slowly, you feel the water around you getting warmer and lighter. There is sunlight on the water now. While everything is getting warmer and lighter, the weight on your throat vanishes. The darkness dissolves and you feel yourself slowly being freed. You have left your body behind you. It is no longer important. You come to the surface and breathe, freely and joyfully.' Work out the image, using waking-dream techniques. For example, have the remigrant drift slowly in a little boat to an island where he is going to feel wonderful. Wait until the remigrant feels free and happy and then let him look at the dying experience, from a distance as it were. Say that he will now understand his past life better.

Remain in constant contact with the remigrant during this intervention. When you suggest that the water is getting warmer and lighter, ask the remigrant if he feels this. The remigrant may add his own sensations. Such a cathartic dying experience is impressive, even for observers who reject reincarnation. It is incomparably more satisfying than to have found out street names and house numbers, even if these are historically documented later.

What should you do when repeated versions of an event are contradictory? This requires 'disentanglement techniques'. First, concentrate on the elements that were exactly the same. For example, the remigrant came to an inn on a horse; the bar-room was full; the barman was fat and looked upset. Send the remigrant back to the beginning of the experience and ask him to describe these elements in detail: where the inn was located, the colour of the horse, if it was his own horse, how big it was, if he could feel and smell the horse, the barman's apron, etc.

You have to do extra anchoring, because apparently the level of reliving was too shallow to channel the emotions of this situation. In between, you may give small suggestions like: it does not matter if you cannot see everything clearly just yet, it does not matter that the stories differ, etc. If a version offers relief, the remigrant can proceed. In past-life therapy there may remain some fabrication, causing a catharsis that is only partial. Here we are in the area of 'screen memories'.

An apparent contradiction may occur because two experiences have become mixed up. If a remigrant was married twice in her life, and we ask her about marriage, strange mixtures may appear in the reliving experience, especially if she was married in the same place twice, for example. The same is true when the remigrant was at the same inn twice, and on both occasions something important happened.

In the 'dating technique' the remigrant goes back to the moment just before the occurrences and makes careful note of the time of day, how he felt, what happened before, etc. When he enters the occurrence step by step, there is a good chance he will get through it unaffected by extraneous elements. Artificial 'tracers' can help to disentangle different versions. Have the remigrant imagine that he is holding, say, a golden ball tightly in his left hand while he enters the experience, and that he has to hold on to this golden ball. When something paradoxical or contradictory happens, ask the remigrant if he still holds the golden ball. Apparently, the film track of past lives has a side track that can tape things temporarily, or erase them. Entanglements and disturbances in the track of time are common in drug users. Here, disentanglement takes time. First, you establish the 'emotional differential' of each drug: what drug is connected to what emotions. Then you have to take each emotional line and clean it up.

What is to be done when remigrants associate themselves with a historically famous person? Be reserved, if only because the chances it is true are minimal. When fantasy is out of the question (chapter 17 will give some techniques to test this), the remigrant may have been close to this person. Ask the remigrant to go back to a situation where many people surrounded this famous person, and ask if anybody there catches his attention or seems related. Sometimes, this is an ordinary bystander, and the remigrant comes back as this person in the second version of his experience. Some examples can be found in Ron Hubbard (1958). A cannon-boy on one of Nelson's ships identifies with Nelson in the first regression; a doorman during one of Beethoven's concerts identifies with an aristocrat in the audience, and then with Beethoven himself. Keep your cool, remain objective, and accept it only as a remote but interesting possibility. When a remigrant thinks he has been some great person, do not argue with him to bring him back to reality. First, this is in bad taste, and second, he just might be right, and you would have insulted a prominent client.

If the remigrant is constantly wondering whether what he sees is right, you may instruct him to change random details. For example, he sees a white house with a red roof, and you ask him if he can change it to a dark brown house with a green roof. Or he sees himself as a lady dressed in dark blue walking next to a gentleman in a light suit, and you ask him if he can experience himself as the gentleman, or if he can change the colour of the clothing, and so on. If a remigrant does this without trouble, the chances are that the image was a fantasy. If a person cannot do this, this indicates that the experience is at least psychically real and not random. It is a reasonable indication of a real memory.

When rewinding, tracing, and other techniques fail to clear up obviously paradoxical or impossible events, use finger signals to ask if this has been a dream, a fantasy, the play the remigrant saw, or a book he read in his past life. When you get negative answers on all of them, deal with the experience as a psychodrama, and let the pseudo-remigrant work it out as such.

Special cases

A remigrant may go back so intensely that he places the questions from the counsellor within his past life. Chapter 6 called that 'identification'. Edith Fiore gives the example of the remigrant who relived herself as an Indian girl with a knowledge of herbs. When she asked her to talk about this, the remigrant became afraid because somebody was trying to steal her secrets, and because she could not understand such dishonourable conduct (Fiore 1978: 11). Go along with such situations, ask only questions that are acceptable to this person in this situation, and wait until the retrospect to try to get more information.

'Recursive indications' in regressions, referring to the present regression situation, are rare. For example, the remigrant meets a person and suddenly identifies him with you. Accept it as a possiblity, but beware of transference. Netherton responds: 'This information has no meaning to me, but please continue with the regression.' Sometimes the counsellor is so curious about himself that he disrupts the development of the regression. Remember, you are there for the remigrant, not the other way round.

Other special cases are mediumistic people. They usually have strong somatics. When you have any indication of mediumship, give a clear hypnotic anchoring at the beginning. Usually, their trance is deep enough during relaxation to let these instructions work. One important instruction is to remain in constant contact with the counsellor and to continue to understand the counsellor. We can see with finger signals whether a regression can be experienced well. Finally, establish beforehand some trigger word or physical contact that will make a person come back calmly and quickly. Such safety measures prevent a regression from changing into an uncontrollable out-of-body experience. A mediumistic out-of-body experience leaves the body cold and rigid. In that case, touch it, preferably in the chakra regions.

Such situations are rare, but impressive, and many counsellors are afraid of them. If you use magnetism, you may seal the chakras, for example at the stomach and on the head. This is sufficient to make a person return, or to prevent them leaving their body. If you doubt whether you can magnetize, and the remigrant is new to you, look for psychic dispositions in a preliminary meeting. Indications are: previous spontaneous out-of-body experiences, sensing the presence of discarnate people, involuntary psychic impressions, and physical response to the physical and psychological problems of others. When in doubt, build in some extra safety devices.

If the finger signals were fixed beforehand, if the remigrant experienced a place where he could be himself, and if he started his voyage of his own accord, nothing can go wrong. Besides, a counsellor who remains self-possessed has few things to fear.

Further reading

There are as yet few good text books on past-life exploration. The best books are Glaskin (1974) and McClain (1986). A large part of what little else there is covers induction techniques: hypnosis and visualization.

Handbooks on hypnosis-induction have been written by Leslie Le Cron (1976), Hubert Scharl (1977), and Kurt Tepperwein (1977), among many others. A few books on hypnotherapy will be discussed in the next chapter. Visualization as an introduction to regression is described by Bennett (1937), Brennan (1971), Jamieson (1976), Moore (1976), and Langedijk (1980). Examples from sessions are given by Bernstein (1956), Bloxham (1958), Hubbard (1958), Moss and Keeton (1979), Langedijk (1980), Goldberg (1982), and Williston and Johnstone (1983).

16 Past-life Therapy

Past-life therapy is the treatment of present psychic and psycho-somatic problems that originate from past lives. Past-life therapy heals karmic psychosomatic illnesses and solves karmic psychological problems. Chapter 12 defined karma as liabilities from past lives: the retention of complicated relations or negative psychological reactions and the repercussions of traumas and postulates. Chapter 10 and 11 gave examples of these.

Past-life therapy has a sister, 'past-life deployment': finding, de-veloping, and learning to use more or less dormant talents from past lives. That does not solve karma; it liberates dharma. I have found neither methods, nor results, nor research on this topic. According to Joan Grant, awakening sleeping talents occurs when animating the 'supra-physical' (presumably a permanent extract from the etheric body) from a past incarnation (Kelsey and Grant 1967). Taken in this sense, past-life deployment would be the counterpart of the treatment of 'hangovers', which this chapter will discuss.

Four karmic repercussions: traumas, hangovers, pseudo-obsessions, and postulates

Different karmic repercussions require different therapeutic re-sponses. There are basically four types: traumas, hangovers, pseudo-obsessions and postulates. Real obsessions are a fifth chal-lenge, but the majority are not karmic and their treatment is quite distinct. This chapter only broaches this subject. However, a past-life therapist should be able to diagnose obsession and refer his patient to an obsession therapist. Some therapists are able to treat both. Some of them, like Louise Ireland-Frey (1986), always start by looking for obsessions, to avoid regressing the obsessor instead of the patient.

Traumas are the unhealed wounds left by a terrible experience of physical pain, despair, and stupefaction. The worst, most extreme traumatic experience is that of being slowly tortured to death, or of watching a person whom you love dearly being tortured to death. Less terrible traumatic experiences are frightful and painful deaths, like being attacked by a wild animal, dying in combat, and violent accidents. Another horror is the sudden loss of a family member: a spouse who dies in flames, a child hit by a car, a sister who is sold as a slave. The most common severe traumas found in past-life regressions are: witches and heretics being tortured and displayed, concentration-camp experiences, and small children dying in panic during bombing raids.

A trauma's power derives from the energy of the suppressed negative experience: pain, fear, hatred, disgust, jealousy, despair. Traumas may lend a horrible and sometimes frightful taste to otherwise tolerable situations when these situations show similarities to the original trauma. If inquisitors shouted at you and hit you in a place lit by flickering torches, then your father, who hits you and shouts at you while walking across the campground with a lantern, may restimulate the forgotten experience and scare you to death. Someone sees her house burning down. She loses control, for she unconsciously remembers a fire in which she died together with others. The shadow of this terrible experience looms up, even if there is nobody in the present burning house. Traumas from past lives often manifest themselves in the form of hypersensitivity to particular situations. For example, if a phobic finds that searches in present-life regressions only bring trivial causes, and reliving them does not remove the phobia, this points to a trauma from a past life.

If you compare your inner field with a garden or a farmyard, it will have well-tended and neglected spots. In one corner you walk on a perfect lawn, and in another corner you trip over roots or get struck in the mud. Other pitfalls are hidden. These are your karmic 'manholes'. Because you have forgotten them, falling into them is a horrible, unexpected experience: an inexplicable fear arises, a dark threat suddenly seems to loom over you, a strangling jealousy pops up after a small incident, somebody brushes your neck and you break into a sweat.

Traumas are like hidden manholes, postulates are like treadmills, whirlpools, knots, or vicious circles in the paths of your psychic garden. They are ingrained in you as fixed programmes: 'If I lose control, I'm lost.' 'If I escape, I will be free.' 'I cannot think because I am a woman.' No postulate can be overcome just by reliving the original situation that triggered the programme. Each postulate has to be recognized, understood, and renounced freely.

Our strongest postulates are intensely engraved, concern existential issues, and imprison us in paradoxes. When our psychic resistance crumbles after lengthy torture, and the inquisitor thunders in a brass voice that we are children of the devil, our confused mind absorbs this as the ultimate truth, embracing it as a rescue from disintegration. Countless people have postulates like:

- 'I am a whore.'
- 'There will be no mercy for me.'
- 'I am lost forever.'
- 'I am dark and evil inside.'

Self-satisfied, 'positive' postulates are:

- 'I can do as I like.'
- 'Everybody loves me.'
- 'I am the most beautiful.'
- 'I can help everybody.'

A third type of karmic problem are 'hangovers'. These are re-percussions of entire lives. A female remigrant finds herself as a woman in eighteenth-century South America on an isolated hacienda. Looking back on this life, the overriding impression is one of bareness. The courtyard is bare, the surroundings are bare, the houses are bare, her whole life is bare. The one overpowering feeling is of bareness, dullness, stuffiness, shallowness, and emptiness. It is a suffocating blanket covering the entire life. Formulated as a postulate, it could be described as: 'Everything is bare.'

Another remigrant experiences a life that burdened him with superstitious fears about everything from his childhood onward. Another person experiences a life that consisted only of hard work from early morning to late evening. A fourth experiences a life where he had to toil for other people, and never had anything of his own.

Such experiences lead to general feelings about life: 'Everything is dangerous; you are never safe.' 'Life is exhausting.' 'I have nothing

343

that is my own.' Such feelings are suffocating energy gluttons, wet blankets, spider webs, and dark fogs that make the whole garden sombre and unpleasant. Reliving such a life explains where this feeling originated. This in turn provides intellectual comfort, but sometimes strengthens rather than weakens the feeling, until it is disconnected from the present life.

'Pseudo-obsessions' result from an incomplete death, rather than from an overriding negative feeling about life. The personality from the previous life has not found peace, has not been integrated in the larger self, in the total personality. The earlier personality haunts us. In Joan Grant's words: 'the supra-physical from a past life haunts our aura.' A characteristic difference between a hangover and a pseudo-obsession is that a wide range of (mostly non-specific) psychosomatic complaints accompany a pseudo-obsession. A person's stomach gives problems, and when these are healed, emotional crying fits result. When these crying fits are over, the person gets skin problems. If the skin problems are treated, leaden legs or anorexia follow. Here too, to find the unfinished business, look for the fundamental postulates. A common psychosomatic symptom is allergy. Kelsey and Grant (1967) give a convincing example. Whitton and Fisher give an interesting and instructive case about a woman who is allergic to just about everything: 'I cannot help but feel that I'm allergic to life itself' (1986: 100).

Indications for past-life therapy

Being a cognitive therapy, the effectiveness of past-life therapy depends on the patient's sincere desire to be healed. People with a typical patient mentality usually achieve only minimal improvement, even after successful regressions. According to research by Johannes Cladder (1983), phobics with compulsive behaviour are less sensitive to past-life therapy than phobics without compulsions.

People who struggle actively with their psychic or psychosomatic problems are, almost without exception, good candidates for past-life therapy. Every psychic problem or psychosomatic problem whose origin cannot be found in the present life, and which does not respond to other psychotherapy, is a possible case for past-life therapy. Many other problems are as well. Opinions differ on the percentage of psychic and psychosomatic problems that past lives cause. Dethlefsen concludes that past lives contribute to a large portion of psychic problems (1974: 99).

According to Hubbard (1958), 82 per cent of cases improve unequivocally, psychologically and physically, after past-life therapy. My own estimate is also that, of those who have comparable experiences in regressions, about 80 per cent improve considerably. General belief in reincarnation does not affect the success of the therapy. The only important thing is to accept the experiences from other situations in a different time, without worrying whether or not they are fantasies. An interesting detail from Cladder's work is that regressions to past lives tend to make the patients less psychotic and give them a greater sense of reality. Extroversion increases, and the patients' sense of orientation seems to improve.

What are the indications for past-life therapy? First of all, the patient has to be motivated to explore himself. Those who attach too much importance to being a patient are better off with 'anti-therapies' which break the patient-therapist relationship. On the other hand, people who refuse the role of a patient are also unfit for explorative, cognitive therapy. They refuse to relax, and give interpretations, comments, and rationalizations on everything that even resembles a real experience or a real emotion. This may be satisfying as a form of intellectual chess, but is useless for liberating experiences and insights. People who just want to get rid of their problems without getting into the causes can sometimes be helped by anti-therapy, and more often with behavioural or suggestive therapy.

A successful regression needs either an entry point or sufficient relaxation. The best entry points for regression therapy are irrational fears, peculiar somatics, recurrent dreams, and repetitive phrases that indicate postulates. Provoking the feeling, the somatic, or the dream, or repeating the postulate, while instructing the remigrant to go back to the situation that caused this feeling or the place where the postulate was literally spoken or was literally true, usually induces a regression. The regression may lead to a situation in this life or in a previous life.

People in trance can indicate whether the problem originates in this life or in a past life via ideo-motoric finger signals. The number of relevant lives can be indicated as well. The finger signals of a remigrant with the postulate 'I am branded' indicated seven lives involved in this complex. The first of these lives was that of a middle-aged man who got leprosy when he had left his family and saw this as a punishment for his lack of love for them. The last of these lives was a life as a prostitute. The remigrant was now neither branded, nor a leper, nor a prostitute, but was overshadowed by seven branded lives, fused by restimulation into one karmic complex.

Typical postulates from past lives are:

- 'If I make love with a man he will murder me.'
- 'They have forgotten me. I have nowhere to go.'
- 'They let me sit here and rot.'
- 'See what has become of me.'

Other indications for a past-life cause is a feeling of having ended up with the wrong parents, and a mono-symptomatic neurosis: a healthy and well-balanced person who has just one inexplicable problem (Kelsey). Cladder sums it up clearly: 'It is as if past lives are most essential for phobics with the least problems' (1983).

When you work with relaxation or visualization, the following are indications that people will end up in past lives: a general body relaxation in which heart-beat is felt in all limbs (Langedijk); a successful visualization of leaving the body, going up, and landing again (Glaskin, among others). Contra-indications are an inability to relax, or to associate freely with words and sentences, lack of trust in the therapist (as in all forms of psychotherapy), and strong lack of self-confidence.

Psychotic or depressed people are usually bad candidates for regression therapy, and few reincarnation therapists like to work with drug addicts. The imagery of addicts is normally chaotic and tedious, as though their tapes have got mixed up and stuck together. According to scientologists, each drug has to be connected with a specific emotion and these emotion tracks have to be worked out one by one. Heavy use of medicines is also obstructive.

Since the therapist accompanies the patient closely during regression, there is a bond between the therapist and the patient. Most therapists relate to some types of patient with difficulty. One may dislike cancer patients, the next may dislike patients who have worked with black magic in their past life. The therapist has to give special attention to sensitive, and especially mediumistic, people. They have a tendency to leave the body during regressions. The therapist has to know how to respond to this, to avoid unpleasant psychic and physical consequences.

Causes of traumas and postulates

Traumatic (literally: wounding) experiences are overwhelming experiences we were able neither to digest nor to ignore. This is because the emotions burned us so deeply that we were unable to detach ourselves from them, and at the same time they were too terrible to accept, to attach to and integrate into our life and our identity. They become undigested experiences with great psychic mass, not absorbed into the normal memory, but leading a life of their own. Hubbard's work (1950) has shown how each traumatic experience is a clear episode with a precise beginning and end. The result he calls an 'engram', something engraved. The interesting aspect of engrams is that, besides episodes with physical pain or strong negative feelings, they encompass verbal contents: words and sentences.

Traumas are usually undigested and suppressed because the original experience was insupportable: terror, torture, inquisition, witch hunts, concentration camps, etc. But less horrible situations can be traumatic too, through lack of opportunity to come to terms with them, because of sudden death, or because the mind was dominated by some warped view or inhibiting command. This leads to suppressed understanding, misunderstanding, or lack of understanding. Often we have learned the misunderstanding from somewhere. Sometimes we acquired it ourselves: from some vow we made, a postulate that made understanding and digestion impossible. Thus, we can have a warp (wrong interpretation), confusion and perplexity (lack of interpretation), and a postulate (rigid interpretation). Netherton provides good examples of wrong interpretation (Netherton and Shiffrin 1978: 34, 75, 76).

Dying experiences show that, if all goes well, cardinal events are confronted and digested during the second retrospect. Therefore, traumatic situations which haunt us in following lives indicate

347

inadequate dying processes. When negative emotions like fear, hatred, and terror are combined with intense physical pain, a trauma can hardly be avoided because of physical and psychical incapacitation. Victims may even adopt feelings of dependency for their torturers. This results in a warped digestion and so in a sore karmic gnarl: a trauma-postulate complex. Other victims try to understand the hellish experience as a punishment for their sins, or as God testing their strength. This too, results in a trauma-postulate complex. Hubbard (1958) gives the example of an aristocratic girl who is kidnapped and tortured by people who want to find her father's treasures. She does not know where these are to be found, but is unable to convince her torturers of this. During the questioning and the torture the conspirators constantly tell her she is, like every woman, stupid and irresponsible. This etches the postulate: 'A woman is stupid and irresponsible' in her naive, confused, and exhausted spirit, and then: 'This is what happens to you when you are a woman.'

In a later incarnation, such an experience may lead to such difficulties as not menstruating (not wanting to be a woman); being a bad pupil at school (women are stupid); being messy and confused (women are irresponsible); and having fears (anything may happen to you). In key sentences especially, pay attention to paradoxes, double-binds, super-generalizations, and recursive sentences (that may refer to the exploration and the therapy itself).

Examples of paradoxes are:

1 'If I find myself, I am lost.'
2 'I can't do anything if I escape.'
3 'I hate people who get too close to me.'
4 'I desperately want to be spontaneous.'

Examples of double-binds are:

5 'If I am successful, I am afraid I will mess it up.'
6 'I hate people who impose upon me, and people who let me down.'

Examples of super-generalizations are:

7 'All men are the same.'
8 'Nothing ever goes right for me.'
9 'Nobody understands me.'

Examples of recursive statements are:
10 'I cannot get out of it.'
11 'I do not know what I want.'
12 'I do not trust anybody. Including you.'

Examples 1, 2, 3, 5, 6, 8, and 9 may also be recursive, as may 7 if the therapist is male.

When we are about to be born again we take the traumas and engrams from past lives with us. Events during the pregnancy or the birth may restimulate them. Take again the example of the aristocratic girl. She is going to incarnate again as a woman. Her mother, who is not married, has to tell her own parents that she is pregnant. The mother bursts into tears, and cries: 'Why were you so terribly irresponsible?' The incarnating girl identifies with this and so the karmic engram is restimulated. Later in her life another situation may restimulate this. Often, one restimulation is enough to restart the vicious circle. Some boys are chasing her on the school grounds and tie her up. When she protests, they answer that she was stupid enough to get caught. This may cause her to scream in panic, to have nightmares, stomach cramps, and spots on her face (places where she was hurt in her previous life) as the karmic sore bursts open. People are often deeply wounded by things that hardly seem to affect others. The striking psychology of everyday life calls this 'putting on a show' or 'putting yourself out'.

Always remember the importance of a warped interpretation, because we tend to regard the objective occurrences as decisive. Certainly, there are horrors in which only the sick can remain healthy. However, interpretation remains essential. This is important because many therapists believe that repeating the regression of the situation more or less intensely ('flooding') is enough to cure the patient. The trauma would just wear out. However, repeating and flooding a falsely interpreted experience may solve the symptom and aggravate a deeper problem.

Catharsis is the result of the triad of emotional, physical, and intellectual liberation. Catharsis restructures the Gestalt of an experience, it is an 'Aha-Erlebnis', a Eureka! A sure sign of a successful catharsis is peace: emotional peace, physical peace, and spiritual peace. Only insight gives peace of mind. Somatics are observable, and therefore important for the therapist. The patient blushes or turns pale, breathes differently, gets hot or cold, has cramps or shocks. Even his smell may change. On a few occasions patients reliving a traumatic death exude a penetrating scent. Others drip in sweat. The face tightens during the recall of a trauma. During a real cathartic session, patients first become ugly, and then beautiful.

An engram registers all the perceptions, feelings, and thoughts from a distinct event. Therefore, have the experience relived as realistically as possible. Somebody who gets sick with fear as a lion runs towards him in an arena should be allowed to begin with a diluted version of the experience, but it remains important for him to hear the lion's snarl and to smell his scent, in order fully to overcome his fear of lions and related feelings. Even more important is understanding, the correction of incorrect or insufficient interpretation, and the realization that the postulates engraved during this situation may have been comprehensible and correct of the particular situation but are not eternal truths and have to be relinquished as generalities. Pay attention to the reality content of the experience, but also to its emotional and intellectual interpretation, and to possible postulates formed or attached to it.

The engram contains the complete registration of the experience, but also an interpretation or label classifying it as 'indigestible'. Hubbard was the first to point out this interesting characteristic of engrams (1950). If somebody screamed 'I cannot reach it!', or 'I am at a complete loss', or 'I do not believe it', these sentences may seem to refer to the whole experience. They lock the experience, because the patient feels he cannot reach it, is at a loss about it, or does not believe he ever had the experience.

Besides insupportable traumatizing experiences and undigestible interpretation, recursive labels are an important cause of locking difficult experiences in suppressed engrams which haunt our unconscious in the form of karmic manholes. They are fragmented, isolated, and suppressed pieces of our life-story.

At the beginning of a regression therapy, such engrams often blanket the unconscious. This cover is always present when the patient trusts the therapist, but still fails to relax or see anything. The therapist simply asks the patient how he feels when he is unable to relax or see anything. He takes the answers as postulates labelling and at the same time hiding an experience.

R: I would like to see something, but it keeps slipping away. I cannot keep a grip on anything.

C: Repeat five times, with increasing concentration: I cannot keep a grip on anything. Pay attention to the feelings and physical sensations you have.

R: I cannot keep a grip on anything. I cannot keep a grip on anything. I cannot keep a grip on anything. Oh, I feel a fear in my stomach and a stinging pain in my right temple.

C: Now you are going to go back to the situation in which you were unable to keep a grip on something. You feel fear in your stomach. You feel a stinging pain in your right temple. You are now in the situation.

R: Oh God! She is sinking. She is sinking! She is drowning and I am unable to do anything. I feel my strength ebbing away. I can hardly hold the trap-door any more. My head hurts. I am losing blood.

And so on.

Patients who are unable to see anything end up in situations where it is dark, where they are blindfolded, are blind, or are not allowed to see something. Patients who feel tense end up in situations where they have desperately exerted themselves; a patient whose head feels heavy ends up in a situation with head wounds, etc.

Whenever a patient is unable to relax, cannot see anything, or (when applying hypnosis) is unable to enter trance, even though he trusts the counsellor, the barrier is in fact a block. Do not try to overcome or avoid this block; use it as a lead instead. The people with the greatest barriers often enter regression most easily. A barrier is not an obstruction, but an invitation to dance.

The regression or reliving is like a vaccination after the disease. The patient relives his misery, but at a safe distance, in another body, with a therapist he trusts. This makes the experience digestible. A patient may be thankful to you for having helped him free himself from an experience, but keep in mind that, ultimately, we can only free ourselves from situations by accepting them completely. In the jargon of individual-psychology: we have to experience it as a 'subject', not as an 'object'. The patient has to accept it as a part of his past, and he has to accept his responsibility inasmuch as he had any. As long as he feels that the situation was incidental or meaningless catharsis will not come. A man could have failed an important mission because he fell off his horse. He might have to realize that this was not fortuitous, because he already feared failure. He will have to see himself as someone who invited failure with his fear of it, and will have to accept this.

The deeper the wound, the higher the healing. A healing experience can be generalized to a more open and more positive attitude, well into the future, and encompassing others as well. The liberation from deep traumas may have an especially humanizing, religious, or cosmic aspect. If catharsis is complex, you have to guide the patient through it, strengthen and consolidate it. Verbalizing the healing in the right words is important. If you understand the patient's experience you can speak the words that liberate.

Some therapists have the patient express and work off his suppressed emotions out loud or silently (silent 'abreaction'). This works only when it gives the patient a break to understand and find his bearings more easily. For the rest, abreaction is a rough, dead-end method. There are better ways to put a person's energy in balance.

Sometimes, it helps to renovate experiences, fantasize systematically another version of the experience. Rather than being overwhelmed by everything that happens, the patient deals with it successfully. A woman has been atrociously raped in a dark forest, and is left with fear and hatred. During the difficult and incomplete regression, the therapist notices that unconsciously she feels guilty because she ignored a warning, and did not defend herself. He helps her confront the situation again, this time defending herself successfully, and after that experiencing a version in which she heeded the warning. Such renovations may occur spontaneously, as protection. The patient may joyfully recount how successfully she protected herself. If such screen memories are coupled with self-satisfaction, there is considerable work for the therapist.

Renovation is essential with incomplete dying experiences. Marianne DeJong made it plausible that agoraphobia (anxiety about open spaces, with feelings of loneliness, disorientation, anonymity, and powerlessness) is the result of incomplete dying, where a soul remains wandering, without finding rest. The light and peace remigrants describe beside a complete dying experience is simply the catharsis of the difficulties and the unfinished business of a whole life. If this did not happen then, the remigrant may experience it now in therapy. The therapist helps the patient to find the light now. This is not just relevant to agoraphobia, but is also essential with hangovers and pseudo-obsessions. In renovations the present person enters the past and intervenes, as with regressions in the present life.

R: I still see myself as a baby. I am screaming. I feel like I am going crazy. They will not help me, and he has hit me to boot. Oh God, what misery!

C: Step out of yourself and see this screaming baby. Imagine yourself as you are now, entering the room. Give the baby what you feel it needed just then.

R: I can go no further. I feel as though I'm stuck in a cold, grey mist. I know there is light somewhere, but I cannot reach it. I'm not even sure if I want to. I feel jealous, wounded, unappreciated. I hate everything and everybody.

C: Look at yourself sitting in this mist. You, as you are now, are there. What is your impression of that sitting person (who is you)? What does he need? Try to get near to him.

Renovation is possible without dissociation. A remigrant experiences herself as a little girl who is violently drowned by a masked man. There is an epidemic, and she has contracted the disease, but she does not understand this. Her only experience is the terror, crying and screaming as she dies. She has an enormous fear of water. The therapist confirms that she has died, that it is all over. Everything is peaceful and good now. She is floating in wonderfully sun-drenched water. She slowly rises in the ever more sunny and wonderful water, and is drifting on it. By now, she has a boat, and she drifts to an idyllic island in the river. She lands on the island. It is all hers. The therapist invites her to see the island as she would like to have it: a beautiful birch tree, twittering birds, sun on the grass, and . . . what a lovely kitten she is holding in her lap!

Renovating an experience is drastic. Be well aware of what you are doing and how you do it. Sketch only outlines and let the patient elaborate them. It is useless to bring the patient into your own world. He has to stay in his own world. Use your intuition, your sensitivity, your common sense and your good taste. Have an idea of what the patient is going to see, using your experience and skill.

Therapeutic indications from others, unintended therapeutic moments

The most famous examples of therapeutic indications based on re-incarnation insights are Edgar Cayce's life-readings. He explained many problems in the present life by occurrences in past lives. Among others, he did this with people who had chronic painful physical complaints and wondered what they had done to deserve such a fate.

Cayce looked into physical deficiencies, weaknesses, and diseases, psychic and relationship problems, setbacks and accidents, and every other aspect of fate. He often gave specific career and health advice but his greatest therapeutic merit was the insight and overview he gave to his clients. Muller also gives examples of such advice (Muller 1970: 210–12, 214).

Regressions may have an unintentionally therapeutic effect. The first memory of a past life is often the dying experience. As a result, the remigrant may lose some of his fear of dying. He experiences himself after death as a conscious, active being, and usually he experiences how pleasant and liberating dying is. Of course, this only happens when the counsellor allows him to go on to the experiences after the death.

When the first memory of a past life is not the moment of death, but an apparently random episode from an apparently random life, this memory usually rings a relevant bell in the present life. Glaskin recounts his first experience with the Christos experiment: he finds himself in early classical Egypt, struggling to express himself in primitive hieroglyphs. The limitations of language, especially written language, frustrated him. Just at this time, Glaskin was struggling with a writer's block, but this experience made him aware of the wealth of our present written language. His block vanished, and for the first time in years, he was able to write again (Glaskin, 1974: 207). This could be used to explain the regression as a psychodrama, but the experience is so real, he feels himself so strongly in another body, another time, and another mentality, that at least the subjective evidence is strong. Later, Glaskin procured objective evidence (Glaskin 1979).

Remigrants who go back out of curiosity sometimes end up in traumatic experiences that are relevant to the immediate problems of their present life. When this happens spontaneously, the remigrant is ready for it. A counsellor should only stop these experiences if they make him feel insecure. Another unintentional therapeutic effect is breaking through prejudices with regressions. A student who experiences a life in which he was sick to death of the monotonous food he had to eat, has since then never said anything negative about McDonald's again. An athletic, progressive young man who is a health freak, finds himself a stout family father who is as proud as a peacock of his family. Hatred of Romans, Germans, Jews and blacks may vanish after reliving lives with negative experiences with persons from these groups. The prejudice is attached to real experiences, and seen in perspective: 'That was then. And it only concerned those people.'

Finally, working on one problem, quite another problem may disappear. Netherton gives examples of working on the feelings of being alone, unloved, and unlovable of homosexual men. Later he works on feelings of guilt, and so may discover and resolve the original response that triggered homosexuality. In this way homosexuality may dissolve, although this is not to say that all homosexuality is caused this way. Nor does it imply that changing sexual orientation is an aim of therapy.

General remarks about past-life therapy

Past-life therapy is an effective form of psychotherapy, and often resolves problems that other forms of therapy could not. The basic method, regression, is simple. A lay hypnotist without experience can immediately have some success, if he inspires trust, gives good guidance, can handle emotions, has common sense and, advisably, has some knowledge of other psychotherapies.

Regression is primarily a way to detect and relieve traumas. A therapist who does not believe in reincarnation may still use regression as a diagnostic psychodrama leading up to other forms of psychotherapy. Ability to apply insights and methods from other therapies during recall and digestion is useful for a past-life therapist. For example, experience with individual-psychology or ego-state therapy is highly recommendable. Past-life therapy lends itself well to combination with other forms of cognitive therapy. Tracking down traumatic experiences and flooding them, and closing them with positive suggestions is sometimes effective enough, but a practising past-life therapist has to have many more marbles in his pocket.

Past-life therapy starts just as present-life regression therapy does. Traumas, postulates, and to some extent hangovers, can originate in this life also. In the rare cases of split personalities even symptoms similar to pseudo-obsessions can originate in this life. The therapy has to build an emotional, somatic, and postulate bridge to trace these four types of difficulty. It will gradually make clear to what extent these difficulties originate in the present or in past lives. A patient sometimes has to work out a traumatic death before tackling the problems in the present life, at other times the reverse is true.

The fine art of therapy is to map the patient's psychic field and to locate the problems which, when solved, will release the most psychic energy. This energy will be needed to work out heavier or deeper difficulties later. The past-life therapy techniques in this chapter are more broadly applicable, and are related to techniques from other forms of psychotherapy. The only exclusive methods of past-life therapy are the use of post-mortem and prenatal experiences. These are essential with hangovers and pseudo-obsessions.

Induction, consisting of relaxation, visualization, or hypnosis, is usually superfluous. What counts is to find the right bridge. The simplest way is to use actual emotions or, in the absence of emotions, actual somatics, and in the absence of somatics, to identify key sentences or 'postulates'. Traumas, hangovers, and pseudo-obsessions have almost always a grain of postulates in them that can be used to track them down. With a postulate, the key sentence is essential. With a trauma, the key sentence is less important than the emotional contents of the traumatic experience.

My experience with past-life therapy has shown me seven basic steps or principles:

1 Determining if this type of therapy is adequate:
    Not with patients who do not communicate
    Not with people who refuse to be a patient

Not with people who want to remain a patient.
2 Checking if a basis of trust can be built up between patient and counsellor:
   Not with people who aggravate the therapist's energy.
3 Diagnosing what the patient shows:
   Actual emotions
   Actual somatics: bodily feelings
   Recurrent dreams or images
   Postulates.
4 If the patient's account is too full or too vague, there should be a general, in-depth diagnosis via the body or via postulates. Bring somatics, emotions, and postulates together.
5 If the exploration fails: precede the session with relaxation and/or visualization.
6 The surest entry into regression is crossing an emotional and somatic bridge.
7 The therapist's guidance should be emotional and physical as well as rational, and he should always steer towards catharsis: emotional and physical relief and peace of mind.

Success is more than just using the right techniques. Past-life therapy is a craft, and also an art, and more than that, a healing presence. A good therapist is weathered and mild, friendliness and scars all over.

Further reading

The classics on past-life therapy are by Edith Fiore (1978), and Morris Netherton and Nancy Shiffrin (1978). Adrian Finkelstein has written a rambling book with some interesting cases, but weak on therapy (1985). His induction technique is highly ideological, and his miscellaneous descriptions and thoughts about spiritual healing are unrelated to regression work. He rightly considers self-help and a positive mental attitude as essential, but forgets the most important factor: true understanding. Whitton and Fisher (1986) are interesting and enlightening, but use classic hypnotic regression with classic psychiatry, and offer little on specific methodology. Karl Schlotterbeck (1987) is also interesting because he makes it very clear how necessary a full psychotherapeutic understanding of regression material is. He approaches the subject from many different angles, but often, when you expect a conclusion, he moves over to the next chapter. Much of it is more journalistic than analytic, but it is the journalism of an experienced and sensible practitioner.

Preceding these books are those by Alexander Cannon (1936) and Denys Kelsey and Joan Grant (1967), but they lack examples of sessions. Isola Pisani dedicates a whole book to somebody doing regression therapy with Kelsey (1978) – a bit romantic and philosophical, but a good and sympathetic inner-travel story.

Strict regression therapy was first explored in *Dianetics* by Ron Hubbard (1950), a long and controversial book by an author who has succeeded in becoming more controversial since. For the true student of regression therapy this book is a must, in spite of the exaggerated scope and headstrong attitude that appears to be inherent in pioneer literature. Hubbard's later work (1958), conversely, has limited scope, especially about regressions, and is unfortunately badly written.

Langedijk (1980), Goldberg (1982), and McClain (1986) present examples of more or less therapeutic sessions. Muller presents cases of spiritist past-life therapy, concentrating on obsessions with karmic origin (1970). Books on hypnotherapy, like those by Herbert and David Spiegel (1978) and Gerald Edelstien (1981), should be part of a practising reincarnation therapist's training. More information on the usage of finger signals can be found in Edelstien.

17 Reincarnation Research

This chapter discusses current reincarnation research and indicates directions for further research. Why is research needed? Holzer puts it politely: 'There is no need to disregard scientific standards in this field, where such standards are the only safeguard against delusion, whether perpetrated by others or by oneself' (1985: 204).

What research is being done today? The most obvious form of reincarnation research is the exploration of the question of whether reincarnation is plausible or whether there are alternative explanations for the ostensible memories of past lives. Most research concentrates on verifying apparent reincarnation memories in individual cases. In principle, reincarnation, an unacceptable or unprovable idea in the eyes of most people, can be proven by verifying it in a few cases. Testing reincarnation cases is one kind of research, which I will illustrate with some examples. Another line of research is used by, for example, Wambach. This method produces so many apparent memories of past lives that the plausibility or implausibility of various hypotheses can be tested statistically.

Even if you believe in reincarnation, a regression sometimes produces material whose historical or personal character is dubious. This may be true for part of the regression or for a whole session. Testing episodes and elements of sessions is the same as testing whole sessions or series of sessions.

So far, little research has been done to find patterns and regularities in reincarnation processes. Chapters 10, 11, and 12 of this volume are just a first attempt at classification. Although a lot has been written about reincarnation processes, most of it is limited to global remarks lacking substance, based on loose analyses of a small portion of the available empirical material.

Another line of research is to look for patterns and regularities in the recall process: how do we remember and forget? How is our memory organized? Where is it located? This is a virtually untouched field although the empirical material available allows the formulation of some ideas.

A separate line of investigation is that of finding the present incarnations of people who have died. Such identification procedures can be found in Tibet and Africa, when people want to find the new incarnation of a deceased Dalai Lama or tribal chief, or want to establish the past incarnation of a newborn.

The lines of research discussed in this chapter are:

1 Verifying reincarnation in individual cases.
2 Testing dubious material.
3 Proving reincarnation in general.
4 Development of the evaluation of and methods for past-life therapy.
5 Research into the process of recall.
6 Identification procedures.

Verifying reincarnation in individual cases: testing dubious material

A remigrant elaborately tells his counsellor in great detail about a life in thirteenth-century Italy or in an unidentified, primitive village 'long ago'. Another recounts being a chambermaid in the court of Catherine the Great. How can we check the reality content of such claims? The verification of claims means checking against alternative explanations. Chapter 1 mentioned some alternative explanations. We will leave out the question of a genetic memory here, as we have already shown the impossibility of this hypothesis.

Figure 10 gives 21 indications to test the plausibility of 10 different explanations of recollections. The figure shows that clairvoyance (ESP) and obsessions are the most difficult to differentiate from reincarnation memories. It also shows that the strongest indications for a reincarnation memory are: catharsis, constancy of the memories under different sequences, and the absence of large psychosomatic problems. Historical confirmation is nice, and shows that the experience is no psychodrama, but it takes time, is difficult, and does not discriminate reincarnation from obsession, clairvoyance, telepathy, or a collective unconscious.

INDICATORS	A	B	C	D	E	F	G	H	I	J
CONTENTS										
Resistance and Catharsis and therapeutic effect	+	+	-	-	-	+	(-)	-	-	-
New experiences and breaking through prejudices	+	-	+	+	+	-	+	-	-	-
New body sensations	+	+	+	+	+	(-)	+	-	-	-
Film-like memories	+	+	+	+	+	+	+	-	(-)	-
CONCOMITANTS										
New abilities, e.g. xenoglossy	+	+	+	+	(+)	-	-	-	-	-
Somatic changes	+	+	-	+	-	+	-	-	-	-
Indications of new abilities	+	+	+	+	+	-	+	-	-	-
Voice changes	+	+	-	+	-	+	+	-	(+)	-
Changed skin resistance or brain-wave length	+	+	+	+	(+)	+	-	-	-	(+)
Weak xenoglossy	+	+	+	+	+	-	+	+	-	-
PERSONAL CHARACTERISTICS										
Stigmata	+	+	-	-	-	+	+	-	+	-
Appears only after induction	+	+	+	+	+	+	+	+	-	-
Absence of paranormal talents	+	+	-	-	+	+	+	+	+	+
Absence of psychosomatic problems	+	(-)	+	+	+	+	+	+	+	+
GUIDANCE CHARACTERISTICS										
Inducing varying time-sequences	+	(-)	(+)	-	-	-	-	-	-	-
Trance without foreknowledge	+	+	+	+	+	+	-	+	+	-
Various hypnotists	+	+	+	(+)	+	+	+	+	+	-
CHECKS										
Significant historical confirmation	+	+	+	+	+	-	-	-	-	-
Confirmation of child cases	+	+	+	+	+	-	-	-	-	-
Multiple independent viewpoints	+	(-)	+	+	+	-	+	-	-	-
Weak historical confirmation	+	+	+	+	+	-	+	+	-	-

ALTERNATIVE EXPLANATIONS:

A: Reincarnation	F: Psychodrama
B: Obsessions	G: Deceit
C: Clairvoyance	H: Pseudo-memory
D: Telepathy	I: Imagination
E: Collective unconscious	J: Déjà-vu

+ : *not conflicting*   **–** : *conflicting*

(+): *improbable combination*   **(–)**: *probably conflicting*

Figure 10 Testing individual cases of past-life memory

A regression experience has to satisfy several criteria to establish whether it is a reincarnation memory: such as emotional resistance, catharsis, and a permanent therapeutic effect after the recall and digestion of a difficult and burdening situation. Also, new experiences and breaking down prejudices are important indications. A third important indication is whether the remigrant experiences a different body, with regard to health, constitution, age, or sex. A fourth aspect is whether or not the recall of a life is complete, rather than a smattering of loose fragments.

Fragments with a clear emotional and cathartic character and therapeutic effect contradict explanations such as *déjà vu*, imagination, and pseudo-recall. They also contradict a collective unconscious, and telepathic or psychic information, because such fragments tell of personal experiences connected with the remigrant's personal characteristics and problems. Also, if the remigrant were deceiving the counsellor or imagining the experience, this would require considerable acting talent and preparation. However, explanations such as psychodrama and obsession remain plausible.

A different body experience in regressions indicates nothing about collective memory, telepathy, or clairvoyance, but does make a psychodrama unlikely. Film-like memories exclude *déjà vu* and pseudo-recall, and make imagination unlikely.

A regression often has concomitants such as a voice change. A girl describing a male incarnation may start speaking in a deeper voice, and an old person describing a childhood may start to speak in a child's voice. These changes may be distinct during hypnosis, but they also occur without hypnosis. Other concomitants are somatic changes: the breathing rhythm changing, the posture becoming strained, the face turning red or pale. This is especially common with birth experiences, dying experiences, and situations with intense pain, or intense and long physical discomfort. In less than 1 per cent of cases remigrants speak in a different language belonging to a past life, which includes languages they have never learned or heard in this life (xenoglossy). It is more common for the remigrant to remember a few words in the language, even if he has no idea what language it may be.

Voice changes and physical changes are unlikely with clairvoyance, deceit, pseudo-memory, *déjá vu*, and the collective unconscious. A remigrant may be able to change his voice when he is deceiving the counsellor or imagining vividly, but not to conjure up red stripes on his skin as he describes being whipped. Such phenomena are possible in a deep hypnotic trance if the counsellor suggests them, and when these suggestions in no way conflict with the instruction to recall a real past life. Voice changes and posture changes are possible during an intense psychodrama, xenoglossy is not. When a remigrant speaks an unknown language, clairvoyance is improbable, because it is unlikely for clairvoyants to have access to such impersonal information. Xenoglossy is especially convincing when a remigrant with little formal education recites whole passages in a forgotten or exotic language.

Besides checking the contents of the experiences, the concomitants, and the results, the counsellor can build in some controls to check what kind of experiences the remigrant has. In a deep trance, the counsellor can ask the remigrant to do something that requires learning that the remigrant can have only acquired in the past life: to play music, dance or sing. Another important control is to have the remigrant go through his lives in varying order during different sessions. This was done by Wilder among others (Underwood and Wilder 1975). The results are especially impressive when voice changes accompany the recall. Obsession and clairvoyance cannot be precluded, but telepathy can, because recurrent telepathic contacts will not lead to identical results. Psychodramas are unlikely. Experiencing a psychodrama leads to emotional development, changing a subsequent replay. Deceit, imagination, and *déjà vu* are implausible explanations when time and again, in different sequences, identical results are obtained. The cinematic character of memory presumed by this procedure precludes pseudo-memory.

Other important controls are the skin-resistance meter and the brain-wave meter. These are sure tests to preclude at least deceit, pseudo-memory, and imagination. The counsellor can hypnotize the remigrant without telling him what will be expected of him. This precludes deceit and *déjà vu*. To preclude telepathy and the counsellor's suggestion, the remigrant can be tested with different counsellors and hypnotists.

Recollection is tested afterwards by confrontation with historical facts. A wealth of obscure historical details, such as the coins used in Egypt a century after Alexander, or the measuring system used by the Kirghiz in the sixteenth century, is convincing. The literature provides many examples of historical testing. Netherton gives the fine example of the ship *Republic* (Netherton and Shiffrin, 1978: 168). However, many convincing cases cannot be historically verified. Without verifiable facts, deceit cannot be precluded, but usually the many details make deceit highly unlikely. The most convincing regressions are those where the remigrant recounts things yet unknown, which are later verified by new archaeological excavations or new research. The same is true for accounts that contradict actual historical knowledge, but are confirmed later. Guirdham gives the case of a woman who had had Cathar memories since her youth. She described the '*bonhommes*' wearing blue. The historians denied this, but years later they found out that dark blue was worn (Guirdham 1970: 10). Schlotterbeck gives the interesting example of somebody who was searching for confirmation of his recollections coming across a book giving the full history of the town where he once lived. He finds his own story confirmed in almost all details, except that many of the names were wrong, and his three daughters appeared to have been three adopted girls (Schlotterbeck 1987: 43). The wrong names are important, because often they are the first means of entry to the search. Although many names remembered in regression have been verified and identified later, lack of success in historical confirmation does not necessarily invalidate the claim for historical reality.

Checking historical facts is comparable to checking geographical facts. Stevenson checked what proportion of what is told about a past life is consistent with reality. The methods used to preclude deceit and pseudo-memory can be compared with a judicial investigation and cross-checking witnesses claims in general. Stevenson carefully researched the methods used to check the plausibility of the latter (Stevenson 1975: 1).

One interesting check is when different remigrants who did not know each other and had never met describe historically unknown conditions and facts consistently with one another. Netherton describes an interesting example of what he calls 'multiple viewpoints'. The best procedure is to lead remigrants who have the feeling that they have met before through a number of lives in separate sessions. Ask for details and check the similarities and differences. Naturally, the remigrants should not be able to communicate with each other between sessions. Although the multiple-viewpoint technique does not preclude telepathy, it does preclude obsession, unless the same spirit can obsess several people, or a group of spirits are playing some game.

Goldberg treated two patients, the second long after the first, who apparently had been acquainted in a past life. One was a sadistic goldsmith and the other his abused apprentice. Goldberg wonders what would happen if they were to meet, but he would not think of bringing them together. First of all, he says, if they are karmically destined to meet each other, then they will; second, he does not want to play God with his patients: bringing them together might influence their karma too strongly (Goldberg 1982: 126). This view is short-sighted and inconsistent. He is also playing God (as we all do, with almost everyone we know) by refusing to bring them together. In addition, if they are not meant to meet each other, they might never have ended up with the same therapist; and Goldberg also does not consider the simplest and most obvious course of action: to ask the two remigrants if they would be interested in meeting. If they both were, then it would be at least an interesting and probably a meaningful experiment.

Important instances of individual characteristics are birthmarks and stigmata because they preclude explanations such as clairvoyance, telepathy, collective unconscious, and pseudo-recall. A remigrant may use his birthmark or stigma to deceive the counsellor, to imagine a regression or a psychodrama. The absence of psychic gifts makes clairvoyance and telepathy unlikely, and the absence of deep psychosomatic problems and identity crises makes obsession unlikely. Flournoy showed that would-be remigrants can conjure up a lot of imaginary lives. Oddly enough, these fantasies may contain a lot of plausible material (Shirley 1924: 145).

Figure 10 (p. 361) can also be used to test episodes or elements of episodes. First, the counsellor can have the remigrant repeat the experiences. Differing accounts are usually caused by a block (see chapter 15), unless the remigrant is in light trance and the counsellor poses suggestive questions inducing the remigrant to imagine something. The remigrant may sublimate or shift an experience if he wants to avoid confronting unpleasant things he has done, or his own responsibility for ending up in an unpleasant situation. Hubbard has the remigrant repeat the experience over and over until it remains the same. With each repetition he focuses on the elements that are consistent with the previous versions.

The counsellor keeps an eye on the E-meter. If the remigrant speaks in an unemotional tone of voice while the E-meter shows a strongly decreased skin resistance, he is not telling what he is seeing or is about to see. If the remigrant speaks emotionally and the E-meter shows no changes, he is probably imagining the scenes. When there is no deceit or imagination, and the counselling is reasonable, differing versions of an experience usually indicate sublimation.

Effects of past-life therapy

Regressions to apparent situations in past lives leading to catharsis or permanent therapeutic success indicate reincarnation memories, obsession, or psychodrama. Research into the effects of past-life therapy is therefore of great importance, first, because each effective form of therapy is itself important, and second, because it will support the reincarnation hypothesis. There seems to have been little research done to date. A sketchy overview of some research being done in Brazil shows a table of the duration and success of each individual therapy.

In the Netherlands Johannes Cladder (1983) has done more concrete research. Cladder investigated the effectiveness of a particular form of regression therapy using hypnosis and behaviour therapy techniques. It turned out to be a quick and effective method for phobics who had had no success with other methods. Eighty per cent of the phobics were doing better within 22 sessions, with an average of 11 sessions. Of the patients who believed in reincarnation 70 per cent regressed to a past life; of those who did not 50 per cent did. If the patients were divided differently, into people who accepted reincarnation and those indifferent or sceptical, the percentages were 64 and 57 respectively. The patients with past-life memories had more psychosomatic and diverse complaints than the others. Their sense of reality increased. The treatment, consisting of flooding the patient with regression material, benefited phobics with compulsive behaviour very little.

Testing reincarnation in general

A reasonable number of plausible reincarnation memories, using the criteria for checking alternative explanations from above, would be a reasonable proof of reincarnation. But only mathematics offers absolute proof, that is, after accepting some axioms.

The most substantial anti-reincarnation book to date is *Mind out of Time? Reincarnation Claims Reinvestigated* by Ian Wilson (1981). He compares regressions to past lives with the symptoms of multiple personalities. Except for the historical framework, these phenomena are, in his opinion, directly comparable, and caused by 'an unknown, powerful and unconscious psychic mechanism' (Wilson 1981: 157). Reading Wilson's testing of historical facts reminds one of Glenn Williston's experiences. Williston tried to check the historical validity of regression material and wrote a colourful and humorous account of his efforts (Williston and Johnstone 1983: 137).

Wilson's book suffers from the same weakness as the works of reincarnation supporters: it tries to prove something. However, Wilson did his homework better than most of the latter, and collected real data. In my opinion, this makes him obligatory reading for all reincarnation fans, especially those full of enthusiastic gullibility who immediately gather names and dates in regressions.

In general, the success rate of past-life therapy strongly underpins the reincarnation hypothesis. The sublimations and shifts, the catharsis and permanent therapeutic effects, the voice changes and bodily changes during regressions all make explanations such as clairvoyance, telepathy, or a collective unconscious implausible. The regression experiences indicate either regression or a meaningful psychological process. The main arguments against the idea of a pure psychological process are new experiences as of being in another body, tasting things never tasted before, and experiences contradicting present preferences and prejudices. Such experiences do not happen in waking dreams or psychodramas. An extra argument in favour of reincarnation is the example of historical confirmation.

Dethlefsen writes (I have abbreviated his text):

The idea that apparent former lives are projections is untenable. A psychodrama only exists as the result of a projection, conscious or unconscious, of inner conflicts. This cannot explain the phenomena described below.

One remigrant, a radio reporter in his present life, a textile merchant in 1755, gave the exact length of material needed for a suit measured in yards, counted money in guilders, and described a famine in 1732, later verified in a historical chronicle. Another remigrant spent most of the sessions explaining everything about measurements, calculations, and distances. He had been an architect. He described the minutest details of buildings he had built, and only later recounted personal facts. His profession came first. I doubt whether these accounts can be explained as a projection of present inner conflicts.

When a counsellor goes through various lives with a remigrant, these lives turn out to have such different contents that they cannot be the product of one life's projection. A 20-year-old student gives a precise account of an abortion she had in a past life, although she had never been confronted with abortion or pregnancy. The same remigrant experienced her menopause in a session. Afterwards, she said it was an odd feeling, and deepened her understanding of her mother.

Descriptions of past lives are not conglomerates of problems, conflicts, and clichés. They contain too many personal, historically specific observations and abilities to rule out the explanation of psychodrama. Remigrants tell us how long it took to travel a particular distance by coach, how bread was baked in the seventeenth century, and what herbs were used in 1687 to stop bleeding (Dethlefsen 1977: 108).

The explanation most difficult to disprove is obsession: the souls of people who lived in the past haunting those living now. According to the spiritist literature, obsessions are accompanied by serious psychosomatic complaints and identity crises. But many regressions are liberating and make the remigrant healthier, stronger, and more self-aware. Furthermore, the similarities between different, independent lives in comparable circumstances make the obsession hypothesis seem less likely. The pure repetition of regressions, each time in a different sequence, indicates that the remigrant is drawing from a constant, organized memory.

Another line to follow is the statistical analysis of large numbers of comparable regressions. Helen Wambach (1978, 1979) has done the most significant research in this direction. For example, she looked at the social classes the remigrants had lived in. If experiences of past lives were compensation, then many remigrants would remember having led important lives. In the historical regression experiments she conducted, 60 to 80 per cent of the regressions were to lives in the lowest social class. Lives in the highest social classes were found in only 2 per cent (in around AD 800) to 10 per cent (in around AD 1700) of the cases. The remaining portion were lives in the middle classes.

Wambach registered the frequency distribution of race, sex, dress, shoes, food, pottery, etc. All of these distributions were a reasonable reflection of the actual distributions of the periods under consideration. For example, Wambach asked her remigrants what was on the table, whether they had their hands in their lap when they ate, what they ate from and with. She asked if the utensils were wooden, baked clay, or metal, and what they looked like, etc. Some remigrants gave answers like: there was no table, we ate with our hands, we took the food from a common pot with our hands, we ate with leaves, etc. Such answers refute the oft-mentioned 'suggestibility' during hypnosis. The frequency of lives in the five historical periods itself accurately reflected the estimated development of mankind.

Research into the nature of past-life memory

If reincarnation is general, it may be possible to induce past-life recall in everybody, unless it is a talent slowly developed in the course of lives. The success rate for inducing past-life recall varies between 70 and 90 per cent. It would be interesting to identify the circumstances of recall since this could give indications about the nature of past-life recall.

The first point in the investigation into the nature of past-life recall is that people without spontaneous recall can be induced to recall with proper guidance. The first barrier seems to be ignorance, uncertainty, or disbelief. Someone who has never heard of reincarnation, or thinks it is nonsense, is unlikely to recall past lives. Generally, past lives can be recalled when the remigrant is in a certain trance, or is at least relaxed.

Wambach investigated a small sample of 10 people who were unable to have past-life recall during her group sessions (1978). Of these, 2 did have past-life recall in individual sessions, and 4 resisted because they feared a death experience. When this fear was hypnotically blocked, they did have past-life recall. The other 4 resisted every form of psychological exploration, including free association.

Netherton found that only a few patients can remember nothing from a past life (1978). When a patient said he did not see or hear anything, this usually indicated that he was blind, blindfolded, deaf, or sworn to secrecy. The question 'Is something wrong with your eyes or with your ears?' often leads to a breakthrough. Netherton describes a patient who was unable to remember anything from a past life. Her mother, when she had been pregnant with her, was converted to a religion denying all forms of pain and negative feelings. Apparently, this was a strong shut-off command for the foetus.

Past-life memories seem to have two different modes of entry. The first level is similar to our normal memory. It seems to be subject to the same laws of association, forgetting and remembering, sublimation and shifting, and pseudo-memories as our present life memory. The other level is called the higher self in theosophical terms. On this level, memory is complete and objective. This complete, more objective memory also exists for the present life and plays a role in, for example, transactional analysis.

One interesting observation from spontaneous memories of past lives is that more women remember changing sex than men. Psychics who see other people's past lives also mention more women with past lives as men than the reverse (Muller 1970: 277). Apparently the female lives of men are less accessible. Men may resist remembering female lives. Male lives also tend to be more dramatic, more varied, and more karmic than female lives. Lives with a lot of action and drama are more easily remembered than boring lives. This is consistent with our normal memory. However, with enough hypnosis, this difference disappears. Wambach found an equal number of past lives in both sexes, even in groups with an uneven male-female distribution (Wambach 1978: 135). At a certain level of trance, a more objective memory is activated.

Memories of past lives can take on different forms and varying degrees of completeness. 'Fragmentary memories' are feelings associated with a name, or impressions of a landscape, a house, a road, or a windmill. 'Episodic memories' contain a few clear snapshots, without information about the previous occurrences or the circumstances. In 'film memories', episodes from past lives are strung together into a cohesive story of the most important and impressive situations in that life (except those too impressive). Usually, the counsellor can instruct the remigrant to bring such film memories to a stop, to zoom in or out, or to step back to get an overview. 'Total memories', may contain every detail of a particular life. For example, the counsellor can instruct the remigrant who recalls a wedding to jump 3 days ahead, or 13 days, or 3 months. If anything interesting happened in the interim, the counsellor asks the remigrant to go back 2 days. The memories are clear, and remain consistent when repeated. A rarer form of past-life recall are the 'panoramic memories' where the remigrant oversees his whole life as if he were surveying a wide landscape. Probably, such memories are identical with the first retrospect just after death.

The organization of past-life memory allows the reproduction of feelings, observations, and ideas more easily than exact dialogues, names, dates, and other facts. Some people live through intense lives without giving a thought to dates or geographic locations. A counsellor can ask about such things, but if the remigrant did not know the answers even during that life, another memory has to be activated. In regressions this usually happens after the death experience, during the retrospect, and sometimes when the higher self intervenes and the remigrant 'rises above himself'.

Distortions are more common in the first level of memory. Moss and Keeton (1979) describe cases with a mixture of historically correct and incorrect facts. A few obscure historically correct details do not prove that all other information is historically correct. Conversely, a few incorrect details do not prove that all other information is incorrect.

Presumably, the accessibility of the memory is connected to psychic talents.

Identification procedures

A somewhat exceptional form of reincarnation research is that of finding the present incarnation of people who have died, and the past incarnation of infants. Tibet has a centuries-long tradition of looking for the present incarnation of important lamas a few years after they have died. The present incarnation can then continue where the past one left off (a horrible thought). The Tibetans assume that advanced souls can transpose themselves on to a new incarnation, whereas the ordinary soul more or less crumbles after death. These identification procedures are described by Alexandra David-Neel (1961) and Rato (1977). Rato's description follows here.

During the lama's cremation the Tibetans establish in which direction the smoke disappears. The next incarnation will be in that direction (assuming, by the way, a primitive population I process). The lama's most prominent pupil then writes a prayer or a poem about the lama to aid in the search for the new incarnation. This prayer or poem is distributed among the monks. The most important lamas, including the Dalai-Lama, are asked to pray that the new incarnation will be found quickly. Information about extraordinary children, or extraordinary circumstances surrounding the birth, and about the births of children in the area passed by the smoke, is collected.

One example of a pregnancy with extraordinary signs is the following: a pregnant woman dreamt that the guiding deities poured water over her head. This means that all the child's sins will be absolved. During the last month of her pregnancy she became nauseous when she entered a temple, but the god caught her and set her down. A third sign was a dream that the moon and the sun united, meaning the child would be extremely intelligent. During the birth, a rainbow touched the house: a happy sign.

Such indications are put before mediumistic monks who act as oracles. They choose the three most likely prospects for the new incarnation. The three cases are considered in trance and then the verdict is read. The Dalai-Lama confirms the verdict, and the child is brought in. The child often has to select objects belonging to the past incarnation from a large display. The procedure of selecting objects is also used in Africa to identify young children.

Apart from dreams and signs, the heart of the procedure seems to be the consultation of a recognized trance medium, and the child's selection of objects that belonged to the deceased (Rato 1977: 17).

Suggestions for further research

Ian Stevenson contributed greatly to the scientific verification of the reincarnation hypothesis in his pioneer work with child cases. A comparable research programme is needed for induced regressions. Helen Wambach made important steps in this. Hypnotic regression will remain the main tool of investigation, since trance induces objective phenomena such as voice and skin resistance changes, different brain-wave patterns, etc. Using different hypnotists, inducing trance without foreknowledge, repeating the regression post-hypnotically, where the remigrants forget what happened during the regression, strengthen the research. These procedures can rule out deceit, pseudo-memories, imagination, and *déjà vu*. See too Chet Snow's work with French subjects (Snow 1986a).

The most promising developments in reincarnation research are

373

identifying regularities and laws governing reincarnation processes, and analysing the workings of the memory. Research to establish whether reincarnation is a fact is not promising. It is only done for people who probably will not change their beliefs anyway. In general, it is better to let diehards slowly become extinct. Science follows the same procedure.

The investigation of what happens in apparent regressions to past lives is more interesting. The worst finding would be that things are different or more complicated than we expected. At any rate, the field covers an interesting range of human experience. Its reconnaissance is more fruitful than endless proofs of the reincarnation hypothesis. If reincarnation is true, we will have to find many convincing individual cases, but also statistical relationships between regressions.

Fields of research into the laws and regularities of reincarnation processes are:

- the reasons why some people have spontaneous recall and others do not
- which characteristics, talents, and psychosomatic problems can be influenced by past lives
- changes in reincarnation processes over time, for example, whether the intermissions became shorter
- the causes and effects of sex changes.

Disproving hypotheses like imagination, pseudo-memory, and deceit is neither useful nor interesting. Of course, every researcher has to take pains to reduce their likelihood, as a matter of common sense, prudence, and research methodology. But do not look for waterproof arguments against sceptics to break through paranoid attitudes. Ideas about genetic memory and the collective unconscious are speculations which do not require extensive refutation. It suffices to point out the phenomena that contradict them. Finally, the super-ESP hypothesis is useless. More common forms of clairvoyance can be shown to be plausible or implausible in analysing a particular case. But speculating about forms of clairvoyance transcending space, time and identity creates a hypothesis that can explain every last human phenomenon that cannot be explained by direct observation. Regressions are no potpourri of random titbits taken from a collective cauldron of memories; they consist of clearly individual lives that are described as truly personal experiences, and usually have something to do with the present life and personality.

A good example of how regression research and common inquiry may combine is Dick Sutphen's story of his reconstruction of the life of Ed Morrell in his epilogue to the new edition of *The Star Rover* (London 1915). For sceptics such a story is not convincing, but the interesting and essential point is that regression evidence can (and should) stimulate the search for hard evidence, not supplant it.

From a practical point of view, procedures to differentiate personal past-life memories from those of others, whether attached or obsessing, is important: see Holzer (1985) and Goldberg (1982).

Reincarnation research can also be of considerable practical use with problems such as:
- phobias
- allergies and asthma
- anorexia and bulimia
- chronic, atypical forms of psychosomatic disturbance
- alcoholism and drug abuse
- homosexuality
- epilepsy
- cancer
- sadism and masochism.

An interesting line of research is Netherton's 'multiple-viewpoints' approach. With unknown cultures especially, it would be interesting to find remigrants who lived in the same period. The size of the sample and a reasonable spread – perhaps international – are important, as well as the usual precautions to preclude deceit. Wambach's reports at the end of each session provide excellent models, but can doubtless be refined in form and content. Langedijk gives a few interesting suggestions for historical research via regressions (Langedijk 1980: 53):
- the pronunciation of languages only known in writing
- lost civilizations
- ancient religions
- ancient civilizations which gave rise to paranormal gifts.

I would add that our knowledge of daily life in early civilizations can be greatly enriched, even for such recent periods as the last century. Reading about life in the slums of Liverpool in 1850 is as interesting and moving a text as I have ever read (Moss and Keeton 1979: 41).

The number of books about karmic astrology continues to increase without any improvement in quality. A statistical analysis of the correlation between natal charts and regressions to directly preceding lives would be a welcome change. It is sometimes possible to investigate the relationship the other way round. If a recent life is identified and birth registration found, we can compare the previous and the present natal charts. McClain writes: 'As proficiency builds, some individuals may be able to remember such detailed information as exact birthdate and time in some of the more recent lifetimes. Astrological birth charts of previous lifetimes often provide interesting insight into the present lifetime' (McClain 1986: 48). This seems to me to be an overstatement. If an actual natal chart does not provide enough interesting insight, the chart of a previous life certainly will not. Also, why calculate and interpret when there is an incomparably more direct and more convincing way: regression to life retrospects and life blueprints?

Further reading

The oldest type of research is that of testing regressions against historical facts. Bridey Murphy's case is the first (Bernstein 1956, Kline 1956). This is followed by Guirdham's investigation of Cathar cases (Guirdham 1970, 1974). Regressions by Bloxham (Iverson 1976), Glaskin (1979), Moss and Keeton (1979), and a few by Williston and Johnstone (1983) were also tested.

Research into child cases is dominated by Ian Stevenson's work (1966, 1975, 1977, 1980, 1983). Other publications come from Gupta *et al.* (1936), Andrade (1973), and Story (1975). Statistical research on regressions was carried out by Wambach (1978, 1979).

Cladder (1983) researched the effects of past-life therapy. Manly P. Hall wrote a few words about research (1964) and Christie-Murray wrote a study guide on the topic (in about 1975). Ian Wilson researched reincarnation cases and concluded that the reincarnation hypothesis is unsubstantiated (1981). Related to research, is theory-building and model-building. One of the few attempts so far is that by the Brazilian Hernani Andrade (1983).

Epilogue: The Practical Consequences of Belief in Reincarnation

Little has been written on the consequences of the belief in reincarnation. Thea Stanley-Hughes points out a few social consequences (1976: 66) and Arthur Osborn (1966) points out personal consequences. Interest and involvement in reincarnation alone may mean nothing at all. It can be misused to make life seem more sensational. Your new lover is your true soul-mate, and the karma between your wife and yourself has just been worked out. Margaret Thatcher cannot help being the way she is because she is the reincarnation of the medieval Black Prince (Baker 1981: 48). And of course, people who are born on the brink between two periods are showered with gifts: better hearing, eyesight, sense of smell, taste and intuition (Rolfe 1975: 54).

Or even:

I see myself as a child that is exercising levitation. Three children all alone in the Black Forest playing with the energy of the gods and humanity. We fly among the trees, lift heavy objects by power of will alone and participate in the design of the universe. But the forces we play with are too strong for us, and we are smashed by an avalanche we accidentally cause (Moore 1976).

Belief in reincarnation may mean as much or as little as a belief in something else. To fatalistic people it gives an excuse for their fatalism, to active people it gives impetus for their activism. Henry Ford said:

I adopted the theory of reincarnation when I was 26. Religion offered nothing to the point. Even work could not give me complete satisfaction. Work is futile if we cannot utilize the experience we collect in one life in the next. When I discovered reincarnation . . . time was no longer limited. I was no longer a slave to the hands of the clock . . .

I would like to communicate to others the calmness that the long view of life gives to us (Head and Cranston 1977: 355).

A belief is one thing, personal memories of past lives another, and experiencing the retrospect of the prenatal preparation in a regression another thing again. What do such experiences do to people? They bring an abrupt increase in the knowledge of the art of living, I believe, and consequently an improvement in spiritual health, in education, in ethics, and in social activities. I summarize these consequences in the ten points below:

1 The experiences of the retrospect after death and the prospect before birth put our life into a meaningful perspective: we are going somewhere and coming from somewhere. Birth and death remain drastic and dramatic changes, but they lose the power to terrorize us with fear, and to incapacitate us with the prospect of an unimaginable and futile vacuum.

2 The awareness of a planned life course. The realization that we do not have to do everything at once. Every life has a main theme, a main direction. Life is less arbitrary and coincidental. We understand and accept our circumstances better and we may feel that we are on course.

3 Learning and development never end. Living again and again means experiencing and doing new things and looking back on them. 'Up there' we evaluate, think, and steer. 'Down here' we put ourselves and our ideas to the practical test, and we consolidate our gains.

4 Our body is not a prison, but a diver's suit to enable us to operate 'down here'. Moreover, it is a living robot constructed for the development of self-awareness in it. We cannot be aware of ourselves before we have developed our self-awareness in our body.

5 More advanced people help less advanced people and are helped by more advanced people. Human relationships continue beyond death and birth. Through all the muddle human relationships flower. We learn to be considerate to others ('Do not unto others what you will not have done unto you. Do unto others what you

will have done unto you.'), to empathize and sympathize with others, and with and through others we learn acceptance, respect, and trust, also in ourselves. Our sense of responsibility is developed.

6 Differing lives bring different experiences: one time as a man, the next as a woman; one time as an extrovert, the next as an introvert. One life poor, the next one rich. One life meek, the next assertive. Wealth and poverty, man or woman; everything has advantages and disadvantages. We learn to see things in perspective. It makes us less dogmatic, less prejudiced, less complacent, less nationalist, less racist, and less sexist.

7 Reincarnation means an ever-growing wealth of experience. It means a sometimes difficult and exhausting but apparently never-ending road leading to more insight, deeper emotions, richer talents, and to being more ourselves, more related to others. It lends us, and humanity in general, human worth and human nobility. The imperfect is a road to perfection.

8 The break caused by death is often the release from intensely limiting and intensely painful conditions. Checking out regularly maintains our stamina.

9 The future of our planet is our responsibility, our shared lot. History becomes a more continuous stream for us.

10 We see our children as newcomers on the front, people who have to find their own way, learn their own lessons, and make their own contributions.

I would like to add a few lines from T. S. Eliot's *Four Quartets*:

This is the use of memory:
For liberation – not less of love but expanding
Of love beyond desire, and so liberation
From the future as well as the past . . .
'Little Gidding' III

And:

We shall not cease from exploration
And the end of all our exploring

Epilogue

Will be to arrive where we started
And to know the place for the first time . . .

And all shall be well and
All manner of thing shall be well
When the tongues of flame are in-folded
Into the crowned knot of fire
And the fire and the rose are one.
'Little Gidding' V

I have experienced my patients in the terrors of the Inquisition, of witch hunts, of concentration camps, and as frightened children during bombings, crying for their parents. There is much fire and darkness in the world, and probably more to come. Ultimately, the point is humanity and inhumanity: a long and sad story. This book is about the long breath we need for that. 'I would like to communicate to others the calmness that the long view of life gives to us.'

In the final words of Dante's *Paradiso*: 'All that I spoke of is one single flame.'

Glossary

See the indexes for references to the text and for words not included in this glossary.

Akasha record A theosophical idea also used by other schools of thought. Everything occurring in this world is registered in the 'memory of nature'. This memory is in a supersensory, all encompassing etheric field: akasha (original meaning, radiant; later, heaven). How this happens is unclear. The ability to see impressions of the past is regarded as a form of clairvoyance, called 'reading the akasha record'.

   Impressions of situations occurring previously to this life may be explained as impressions from the akasha records rather than as personal memories. This does not explain the personal character of memories.

   The idea of akasha records is vague and undetailed. It is worth little as an alternative explanation of past-life recall, being a more speculative and complex explanation.

Anatta (an-atta; literally, not-self) A Buddhist doctrine, common in Theravada Buddhism. There is reincarnation, but not of the self. Only 'psychic patterns' are imprinted on the new person. Identity of being does not have to co-exist with identity of awareness. A person's present sense of self is not at all identical with the reincarnating soul. Historically, the idea is a reaction to the earlier unsophisticated ideas about the reincarnating self.

Art of living From the perspective of reincarnation this means: developing a sense of your life line or life plan; treating others humanely; keeping negative emotions under control; accepting your fate without losing initiative; taking the time needed for the maturation of judgement or will; neither too many nor too few ambitions; never purposefully inducing negative emotions in others.

Awareness A psychological feature that, at least for the majority of souls, is apparently developed in the incarnate state. Once a person has attained self-awareness, he can take it with him to the discarnate state. The incarnate state can promote self-awareness but also block it.

Self-awareness is the continually shifting result of identification processes. Trance shifts the attention inward. One becomes self-absorbed, and the sense of time diminishes. During a regression, this shift characteristically moves into the past. During dissociation awareness may separate into two focal points simultaneously, resulting in an 'elliptic' consciousness.

Barrier Resistance to relaxing and centring; more specifically, resistance to entering regression. Without barriers, induction is just a piece of cake. Barriers are blocks extending themselves beyond the content to the induction itself. In other words, the induction itself restimulates blocks, often because of recursive postulates. Latent regression experiences may also be threatening and lead to barriers. A death experience just beneath the surface may evoke fear of death. A regression experience may contain shut-off commands.

Barriers may be dissolved by recognizing the specific shut-off commands and other blocks; by going deeper into trance; by practising relaxation at home; or sometimes by improving the trust between remigrant and counsellor.

Blocks Resistance to certain experiences during the regression. The experiences are suppressed and resist being brought back and remembered. Usually the regression halts. The experience is sometimes blanketed by a screen memory, or is remembered in a shallower form – moving out of regression into reliving, memory, or even recollection.

The counsellor has to get around the blocks, but he needs to respect them. Blocks are often the best leads in therapy, especially if they appear early. When the trance is deep enough, finger signals can be used to ask what should be done with the blocks.

Bodhisattva Buddhism sees the incarnate state as imperfect and unsatisfactory. Unless a person follows a specific road each life will irrevocably have consequences for the next incarnation. The Wheel of Life and Death turns on and on without end. A person may strive for liberation, following the eight-fold path, and attain release from the Wheel of Life and Death, and no longer need to reincarnate. He has then attained Nirvana. He continues to exist, but loses his self-consciousness.

Rather than enter Nirvana, a person can continue to reincarnate out of mercy and love for his unliberated brothers. Such a person is a Bodhisattva. Even after entering Nirvana and attaining the Buddhic state, he may choose to remain there as a Pratyeka Buddha, or return as a Buddha of Compassion. The Hindus call the state of liberation *moksha*. They think more of a gradual ascent during many incarnations. Before somebody attempts to attain spiritual peace, he can grow, progress, and attain wisdom through many incarnations. The Buddhist view of reincarnation as a wheel is more pessimistic. The 'periodic return of the perfected', found among the Ismaelites, is a similar thought to that of the Buddhist Bodhisattvas and the Hindu Avatars. The return of Elijah as John the Baptist can be seen in these terms. Such thoughts are found in cultures which do not believe in the reincarnation of common people. However, regressions show that voluntary incarnation with a mission is relatively common. See also *Free will*.

Catharsis Purification. A liberating experience resolving ignorance and negative emotions (e.g. fear, hate, jealousy, anger, powerlessness, guilt, shame, indifference) and replacing them with understanding, acceptance, and peace, often with joy and a sense of freedom. Every therapeutic episode in a regression therapy strives for catharsis.

Catharsis is a mini-retrospect in peace and radiance. The healing retrospect as the temporarily clinically dead report is a kind of 'big catharsis'. Catharsis possibly always contains (usually unconscious) dissociation, and even out-of-body experience. Catharsis is purification, a death as well as a rebirth.

Christos experiment This is the most careful and elaborate induction method for non-therapeutic regressions to past lives. It has characteristic step-by-step procedures with built-in safety measures, and is described by Glaskin (1974).

Compensation theory People who believe they remember a past life are doing so because they need to compensate for the limitations and difficulties in their present life. This theory is only relevant when the remigrant claims his past life was more pleasant or more important. The number of remigrants who believe they were important or even famous people is small. The theory does not explain verified details from the past life which could not have been known from study or communication.

Counselling Conducting the regression of other persons and leading them through the regression experiences with questions and instructions, outside of therapy. This can be done for various reasons and using various methods. Counselling starts with induction. Its basic technique is a mixture of non-directive counselling and direct (but open) guidance, and uses open questions, in-depth questions, repetitions, summaries, and open and specific suggestions.

Deepening is achieved by anchoring in the body, in sensory perceptions, and in feelings, and by working out identity, orientation, relations, and meaning. The episodes in the regression are chosen using winding techniques. Counting instructions, flash answers, and finger signals are common tools. Sometimes experiences stop (blocks), become thin (coming out of regression), go too fast (rush), or cause strain (stress).

When an experience becomes confused, unravelling techniques such as dating and tracing are called for. Working out the correct measures for a confusing or contradictory episode is called 'searching bottom'. Special techniques are needed for psychic people because they may leave their body.

Also important in counselling is building in safety measures to avoid the need for therapeutic interventions. Therapy uses counselling techniques but demands a psychotherapeutic repertoire, as well.

Descent The shift of consciousness from outside to inside the foetus. Sometimes an etheric thread connects the psychic body with the foetus while the consciousness remains outside. As the birth approaches, the thread shortens. Often, the soul is alternately in the body and outside it. It seems that the brain has to be developed sufficiently to be in the body. The main descent is usually in the last two months of pregnancy, or during or just after birth. After the descent the soul can still depart, but it becomes more and more difficult.

Determinism Each event is predetermined by past events. Thus present events determine future events. Coincidence and free will are illusions. A complete knowledge of the past would enable perfect prediction of the future. The religious form of determinism is predestination. In reincarnation determinism sometimes forms part of a karma doctrine. Although regressions show that karma is not fixed by natural laws but works psychologically, the idea of determinism has not been disproven. Determinists would argue that each psychological reaction only looks arbitrary; essentially, it can be computed beforehand. But if each outcome results from a specific psychological constellation, how do we determine this constellation? By its outcome. Jack beats John because Jack is better. How do we know he is better? Because he won. This is running in circles. An empirical underpinning of determinism would be correctly to predict huge numbers of events. This has not been done so far. On the other hand, the empirical refutation of determinism is impossible. This makes determinism an intellectual game or an ideology, not a scientific or practical concept.

Deva An angel-like discarnate being inhabiting and possibly influencing nature. It resembles a personification of natural powers, but quite a number of remigrants have deva-like experiences as their oldest memories. Apparently some sensitives perceive them. Vague, aesthetic world benefactors may be obsessed by devas. As far as reincarnation is concerned this is still a fringe area.

Dharma (1) Rough meaning: inner law. Obligations that we take upon ourselves voluntarily and consciously, maybe because we owe it to ourselves: '*Noblesse oblige*'. It is the 'nobility' a person has acquired as the strength and ability to act not arbitrarily or blinded by immediate impulse, but in harmony with the situation and with his or herself. Dharma is the reverse of karma, which implies involuntary actions imposed by external circumstances and the past. Dharma affects this incarnation and other incarnations, as well as the preparation of an incarnation.

(2) The assets: talents and strengths carried over from past lives. The opposite of karma which includes the liabilities from past lives. Sometimes dharma is carried over involuntarily, and sometimes the incarnating soul chooses to carry it over in accordance with the life plan and the feeding incarnations selected for the coming life. Dharma, like karma, can probably be found in the vehicle of vitality, the chakras, and the aura.

Dissociation Loosening or separating, the opposite of association.
1 Liberation from identifying with a past experience. 'That happened then. I don't have to be afraid of that any more. Now I don't have to do that any more.'
2 Separating a part of the personality from an experience. Being an actor and an observer simultaneously.
3 Introducing the present self into a past experience to aid healing and acceptance.

Dissociation is a temporary aid to achieving an elliptic consciousness and facilitating catharsis, or to breaking an undesirable bond or identification with the past, and is, as such, essential for catharsis.

Drugs Related to reincarnation and regression in three ways:
1 Often drug addiction continues through lives.
2 Drugs may be used to induce memories of past lives. In general, drugs are clumsy because the experiences are almost impossible to guide and work out; but they might lead to interesting findings.
3 Drug addiction complicates regressions and regression therapy. Apparently drugs confuse the retrieval system. Memories get mixed up. Only after an analysis of each drug's effect on emotional restimulation chains can they be unravelled.

Engram The registration of an undigested, sharply defined episode with all the physical, emotional, and intellectual consequences thereof. Engrams are connected to other engrams by association and restimulation.

Etheric body A good characterization is Crookall's term 'vehicle of vitality', the link between the soul and the body, not a vehicle of consciousness. A person is self-aware either in his soul or in his body. When the soul and the body are separated in death, a part of the ether remains in and with the body. Another part is cast off by the soul after death and slowly disintegrates. A third part probably remains with the soul, and contains at least the chakras and all the karma and dharma.

Evolution (1) The experiences, lessons, and emancipation gathered in subsequent lives. Often, two stages are distinguished: the involution stage, where humanity is developed by other powers or beings to the point where people are able to experience their incarnations independently and carry the responsibility for their development; and the actual evolution stage where mankind has to find its own destiny. The involution is normally seen as a process of ever deeper, and more material incarnations, and evolution as ever thinner, more immaterial, and spiritual incarnations (if all goes well). There are three evolution models, each underpinned by regression material:

1 Animal souls evolve into human souls. The idea that souls evolve via minerals, plants, and animals to humans is more specifically called 'transmigration'.
2 Discarnate souls descend into human or humanoid bodies.
3 People from other planets land here either in discarnate or in incarnate form.

(2) More specifically, evolution is the natural development resulting from ever changing experiences during incarnation, in challenging circumstances, with the exertions, choices, and risks involved in them; always learning, in spite of yourself. It precedes education and self-development and never ends.

Free will In reincarnation, free will begins when a person is sufficiently aware during the intermission to make choices about his coming incarnation. The simplest form of free will is the acceptance or refusal of a life plan proposed by somebody else. Free will increases when we are able to design our own life plans. Naturally, freedom increases as karmic obligations and relations decrease. During incarnation free will consists of the choices we make in our actions, and our interpretations and evaluations. For example, we can give in to our moods or get over them. We can look at things pessimistically or optimistically.

Genetic memory One of the hypotheses used to explain ostensible past-life recall. The personal memories of people who lived in the past are genetically stored and inherited. This hypothesis is speculative: first, because memory inheritance has not been established (although apparently some learning may be passed on); second, because it is usually unlikely and in many cases impossible; third, because its capacity is much too small; and fourth, because only memories up until conception can be transmitted. But almost all past-life memories include recollections of death.

Gnosticism Everybody, given the right mental development, can find a direct inner truth which will enlighten, liberate, or transform him. The best method is to study the works of those who are already enlightened. When more emphasis is given to experience, gnosticism tends towards mysticism. When formal apprenticeship within a school or church is emphasized, enlightenment is usually termed 'initiation' and the ideas will probably be esoteric. When the development of paranormal talents is emphasized, the tendency is towards occultism. These three varieties are found in any combination. The fundamental idea is that the person has to rise above material limitations and common sense. In other words, the person should rise above the intellectual limitations of the incarnate state.

Group karma The idea that we are not only affected by the consequences of our own acts, but also by those of the collective we belonged or belong to: fertile ground for generalizations and speculations. So far, regressions have presented no evidence to support the idea. On the contrary, karma appears to be personal. A group of people with a particularly strong bond may reincarnate together and develop a common destiny, but this is rather group dharma than group karma. The idea of group karma often coincides with ideas of national souls, collective horoscopes, and so on.

Guides (1) During an induction with visualization the counsellor can ask the remigrant to imagine a guide as an inner travelling companion and adviser. This guide may have either psychological or objective reality.

(2) Some counsellors believe that in regressions to past lives discarnates function as guides. These can be called upon as protectors, or consulted via mediumistic people or via the patient himself.

Hangover A past life undigested as the result of general emotional malaise: loneliness, boredom, heaviness, hopelessness, meaninglessness.

Heredity Usually of limited import. The body should be suitable to the incarnating person. The composition made from the genetic material of the parents is often subject to choice. Many incarnating people help shape the embryo, giving the infant many characteristics of the incarnating person. Notable talents are not inherited, but brought in. The physique suitable to these talents, like musicality, is based on genetic material. Genes are of secondary importance in parental choice.

Hypersentience The induction method developed by Marcia Moore: a mixture of relaxation and visualization, supplemented by some magnetization and slight hypnotic trance. Characteristic of this method are rather exalted visualizations and regression goals.

Hypnosis This is used here to mean the induction of a trance using verbal and other sensory suggestions. Like magnetization, hypnosis often leads to real regression (level 4), while relaxation, and emotional, somatic, and postulate bridges often result in reliving (level 3).

Identification Adopting or determining an identity.
1 Absorbing experiences, feelings, thoughts, and examples in our self-image. Changing our ideas about ourselves, so that we are able to say 'I am not a second-rate artist', or 'I can fix things just as well as my father'.
2 Deep absorption in an experience, forgetting what has happened since then, and including the present occurrences in the past situation (level 5).
3 Identification with another person: the impression that we are

somebody else, or were somebody else in the past. In Britain, women often identify with Mary Stuart, and on the continent with Marie Antoinette.

4 Establishing which infant is the new incarnation of a deceased notable, or what was the previous incarnation of the infant. An example of the former is the identification of the new Dalai Lama.

Incarnation The process of creating the bond with the foetus, the descent into the foetus or the infant, the reciprocal influence between the soul and the foetus or infant, and the increasing identification with the young child. The incarnation begins some time between the sixth month of pregnancy and just after the birth, and ends some time after the birth.

Incarnation guides Many remigrants experience having been guided by advisers before their birth, varying from one adviser to a whole circle, and from a good friend giving just a note of advice to professionals who design a whole life plan.

Incarnation preparation This usually begins with the consideration or the hint that it is time to return to the front, continues with the life plan, often advised by and discussed with others, and ends with the choice of parents, contact with the foetus, and sometimes a preview of the coming life.

Induction In general, inducing a trance. Here, more specifically, gaining entry to experiences from past lives. The following induction methods are used:

1 Magnetism: using magnetic passes. Hardly any longer used.
2 Hypnosis: usually through suggestions and pseudo-suggestions and then with direct instructions to go back to a past life.
3 Relaxation and visualization: physical and mental relaxation, concentrating on the body, evoking images, often coinciding with a swinging or floating feeling, or with an imagined out-of-body experience. After a symbolic border, or a landing after floating, the remigrant enters an experience from a past life.
4 Evoking recollections and intensifying these to reliving. Going further and further back to the first years, the birth, just before the birth, and then on further.

5 Via the emotional bridge: evoking an emotion and deepening it, then instructing the remigrant to go back to a situation that caused and imprinted this emotion.

6 Via the somatic bridge: amplifying a well-defined and localized bodily sensation and then instructing the remigrant to go back to the situation that caused and imprinted this sensation. It also works well after relaxation as an alternative to visualization.

7 Via the image bridge: taking a recurrent image or dream, or an image coming up spontaneously at the beginning of the session.

8 Via the postulate bridge: having a probable postulate sentence repeated with steady and increasing concentration, then instructing the remigrant to go back to the situation that imprinted this postulate.

Involution The progressive inhabitation of the body by the soul, from the first stage of overshadowing the body to a complete awareness in the body, often leading to loss of recollection of the discarnate state. In this line of thought, evolution is the development of material bodies until they are ready to be inhabited by human souls which can develop self-awareness and humanity (intelligence, empathy, and independence) in them, perhaps also regaining discarnate awareness in the incarnate state.

Karma Originally, action; later, the consequences of action throughout lives. The repercussions or 'liabilities' left from past lives, consisting of direct and indirect somatic effects, of remedial interventions, negative and incomplete psychological reactions, entanglements, and voluntarily accepted debts.

Karmic astrology Reading a person's past life, multiple past lives, or karma from past lives, from the natal chart. Indications for this vary from author to author: the solar signs; the lunar nodes; intercepted signs; the retrograde planets, mystery planets, Saturn, the sun, the moon; squares and opposites; Virgo, Pisces and Scorpio; the fourth, the eighth, the twelfth houses. All of these considerations are speculative. I do not know of any empirical material.

Life goal When people regress to the incarnation preparation or the post-mortem experiences they usually find a main goal for the coming or the just-ended life. Almost certainly there are usually several goals. The generic life goals seem to be: growth in understanding, sympathy, proficiency, and independence.

Life plan The goals of the coming life, important encounters, karma to be worked out and talents to be developed; all are set down as preprogrammed reactions and drives.

Life retrospect After death. First, a quick chronological overview of the past life, with questions like: What did you learn from this? Are you satisfied with it? Did you feel related to certain people? The second retrospect goes per situation, the deceased empathizing with the people he met. This is a deeper, more personal reliving and evaluation. The first retrospect can be so quick that the images are almost parallel with one another, making for one grand life panorama. By exception, one sees a number of previous lives as if looking in multiple mirrors simultaneously.

Moksha Liberation from the limitations of the incarnate state: limited awareness, blindness to and inactivity in the spiritual world, poor paranormal talents. It is often interpreted as the liberation from personal existence, as reunion with the divinity we originated from, and the end of our need to reincarnate.

Obsession Used here in the original meaning: being obsessed by a foreign discarnate personality. Some obsessors have karmic relation with the obsessed person. The obsessor can be an intentional or accidental disturbance: active or passive obsession.

An obsessor can be in the aura – attachment, or in the organism – true obsession. The obsessor may even take over the 'driver's seat' – possession.

Out-of-body experience The soul's temporary departure from the body, also called 'astral projection'. With 'simple' out-of-body experiences only the psychic body departs from the physical body. With a 'complex' out-of-body experience, part of the vehicle of vitality also leaves. Many induction techniques make use of virtual out-of-body experiences: the remigrant visualizes leaving the body. This is usually without objective perception of the physical environment. During such a mental out-of-body experience, the counsellor continues to communicate with the remigrant, who remains aware of his own body, in an elliptic consciousness. With a simple out-of-body experience the person seems to be asleep and is incommunicado. Afterwards, he is able to describe his experiences. A complex out-of-body experience induces a degree of catalepsy: the body becomes colder and stiffer, and breathing and circulation slow down more than during normal sleep, probably similar to hibernation.

Overlapping incarnations Most examples of overlapping incarnations are people who enter a child rather than a foetus. Usually this happens when the soul who had been in the child up until then is either just leaving or has only taken weak possession of the body, for example Jasbir (p. 286). The case of Hermann Grundei (p. 109) may be an exception, because his looks in the new life were so similar to the old one. A real overlapping incarnation is a form of parallel incarnations. Evidence for this is scant.

Parental choice The many different considerations fall into the following categories:
- availability of a nearby foetus (unplanned incarnations of population I: see *Reincarnation patterns*
- karmic entanglements with one or both of the parents
- a good relationship from a past life with one or both of the parents
- an opportunity for development fitting with the life plan
- suitable genetic material.

Past-life recall This type of recollection is graced with many names to distinguish it from common recollection: pre-memory, far memory, retro-cognition, paranormal memory, extra-cerebral memory. The memory can be vague, merely a feeling of having lived before with vague recollections of some situation long ago. It may consist of images, which can be static like photographs, or moving, from fragments up to an entire film memory. The visions are sometimes accompanied by sound and touch, and, less frequently, smell and taste. The feelings and thoughts from that time often re-emerge as well. Memories of conversations may be without sound, as if telepathically replayed. There are sometimes accompanying memories of names, places, or dates. At other times there is some kind of commentary, and in rare cases one can even communicate with the commentator.

Recollection can intensify to reliving an experience, as if you are back in the situation. You can remain an outside observer or be a participant, or both simultaneously: remaining outside looking at what is happening and being in it. This sometimes happens in dreams as well. The sense of being inside the memory, perceiving it as your own memory, is called 'personification', an important characteristic of almost all past-life recall. The presence or absence of personification forms the main difference between real memories and telepathic impressions.

In a few cases you see the images simultaneously, as parallel. This is called a panoramic memory. The phenomena of life panoramas became known through people who were in near-fatal accidents or briefly clinically dead. A panoramic memory of a past life may be a reproduction of a life retrospect.

Memories of past lives can come up spontaneously, without immediate cause, or be triggered by particular circumstances. They often come up following feelings of recognition and familiarity in a new city or region, or with a stranger. Memories can emerge in dreams, during illness, or in accidents, and with loss of consciousness (out-of-body experiences).

Past-life therapy Regression therapy accepting and often seeking regressions to apparent past lives and to experiences after death and before birth.

Precipitation The deposit in the body of psychic (and etheric) charges from a past life (karma and dharma). Various forms are:

1 Psychosomatic complaints resulting from dubious or perverse practices in a past life (terrorism, torture, deceit, abuse of power, sexual abuse); this includes reversals.
2 Psychosomatic complaints resulting from the repercussions of trau-

matic experiences (severe victimization, undigested dying experiences, etc.).

3 Care, attentiveness, harmony, and a sense of beauty which may lead to a healthy, balanced and beautiful body.

4 Psychosomatic complaints resulting from postulates.

Progression Pre-experiencing the future of this life or a coming life. There are examples of plausible progressions in this life. Progressions to coming lives seem to be sensitive to the unconscious expectations of the counsellor and the 'promigrant'.

Pseudo-obsession Obsession by the personality of a past life. If a particular life has not been worked out because of incomplete dying, that personality is unable to integrate in the larger personality or higher self. In a new incarnation, this past personality can be taken along as it is, undigested, and haunt the aura or the body. As with real obsession, this causes psychosomatic complaints. A treatment of this personality leads to harmonization (it becomes a regular feeding personality) and integration. Sometimes, it is altogether purged and departs to the 'light' of the higher self. Psychic and psychosomatic complaints typical of pseudo-obsession are, for example, autism and anorexia.

Psychodrama The visualization of some psychological tension in the form of a story, spontaneous or conscious. Many dreams are psychodramatic. A psychodrama can be induced in a waking dream. It can lead to a spontaneous trance with an intensity and clarity that is as distinct from a regular fantasy as reliving is from a regular memory.

Psycho-plastic A characteristic of the psychic (or astral) world. The surroundings correspond to our mental state. This can be subjective: we create our environment to suit our own thoughts, feelings, wishes, and fears; but also objective: we get to a place or visit a person by thinking of them intensely. The body experience is also psycho-plastic: our self-image and appearance depend on how and what we think and feel.

Psychosomatic Somatics heavily influenced by psychology. A person who is allergic to roses may sneeze when he sees plastic roses. Placebos are sometimes just as good as, or even better than, real medicine, especially if expensive and prescribed by somebody the patient trusts.

Diseases like cancer, and cardiovascular diseases, have a psychosomatic aspect: certain personality traits increase the likelihood that certain diseases will manifest themselves. With infectious diseases susceptibility is probably a psychosomatic factor.

In a deep trance, blisters can appear, bleeding can start, warts can disappear, etc.

Regression In general, going back in time; more specifically, a form of reliving while forgetting everything that happened after the relived situation. Reliving and real regression are usually done with a counsellor. Bodily reactions belonging to the relived situation can occur during regression. Regressions can have different purposes and be done in different ways.

Regression therapy Re-experiencing and digesting situations which were traumatic and/or resulted in the formation of postulates, and attaining catharsis.

Reincarnation Returning to a human body many times. It can be a religious doctrine, an argued conviction, or an experience: spontaneous memories or induced regression. Alternative designations are: metamorphosis, palingenesis, transanimation, transcorporation, transmigration. Colloquially, the most common terms are:
- reincarnation: continual rebirth as a person
- metempsychosis: rebirth either as a person or as an animal
- transmigration: developing from mineral to plant to animal to human and higher incarnation forms.

Reincarnation patterns Various types of incarnation processes.
1 Population I: Unaware or vaguely aware; unplanned; based on the availability of a nearby foetus; intermission of a few years.
2 Population II: Reincarnation following a life plan usually recommended and with strong educational concerns. Intermission is normally a few decades.

3 Population III: Reincarnation according to a self-designed life plan, often with some self-chosen or accepted mission.

Restimulation The renewed stimulation of an existing postulate or trauma in a situation associated with the original situation causing the trauma or triggering the postulate. In general, restimulation fortifies the existing trauma or postulate. Restimulation results in 'chains': a series of experiences sharing the same trauma or postulate. Presumably, restimulation during life is facilitated by preceding restimulation during pregnancy and birth. The therapy situation itself may restimulate traumas and postulates, especially those connected with passivity, dependence, and manipulation.

Retention Continuity throughout lives. Everything we take with us directly from past lives. It can have more or less influence, but it remains unchanged. This can apply to talents, idiosyncrasies, tendencies, appearance, and relations.

Sex choice The sex of an incarnation can be determined to a fixed pattern, chosen arbitrarily, or come about by accident. The first option usually means that the sex remains the same or alternates according to fixed rules – for example, a different sex every incarnation. Many people believe in such a regular alternation.

The published cases show sex change to be common, but not universal. Apparently sex is often chosen, but is more often determined without the incarnating person's intervention, either systematically or arbitrarily, and may sometimes be entered on rashly or mistakenly.

Singularization An existing personality splitting off another personality or sub-personality.

Soul The continually reincarnating entity, becoming conscious and self-aware via its incarnations. It is the real person, the real individual.

Stigmata Birthmarks, usually in the form of blotches or scratches on the skin. The best known birth stigma is a skin blotch where the previous incarnation was fatally wounded; for example, a red line on the neck if they were decapitated, or a red spot on the back where a spear entered. Presumably, stigmata are more common when the deceased intensely experienced the wound just before or just after his death, integrated it into his self-image, and subsequently entered the foetus early in its development without leaving the past life behind. A clear example of such a psychosomatic effect is the person whose fingers had grown together, and who remembered a lengthy fight leading to his death where his hands were so bloody that his fingers were stuck together.

Other stigmata are memory aids: something facilitating the memory of a past life, or something which will indicate to others the previous identity. Such memory aids are especially common in tribes believing in rebirth close to where the past incarnation died, and accepting wishes for the next life and prophetic dreams as natural.

A third kind of stigma is purely karmic, for example Wijeratne who had a shrivelled arm and saw this as the result of having killed his wife with that arm in his past life (see p. 247).

In regressions with strong somatics, temporary stigmata may appear, for example a person who suddenly has red stripes on his back when he re-experiences a thrashing.

Super-ESP Super-extra-sensory perception, a proposed form of clairvoyance to explain apparent past-life recall and apparent messages from the deceased. Such clairvoyance clearly exceeds the talents of the usual paragnostic, hence 'super'. This explanation is normally used by parapsychologists who do not believe in a discarnate existence before or after death, or who think that accepting this will endanger the precarious scientific status of parapsychology. As with many mental constructs, super-ESP can hardly be disproven, since all counterindications can be explained as part of the character of super-ESP. This includes the personal identification of deceased people, or the experience of personal memories of a past life. The theosophical idea of the possibility of reading the akasha records is virtually identical with the idea of super-ESP.

Temple training This entails every form of training in the development of paranormal abilities. The regressions of people who have natural paranormal abilities in this life indicate paranormal training in earlier lives. Since most of this training entailed a shift of consciousness, paranormal abilities have a tendency to remain with the person through death and birth. Much of the temple training that comes up took place in Egypt, in the Indian cultures of central and south America, and in Atlantic cultures. Less common areas of temple training are India and the Far East, and early or prehistoric Greece. Other temple trainings are difficult to place historically or geographically. Some of the training took place outside official institutions. The concept 'temple training' therefore, has to be taken in a broad sense.

Throughth The fourth (or first) dimension. The deceased feel able to pass through objects and people. Perceived three-dimensionally, they are in the same place but in the fourth dimension they are not. Contact in the fourth dimension results in interaction: people become aware of the deceased. This is what happens with telepathy, obsession, and such. Clairvoyants see three-dimensional sections of the four-dimensional aura. This explains why different sensitives see different things, besides reasons of common imprecision, imagination, and unconscious interpretation.

Trance Originally, a state resembling deep sleep entered by a medium or subject through deep magnetization or hypnosis; more broadly, any state of changed consciousness in which a person has less attention for his immediate surroundings. Within the framework of regressions, trance is a consciousness shifted from the exterior to the interior world, and from the present to the past, and includes physical changes in muscle tension, skin resistance, and brain-wave rhythms, as well as mental changes such as relaxation, an altered sense of time, reduced power of observation, and increased power of imagination. Trance depth can vary.

A trance medium is a person who can bring himself into a trance enabling communication with discarnate entities; more generally a person whose paranormal abilities surface in trance.

Vehicle of vitality A term coined by Crookall to designate the intermediary between the psychic body and the physical body. It is often called the etheric body. Crookall preferred 'vehicle' because apparently we cannot be self-aware in this body, whereas we are self-aware in the physical and the psychic (or astral) body. Apparently the vehicle of vitality does not have its own independent organization. Many observations indicate that the 'silver cord' does not have an organic structure, but looks like any string resulting from stretching an elastic substance.

Bibliography

Every attempt has been made to provide full references for the works listed in the Bibliography, which aims to be as complete as possible. The author apologizes for any omissions and would be interested to receive any further details which readers can supply.

Works on reincarnation in English

Abhedananda, Swami (1899) *Reincarnation*, Calcutta: Ramakrishna Vedanta Math, 1964.

Allen, Eula (1965) *Before the Beginning*, Virginia Beach: ARE.

Anderson, Jerome A. (1894) *Karma: A study of the law of cause and effect in relation to re-birth or reincarnation, post-mortem states of consciousness, cycles, vicarious atonement, fate, predestination, free will, forgiveness, animals, suicides, etc.*, San Francisco: Lotus.

—— (1894) *Reincarnation: A study of the human soul in its relation to re-birth, evolution, post-mortem states, the compound nature of man; hypnotism, etc.*, San Francisco: Lotus.

Andrade, Hernani Guimarães (1973) *The Ruytemberg Rocha Case*, São Paulo: Brazilian Institute for Psychobiophyscial Research.

Anon (1909) *Reincarnation and Christianity, by a Clergyman of the Church of England*, London: Rider.

Arundale, Francesca (1890) *The Idea of Re-birth*, London: Kegan Paul.

Atkinson, W. W. (1908) *Reincarnation and the Law of Karma*, Chadwell Heath, Romford: Fowler, n.d.

Aurobindo, Sri (1952) *The Problem of Rebirth*, Pondicherry, 1973.

Austen, A. W. (1938) *Teachings of Silver Birch*, London: Psychic Press.

Baker, Douglas M. (1977) *Karmic Laws*, Wellingborough: Aquarian, 1982.

—— (1978) *The Wheel of Rebirth*, Wellingborough: Aquarian.

—— (1981) *Reincarnation: Why, when and how we have lived before*, Potters Bar: D. Baker.

Banerjee, H. N. (1979) *The Once and Future Life*, New York: Dell.

—— (1980) *Americans Who Have Been Reincarnated*, New York: Macmillan.

Banerjee, H. N. and Dusler, W. (1974) *Lives Unlimited: Reincarnation east and west*, New York: Doubleday.

Baronti, Gervée (1936) *You Have Lived Before!* London: Pearson.

—— (1937) *The History of the Soul*, Chesham: Baronti.

Bendit, Laurence, J. (1965) *The Mirror of Life and Death*, Wheaton: Theosophical Publishing House.

Bibliography

Bennett, Colin (1937) *Practical Time-travel: How to reach back to past lives by occult means*, Wellingborough: Aquarian, 1980.

Bernstein, Morey (1956) *The Search for Bridey Murphy*, New York: Doubleday, 1978.

Bertholet, Alfred (1904) *The Transmigration of Souls*, New York: Harper, 1909.

Besant, Annie (1895) *Karma* Adyar: Theosophical Publishing House, 1975.

—— (1898) *Reincarnation*, Adyar: Theosophical Publishing House, 1924.

—— (1904) *Reincarnation a Christian Doctrine*, London: Theosophical Publishing House.

—— (1912) *A Study in Karma*, Adyar: Theosophical Publishing House, 1917.

Besant, Annie and Leadbeater, C. W. (1913) *Man: Whence, How and Whither*, Adyar: Theosophical Publishing House, 1971.

—— (1924) *The Lives of Alcyone*, Vol 1. and 2, Adyar: Theosophical Publishing House.

Blakiston, Patrick (1970) *The Pre-Existence and Transmigration of Souls*, London: Regency.

Blavatsky, Helena P. (1886) 'Theories about reincarnation and spirits', *The Path*, November.

Bloxham, Arnall (1958) *Who was Ann Ockenden?* London: Neville Spearman.

Blythe, Henry (1956) *The Three Lives of Naomi Henry*, London: Frederick Muller.

Bowen, Francis *Christian Metempsychosis*.

Box, Sushill Chandra (1959) *Your Last Life and Your Next*, Calcutta.

Brennan, J. H. (1971) *Five Keys to Past Lives: Practical aspects of reincarnation*, Wellingborough: Aquarian, 1978.

Brownell, George B. (1946) *Reincarnation*, California.

Bryce, James (1978) *Reincarnation Now!*, Vancouver: Fforbes.

Cannon, Alexander (1936) *The Power of Kharma*, London: Rider.

Carr, Donald (1968) *The Eternal Return*, New York: Doubleday.

Cayce, Edgar Evans (1968) *Edgar Cayce on Atlantis*, New York: Paperback.

Cayce, Hugh Lynn (1964) *Venture Inward*, New York: Harper.

Cerminara, Gina (1950) *Many Mansions*, New York: Sloane, 1970.

—— (1963) *Many Lives, Many Loves*, New York: Sloane.

—— (1967) *The World Within*, London: Daniel, 1973.

Challoner, H. K. (1935) *The Wheel of Rebirth: Some memories of an occult student*, London: Theosophical Publishing House, 1969.

Challoner, H. K. and Northover, Roland (1967) *Out of Chaos*, London: Theosophical Publishing House.

Chinmoy, Sri (1974) *Death and Reincarnation*, Jamaica, New York State: Agni.

Christie-Murray, David (*c.* 1975) *Reincarnation*, London: Social Psychology Research Study Guide.

—— (1981) *Reincarnation: Ancient beliefs and modern evidence*, Newton Abbot: David & Charles.

Cladder, Johannes M. (1983) 'Past-life therapy with difficult phobics', *Journal of Regression Therapy*, 1986, 1:2, pp. 81–5.

Cohen, Daniel (1975) *The Mysteries of Reincarnation*, New York: Dodd, Mead & Co.

Cooper, Irving Steiger (1917) *Reincarnation: The hope of the world*, Wheaton: Theosophical Press, 1972.

Cranston, S. L. and Williams, C. (1984) *Reincarnation: A New Horizon in Science, Religion and Society*, New York: Julian Press.

de Silva, Lynn A. (1968) *Reincarnation in Buddhist and Christian Thought*, Colombo: Christian Literature Society of Ceylon.

Desmond, Shaw (1940) *Reincarnation for Everyman*, London: Dakers.

Dethlefsen, Thorwald (1977) *Voices From Other Lives*, New York: Evans.

Devlin, Barbara Lynne (1984) *I am Mary Shelley*, New York: Condor.

Dewitt Miller, R. (1965) *Reincarnation*, New York: Bantam.

Ducasse, C. W. (1960) *A Critical Examination of the Belief in Life After Death*, Springfield: Thomas.

Ebon, Martin (1970) *Reincarnation in the Twentieth Century*, New York: Signet.

Edmonds, I. G. (1979) *Other Lives: The story of reincarnation*, New York: McGraw-Hill.

Eichhorn, Gustav (1909) *Heredity, Memory and Transcendental Recollection as seen by a Physicist*, 1959.

Encausse, G. (Papus) (1929) *Reincarnation*, London: Rider.

Evans, W. H. (1953) *Reincarnation: Fact or fallacy*, London: Psychic Press.

Finkelstein, Adrian (1985) *Your Past Lives and the Healing Process: A psychiatrist looks at reincarnation and spiritual healing*, Farmingdale: Coleman.

Fiore, Edith (1978) *You Have Been Here Before*, New York: Ballantine.

Fisher, Joe (1985) *The Case for Reincarnation*, London: Grafton Books, 1986.

Flournoy, Theodore (1900) *From India to the Planet Mars*, New York: University Books, 1963.

Fox, Emmett (1939) *Reincarnation: Described and explained*, London: Harper & Row, 1967.

Frieling, Rudolf (1974) *Christianity and Reincarnation*, Edinburgh: Floris, 1977.

Geley, Dr Gustave (1930) *Reincarnation*, London: Rider.

Glaskin, G. M. (1974) *Windows of the Mind*, London: Arrow Books.

—— (1978) *Worlds Within*, London: Arrow Books.

—— (1979) *A Door to Eternity*, Wildwood: Book Wise.

—— (1974) *We Are One Another*, Jersey: Neville Spearman.

—— (1976) *The Lake and the Castle*, Jersey: Neville Spearman.

—— (1980) *The Island*, Jersey: Neville Spearman.

Goldberg, Bruce (1982) *Past Lives, Future Lives: Accounts of regressions and progressions through hypnosis*, North Hollywood: New Castle.

Goudey, R. F. (1928) *Reincarnation: A universal truth*, Los Angeles: Aloha.

Graham, David (1976) *The Practical Side of Reincarnation*, Englewood Cliffs: Prentice Hall.

Grant, Joan (1937) *Winged Pharaoh*, London: Landsborough Publications, 1958.

—— (1939) *Life as Carola*, London: Methuen.

—— (1942) *Eyes of Horus*, London: Diploma, 1974.

—— (1943) *Lord of the Horizon*, London: Diploma, 1974.

—— (1945) *Scarlet Feather*, London: Methuen.

—— (1947) *Return to Elysium*, London: Methuen.

Bibliography

—— (1952) *So Moses was Born*, London: Diploma, 1974.

—— (1956a) *Time out of Mind*, London: Barker.

—— (1956b) *Far Memory*, New York: Harper & Row.

Gregor, Norman *Thoughts on Reincarnation*, Tunbridge Wells: Cregor.

Grossi *Reliving Reincarnation Through Hypnosis*.

Guirdham, Arthur (1970) *The Cathars and Reincarnation*, London: Neville Spearman.

Gunaratna, V. F. (1971) *Rebirth Explained*, Kandy: Buddhist Publication Society.

Gupta, I. D., Sharma, N. R., and Mathur, T. C. (1936) *A Case of Reincarnation*, Delhi: International Aryan League.

Haich, Elisabeth, Robertson, John P. trans. (1965) *Initiation: Priestess in Egypt*, London: George Allen & Unwin.

Hall, Manly P. (1939) *Reincarnation: The cycle of necessity*, Los Angeles: Philosophical Research Society, 1978.

—— (1964) *Research on Reincarnation*, Los Angeles: Philosophical Research Society.

—— (1979) *Death to Rebirth*, Los Angeles: Philosophical Research Society.

Hanson, Virginia (ed.) (1975) *Karma: The universal law of harmony*, Wheaton: Theosophical Publishing House.

Hartley, Christine (1972) *A Case for Reincarnation*, London: Hale

Head, Joseph and Cranston, S. L. (1961) *Reincarnation, an East-West Anthology*, New York: Julian Press.

—— (1967) *Reincarnation in World Thought: A living study of reincarnation in all ages; including selections from the world's religions, philosophies, sciences and great thinkers of the past and present*, New York: Julian Press.

—— (1977) *Reincarnation: The Phoenix Fire Mystery: An east-west dialogue on death and rebirth from the world of religion, science, psychology, art and literature, and from great thinkers of the past and present*, New York: Julian Press/Crown Publishers.

Henderson, A. (1935) *The Wheel of Life*, London: Rider.

Hick, John (1976) *Death and Eternal Life*, London: Collins.

Hodson, Geoffrey (1951) *Reincarnation: Fact or fallacy?* Wheaton: Theosophical Publishing House, 1972.

Holzer, Hans (1970) *Born Again: The truth about reincarnation*, Folkestone: Bailey & Swinfen, 1975.

—— (1974) *Patterns of Destiny*, Los Angeles: Nash.

—— (1985) *Life Beyond Life: The evidence for reincarnation*, West Nyack: Parker.

Howard, Alan (1980) *Sex in the Light of Reincarnation and Freedom*, Spring Valley: St Geroge.

Howe, Jr, Quincy (1974) *Reincarnation for the Christian*, Philadelphia: Westminster.

Hubbard, L. Ron. (1958) *Have you Lived Before This Life?*, Copenhagen: Scientology Publications, 1977.

—— (1973) *Mission into Time*, Copenhagen: Permald & Rosenqueen.

Humphreys, Christmas (1943) *Karma and Rebirth*, London: Curzon, *c.* 1983.

Ingalese, Richard and Isabelle (1908) *From Incarnation to Reincarnation*, New York: Watkins.

Ireland-Frey, Louise (1986) 'Clinical depression: Releasement of attached entities from unsuspecting hosts', *Journal of Regression Therapy*, Vol. 1, No. 2, pp. 90–101.

Iverson, Jeffery (1976) *More Lives Than One?*, New York: Warner, 1977.

Jamieson, Bryan (1976) *Explore Your Past Lives*, Van Nuys: Astro Analysis Publications.

Jinarajadasa, C. (1915) *How We Remember Past Lives, and Other Essays on Reincarnation*, Adyar: Theosophical Publishing House, 1973.

Johnston, Charles (1899) *The Memory of Past Births*, New York: Theosophical Society, 1904.

—— (1900) *Karma, Works and Wisdom*, New York: Theosophical Society.

Jong, Marianne de, *Agoraphobia: Trauma of a Lost Soul*, not yet published.

Kardec, Allan (1857) *The Spirits' Book*, London: Psychic Press, 1975.

Kelsey, Denys and Grant, Joan (1967) *Many Lifetimes*, London: Corgi, 1976.

Klausner, Margot (1975) *Reincarnation*, Massada: Ramat-Gan.

Kline, Milton V. ed. (1956) *A Scientific Report on the Search for Bridey Murphy*, New York: Julian.

Knight, Marcus, (1950) *Spiritualism, Reincarnation and Immortality*, London: Duckworth.

Kolisko, Eugen (1940) *Reincarnation and other Essays*, Bournemouth: Kolisko Archive, 1978.

Krutch, Joseph Wood (1962) *More Lives than One*, New York: Morrow.

Langley, Noel (1967) *Edgar Cayce on Reincarnation*, London: Howard Baker, 1969.

Leadbeater, C. W. (1899) *Clairvoyance*, London: Theosophical Publishing Society.

—— (1910) *The Inner Life*, Vols. 1 and 2, in *Theosophical Talks at Adyar*, London: Theosophical Publishing Society.

—— (1930) *Reincarnation*, Harrogate: Theosophical Publishing Committee.

—— (1941) *The Band of Servers: A Record of Past Lives and the Karma Thereof*, Adyar: Theosophical Publishing House.

—— (1941–50) *The Soul's Growth through Reincarnation*, C. Jinarajadasa ed., Vol. 1: Lives of Erato and Spica; Vol. 2: Lives of Orion; Vol. 3: Lives of Ursa, Vega and Eudox; Vol 4: Lives of Ulysses, Abel, Arcor and Vale, Adyar: Theosophical Publishing House.

Leek, Sybil (1974) *Reincarnation: The second chance*, New York: Stein & Day.

Lenz, Frederick (1979) *Lifetimes: True accounts of reincarnation*, New York: Ballantine, 1986.

Livingstone, Marjorie (1930) *The New Nuctemeron*, London: Rider.

London, Jack (1915) *The Star Rover*, Malibu: Valley of the Sun, 1987.

Luntz, Charles (1957) *The Challenge of Reincarnation*, St Louis: Luntz Publications.

Lutowslawski, Wincenty (1928) *Pre-existence and Reincarnation*, London: Allen & Unwin.

MacGregor, Geddes (1978) *Reincarnation in Christianity*, Wheaton: Quest Books.

Bibliography

MacReady, Robert (1980) *The Reincarnations of Robert MacReady*, New York: Zebra.

MacTaggart, John M. E. (1917) *Human Immortality and Pre-existence*, New York: Kraus, 1970.

Martin, A. R. (1942) *Researches in Reincarnation and Beyond*, Sharon.

Martin, Eva (1927) *The Ring of Return: An anthology of references to reincarnation and spiritual evolution: from prose and poetry of all ages*, Albuquerque: Sun, 1981.

McClain, Florence Wagner (1986) *A Practical Guide to Past Life Regression*, St Paul: Llewellyn.

Meyer, Louis E. (1937) *Reincarnation*, Unity Village, Missouri: Unity School of Christianity.

Mirza, N. K. (1927) *Reincarnation in Islam*, Adyar, Theosophical Publishing House .

Misra, M. D. (1927) *Reincarnation and Islam*, Madras.

Montgomery, Ruth (1968) *Here and Hereafter*, New York: Howard MacCann; Greenwich: Fawcett.

—— (1974) *Companions Along the Way*, New York: Fawcett.

Moody Jr, Raymond A. (1975) *Life after Life*, New York: Bantam/Mockingbird.

—— (1977) *Reflections on Life after Life*, New York: Bantam/Mockingbird.

Moore, George Foot (1914) *Metempsychosis*, Cambridge: Harvard University Press.

Moore, Marcia (1976) *Hypersentience*, New York: Crown.

Moore, Marcia and Mark Douglas (1968) *Reincarnation: Key to immortality*, York Harbor: Arcane.

Morrell, Ed (1924) *The Twenty-Fifth Man*, New York: Vantage, 1955.

Moss, Peter and Keeton, Joe (1979) *Encounters with the Past: How man can experience and relive history*, London: Sidgwick & Jackson

Muller, Karl E. (1970) *Reincarnation, Based on Facts*, London: Psychic Press.

Netherton, Morris and Shiffrin, Nancy (1978) *Past Lives Therapy*, New York: Morrow.

Nyantiloka, Mahathera (1959) *Karma and Rebirth*, Kandy: Buddhist Publishing Society.

O'Connor, Dagmar (1956) *The First Pharaoh*, London: Regency Press.

O'Flaherty, Wendy Doniger ed. (1980) *Karma and Rebirth in Classical Indian Traditions*, Berkeley: University of Berkeley Press.

Pakenham-Walsh, W. S. (1982) *A Tudor Story: The Return of Anne Boleyn*, Cambridge: James Clarke & Co.

Palmer, Cecil ed.(1921) *Reincarnation: The True chronicles of rebirth of two affinites, recorded by one of them*, London: Palmer.

Paramananda, Swami (1919) *Reincarnation and Immortality*, Boston: Vedanta Centre, 1923.

Parameswara, P. (1973) *Soul, Karma and Re-birth*, Bangalore: Parameswara

Pascal, Théophile P. (1895) *Reincarnation: A study in human evolution*, Theosophical Publishing Society, 1950.

Perkins, James Scudday (1961) *Through Death to Rebirth*, Wheaton: Theosophical Press.

—— *Experiencing Reincarnation*, Wheaton: Quest Book.

Praed, Rosa Caroline (1914) *Nyria*, London: Rider.

Priestley, J. B. (1938) *I Have Been Here Before*, London: Heinemann.

Pryse, James Morgan (1900) *Reincarnation in the New Testament*, Mokelumne Hill: Health Research 1965.

Reyna, Ruth (1975) *Reincarnation and Science*, New Delhi: Sterling.

Rinbochay, Lati and Hopkins, Jeffery (1979) *Death, Intermediate State and Rebirth in Tibetan Buddhism*, Ithaca: Snow Lion, 1985.

Rolfe, Mona (1975) *The Spiral of Life: Cycles of reincarnation*, Suffolk: Neville Spearman.

Ryall, E. W. (1974) *Second Time Round*, Jersey: Neville Spearman.

Schlotterbeck, Karl (1987) *Living Your Past Lives: The Psychology of Past Life Regression*, New York: Ballantine.

Sharma, I. C. (1975) *Cayce, Karma and Reincarnation*, Wheaton: Theosophical Publishing House, 1982.

Shelley, Violet M. (1979) *Reincarnation Unnecessary*, Virginia Beach: ARE Press.

Shirley, Ralph (1924) *The Problem of Rebirth*, London: Rider, 1938.

Smith, Susy (1967) *Reincarnation for the Millions*, Los Angeles: Sherbourn.

Snow, Chet B. (1986a) 'A comparison of French and American past-life recall', *APRT Newsletter*, Spring.

—— (1986b)'Beyond the millennium – new age or brave new world?', *Journal of Regression Therapy*, Vol. 1, No. 1, Spring.

Stanley-Hughes, Thea (1976) *Twentieth Century Question: Reincarnation*, London: Movement.

Stearn, Jess (1969) *The Second Life of Susan Ganier*, London: Leslie Frewin.

—— *A Matter of Immortality*.

Steiger, Brad (1967) *The Enigma of Reincarnation*, New York: Ace, 1973.

Steiger, Francie and Steiger, Brad (1981) *Discover Your Own Past Lives*, New York: Dell.

Stein, W. J. (1932) *The Principle of Reincarnation*, London: Anthroposophical Publishing Co., 1947.

Steiner, Rudolf (1960) Osmond trans., *Reincarnation and karma*, London: Anthroposophical Publishing Company.

Stevenson, Ian (1961) *The Evidence for Survival from Claimed Memories of Former Incarnations*, Burg Heath: Peto.

—— (1966) *Twenty Cases Suggestive of Reincarnation*, University Press of Virginia, 1974.

—— (1975–83) *Cases of the Reincarnation Type*, Volume 1: Ten Cases of India (1975); Volume 2: Ten Cases in Sri Lanka (1977); Volume 3: Twelve Cases in Lebanon and Turkey (1980); Volume 4: Twelve Cases in Thailand and Burma (1983), Charlottesville: University Press of Virginia.

Stevenson Howell, Olive (1926) *Heredity and Reincarnation*, London: Theosophical Publishing House.

Stewart, Ada J. (1970) *Falcon: The autobiography of His Grace James IV, King of Scots*, London: Davies.

Story, Francis (1959) *The Case for Rebirth*, Ceylon.

—— (1975) *Rebirth as Doctrine and Experience*, Kandy: Buddhist Publishing Society.

Sutphen, Dick (1976) *Past Lives, Future Loves*, New York: Pocket Books.

—— (1978) *You Were Born Again to be Together*, New York: Pocket Books.

Sutphen, Dick and Taylor, Lauren (1983) *Past-life Therapy in Action*, Malibu: Valley of the Sun.

Talbot, Michael (1987) *Your Past Lives: A reincarnation handbook*, New York: Harmony Books.

Tatz, Mark and Kent, Jody (1977) *Rebirth: The Tibetan game of liberation*, New York: Anchor.

Tingley, Katherine (1907) *Reincarnation*, Albuquerque: Sun, 1981.

Toyne, Clarice (1976) *Heirs to Eternity: A study of reincarnation with illustrations*, London: Neville Spearman.

Underwood, Peter and Wilder, Leonard (1975) *Lives to Remember: A case book on reincarnation*, London: Robert Hale.

Van Auken, John (1984) *Born Again . . . and Again: How reincarnation occurs, why, and what it means to you!*, Virginia Beach: Inner Vision.

—— *Past Lives and Present Relationships*.

Van Pelt, G W. (1977) *Karma: The law of consequences*, Pasadena: Theosophical University Press.

Van Waveren, Erlo (1978) *Pilgrimage to the Rebirth*, New York: Weiser.

Wachsmuth, Gunther (1933) *Reincarnation as a Phenomenon of Metamorphosis*, New York: Anthroposophic Press, 1937.

Walker, Benjamin (1981) *Masks of the Soul: The facts behind reincarnation*, Wellingborough: Aquarian.

Walker, E. D. (1888) *Reincarnation: A study of forgotten truth*, New York: University Books, 1965.

Wambach, Helen (1978) *Reliving Past Lives: The evidence under hypnosis*, London: Arrow Books, 1980.

—— (1979) *Life Before Life*, London: Bantam.

—— (1986) 'Past-life therapy: the experiences of twenty-six therapists', *Journal of Regression Therapy*, Vol. 1, No. 2, Autumn.

Weatherhead, Leslie (1958) *The Case for Reincarnation*, Tadworth: Peto, 1971.

Weisman, A. (1977) *We immortals: The Dick Sutphen past life hypnotic regression seminars*, New York: Pocket Books, 1979

Whitton, Joel and Fisher, Joe (1986) *Life Between Life: Scientific explorations into the void separating one incarnation from the next*, Garden City: Doubleday.

Williston, Glenn and Johnstone, Judith (1983) *Soul Search: Spiritual growth through a knowledge of past lifetimes*, Wellingborough: Turnstone.

Willson, Martin (1984) *Rebirth and the Western Buddhist*, London: Wisdom, 1987.

Wilson, Ernest C. (1936) *Have We Lived Before?*, Lee's Summit: Unity School of Christianity, 1953.

Wilson, Ian (1981) *Mind Out of Time? Reincarnation Claims Investigated*, London: Gollancz.

Wood, Frederic Herbert (1937) *Ancient Egypt Speaks*, London: Rider.

—— (1953) *After Thirty Centuries*, London: Rider.

—— (1955) *This Egyptian Miracle*, London: Watkins/Rider.

Woodward, Mary Ann (1972) *Edgar Cayce's Story of Karma*, New York: Berkeley Publishing Co.

Woolger, Roger J. (1987) *Other Lives, Other Selves: A Jungian psychotherapist discovers past lives*, New York: Doubleday.

Wright, Leoline L. (1975) *Reincarnation: A love chord in modern thought*, California: Theosophical University Press, 1977.

Karmic astrology

Arroyo, Stephen (1978) *Astrology, Karma and Transformation: The inner dimensions of the birth-chart*, Vancouver: CRCS Publications.

Baronti, Gervée (1938) *Your Previous Life on Earth: Reincarnation simplified*, London: Jenkins.

George, T. (1977) *The Lives You Live as Revealed in the Heavens: A history of karmic astrology and pertinent delineations*, Arthur.

Hall, M. P. (1975) *Astrology and Reincarnation*, Philosophical Research Society.

Hodgson, Joan (1943) *Wisdom in the Stars*. Reprinted as: *Reincarnation Through the Zodiac*, Vancouver: CRCS Publications, 1979.

Luxton, L. K. (1978) *Astrology, Key to self-understanding: A guide to karma, reincarnation and spiritual astrology*, St Paul: Llewellyn.

Manik, Chand Jain, *Karmic Control Planets*, Astrological Publications.

Moore, Marcia and Douglas, Mark *Karmic Astrology*, York Harbour: Arcane.

Palmer, Martin, Man-Ho, Kwok, and Brown, Kerry trans. eds. and (*c.* 1600) *Three Lives*, London: Century, 1987.

Robertson, M. *Time Out of Mind: The past in your astrological birth chart and reincarnation.*

Schulman, Martin (1976–8) *Karmic Astrology*, Vols. 1–4, New York: Weiser.

Yott, D. H. (1977–9), *Astrology and Reincarnation*, Vols. 1–3, York Beech: Weiser.

Koechlin de Bizemont, Dorothée (1983) *L'Astrologie Karmique*, Paris: Laffont.

Weiss, S. *Karma-Astrologie: Esoterische Studie über die Planeten Saturn und Neptun.*

Other quoted works in English

Addison, James Thayer (1933) *Life Beyond Death in the Beliefs of Mankind*, London: George Allen and Unwin.

Ansbacher, Heinz and Ansbacher, Rowena eds. (1982) *The Individual Psychology of Alfred Adler: A systematic presentation in selections from his writings*, New York: Basic Books.

Blavatsky, H. P. (1877) *Isis Unveiled: A master-key to the mysteries of ancient and modern science and theology*, Vols. 1 and 2, Pasadena: Theosophical University Press, 1963.

—— (1888) *The Secret Doctrine: The synthesis of science, religion and philosophy*, Vols. 1 and 2, Pasadena: Theosophical University Press, 1963.

Boswell, Harriet A. (1969) *Master Guide to Psychism*, West Nyack: Parker.

Chapple, Christopher (1986) *Karma and Creativity*, New York: State University of New York.

Crookall, Robert (1961) *The Supreme Adventure*, London: James Clarke.

—— (1965) *Intimations of Immortality*, London: James Clarke.

—— (1966) *The Next World – and the Next: Ghostly garments*, London: Theosophical Publishing House.

—— (1967) *Events on the Threshold of the After-life*, Moradabad: Darshana.

—— (1978) *What Happens When You Die*, Gerrards Cross: Smythe.

Currie, Ian (1978) *You Cannot Die*, New York: Methuen.

Dahl, Roald (1977) *The Wonderful Story of Henry Sugar: and six more*, Harmondsworth: Penguin, 1982.

Dean, Geoffrey and Mather, Arthur (1977) *Recent Advances in Natal Astrology: A critical review 1900–1976*, Cowes: Recent Advances.

Edelstien, M. Gerald (1981) *Trauma, Trance and Transformation: A clinical guide to hypnotherapy*, New York: Brunner/Mazel.

Eliot, T. S. (1969) *The Complete Poems and Plays*, London: Faber and Faber.

Encyclopaedia Britannica (1964) *Second Council of Constantinople*, Vol. 6: 636, London: Encyclopaedia Britannica.

Fielding, Hall (1898) *The Soul of a People*, London: Macmillan.

Fox, Oliver (1939) *Astral Projection*, London: Rider.

Hardin, Gordon (1969) 'The tragedy of the commons', *Administrative Science Quarterly*.

Hearn, Lafcadio (1897) *Gleanings in Buddha Fields*, Tokyo: Tuttle, 1972.

Hubbard, L. Ron. (1950) *Dianetics: The modern science of mental health*, Copenhagen: New Era, 1982.

Keyes, Charles F. and Daniel, E. Valentine eds. (1983) *Karma: An anthropological inquiry*, Berkeley: University of California Press.

Korzybski, Alfred (1933) *Science and Sanity: An introduction to non-Aristotelian systems and general semantics*, Lakeville: International Non-Aristotelian Library, 1958.

Le Cron, Leslie ed. (1952) *Experimental Hypnosis*, New York: Macmillan.

Lindbergh, Charles (1953) *The Spirit of St Louis*, London: Hamilton, 1957.

Mehta, Rohit *The Journey with Death*, Delhi: Motilal Banarsidass, 1977.

Millard, Joseph (1961) *Edgar Cayce, Man of Miracles*, London: Neville Spearman.

Monroe, Robert A. (1977) *Journeys of the Body*, New York: Doubleday.

Montgomery, Ruth (1971) *A World Beyond*, New York: Fawcett.

Nietzsche, Friedrich, *The Joyful Wisdom*, Gordon Press, 1974.

—— (1889) R. J. Hollingdale trans. *Ecce Homo: how one becomes what one is*, Harmondsworth: Penguin, 1979.

Osborn, Arthur W. (1966) *The Meaning of Personal Existence, in the Light of Paranormal Phenomena; The Doctrine of Reincarnation and Mystical States of Consciousness*, Wheaton: Theosophical Publishing House, 1967.

Ouspensky, P. D. (1911) Bessaraboff, N. and Bragdon, C. trans. *Tertium Organum*, London: Kegan Paul, 1934.

Poortman, J. J. (1978) *Vehicles of Consciousness*, Vols. 1–4, Adyar: Theosophical Publishing House.

Powell, Arthur E. (1925) *The Etheric Double and Allied Phenomena*, London: Theosophical Publishing House, 1979.

—— (1926) *The Astral Body and Other Related Astral Phenomena*. London: Theosophical Publishing House.

—— (1927) *The Mental Body*, London: Theosophical Publishing House, 1975.

—— (1928) *The Causal Body and the Ego*, London: Theosophical Publishing House, 1978.

Praed, Rosa Caroline (1914) *Nyria*, London: Rider.

Rato, Khyongla Nawang Losang (1977) *My Life and Lives: The story of a Tibetan incarnation*, New York: Dutton.

Roberts, Jane (1972) *Seth Speaks*, New York: Bantam Books.

Sagan, Carl (1977) *The Dragons of Eden: Speculations on the evolution of human intelligence*, New York: Ballantine.

Sinnett, A. P. (1883) *Esoteric Buddhism*, Minneapolis: Wizards Bookshelf, 1973.

Smith, Huston (1958) *The Religions of Man*, New York: Harper & Row.

Spearman, Neville ed. (1953) *The Boy Who Saw True*, London: Neville Spearman.

Spiegel, Herbert and Spiegel, David (1978) *Trance and Treatment*, New York: Basic Books.

Sugrue, Thomas (1942) *There is a River*, New York.

Verney, Thomas with Kelly, John (1981) *The Secret Life of the Unborn Child* New York: Summit.

Von Glasenapp, Helmuth (1942) *The Doctrine of Karma in Jain Philosophy*, Bombay: Bai Vijibai Jivanlal Charity Fund.

Von Reichenbach, Karl Baron (1849) *Researches on Magnetism, Electricity, Heat, Light, Crystallization and Chemical Attractions in their Relations to the Vital Force*, Seacaucus: University Books, 1974.

Watkins, J. and Watkins, H. (1979) 'The theory and practice of ego-state therapy.' in Caryson, H. ed. *Short-term Approaches to Psychotherapy*, New York: National Institute for the Psychotherapies and Human Sciences Press.

Walli, Koshelva (1977) *Theory of Karma in Indian Thought*, Varanasi: Bharata Manisha.

Wheeler, Dave (1977) *Journey to the Other Side*.

Quoted works on reincarnation in other languages

Andrade, Hernani Guimarães (1983) *Morte, Renascimento, Evolução: Uma biologia transcendental*, São Paulo: Pensamento.

—— (1988) *Reencarnação no Brasil: Oito casos que sugerem renascimento*, São Paulo: O Clarim.

Aranco, S. (1982) *Tres pontos basicos sobre reencarnação*, Lisboa: Fraternidade.

Bertholet, Ed (1949) *La Réincarnation*, Paris: Aryana.

—— *Petite Iconographie de la Réincarnation*, Paris: Delachaux et Nestle.

Bibliography

Bjørkhem, John (1942) *De Hypnotiska Hallucinationerna*, Stockholm.

Bock, Emil (1932) *Wiederholte Erdenleben: Die Wiederverkörperungsidee in der deutschen Geistesgeschichte*, Stuttgart: Verlag der Christengemeinschaft.

Brazzini, Pasquale (1952) *Dopo la Morte si Rinasce?* Milan.

Brouwer, Els (1978) *Mozaïek van vorige levens*, Deventer: Ankh-Hermes.

Costa, Giuseppe (1923) *Di là della Vita*, Turin: Lattes.

David-Neel, Alexandra (1961) *Immortalité et Réincarnation. Doctrines et pratiques: Chine, Tibet, Inde*, [Monaco]: Editions du Rocher, 1978.

Delanne, Gabriel (1894) *Documents pour Servir à l'Étude de la Réincarnation*, Paris: Editions de la B P S, 1924.

—— *Les Preuves de la Réincarnation.*

de Rochas, Albert (1911) *Les Vies Successives*, Paris: Chacornac, 1924.

Des Georges, A. (1966) *La Réincarnation des Âmes selon les Traditions Orientales et Occidentales*, Paris: Michel.

Desjardins, Denise (1977) *De Naissance en Naissance: Témoignage sur une vie antérieure*, Paris: La Table Ronde.

—— (1980) *La Mémoire des Vies Antérieures*, Paris: La Table Ronde.

Dethlefsen, Thorwald (1974) *Leben nach dem Leben*, De Bilt: Fontein.

—— (1976) *Das Erlebnis der Wiedergeburt: Heilung durch Reinkarnation*, München: Bertelsmann.

—— (1979) *Schicksal als Chance: Esoterische Psychologie – Das Urwissen zur Vollkommenheit des Menschen*, München: Bertelsmann.

Eckhart, K. A. (1937) *Irdische Unsterblichkeit: Germanischer Glaube an die Wiederverkörperung in der Sippe*, Weimar: Böhlau.

Encausse, G. 'Papus' (c. 1920) *La Réincarnation. La Metempsychose. L'Évolution Physique, Astrale et Spirituelle*, Paris: Dorbon-Aine.

Ferreira, Dr Inacio (1955) *Psiquiatria em Face de Reencarnaçao*, Uberaba.

Hondius, J. M. (1957) *Ontmoeting met vorige levens*, Deventer: Kluwer.

Husemann, Frederich (1938) *Het gezicht van de dood: Een fundamentele blikverruiming*, Rotterdam: Christofoor.

Langedijk, Pieter (1980) *Reïncarnatie, psychotherapie en opvoeding*, Deventer: Ankh-Hermes.

Neidhart, Georg (1959) *Werden wir wiedergeboren?* München.

Penkala, Maria (1972) *Reïncarnatie en preëxistentie*, Deventer: Ankh-Hermes, 1973.

Pisani, Isola (1978) *Mourir n'est pas Mourir*, Paris: Laffont.

—— (1980) *Preuve de Survie: Croire ou savoir*, Paris: Laffont.

Reepmaker, M. (1902) *Reïncarnatie*, Rotterdam.

Rittelmeyer, Friedrich (1931) *Wiederverkörperung im Lichte des Denkens, der Religion, und der Moral*, Stuttgart: Verlag der Christengemeinschaft.

Snowden-Ward, H. *Karma en Re-incarnatie*, Amsterdam: Ned. Theos. Ver., n.d.

Steiner, Rudolf *Gesamtausgabe*, Dornach: Rudolf Steiner/Nachlassverwaltung.

  GA 9 (1904) *Theosophie*, pp. 61–90.

  GA 16 (1912) *Ein Weg zur Selbsterkenntnis des Menschen*, pp. 78–85.

  GA 17 (1913) *Die Schwelle der geistigen Welt*, (pp. 30–3).

GA 26 (1924–5) *Anthroposophische Leitsatze*, pp. 34–40, 72–5, 177–96.

GA 34 (1903–8) *Luzifer-Gnosis*, pp. 67–91, 92–107, 361–3, 371–7, 381–3, 404–6.

GA 53 (1904) *Grundbegriffe der Theosophie*, pp. 42–58.

GA 54 (1906) *Weltratsel und Anthroposophie*, pp. 279, 306.

GA 93a (1905) *Grundelemente des Esoterik*, Vortrage 8, 16, 21, 22, 29.

GA 95 (1906) *Vor dem Tore der Theosophie*, Vortrage 6, 7, 8.

GA 97 (1906) *Das Christliche Mysterium*, Vortrag 14/6/1906)

GA 99 (1907) *Die Theosophie des Rosenkreuzers*, Vortrage 6, 7).

GA 100 (1907) *Menschheitsentwicklung und Christus-Erkenntnis*, Vortrage 7 und 8 von *Theosophie und Rosenkreuzertum*.

GA 109/111 (1909) *Das Prinzip der spirituellen Oekonomie in Zusammenhang mit Wiederverkörperungsfragen*, Vortrag 21/1/1909, Vortrag 7/3/1909, Vortrag 12/6/1909.

GA 114 (1910) *Das Lukas-Evangelium*, Vortrag 10.

GA 120 (1910) *Die Offenbarungen des Karma*.

GA 130 (1912) *Das esoterische Christentum und die geistige Führung der Menschheit*, Vortrag 8/2/1912.

GA 131 (1912) *Wiederverkörperung und Karma*.

GA 133 (1912) *Der irdische und der kosmische Mensch*, Vortrag 5.

GA 134 (1911–12) *Die Welt der Sinne und die Welt des Geistes*.

GA 153 (1914) *Inneren Wesen des Menschen und Leben zwischen Tot und neuen Geburt*.

GA 157 (1914–15) *Menschen Schicksale und Völker Schicksale*.

GA 181 (1918) *Erden, Stirben und Welterleben*.

GA 235 (1979) *Esoterische Betrachtungen Karmischer Zusammenhange: I Band Geesteswetenschappelijke beschouwingen van het karma*.

GA 236 (1924) Idem. II. Band (I) Vortrage: 8 t/m 20

GA 237 Idem. III. Band (I) Vortrage 2

GA 238 Idem. IV. Band (I) Vortrage 2. 7 und 8

GA 239 Idem. V. Band (I) Vortrage 8 t/m 16

GA 240 Idem. VI. Band (I) Vortrage 7 und 8

Steiner, Rudolf (1961) *Reinkarnation und Karma: Gesammelte Aufsatze 1903–1923*, Dornach: Rudolf Steiner/ Nachlassverwaltung.

TenDam, Hans (1982) *Reincarnatie: Denkbeelden en ervaringsfeiten. Rondetafelgesprek*, Bres 92 en 93.

Van Ginkel, H. J. (1917) *Leeft men meer dan eenmaal op aard? Een bijdrage tot toelichting van het reincarnatieprobleem* Amsterdam: Theosophische Uitgeversmij.

Van Holthe tot Echten, R. O. (1921) *Reïncarnatie: Historische, ethische, wijsgerige en wetenschappelijke beschouwing*, Bussum: Van Dishoeck.

Veltman, W. F. (1974) *Karma en Reïncarnatie*, Zeist: Vrij Geestesleven.

Verbrugh, Hugo S. (1980) *Een beetje terugkomen: Reïncarnatie als denkbeeld en ervaringsgegeven*, Rotterdam: Christofoor.

Victor, Jean-Louis (1980) *Réincarnation et peintres mediums*, Paris: Édition du Nouveau Monde.

Weden, W. and Spindler, W. (1978) *Ägyptische Einweihung: Erinnerung an ein Leben als ägyptischer Priester*, Frankfurt: Fischer.

Other quoted works in other languages

Arenson, Adolf (1950) *Leitfaden durch 50 Votragszyklen Rudolf Steiners: (Zie trefwoorden 'Karma' en 'Wiederverkörperung')* Stuttgart: Freies Geistesleben.

Bezeira de Menezes, Adolpho (1946) *A loucura sob novo Prisma*, Rio de Janeiro.

Fechner, Gustav Theodor *Van het leven na de dood*, Den Haag: Servire.

Hampe, Johann Christoph (1975) *Sterben ist doch ganz anders: Erfahrungen mit dem eigenen Tod.*

Le Cron, Leslie (1976) *Hypnose*, Antwerpen: Ned. Boekhandel.

Lefebvre, Francis (1959), *Expériences Initiatiques*, Vol. 3, Paris.

Nietzsche, Friedrich *De symptomen van het verval*, Aphorisme 23 uit: 'De vrolijke wetenschap', Boek I, Amsterdam: Arbeiderspers, 1976.

Sartre, Jean-Paul (1938) *La Nausée*, Paris.

Scharl, Hubert (1977) *Moderne Hypnose-techniken für Mediziner*, München: Marczell.

Schreiber, Flora-Rheta (1973) *Sybil: Het ware verhaal van een vrouw met 16 persoonlijkheden*, Haarlem: Gottmer, 1974.

Stephenson, Gunther (1980) *Leben und Tod in den Religionen: Symbol und Wirklichkeit*, Darmstadt: Wissenschaftliche Buchgesellschaft.

TenDam, Hans (1980) *Orakels en inspiraties: Spirituele mogelijkheden tot de beantwoording van levensvragen*, Katwijk: Servire.

Tenhaeff, Dr W. H. C. (1936) *Het spiritisme*, Den Haag: Leopold, 1972.

—— *Ontmoetingen met paragnosten*, Utrecht: Bijleveld.

Tepperwein, Kurt (1977) *Handboek van de Hypnose*, Amsterdam: Meulenhoff, 1980.

Van Nes, C. (1958) *Over dood en leven*, Den Haag: Van Stockum.

Further reading in other languages

Baer, Emil (1926) *Das Geheimnis des Wiedererkennens*, Zürich.

Beaugitte, G. and Neuville, Pierre (1958) *Marie-Lise*.

Besant, Annie *Reïncarnatie en haar noodzakelijkheid en waarom wij onze vorige levens vergeten*, Amsterdam: Theosophische Uitgeversmij, n.d.

Calderine, Innocenzo (1913) *La Reincarnazione: Inchiesta internazionale*, Milano.

Celmar, M. L. (1925) *L'Âme et ses Réincarnations*, Paris.

Cooper, Irving Steiger *Groei door reïncarnatie*, Karma en Reïncarnatie Legioen, n.d.

Delacour, J. B. (1979) *Vom ewige Leben*, Düsseldorf: Egon Verlag.

de Saint-Savin, Charles (1947) *La Réincarnation Universelle*, Paris, Dervy.

Domingo Soler, Amalia *Hechos que Prueban*, Buenos Aires: Ed. Argentina 18 de Abril, n.d.

Falke, R. (1904) *Gibt es eine Seelenwanderung?*, Strien.

Howemann, Friedrich (1938) *Het gezicht van de dood: Een fundamentele blikverruiming*, Rotterdam: Christofoor, 1980.

Hutten, Kurt (1962) *Seelenwanderung*, Stuttgart: Kreuz.

Koechlin de Bizemont, Dorothée (1983) *L'Astrologie Karmique*, Paris: Laffont.

Lacerda, Nair (1978) *A Reencarnação Atraves dos Seculos*, São Paulo: Pensamento.

Liekens, Paul (1982) Reïncarnatie: Sleutel tot de zin van het leven, Deventer: Ankh-Hermes.

Magre, Maurice (1932) *La Mort et la Vie Future*, Paris: Pasquelle.

Martins, Cesso (1976) *Espiritismo e Vidas Successivas*, Rio de Janeiro: Ed. ELO.

Miranda, Herminìo C. (1975) *Reencarnação e Immortalidade*, Rio de Janeiro: FEB.

—— (1981) *A Reencarnação na Biblia*, São Paulo: Pensamento.

Ortt, Felix (*c.* 1947) *Het Reïncarnatie-vraagstuk.*

Pascal, Dr B. *Essai sur l'Évolution Humaine*, Paris: Publ. Theosophiques.

Pezzani, Andre (1865) *La Pluralité des Existences de l'Âme*, Paris, Dider.

Schmidt, K. O. (1956) *Wir leben nicht nur einmal*, Dettenbach: Buddingen.

Van der Meer, B. (1951) *Reïncarnatie in een nieuw licht*, Wassenaar: Servire.

Van Praag, H. (1972) *Reïncarnatie in het licht van wetenschap en geloof*, Bussum: Teleboek.

Index of Names

General Index

ARKANA – NEW-AGE BOOKS FOR MIND, BODY AND SPIRIT

With over 150 titles currently in print, Arkana is the leading name in quality new-age books for mind, body and spirit. Arkana encompasses the spirituality of both East and West, ancient and new, in fiction and non-fiction. A vast range of interests is covered, including Psychology and Transformation, Health, Science and Mysticism, Women's Spirituality and Astrology.

If you would like a catalogue of Arkana books, please write to:

Arkana Marketing Department
Penguin Books Ltd
27 Wright's Lane
London W8 5TZ

ARKANA – NEW-AGE BOOKS FOR MIND, BODY AND SPIRIT

A selection of titles already published or in preparation

Neal's Yard Natural Remedies Susan Curtis, Romy Fraser and Irene Kohler

Natural remedies for common ailments from the pioneering Neal's Yard Apothecary Shop. An invaluable resource for everyone wishing to take responsibility for their own health, enabling you to make your own choice from homeopathy, aromatherapy and herbalism.

The Arkana Dictionary of New Perspectives Stuart Holroyd

Clear, comprehensive and compact, this iconoclastic reference guide brings together the orthodox and the highly unorthodox, doing full justice to *every* facet of contemporary thought – psychology and parapsychology, culture and counter-culture, science and so-called pseudo-science.

The Absent Father: Crisis and Creativity Alix Pirani

Freud used Oedipus to explain human nature; but Alix Pirani believes that the myth of Danae and Perseus has most to teach an age which offers 'new responsibilities for women and challenging questions for men' – a myth which can help us face the darker side of our personalities and break the patterns inherited from our parents.

Woman Awake: A Celebration of Women's Wisdom Christina Feldman

In this inspiring book, Christina Feldman suggests that it *is* possible to break out of those negative patterns instilled into us by our social conditioning as women: confirmity, passivity and surrender of self. Through a growing awareness of the dignity of all life and its connection with us, we can regain our sense of power and worth.

Water and Sexuality Michel Odent

Taking as his starting point his world-famous work on underwater childbirth at Pithiviers, Michel Odent considers the meaning and importance of water as a symbol: in the past – expressed through myths and legends – and today, from an advertisers' tool to a metaphor for aspects of the psyche. Dr Odent also boldly suggests that the human species may have had an aquatic past.

ARKANA – NEW-AGE BOOKS FOR MIND, BODY AND SPIRIT

A selection of titles already published or in preparation

On Having No Head: Zen and the Re-Discovery of the Obvious
D. E. Harding

'Reason and imagination and all mental chatter died down . . . I forgot my name, my humanness, my thingness, all that could be called me or mine. Past and future dropped away . . .'

Thus Douglas Harding describes his first experience of headlessness, or no self. This classic work truly conveys the experience that mystics of all ages have tried to put into words.

Self-Healing: My Life and Vision   Meir Schneider

Born blind, pronounced incurable – yet at 17 Meir Schneider discovered self-healing techniques which within four years led him to gain a remarkable degree of vision. In the process he discovered an entirely new self-healing system, and an inspirational faith and enthusiasm that helped others heal themselves. While individual response to self-healing is unique, the healing power is inherent in all of us.

'This remarkable story is tonic for everyone who believes in the creative power of the human will' – Marilyn Ferguson.

The Way of the Craftsman: A Search for the Spiritual Essence of Craft Freemasonry   W. Kirk MacNulty

This revolutionary book uncovers the Kabbalistic roots of Freemasonry, showing how Kabbalistic symbolism informs all of its central rituals. W. Kirk MacNulty, a Freemason for twenty-five years, reveals how the symbolic structure of the Craft is designed to lead the individual step by step to psychological self-knowledge, while at the same time recognising mankind's fundamental dependence on God.

Dictionary of Astrology   Fred Gettings

Easily accessible yet sufficiently detailed to serve the needs of the practical astrologer, this fascinating reference book offers reliable definitions and clarifications of over 3000 astrological terms, from the post-medieval era to today's most recent developments.

ARKANA – NEW-AGE BOOKS FOR MIND, BODY AND SPIRIT

A selection of titles already published or in preparation

The Networking Book: People Connecting with People
Jessica Lipnack and Jeffrey Stamps

Networking – forming human connections to link ideas and resources – is the natural form of organization for an era based on information technology. Principally concerned with those networks whose goal is a peaceful yet dynamic future for the world, *The Networking Book* – written by two world-famous experts – profiles hundreds of such organizations worldwide, operating at every level from global telecommunications to word of mouth.

Chinese Massage Therapy: A Handbook of Therapeutic Massage Compiled at the Anhui Medical School Hospital, China
Translated by Hor Ming Lee and Gregory Whincup

There is a growing movement among medical practitioners in China today to mine the treasures of traditional Chinese medicine – acupuncture, herbal medicine and massage therapy. Directly translated from a manual in use in Chinese hospitals, *Chinese Massage Therapy* offers a fresh understanding of this time-tested medical alternative.

Dialogues with Scientists and Sages: The Search for Unity
Renée Weber

In their own words, contemporary scientists and mystics – from the Dalai Lama to Stephen Hawking – share with us their richly diverse views on space, time, matter, energy, life, consciousness, creation and our place in the scheme of things. Through the immediacy of verbatim dialogue, we encounter scientists who endorse mysticism, and those who oppose it; mystics who dismiss science, and those who embrace it.

Zen and the Art of Calligraphy
Omōri Sōgen and Terayama Katsujo

Exploring every element of the relationship between Zen thought and the artistic expression of calligraphy, two long-time practitioners of Zen, calligraphy and swordsmanship show how Zen training provides a proper balance of body and mind, enabling the calligrapher to write more profoundly, freed from distraction or hesitation.

ARKANA – NEW-AGE BOOKS FOR MIND, BODY AND SPIRIT

A selection of titles already published or in preparation

The TM Technique Peter Russell

Through a process precisely opposite to that by which the body accumulates stress and tension, transcendental meditation works to produce a state of profound rest, with positive benefits for health, clarity of mind, creativity and personal stability. Peter Russell's book has become the key work for everyone requiring a complete mastery of TM.

The Development of the Personality: Seminars in Psychological Astrology Volume I Liz Greene and Howard Sasportas

Taking as a starting point their groundbreaking work on the cross-fertilization between astrology and psychology, Liz Greene and Howard Sasportas show how depth psychology works with the natal chart to illuminate the experiences and problems all of us encounter throughout the development of our individual identity, from childhood onwards.

Homage to the Sun: The Wisdom of the Magus of Strovolos
Kyriacos C. Markides

Homage to the Sun continues the adventure into the mysterious and extraordinary world of the spiritual teacher and healer Daskalos, the 'Magus of Strovolos'. The logical foundations of Daskalos' world of other dimensions are revealed to us – invisible masters, past-life memories and guardian angels, all explained by the Magus with great lucidity and scientific precision.

The Year I: Global Process Work Arnold Mindell

As we approach the end of the 20th century, we are on the verge of planetary extinction. Solving the planet's problems is literally a matter of life and death. Arnold Mindell shows how his famous and groundbreaking process-orientated psychology can be extended so that our own sense of global awareness can be developed and we – the whole community of earth's inhabitants – can comprehend the problems and work together towards solving them.

ARKANA - NEW-AGE BOOKS FOR MIND, BODY AND SPIRIT

A selection of titles already published or in preparation

Encyclopedia of the Unexplained
Edited by Richard Cavendish Consultant: J. B. Rhine

'Will probably be the definitive work of its kind for a long time to come' – *Prediction*

The ultimate guide to the unknown, the esoteric and the unproven: richly illustrated, with almost 450 clear and lively entries from Alchemy, the Black Box and Crowley to faculty X, Yoga and the Zodiac.

Buddhist Civilization in Tibet Tulku Thondup Rinpoche

Unique among works in English, *Buddhist Civilization in Tibet* provides an astonishing wealth of information on the various strands of Tibetan religion and literature in a single compact volume, focusing predominantly on the four major schools of Buddhism: Nyingma, Kagyud, Sakya and Gelug.

The Living Earth Manual of Feng-Shui Stephen Skinner

The ancient Chinese art of Feng-Shui – tracking the hidden energy flow which runs through the earth in order to derive maximum benefit from being in the right place at the right time – can be applied equally to the siting and layout of cities, houses, tombs and even flats and bedsits; and can be practised as successfully in the West as in the East with the aid of this accessible manual.

In Search of the Miraculous: Fragments of an Unknown Teaching P. D. Ouspensky

Ouspensky's renowned, vivid and characteristically honest account of his work with Gurdjieff from 1915–18.

'Undoubtedly a *tour de force*. To put entirely new and very complex cosmology and psychology into fewer than 400 pages, and to do this with a simplicity and vividness that makes the book accessible to any educated reader, is in itself something of an achievement' – *The Times Literary Supplement*

ARKANA – NEW-AGE BOOKS FOR MIND, BODY AND SPIRIT

A selection of titles already published or in preparation

Weavers of Wisdom: Women Mystics of the Twentieth Century Anne Bancroft

Throughout history women have sought answers to eternal questions about existence and beyond – yet most gurus, philosophers and religious leaders have been men. Through exploring the teachings of fifteen women mystics – each with her own approach to what she calls 'the truth that goes beyond the ordinary' – Anne Bancroft gives a rare, cohesive and fascinating insight into the diversity of female approaches to mysticism.

Dynamics of the Unconscious: Seminars in Psychological Astrology Volume II Liz Greene and Howard Sasportas

The authors of *The Development of the Personality* team up again to show how the dynamics of depth psychology interact with your birth chart. They shed new light on the psychology and astrology of aggression and depression – the darker elements of the adult personality that we must confront if we are to grow to find the wisdom within.

The Myth of Eternal Return: Cosmos and History Mircea Eliade

'A luminous, profound, and extremely stimulating work . . . Eliade's thesis is that ancient man envisaged events not as constituting a linear, progressive history, but simply as so many creative repetitions of primordial archetypes . . . This is an essay which everyone interested in the history of religion and in the mentality of ancient man will have to read. It is difficult to speak too highly of it' – Theodore H. Gaster in *Review of Religion*

Karma and Destiny in the I Ching Guy Damian-Knight

This entirely original approach to the *I Ching*, achieved through mathematical rearrangement of the hexagrams, offers a new, more precise tool for self-understanding. Simple to use and yet profound, it gives the ancient Chinese classic a thoroughly contemporary relevance.

ARKANA – NEW-AGE BOOKS FOR MIND, BODY AND SPIRIT

A selection of titles already published or in preparation

A Course in Miracles: The Course, Workbook for Students and Manual for Teachers

Hailed as 'one of the most remarkable systems of spiritual truth available today', *A Course in Miracles* is a self-study course designed to shift our perceptions, heal our minds and change our behaviour, teaching us to experience miracles – 'natural expressions of love' – rather than problems generated by fear in our lives.

Medicine Woman: A Novel Lynn Andrews

The intriguing story of a white woman's journey of self-discovery among the Heyoka Indians – from the comforts of civilisation to the wilds of Canada. Apprenticed to a medicine woman, she learns tribal wisdom and mysticism – and above all the power of her own womanhood.

Arthur and the Sovereignty of Britain: Goddess and Tradition in the Mabinogion Caitlín Matthews

Rich in legend and the primitive magic of the Celtic Otherworld, the stories of the *Mabinogion* heralded the first flowering of European literature and became the source of Arthurian legend. Caitlín Matthews illuminates these stories, shedding light on Sovereignty, the Goddess of the Land and the spiritual principle of the Feminine.

Shamanism: Archaic Techniques of Ecstasy Mircea Eliade

Throughout Siberia and Central Asia, religious life traditionally centres around the figure of the shaman: magician and medicine man, healer and miracle-doer, priest and poet.

'Has become the standard work on the subject and justifies its claim to be the first book to study the phenomenon over a wide field and in a properly religious context' – *The Times Literary Supplement*

ARKANA – NEW-AGE BOOKS FOR MIND, BODY AND SPIRIT

A selection of titles already published or in preparation

Being Intimate: A Guide to Successful Relationships
John and Kris Amodeo

This invaluable guide aims to enrich one of the most important – yet often problematic – aspects of our lives: intimate relationships and friendships.

'A clear and practical guide to the realization and communication of authentic feelings, and thus an excellent pathway towards lasting intimacy and love' – George Leonard

The Brain Book Peter Russell

The essential handbook for brain users.

'A fascinating book – for everyone who is able to appreciate the human brain, which, as Russell says, is the most complex and most powerful information processor known to man. It is especially relevant for those who are called upon to read a great deal when time is limited, or who attend lectures or seminars and need to take notes' – *Nursing Times*

The Act of Creation Arthur Koestler

This second book in Koestler's classic trio of works on the human mind (which opened with *The Sleepwalkers* and concludes with *The Ghost in the Machine*) advances the theory that all creative activities – the conscious and unconscious processes underlying artistic originality, scientific discovery and comic inspiration – share a basic pattern, which Koestler expounds and explores with all his usual clarity and brilliance.

A Psychology With a Soul: Psychosynthesis in Evolutionary Context Jean Hardy

Psychosynthesis was developed between 1910 and the 1950s by Roberto Assagioli – an Italian psychiatrist who, like Jung, diverged from Freud in search of a more spiritually based understanding of human nature. Jean Hardy's account of this comprehensive approach to self-realization will be of great value to everyone concerned with personal integration and spiritual growth.